SIDE by SIDE

SIDE *by* SIDE

DEAN MARTIN &
JERRY LEWIS
ON TV AND RADIO

BY

MICHAEL J. HAYDE

BearManor Media

2018

Side By Side: Dean Martin & Jerry Lewis On TV and Radio

© 2018 Michael J. Hayde

All rights reserved.

The United States Copyright Office, 2006

Published in the United States of America by:

Bear Manor Media
P. O. Box 71426
Albany, GA 31708

bearmanormedia.com

Typesetting and layout by John Teehan

ISBN—978-1-62933-352-6

DEDICATION

MY MOTHER introduced me to Dean Martin & Jerry Lewis when we watched *Jumping Jacks* (1952) on television one afternoon in the early 1970s. I thought the film was only moderately amusing, and she agreed, adding, "They were much funnier on *The Colgate Comedy Hour*." That sparked a lovely conversation.

As a middle school student living in Baltimore, she enjoyed the *Colgate* shows. She especially recalled a moment when Jerry tossed the microphone toward the floor, and Dean dived for it just as Jerry yanked it back to safety (*Comedy Hour*, November 4, 1951). Two of her classmates, she remembered, could do a decent Martin & Lewis impersonation. They were known to disrupt class from time-to-time, so on the last day of school, the teacher gave them a chance to entertain, which apparently went over very well. After graduating high school, and having moved to New York, she volunteered to take pledge calls during the team's Muscular Dystrophy telethon in June 1956.

When I obtained a copy of a 1952 *Comedy Hour* on VHS, we watched it together. Both of us laughed at Jerry's antics, and then she happened to remark, "I could never see him as 'The Poor Soul.'" "Neither could Dean," I replied. That was the moment I knew I would write this book.

For all this, and (to paraphrase Jerry) for 80 years of joy that she's given to our family and friends, this book is lovingly dedicated to my mother, Margaret Veronica Hayde.

TABLE OF CONTENTS

INTRODUCTION

IF YOU'VE ONLY SEEN MARTIN & LEWIS in their movies, you haven't seen Martin & Lewis.

For over thirty-five years since their 1956 split, the only Martin & Lewis available for mass consumption were the 16 motion pictures in which they starred, most of which shoehorned them into predictable situations that had served nearly every comedy team since the birth of cinema. Consequently, many latter-day critics, having long heard and read about this team's ability to send audiences into *hysteria in excelsis*, wondered aloud what all the fuss was about.

That changed in the early 1990s when Jerry Lewis dove into his collection of kinescopes and emerged with the team's appearances on *The Colgate Comedy Hour*; first as highlights in a three-part documentary for The Disney Channel titled *Martin & Lewis: Their Golden Age of Comedy*, then shortly afterwards in home video releases and airings on Public Television stations. At that point, critics took another look. "To really appreciate Martin & Lewis," declared author Scott Eyman in 2001, "you have to look at the live TV appearances that have survived. They're chaotic, dangerous, manic, obviously unscripted and funny in a Ritz Brothers/Mel Brooks sort of way." An interesting comparison, given that Harry Ritz was an early Lewis influence, while as a filmmaker, Brooks owes *his* career to Lewis' trailblazing success.

Likewise, Tom Shales, critic for the *Washington Post*, wrote the following year, "They didn't so much 'appear' [on *Colgate*] as storm the studio, two merry maniacs whose TV performances were inspired, uproarious bedlam. Kids of that era... looked forward to the Martin and Lewis appearances as they would look forward to a great sports event, because Lewis would run riot through the production, tossing out the script, playing with the cameras and other equipment, wreaking irreverent havoc

Publicity still for *Living It Up* (1954).

and—perhaps, who knows?—paving the way for 'anti-establishment' comedians to come later."

There also survives a body of work that Martin & Lewis did on radio that has been either denigrated or ignored by critics and biographers, yet the best of it closely approaches the *Colgate* hours in laughter and enjoyment. To be sure, a number of these programs, particularly of their first (1949-50) NBC series, are as trite and awkward as their movie plots. It would also be foolhardy to deny that *seeing* Martin & Lewis in action is the preferred way to experience them. Still, their radio guest appearances with Bob Hope and others, and their starring series from 1951-53, convey the ineffable blend of lunacy and charm that captivated audiences to a better degree than their films.

A full appraisal of the team's work in each medium is long overdue, but there's more to the story than a recounting of legendary comedy. For example, Jerry Lewis' relationship with the Muscular Dystrophy Association, which spanned over 60 years, began on *The Colgate Comedy Hour*. He and Dean were the first national celebrities to call attention to the fledging organization, and it was via their TV and radio programs that America became aware of this brace of fatal neuromuscular diseases. According to the MDA's obituary for the comedian: "During Lewis' lifetime, MDA-funded scientists discovered the causes of most of the diseases in MDA's program, developing treatments, therapies and standards of care that have allowed many living with these diseases to live longer and grow stronger." And it all began when Martin & Lewis took a few minutes at the end of a *Comedy Hour* to ask for "just one penny" from each viewer.

The *Colgate* shows are also, at times, a document of an unraveling relationship. Martin and Lewis were partners for ten years. For the first seven, they were two guys who loved their work and each other, and couldn't believe they were receiving so much fame and fortune because of it. The *Comedy Hour* came along just past their fourth anniversary, and many moments throughout its first three seasons depict this love affair at its peak. Over the course of years eight and nine, each man came to believe he was capable of much more than what he'd been doing. They weren't just growing, they were growing apart, and the show occasionally aims a spotlight on the struggle between them. By year ten, both wanted out, yet were bound together by iron-clad contracts, one of which gave them partial ownership of the *Colgate* show. Thus they had to swallow their mutual animus and put on an act that was no more than "an act." They didn't always pull it off successfully.

The story doesn't end with their professional parting, either, for there were additional feuds and reunions over the ensuing years. Even after both were comfortably established as successful solo artists, they wouldn't be permitted to forget each other. When they reunited on live television in 1976, it led off the Ten O'clock News and hit the front page the next morning. It was as if America had been hoping these two would kiss and make up. Over time, that event took on mythic proportions.

All 28 of Martin & Lewis' starring *Colgate Hours* exist, as do three of their guest appearances on the show, a complete two-hour program for MDA, and nearly all of their other post-1949 TV work. At this writing, 80 of their 112 starring radio programs circulate among collectors of old-time radio; most of the rest are in public archives such as the Library of Congress. Through these, plus hundreds of contemporary magazine and newspaper articles and reviews, legacy interviews with Dean, Jerry and their principal associates, and key biographies of both men, this book aims to illuminate the phenomenon that was Martin & Lewis via the work that reached more eyes and ears than any their movies, even when they were among the top ten box office attractions in motion pictures. It also provides insight and context to their split and the interaction that followed. It is, in essence, a treatise on how and why Dean Martin & Jerry Lewis, their partnership and their break up, became legendary.

* * * * *

A brief note on the nomenclature in this book: "Martin & Lewis" refers to the professional unit, whereas "Martin and Lewis" refers to the two men. Also, when quoting from radio and television dialogue scenes, scripted lines appear with quotation marks and ad-libs do not.

PROLOGUE

"Such indeed are the powers of friendship: to breed contempt of death, to overcome the sweet desire of life, to humanize cruelty, to turn hate into love, to compensate punishment by largess; to which powers almost as much veneration is due as to the cult of the immortal gods."

– De Amicitiae Vinculo: The History of Damon and Pythias by Valerius Maximus

"A Handsome Man and a Monkey."
"A Strapping Singer and a Startling Gadfly."
"The Madmen of the Megacycles."
"The Looney and the Tune."

APPELLATIONS SUCH AS THESE have been used to describe the comedy team of Dean Martin & Jerry Lewis. But during their ten years together, beginning on July 25, 1946 at The 500 Club in Atlantic City, only one title mattered: "The Most Successful Act in Show Business."

One was a crooner of Italian descent who called himself Dean Martin. By 1946 he'd evolved into a reasonably professional singer who'd managed to score his own 15-minute radio show over WMCA in New York and a contract with a very small record label, Diamond. Still, he had a lot of rough edges as a performer that were keeping him from the big time. His vocal style was something of a cross between Crosby and Como, mixed with a helping of roguish sexuality that no one, not even Sinatra, could claim. He radiated self-confidence, and could certainly put over a song, but his chatter between numbers tended to be heavy-handed; his put-down of hecklers a bit *too* nasty.

Dean before Jerry.

It was a remnant of his upbringing. Martin, whose real name was Dino Paul Crocetti, was raised in Steubenville Ohio, a town so overrun with mobsters during and after prohibition that it was known as "Little Chicago." An immigrant barber's son who showed little interest in school or legitimate work, Martin went from amateur boxer to blackjack dealer

before some of his gangster pals encouraged him to take his smooth bari-
tone and make a career out of singing. Along the way he married, became
a father, and—in exchange for much-needed cash advances—sold 110%
of his future income to various agents and managers, which finally landed
him in bankruptcy court the previous February.

The other was a Jewish nightclub comic and emcee known as Jerry
Lewis. By 1946, he'd developed a solid reputation for his record act: outrageously comic pantomime while mouthing popular recordings of the day.
He signed with one of New York's better talent agents, Abner Greshler,
and began to add jokes to his repertoire, but the "mute act" was still his

Jerry before Dean.

bread and butter. Although he knew it would take more than pantomime to reach the top, a gnawing fear kept holding him back; a remnant of *his* upbringing.

Lewis, born Jerome Levitch in Newark New Jersey, was the son of two vaudevillian parents. His father, whose stage name was Danny Lewis, was a middlingly successful Jolson-influenced singer; his wife Rae accompanied him on piano. Whenever the couple had to travel, young Jerry was left in the care of several relatives, most of whom simply passed him along until inevitably he'd wind up at his grandmother's house in nearby Irvington. Memories of this nomadic childhood, combined with the task of emerging from his father's self-assured shadow, gave Lewis pangs of insecurity that he would never fully overcome.

Although each was booked into the Glass Hat, a modest nightclub in Manhattan's Belmont Plaza Hotel, beginning September 5, 1944, Martin and Lewis had been officially introduced by mutual friend (and fellow performer) Sonny King while walking along Broadway one afternoon that week. *Variety's* review of the Glass Hat engagement summed up each man's professional standing at the time they became acquainted: Jerry "is a bright youngster" whose record act "is nothing new, but in some of the things he does Lewis is seemingly better than the originals. He needs more schooling as an emcee, but otherwise okay." Dean, on the other hand, "is the show's weak spot; he's got a nice voice but lacks the feel necessary to reach the customers." When the week was up, Dean moved on, while Jerry was held over.

Over the next 18 months, whenever they happened to share the bill, each would clown around during the other's act. Dean made Jerry feel comfortable enough to begin using comic voices and slapstick, and Jerry gave Dean the confidence to relax and hone his own brand of sly comedy. Even when they were merely two solo acts pulling stunts on each other, professionals were impressed: "Lewis's double-takes, throw-aways, mugging and deliberate over-acting are sensational. Martin's slow takes, ad-libs and under-acting make him an ideal fall guy," wrote Bill Smith, *Billboard's* nightclub critic in March 1946, concluding the twosome had "all the makings of a sock act."

When the 29-year-old Martin and the 20-year-old Lewis decided to pair up officially, you couldn't have found two more unlikely partners. About the only thing they had in common was that both were married with children. Yet each brought out the best in the other, and the resulting combination of chemistry, charm and energetic comedy literally knocked audiences out of their chairs. Showbiz veteran Sophie Tucker, appearing at a rival club that same week, caught their craziness at a late-night show and raved the next day. She saw them as "a combination of the Keystone Kops, the Marx Brothers and Abbott & Costello" that "will leave their mark on the whole profession." Within three days there were lines along the boardwalk waiting to see them.

Less than two years later they would debut at New York City's prestigious Copacabana as a supporting act and, after one performance, force management to put them in the headliner's spot. Six months after that, they'd be handed contracts by NBC, Capitol Records, and movie producer Hal Wallis. Three films after *that,* they were the nation's number-one box office attraction. From that point until they decided to call it quits in 1956, Martin & Lewis were guaranteed to gross a minimum of $20 million dollars *annually.* No other individual or team even came close.

From the start, each recognized the other's gifts. "The secret of our success," said Lewis in 1949, "is that we've learned from one another. I was a flop—through fear. Dean knocked that out of me." With tongue only slightly in cheek, Martin added, "And I had trouble speaking. Jerry fixed that. I have to yell to shut him up."

Their first radio series debuted before they'd finished making their first film. NBC gave it an expensive publicity launch, changed the writing staff in mid-stream and kept it on without a sponsor for 39 weeks, but critics had decided that Martin & Lewis had to be seen to be appreciated. Eventually, the expense of airing the series to an indifferent audience proved too great. Fortunately, when the show expired in 1950, Dean and Jerry were given another outlet, one that proved an invaluable ally in their climb to the top: television,

In September 1950, the pair made their first starring appearance on *The Colgate Comedy Hour,* a live variety series with alternating hosts that aired on Sunday nights. They would helm 27 more shows for Colgate through November 1955. These programs, consisting of music, dance, sketches, ad-libs and choice moments from their nightclub act, presented Martin & Lewis in the purest form possible for mass consumption.

By 1951, after the *Comedy Hour's* first season, their hold on the American public was formidable. For a small yet significant example, listen to the close of radio's *Bing Crosby Show* of October 31, after guest Dinah Shore asks, "Who's gonna be with you next week?" Bing replies, "Next week, Dinah, our program assumes a very serious character. A note of solemnity is going to prevail. Rigid decorum will be the keynote

"The Boy With the Tall, Dark and Handsome Voice" is promoted by Dick Richards, one of Martin's many managers in 1944.

as we play host to Dean Martin and Jerry Lewis." A fervent "Ohhhhhh!" and spontaneous applause rises from the studio audience. It's as if Crosby had told an auditorium of first graders that he'd be hosting Santa Claus and the Easter Bunny.

Their first season on television was so successful, NBC gave the team another stab at radio. This second series, which began in October 1951, was a vast improvement over the first, mainly because Dean and Jerry were more confident and less self-conscious, and also because the material was provided by the team's television writers. Catch-phrases, running gags and even an entire sketch or two would alternate between both media. The series was also more successful than its predecessor, and would win an audience award in its first year. Only the irreversible decline of radio as the household's primary entertainment medium kept it from airing more than its two seasons.

What was all the fuss about? More than sixty years later, it's still difficult—if not impossible—to capture the essence of Martin & Lewis on paper. Zany. Wild. Spontaneous. Uninhibited. Choose all of the above, and you're about 25% there. "It is difficult to record just exactly what their act *is*," wrote *Colliers* in 1951, "for they rank among today's leading masters of the ad-lib and the improvised business." That same year, *Pageant* wrote, "The formula ... is a combination of brash and delirious clowning and highly comic pantomime. They are the masters of the zany and the unexpected." And *Quick* added, "The money pouring into Martin and Lewis' pockets came from millions of new fans who have suddenly discovered they enjoy being left dazed and delirious by the pair's violent, bug-house brand of humor."

But that only scratches the surface. Acts that specialize in "brash and delirious clowning" and "bug-house humor" generally lack staying power once the novelty has worn off, yet Martin & Lewis were the top draw in show business right up to their parting. There were other elements to their success. One was that these two jokers were obviously having a lot of fun, and their fun was quite contagious. Some of the biggest laughs in both radio and television come when Dean and Jerry are playing *off* the material; each one trying to break up the other and usually succeeding.

Which leads to another facet, one particularly evident during their first three years on *Colgate*: the obvious affection both men have for each other. Once they became television stars, another appellation was fixed to them: The Damon and Pythias of Show Business. In 1952, *Modern Screen* asserted, "Some people swear that when Dean takes a drink, Jerry reaps a hangover; that if Lewis gulps down a hotdog, Martin is certain to burp; that a day on the beach for Dino spreads a deep tan over the Little Monster, sitting home in the shade. This impression stems from their superbly synchronized shenanigans, and it's true that in the heat of action there's

JERRY LEWIS
SATIRICAL IMPRESSIONS
IN PANTOMIMICRY

In 1946, Lewis was still relying on "Satirical Impressions in Pantomimicry" for work.

telepathy between the pair that could put Western Union out of business."

The evidence is right there on screen. When Lewis fires off an ad-lib, he almost always shoots a glance at Martin with an expression that clearly says he's seeking his partner's approval. Likewise when Martin ad-libs, he'll turn to watch Lewis break up, always flashing a big smile. The warmth between the two is charming—something that cannot be said for other rough-house acts like Abbott & Costello or the Three Stooges. And as they fell in love with each other, audiences fell in love with them. For the length of its run, Dean and Jerry's *Colgate* hours were the only ones guaranteed to top Ed Sullivan's competing CBS show in the ratings, sometimes by a three-to-one margin.

If their magic wasn't lost on audiences, the power it wielded certainly wasn't lost on Martin and Lewis. Indeed, it was mainly the pressure to remain on top that eventually brought conflicting ambitions to the fore. Their chemistry, the affection with which they'd held each other, was so genuine that its waning was instantly noticeable. Gradually their friendship faded before viewers' eyes until all that remained were two professionals trying to fake what had come so naturally a few years before. Sometimes they would rise to the occasion and turn in solid performances (usually when the writing was equal to the task); sometimes they'd be too tired or fed up to bother.

The inevitable end came swiftly. Their final TV appearance took place over the last two days of June 1956 when they hosted a Muscular Dystrophy telethon that is forever lost; Lewis couldn't bear to retain even a minute of what must have been a painful 21 hours. (For much the same reason, he could never bring himself to watch the final Martin & Lewis film, *Hollywood Or Bust*. "It's the single one of my movies that I've never seen, and never will," promised Lewis in 2005.) They closed their joint career ten years to the day after they'd started it, in front of an SRO crowd at the Copacabana. The chronological symmetry was perfect, as was the locale: they'd met in Manhattan, they'd say goodbye there.

The venue, too, was apropos. Nightclubs had given Martin & Lewis a place to build a reputation and be seen by the power brokers of show business. From there, radio provided respectability and a weekly showcase for Martin's songs. Motion pictures put them in the top income bracket and assured them of immortality.

And television made them superstars.

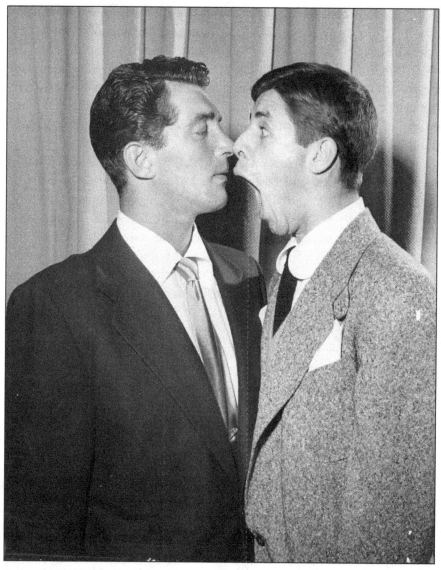

Photo courtesy of the Patti Lewis Collection, Library of Congress.

1 THE ORIGIN:
MARTIN & LEWIS EXPLAIN HOW MARTIN AND LEWIS BECAME MARTIN & LEWIS

JERRY LEWIS: "I was standing on the corner of 54th and Broadway, in New York City. Someone I knew walked up with Dean Martin, and we were introduced.[1] I was doing [my] act at the Glass Hat in New York when I met Dean, a singer on the same bill. I was attracted to Dean almost immediately."[2]

DEAN MARTIN: "I admired Jerry's wit and the fact that he was always in there pushing. Besides, I thought he was a great guy."[3]

JERRY: "I wasn't even thinking about him talent-wise, or from the career angle. I just thought… 'What a wonderful guy.'[3] He was nine years older than I, and I thought of him as the big brother I never had."[2]

DEAN: "Jerry and I became friends and used to have a great time together.[1] He was messin' around with my act and I was messin' into his."[4]

JERRY: "I found that I could make him laugh at my clowning and that he clowned back, and he liked me."[2]

DEAN: "He was appearing at the 500 Club in Atlantic City, and one night the owner found himself minus an act. Jerry suggested me, but the owner protested he didn't want a singer. Jerry explained that I not only sang, but could be funny and played a great straight man for him. We were put on as a team, but nothing funny happened. The manager reminded us both that he didn't need a singer, and we'd better get funny."[1]

JERRY: "We locked ourselves in a hotel room, and four hours later we walked out that door—with nothing, absolutely nothing."[5]

DEAN: "We had such colossal ideas, but none of them jelled on paper. We didn't use a line."[3]

JERRY: "We didn't know what we were going to say or do or sing."[5]

DEAN: "The second night, we went on with a 'who-the-hell-cares-any-way' attitude. It worked wonders. We broke up the joint and everyone howled. It seemed to me that Jer and I were made for each other."[6]

JERRY: "We both had certain assets. Dean had talent and I was fast on my feet. He sang and I ran around yapping like a macaw. He said funny things and I was real loud. And the audience ate it up."[5]

DEAN: "The people went wild. After the show, we went back to the hotel and Jer said something about bein' a team. I said 'Fine.' He said, 'Since you're older and have been in the business longer, let's split 60-40, 60 for you.' I said, 'No, we'll go 50-50. Just give me top billing.' That was fine with him. We never had a contract with each other—just a handshake."[4]

ENDNOTES

1. "Two Serious Comedians" by Jane Pelgram, *Radio & TV Life*, March 6, 1949
2. "I've Always Been Scared," by Jerry Lewis as told to Bill Davidson, *Look*, February 5, 1957
3. "Dean Martin, Vagabond Singer – Jerry Lewis, Sentimental Clown," by Maxine Arnold, *TV-Radio Mirror*, June 1952
4. "Crown Prince of the Clan" by Richard Gehman, *The American Weekly*, August 30, 1959
5. "Will TV's Hottest Combo Split?" by John Maynard, *Los Angeles Examiner*, July 18, 1954
6. "Why Martin and Lewis Fight," by Lloyd Shearer, *Parade*, August 28, 1955

2

1946–1950:
WELCOME TO NBC

DEAN: "Buck up, Jerry. It's our big chance!"

JERRY: "Yeah: the opportunity of a lifetime. The greatest moment of our lives. We go down to NBC, we walk out on the stage, and face all those people. And Dean?"

DEAN: "Yes?"

JERRY: "I wish I was dead."

Dialogue from THE MARTIN & LEWIS SHOW
premiere broadcast, April 3, 1949

IT TOOK A LITTLE WHILE for the newly-minted team to travel from "just a handshake" to the pinnacle of show biz, but for them it moved like lightning. After closing at the 500 Club in September, they went to the Havana-Madrid, where they'd initially begun "messin' into" each other's acts, this time as a bona fide duo with the second half of the evening's entertainment all theirs. It was at this engagement that the major newspaper and trade columnists discovered them. "[The] newly formed team… just about broke up the joint," *Billboard's* Bill Smith assured readers. "As singles they both do well…but together they're terrific. Their bits of biz, the effect of ad libs, their ability to break off one routine, go into another, and then go right back into the first one had customers yowling and limp."

3

Photo courtesy of the Patti Lewis Collection, Library of Congress

"Two youngsters working for small salaries in the Broadway night-clubs, Jerry Lewis and Dean Martin, have teamed up in a comedy act and their combined pay has quadrupled," wrote columnist Jack O'Brian the following month. "They will play Chicago's Latin Casino at $1,500 per week and on their New York return will get $2,000." They also made appearances on local radio shows such as *Merry-Go-Round* over Philadelphia's WDAS and with *Washington Daily News* columnist Arnold Fine over WWDC.

In a late 1990s interview, Lewis described their comedy as "three hours of 'Did you take a bath this morning?' 'Why, is there one missing?'" He wasn't far from wrong. Fine, in his "Tips on Tables" column, printed a fair sample from their December appearance at Paul Young's Romany Room in DC: "Amid a flurry of slapstick antics, Dean Martin points at Jerry Lewis, then turns to the audience and states, 'If this resembles anybody living, it's better off dead'.... Martin is a fairly suave chap who sings a good romantic song. But when Lewis—an anemic, thin, gawky lad—interrupts the crooner, the laughter begins. Martin retaliates with 'It's alright, folks; he's having a chest put in tomorrow.' Then there's the situation involving an irate cab driver (Lewis) arguing with his fare (Martin). When they are on the verge of a slugfest, the erstwhile passenger asks, 'What kind of cab driver are you?' Lewis answers, 'Yellow,' and walks sheepishly away.

"The most hilarious sequence of all is a take-off of Al Jolson's Sonny Boy. Lewis props himself with a set of huge, protruding teeth, an oversized hat, a big cigar. He rolls up his pants legs, climbs on Martin's knee as the warbler sounds out the tear-jerking lyrics. The opening-night crowd yowled and yowled."

Another Washington columnist, Harry MacArthur of the *Evening Star*, discerned one secret of their wide appeal at the same engagement: "When Mr. Lewis sets out to perform, his first heckler is Mr. Martin. If you don't like comics, you're on Dean's side right away. When Mr. Martin sings, it is Mr. Lewis who is out in the audience dropping plates and is otherwise interrupting. If you don't like crooners, you're on Jerry's side. Neither of them alone, nor any single performer, could win an audience that trickily. And once won, an audience is a receptive crowd for the doings of the Lewis-Martin duo."

From nightclubs they progressed to theaters that were still offering vaudeville to accompany motion pictures, beginning with Loew's State, Manhattan in January 1947. *Variety's* 'Wood' was there and penned a review for the "New Acts" section: "Deriving maximum benefit from the fresh, clean, youthful appearance of the pair, the turn does a smart job of tickling the customers' funny-bones at the State.... All-in-all, these two kids have themselves a fine act." *Billboard's* reviewer noted the addition of what would become a staple of their live television performances: "Pair have a new routine... Martin stays on stage for 'Ol' Man River,' while Lewis goes down into the pit to make like an ork (*sic*) leader. Martin played it straight; Lewis mugged it up, quarreling with musicians, and throwing bits of biz around for hilarious results. Pay-off was everything the lads could have wished for."

It was during an engagement at the State that summer (about which *The Billboard* wrote they "had the customers on their feet and yelling for more") that the team made its network radio bow. *Scout About Town*, hosted by disk jockey Barry Gray, showcased talent then appearing at venues around the city on a weekly 15 minute broadcast from the studios of station WOR. Despite its local flavor, the series was carried by the full Mutual Broadcasting System.

Seven years after the fact, Gray remembered the evening of August 5, 1947: "Jerry asked me where the program was heard. I told him 'all over America.' (We had some 400 stations.) He looked numb—'All over America?' and his voice squeaked… In the WOR studios, Jerry nervously went over his script. Then the time for broadcasting approached. Just a moment before we went on the air, Jerry, standing before the microphone, picked up the mike cable and said, 'Through this wire we get all over the country?' When I nodded, all he said was, 'Imagine!'"

The broadcast, which survives and circulates among old-time radio hobbyists, lends credence to Gray's observation. Martin & Lewis are basically an opening act for opera singer Dorothy Sarnoff, whom Gray later introduces as "our really *special* guest." They interact primarily with the host and Ms. Sarnoff, not with each other. Dean gets to sing a chorus of "Peg O' My Heart" and impresses Dorothy with his imperson-ations of Bing Crosby, Cary Grant and Clark Gable; however at other times, it's clear that he's reading lines, taking several awkward pauses. In contrast, Jerry is palpably nervous, twice tripping over his tongue when trying to say "Barry Gray"… although he's quick-witted enough to ad-lib a scolding ("Get off there!") before getting it right on the third try. His tendency to finish sentences like questions, and the soon-to-be catch phrase "Are you for real?" are already present, and a small studio audience can clearly be heard reacting to his antics as he turns away from the microphone.

The finale of each *Scout About Town* featured the presentation of "the Barry Gray Awards of the week" to the guest performers. Gray had no illusions about the importance of these tributes; they were designed for "getting actors to work for scale and sometimes, as they say on Broadway, 'for no.'" Even so, his commendation of a team that had just passed its first anniversary and had yet to appear west of Illinois was more than a little prophetic: "To Dean Martin and Jerry Lewis for their amazingly fresh and

Ad for the team's September 1947 appearance at the Riviera in Fort Lee NJ.

hilarious comedy, which I predict will carry them to even greater successes on the musical comedy stage and on the screen."

Appearances at clubs and theaters between New York and Chicago continued into 1948, culminating in the Copacabana booking in April that was intended for two weeks and ended up lasting nearly three months. The bigwigs of the radio and TV networks got their first look at them there; many were present when their opening night performance turned the headliner, 20th Century-Fox's musical star Vivian Blaine, into an afterthought. In May, CBS floated an 8-week summer replacement radio series, but that idea went nowhere. The following month, though, the network came through with a solid opportunity: Martin & Lewis would make their television debut on the broadcast that would also introduce home audiences to that most ungainly of emcees: Ed Sullivan's *Toast of the Town*.

Sullivan was the gossip columnist of the *New York Daily News*; as such he had a lot of show business connections. He was also no stranger to the microphone, having hosted stage and radio programs over the prior sixteen years. When CBS placed one of its top dramatic talents, Worthington Miner, in charge of television programming in the spring of 1948, they tasked him with creating a variety program that could favorably compare with NBC's forthcoming *Texaco Star Theater*, which would be hosted by a rotating slate of top comedians, starting with Milton Berle for its first four weeks beginning June 8. Miner, in turn, decided the answer was "a variety show where the master of ceremonies is a *discoverer* of talent," and recalled Sullivan's work as host and talent scout of the *Daily News's* annual Harvest Moon Ball.

Concurrently, Sullivan was itching to get into television and had already teamed with producer Marlo Lewis (no relation to Jerry, but whose sister, vocalist Monica Lewis, was then appearing at the Copacabana with the boys) to create a variety show along the lines of the Harvest Moon Ball. Lewis had already pitched the idea to Miner's predecessor, Jerry Danzig, to a less-than-enthusiastic response. But with Miner in command, things moved quickly: "In a matter of hours, we made a deal with Ed."

The "deal," as Marlo Lewis cheerlessly recalled in his 1979 memoir *Prime Time*, was for $400 per week, money that was to cover Sullivan, himself and *all* talent. No amount of cajoling or threats could move CBS from its "take it or leave it" position. Yet when the glum producer outlined the deal to Sullivan, "he was gleeful. With his characteristic damn-the-torpedoes attitude and his headlong drive to get into television, he said, 'Screw 'em! Grab the deal! I don't care what they're offering us. We'll pay for the show out of our own pockets if we have to.'" Sullivan wasn't joking and, according to Lewis, the two of them "subsidized CBS" for the first twenty-six weeks.

According to Miner, Sullivan "brought me back a very limp list of tired performers…second-string all the way down the line. Ed couldn't talk any of the top headliners around into coming on the show. They wouldn't go near it. So I said, 'Ed, you've missed the point. You're in there to discover talent. Nothing will sell this show as much as the fact that you are dealing with the stars of tomorrow—not yesterday. You find me two great bets for *tomorrow*—and we will have a great opening show.' And [with Martin & Lewis] that's what he did."

Marlo Lewis remembered it differently; his first notice on booked talent came during a phone call with Sullivan:

SULLIVAN: "Let me tell you what I've lined up for the show."

LEWIS: "Big names?"

SULLIVAN: "Reeelly big."

LEWIS: "Tell me…I'm ready for some good news."

SULLIVAN: "For openers—only the biggest comedy act in the history of show business! You think twenty-five minutes of Dean Martin and Jerry Lewis will satisfy [CBS]?"

LEWIS: "Fantastic! How much do we have to pay them?"

SULLIVAN: "Are you ready for this? Twenty-five bucks apiece!"

Lewis's memory may also have been faulty; 14 years later, Sullivan recalled paying the team $200, and that it was his daughter Betty who'd discovered them. "She predicted that youngsters all over the country would flip over their lunacies," he told *TV Guide*, "and Betty was so-o right!" The columnist-turned-impresario also finagled Broadway's Richard Rodgers and Oscar Hammerstein II to perform a medley of their hits "for nothing," along with concert pianist Eugene List, dancer Kathryn Lee, boxing referee Ruby Goldstein, and a singing New York City fireman, John

Kokoman. Marlo got his sister Monica for a singing spot, plus six Copa showgirls to sing and prance about as "the Toastettes." Ray Bloch and his Orchestra had already been committed.

There was no question which was the headline act, even though they'd eventually be whittled down from twenty-five minutes to six. Marlo Lewis got on the phone with their agent Abby Greshler and was "met with immediate cooperation. 'Drop over to the Copa tonight,' Greshler suggested. 'Watch the boys work. Then you and Jerry figure out what you want them to do on the show. Dean will leave it up to the two of you.'" After the show, the two Lewises met in a hotel suite above the famous niterie, and Marlo beheld a much more self-assured performer than had Barry Gray: "Irrepressible, breezy and brash, he kidded his way through our conversation. He joked about my relationship with the 'Smiling Irishman' [and] kept calling him 'Abe Solomon.'" Together they hammered out a game plan; when that was done, Jerry "assumed an exaggeratedly serious expression and grabbed a Gideon Bible from the nighttable (*sic*). Putting his hand on the Book, he said, 'Tell Abe Solomon we promise to

Dean and Jerry at the Riviera. Photo courtesy of the Fort Lee Film Commission.

WINS radio's Jack Eigen broadcasts from the Copacabana during Martin & Lewis' engagement; he's joined here by Al Jolson, one of many celebrities who came to see the hot new comedy team. Photo courtesy of the Patti Lewis Collection, Library of Congress.

give him a very nice show. Tell him we do jokes, we dance and we sing, and we're really pretty good!'"

They were more than "pretty good," according to Miner. "They came on and they were dynamite." *Variety* agreed: "Talent, on the whole, was standout. Tops were Dean Martin and Jerry Lewis with their zany comedics." Of the host, however, the reviewer opined, "as an emcee [he] is a good newspaper columnist." But from the start, Sullivan had a quality that even CBS head William Paley couldn't define: "His popularity was magical – beyond explanation," he would write in *As It Happened*. "He couldn't perform in any way. He never tried. All he had to do was talk and he did very little of that." Yet Paley recognized Sullivan's gift as "a showman who could attract the best and most timely performers from all four corners of the world of entertainment."

The premiere took place on Sunday, June 20, 1948. It marked the beginning of Sullivan's 23-year Sunday night reign, one that would endure only one serious threat, from the comedy team he'd gleefully booked for his opener.

* * * * *

In July, Dean and Jerry returned to the 500 Club for their 2nd Anniversary as a team. On August 3, they made their NBC bow on *Texaco Star Theater*, then being hosted by Morey Amsterdam. Little is known about the broadcast, except that *Variety* believed "Amsterdam found it tough to shine" while competing with Martin & Lewis for laughs. Texaco must have agreed, and signed Milton Berle as permanent host three weeks later.

More critical for the team was their Hollywood debut at Slapsie Maxie's a week later, followed almost immediately by a siren song of film offers that Lewis and Greshler would sift through with care. They'd sign a recording contract with Capitol Records on August 20, and a million-dollar motion picture deal with independent producer Hal Wallis a few days later. They also "stole" the club's house band and its leader, Dick Stabile, who would work exclusively for Martin & Lewis until their final joint performance. ("Joint" being an appropriate word for another reason since, according to Lewis, Stabile introduced both he and Dean to marijuana.)

Prior to leaving for the Coast, Greshler had his clients record a radio audition that was scripted by Hal Block. Georgia Gibbs guested, Frank Gallop announced and Ray Bloch and his Orchestra handled the music. Greshler's plan was to submit the recording directly to advertising agencies, but that was pre-empted when outside circumstances quickly forced NBC to take a closer look at Martin & Lewis.

In the early fall of 1948, one-by-one, most of the network's major radio stars defected to CBS. Performers such as Jack Benny, Edgar Bergen, Burns & Allen and *Amos 'n' Andy* were lured away by the opportunity to own their shows and receive a corresponding break on their income taxes. Reluctantly, NBC realized they would have to pursue new talent with exclusive contracts covering both radio and television just to stay in business.

Prior to drawing up any long-term contracts, the first thing the future "Peacock Network" did for the boys was to put them on television. They did the first three weeks of *Welcome Aboard*, a half-hour variety show sponsored by Admiral Television, in October. But the shows were clunky and camerawork was often poor; even the surviving third show, which *Variety* thought their best ("On each successive stint, the boys unloosened more and to advantage"), wasn't visually compelling. In 1948, TV was still a poor stepchild compared to radio.

The week after their third *Welcome Aboard* show, they guest-starred on Bob Hope's weekly radio program, and upon listening it's evident that Dean Martin hadn't solved his inability to sound natural when reading lines, and that Jerry Lewis had come a long way from the uncertain comic who'd guested on *Scout About Town*. Hope sets the scene: the boys are concluding their act at Slapsie Maxie's. Martin sings "Everybody Loves Somebody," a song that would *really* take him places a few years after the split, then trips over his tongue just saying his partner's name. Lewis comes out and the two go into one of their standard bits:

A June 1948 newspaper advertisement. The supporting acts kept changing but the headliners were finishing up their second month.

JERRY: "I'm awfully glad you called on me and because you let me be out here with you like this, I appreciate it?"

DEAN: "You wha-?"

JERRY: "I said, by your calling me like this, I appreciate it?"

DEAN: "Why do you keep the words up in the air? Let it come down, there's a period there. You would say, 'I'm going to the corner.' Not 'I'm going to the corner?'"

JERRY: "Well, you talk your way. I talk that way because, listen?"

Back in their dressing room, somebody knocks on the door. (*Jerry:* "Who's there, boy or girl?" *Hope:* "Bob Hope." *Jerry:* "Answer the question!") Hope wants the boys to appear on his program; Dean's amenable, but Jerry's dead set against it: "I don't care what you say, I'm not going on the radio. I hate the radio, and if you make me go on the radio, I'll swallow my skate key!" Then Hope mentions the $5,000 fee per guest shot. *Hope:* "And if you guys work out, you can come back for five more shots." *Jerry:* "And I want mine with soda! (Laughs) I put one over on him, didn't I? Ain't I the *shifty* one?"

Between Lewis's ad libs ("Hey Dean, light me another cigarette. I swallowed the last one!") and Martin's seeming inability to correctly pronounce words of two or more syllables, Hope has a hard time keeping it together, and it's clear the studio audience is enjoying the proceedings. The prolonged craziness necessitated dropping Hope's usual closing: a special-lyric rendition of his signature tune, "Thanks for the Memories." Fortunately, an original script survives that includes this verse:

> *THANKS FOR THE MEMORY*
> *OF THE MARTIN-LEWIS TEAM*
> *YOU'RE SURE TO GAIN ESTEEM*
> *IT'S TRUE, YOU KNOW, AS SHOWMEN GO*
> *YOU'RE REALLY ON THE BEAM*
> *WE THANK YOU SO MUCH.*

The team returned for a second "shot" four weeks later to similar reaction, and that was proof enough for NBC. On December 17, Dean and Jerry signed a five-year contract for radio, a deal *The Billboard* valued at $150,000. Greshler cannily held out for a non-exclusivity clause for television; thus the network was limited to first refusal rights to meet or exceed anyone else's TV offer. Writers Dick McKnight and Ray Allen and producer/director Robert L. Redd were engaged to concoct a series for the team that was to run a full 39 weeks. On or about December 21,

Dean and Jerry rehearse for their television debut on *Toast of the Town*.

Two excited young men arrive at NBC studios in October 1948. Photo courtesy of the Patti Lewis Collection, Library of Congress.

Martin & Lewis recorded an audition for their own starring show, with Lucille Ball as their guest star.

The audition survives, and was first made available to the public on a record album released during the early 1970's. Today, it circulates in versions derived from a 37-minute unedited tape, and a half-hour, edited-for-broadcast transcription disk. The boys spend the first half trying to work up the nerve to get to the NBC studio for their show, and begin the second half with a discussion that Jerry escalates into a split-up of their partnership. Jerry's penchant for exaggeration is then directed toward their guest:

DEAN: "What's the matter, Lucille?"

LUCILLE BALL: "Don't act like you don't know. You've got some nerve, Dean Martin, asking me to come down here and be a guest on your radio program, after the way you beat up that sweet, adorable little Jerry Lewis. Why, if I weren't a perfect lady, I'd slug ya. The idea: beating up that cute, darling, lamby-pie."

DEAN: "Me?"

JERRY: "Yes, you, Dean Martin!"

DEAN: "But Jerry... hey, where'd he go?"

LUCILLE: "He's behind me, where he'll be safe. He's not going to stay out here where you can knock him down again."

DEAN: "Knock him down?!?"

LUCILLE: "Yes, and kicking him, and throwing dirt in his face, and trying to drive your car over him!"

DEAN: "I did that?"

JERRY: "See, Lucille, he admits it!"

Eventually, Miss Ball succumbs to Dean's charm and after everybody makes up, she invites the boys to a private party:

LUCILLE: "Jerry, I hope you understand, I've invited important people. People of refinement, breeding, culture."

JERRY: "Don't worry about me! Refinement and breeding and culture pour out of me like sweat off a horse's neck!"

DEAN: "Lucille, don't worry. I'll guarantee Jerry."

LUCILLE: "Well, I don't know. I'm afraid he'll be a little raucous."

Red Skelton looks askance as Dean & Jerry feed each other while waiting for their turn on the all-star NBC broadcast *Elgin Thanksgiving Day Greeting to America*, November 25, 1948. Photo courtesy of Kayley Thompson.

JERRY: "Raucous? Me?!? Don't ever worry about Jerry Lewis being raucous. I'll make more noise than anyone there!"

In closing, the three sing "The Money Song," which was the team's first release for Capitol. It also served as the series theme song.

Once the audition was completed, the duo headed to Miami, then the favored winter destination of the East Coast elite, for an engagement at the Beachcomber. Arthur Godfrey, who was then—and would be for years to come—CBS's most lucrative property, caught their show during the first week of January, and on Monday the 10th, devoted about ten minutes of his morning program to raving about the funniest act he'd ever seen. "What Godfrey didn't mention," wrote *Variety*, "and what CBS execs figured he didn't even know, is that the Martin-Lewis combo are (*sic*) NBC's newest comedy acquisition."

As their show drew nearer to its debut date of April 3, 1949, NBC made certain that Martin & Lewis were heard on their part of the dial. They did a spot on a March of Dimes special on January 31. On February 10, they appeared on *Chesterfield Supper Club* with Peggy Lee, and seven days later, they did *Sealtest Variety Theater*, hosted by Dorothy Lamour. According to *Variety*, Sealtest, unhappy with *Variety Theater's* ratings, gave some thought to sponsoring the team's series, but nothing would come of it. Five days before their premiere, they returned to *The Bob Hope Show* for a third round of hijinks.

Somehow, in the slipshod documentation of Dean and Jerry's radio career, the audition with Lucille Ball has been tagged by many radio historians as the series opener. Where this idea originated is a mystery, because the contemporary evidence—newspaper ads and reviews, magazine and trade paper reviews, NBC's files, and the show that aired seven days later—assert that Bob Hope was the guest on the premiere of *The Martin & Lewis Show* on April 3rd. The Hope program used nearly the same script as the audition, although there's some variance in the plot during the second half. It's possible that the misconception arose because the premiere circulates only in a 42-minute unedited tape. As of this writing, the broadcast version has yet to surface.

As in the audition, Dean and Jerry fret about how they'll be received at NBC. In this version, Jerry's even more concerned, given the importance of their guest star:

JERRY: "Gee, I start to shake all over when I think of tonight – being on the same show with Bob Hope! Gee, he's a big star, Dean, and…"

DEAN: "Aw, don't worry, we'll get through it somehow. And by the way Jerry, when you meet Bob Hope, don't make any cracks about his nose."

JERRY: "No cracks about his nose?"

DEAN: "Naw, just shake hands with it and let it go at that!"

An apprehensive Bob Hope prepares to assist these two loons with the premiere of their own series, April 3, 1949.

JERRY: *(Laughing)* "'Shake hands with it!' Hey, that was a *sterling* one! Look, Dean, you're the singer and I'm the comedian, right?"

DEAN: "That's right."

Dean and Jerry at the NBC microphone, April 1949.

JERRY: "You're supposed to sing, and I'm supposed to tell the jokes and get the laughs. And yet, you just told a joke and got a big laugh! Ha-ha-ha-ha-ha-ha! *(Mock seriousness)* Don't do it no more!"

When Hope comes on, it's ostensibly to welcome Dean and Jerry to the network; having hosted them three times before, NBC obviously wanted the audience to accept the team as his protégés. Things move along briskly at first, with plenty of cracks about Jerry's hair (*Hope:* "What does the barber use, scissors or sandpaper?" *Dean:* "Oh, the barber uses scissors, but he works from the inside.") and physique (*Hope:* "You boys are gonna be working pretty hard from now on, so Jerry, you've got to build up your strength." *Jerry:* "What would you suggest, Mr. Hope?" *Hope:* "Put Something in Your Pot, Boy"[1]). At one point, Jerry flubs a line and Hope advises him to "Start over, it's tape. Crosby starts ten times a night!" Inevitably, Dean stumbles on a word, adding, "I get a straight line, can't even read it!" "Funny how those strange words came out alright," replies Hope, laughing; at which point Jerry complains, "I don't want you guys to get upset, but I don't like how well you're working together!"

After that, things come apart quickly:

HOPE: "This kid's really gonna live tonight. At midnight, he'll be drinking Ovaltine from Margaret O'Brien's slipper."

DEAN: (stepping on Hope's laugh) "Well, it's awfully nice of you, Bob, to invite us…" I'm sorry!

HOPE: Please!

JERRY: (to the audience) Well, I hope you folks are enjoying our career!

DEAN: "Well, it's awfully ni-… it's awfully nice—" I'll get this line in yet, Bob!

HOPE: I hope you have it right when you get your chance! Go ahead!

DEAN: It's awfully nice of you to come over for our hour show… and to invite us to your party. Who's gonna be there?

HOPE: We'll need an hour to hatch this thing… where are we? You've got me confused—you've read every line on this page!

---

1. A current song recorded by Les Brown, who was the bandleader for Hope's program.

After all the hype NBC put into its publicity, reviews of the opener pretty much reached the same conclusion: the show needed a lot of work. With its usual astute eye, *Variety* observed: "Bridging the gap from a nitery visual assist into a strictly audio medium still remains a big "but." Chalk it up to a couple of novices working in a new medium... but Sunday's show was off on timing, pace and tempo. It was particularly apparent when they stood up against Hope.... A succession of Martin fluffs didn't kid anyone, nor were they funny. Hope, of course, hopped on them, but brother, there wasn't that Crosby pickup."

Billboard's Sam Chase agreed: "[After] the initial outing, the lads will have to do considerable improving to live up to [NBC's] hopes. Much of the material... was culled from the auditions the comics made, and too much of it was in the same groove which countless spielers preceding them on the airlanes have worn deep.... With five writers credited, there weren't that many fresh gags used." Chase concluded the ball was in NBC's court: "If the scripters can come up with material as fresh as their

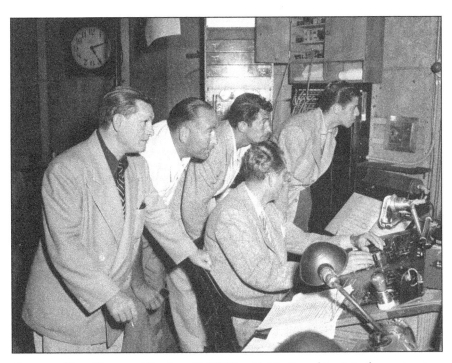

Composer Victor Young and Producer Hal Wallis with Martin and Lewis in the scoring stage at Paramount. Young's presence implies they're observing a session for *The Accused* (1949). Note how intently Lewis is watching; from the start he wanted to learn about filmmaking. Photo courtesy of the Patti Lewis Collection, Library of Congress.

style and talent, Martin and Lewis still may earn all the accolades which were tossed their way before they ever faced a mike."

Radio and Television Life's critic wrote: "Times have changed, and Martin & Lewis are expected to hit the heights with one program. Their first show wasn't so hot. Maybe if we'd never heard of them before and expected nothing much, we might have enjoyed the show more. But no, that tense feeling of do-or-die made us self-conscious listeners – and probably made Martin & Lewis a pair of self-conscious comedians."

Cruelest of all was the *Washington Post*'s Sonia Stein: "NBC is very much at fault, for trying to palm off the Dean Martin-Jerry Lewis comedy show. If it was presented with humility, and a notation that it was the best they could do on short notice, it could be forgiven. But no. An NBC Vice President... suggested I listen. I hope he listened too. A pox on Martin, Lewis and the v.p. Such high points as the script had were ruined by Lewis' delivery, which is all brash and a yard wide. 'Ozzie and Harriet,' who vacated the [time slot] on NBC to fill it at CBS, can't be much worried over this competition."

All told, NBC was spending about $10,000 a week on the show, $2,000 of which went to the stars. There was no sponsor - the only ads were public service announcements for US Savings Bonds (even these ended after the first month). The network's hope was to lure a client after a few solid broadcasts.

The premiere had set the pattern for the series to follow. Not so surprisingly, McKnight, Allen and the handful of other scribes came up with a pseudo-situation comedy. Martin and Lewis portrayed Martin & Lewis, a hot new comedy team, and the "plots" focused on their attempts to get their show on the air, find a sponsor, come up with a new nightclub act, make a new record for Capitol, and so forth. Inevitably, Jerry's nonsense would interfere with the job at hand, and Dean would have to set things straight—if he could. Along the way, they'd interact with a guest star and deal with any number of crazy supporting characters, especially their scatterbrained secretary, Florence, played by Flo McMichaels. Another equally dizzy character was Mrs. Taproot, the president of a Dean Martin fan club for women aged 50 or older. Of course, there would be musical interludes: Dean would sing two songs completely straight. It was a slight reworking of the tried-and-true format bequeathed to numerous radio comics by the master, Jack Benny.

The gags—most of which, unfortunately, got old faster than the writers expected—usually centered around Jerry's hairstyle ("I don't comb it.

I just wake up in the morning and let it ad-lib."), his weight (*Dean:* "A hundred and eighteen and three-quarter pounds—and that's with clothes on. What do you weigh stripped?" *Jerry:* "I don't know—I'm bashful!"), his love life (*Jerry:* "She's the most glamorous, the most gorgeous, the most fascinating, the most beautiful girl in the whole world!" *Dean:* "Oh, my gosh, not another lady wrestler!") and his lack of brain power (*Dean:* "Don't tell me how to be smart. Do I tell you how to be stupid?" *Jerry:* "So what's to tell?"). All this, and a plethora of Lewis catch-phrases: "I wish I was dead" or "Look how they're starin' at me" every time a joke falls flat; along with "I'm only 23 years old – what do *I* know?" "Ooooh, what a *ham!*" "Oh, Dean, I'm so unworthy of you!" "Well, you see… I haven't been too well!" And, at least once in every show, "Are you for real?"

What little comedy remained usually came to a dead halt when Florence the secretary walked in. Flo McMichaels gave her all, but poor writing sabotaged her performance nearly every week. Typical was this exchange:

JERRY: "What you need, Florence, is some real good perfume."

FLORENCE: "Well, that'll make me meet men?"

JERRY: "Sure! And look at these brands here: Savage, Helpless, Quivering, Frantic…"

FLORENCE: "Goodness, I just want to meet a man, I don't want to drive him crazy!"

DEAN: "Well, what perfume do you like best, Florence?"

FLORENCE: "Well, I used to use a perfume that was double-guaranteed to stop men dead in their tracks!"

JERRY: "What was it? LaTene? Twenty Carats?"

FLORENCE: "Oh, no. This wasn't that subtle stuff - this had a direct approach to men!"

JERRY: "What was it called?"

Movie and radio tough guy Sheldon Leonard brings his patented Runyonesque delivery to *The Martin & Lewis Show*.

FLORENCE: "Pucker, Sucker!"

DEAN: "You know, it's nice you two dropped into this drug store—now they've got dopes on both sides of the counter!"

The first four weeks were transcribed from Hollywood, where Dean and Jerry were finishing up their first film for Hal Wallis. This was also radio-related: an adaptation of the popular sitcom *My Friend Irma*, which put them in a somewhat uncomfortable position, the highly-touted new stars of NBC debuting in the movie version of a top 5 CBS radio show and having to promote it on their own series to boot. Adding insult to injury, CBS would receive a percentage of the film's gross box office. If nothing else, it was payback for Arthur Godfrey's generous plug, which both NBC and Martin & Lewis had been using in their press releases.

Once production wrapped on *My Friend Irma* (1949), *The Martin & Lewis Show* moved to New York City. Guests came from the theatre district, along with movie stars who happened to be in town. At the time *Variety* reported, "Several of the guests appearing so far have reportedly been dissatisfied with the final outcome of the program." After having taped her appearance on April 26, actress Madeleine Carroll had immediate second thoughts, and requested that it not be aired. Robert Redd attempted to sign Charles Laughton as a replacement, but Laughton insisted on seeing a script first and wouldn't commit until the following week. The writers hastily turned out a script without a guest, which was taped—but the resulting show was so poor that the one with Miss Carroll had to be used, airing on May 1, 1949.

Nevertheless, Lever Brothers expressed an interest in the team around this time. The soap company was sponsoring Bob Hope's program, suggesting that Hope may have taken his role as the team's mentor straight to Lever's boardroom. Arrangements were made for *The Martin & Lewis Show* to become the summer replacement for Hope's *Swan Soap* program.

A few days later, *Variety* tuned in again to hear the team's program with guest Burl Ives. "Not since their kickoff show—and that was spotty—have the saloon funsters come through in the abstract. The efforts of NBC's comedy white hopes in the pre-7 p.m. Sunday night slot have ranged from poor to terrible. The Burl Ives stint was anywhere in that range." By the time the series moved into Hope's timeslot, Lever had changed its mind about picking up the tab.

In its June 29 issue, *Variety* wrote that the Colgate-Palmolive Peet Company "may latch on to sponsorship of the Dean Martin-Jerry Lewis NBC comedy show in the fall." Intriguingly, the "chief factor motivating Colgate is said to be its reaction to M&L's performance in the new Paramount *My Friend Irma* pic, which was previewed for Colgate execs last week, thus indicating that Colgate has TV plans also in mind for the comics." This deal fell through as well, but seeds were sown for the future.

All told, the team had received offers from fourteen sponsors; unfortunately, they were offers to go on television exclusively. The team declined, claiming they wanted to succeed in radio first. Commenting on this, *Radio and Television Life* magazine added, "How can they be so blind to the fact that they are an extremely dull couple on the air, and extremely funny when seen?" In retrospect, they weren't blind at all—radio was a less risky (and less costly) medium for two comedians that had yet to prove themselves to mainstream audiences.

The problem with *The Martin & Lewis Show* was that it was a situation comedy with too much "situation" and not enough comedy. In some cases, the plots seemed to dare the team to be funny. A perfect example is the program of June 21, 1949, its debut as Hope's summer replacement.

Once again, *Variety* reviewed the show and commented that "there's still considerable polishing to be done."

In this tale, a member of Tony Martin's fan club takes Dean to court to stop him from using the name Martin. Tony Martin himself is critical of the idea, but when Dean and Jerry confront him about it a little *too* belligerently, he immediately changes his mind and welcomes the lawsuit. In court (with Jerry serving as Dean's "lawyer"), the two crooners must "prove" to the judge which one of them is worthy of keeping the name.

Said *Variety*, "Any charm and cleverness that this turn might have had was dissipated by some inept writing. It was surprising that either [vocalist] went for this type of show which virtually forced listeners to make up their minds as to which singer is better. [The] story line also forced Martin and Lewis to work as individuals instead of a team. Lewis was almost lost in the shuffle." As unbelievable as *that* sounds, *Variety's* reviewer was dead-on. Heard today, the whole show seems like an over-long, unfunny lead-in for the finish, when the two Martins sing a duet on "Anything You Can Do (I Can Do Better)."

The following week's show was selected by NBC for a special package directed toward advertising agencies and potential sponsors. It was a strange choice: the crux of the episode focused on Jerry's need to baby-sit a boy genius (the nephew of guest John Carradine) while also on a date with Florence. Both Martin and Carradine are secondary to the plot. Apart from his allotted two songs, Dean is barely there; perhaps it was his turn to be "almost lost in the shuffle."

With the help of their partner, RCA, the network assembled a box set of three 45 rpm records, which contained the episode along with a brief audio sales pitch. The package was sent out during the remainder of summer, but for naught: the lukewarm reviews plus the $10,000 weekly price tag totaled No Sale.

On July 19, the show moved back to Hollywood. Ben Alexander, later to become famous as the rotund partner of Sgt. Joe Friday on *Dragnet*, took over as announcer. More importantly, Sheldon Leonard came aboard as a new running character: Soapie, a neighbor who involves the boys in some crazy, expensive schemes - one of which led to a storyline that lasted several weeks, beginning with the show of August 16, where he convinces them to buy their own nightclub. Leonard's character, and his patented Damon Runyonesque voice, definitely added some life to the show, but too often both Dean and Jerry played straight for him. When a supporting player gets bigger laughs than Martin & Lewis, something's wrong:

DEAN: "Well, I'll admit that I'd like to be in business for myself, Soapie, but how could Jerry and I ever own a nightclub?"

SOAPIE: "Well now, I happen to know of a nice little club that you could lease real cheap: four thousand bucks!"

JERRY: "Gee!"

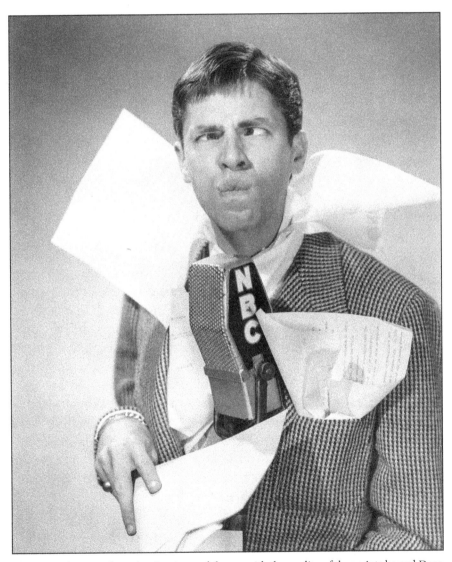

This was only a gag photo, but Lewis wasn't happy with the quality of the scripts he and Dean were getting. Photo courtesy of the Patti Lewis Collection, Library of Congress.

SOAPIE: "That's one of 'em. Keep going kid; just three more 'G's' and you're in escrow."

After twelve weeks in Bob Hope's spot, and still no sign of a sponsor, NBC took the show off after the broadcast of September 6. Meanwhile, *My Friend Irma* opened. Most critics hated the movie but loved the team, and finally Mr. and Mrs. Average American discovered that these two guys really were funny. Dean and Jerry did personal appearances with the film's New York booking and took the opportunity to talk about their radio program with the *Philadelphia Inquirer's* Frank Brookhouser:

> "*There's only one thing wrong with radio,*" *said Dean.*
> "*We're on it,*" *shouted Jerry.*
> "*It's not for sight,*" *said Dean. "Unless you see Jerry's puss, he has nothing. He is for sight. I've been carrying the whole radio show for 23 weeks. But I don't mind holding it up. I've been doing fine.*"
> *Severe pain, rank amazement and sheer incredulity stampeded across Jerry's face.*
> "*Jerry always wants to quit, but I keep him on,*" *Dean continued, deadpanned. "I split the money with him. I'm fair about it. I get 60%, he gets 40. He may get better on television.*"

Behind closed doors, Martin and Lewis did more serious griping. *Variety* reported that the team believed NBC had shortchanged them on production matters, particularly the quality of the writing. The network countered that "the best talents available have been assigned to the production end of the show," and that if their ratings haven't been "everything that was desired, the fault lies elsewhere."

While *My Friend Irma* rocked the box office, NBC brought *The Martin & Lewis Show* back to the air on Friday October 7 at 8:30pm. Capitulating to the stars, the network assigned all new writers, including Charley Issacs, Hal Goodman and Jack Douglas; plus, according to *Variety*, "[vested] Lewis with powers to sit in on story conferences and lend an assist." Dean and Jerry, for their part, plugged their return by appearing on TV with Uncle Miltie on October 18.

None of which helped, as it was pretty much the same show, with the same tired situations and running gags offset by an occasional belly-laugh. The funniest moment in the October 7 program may have been an accident. Dean and Jerry are discussing how to make their nightclub successful:

DEAN: "If you and I want to stay in show business, and become a great success, we've got to have a story to tell."

JERRY: "You mean, it isn't enough to have good food and drinks?"

(Long Pause)

JERRY (his natural voice): "It's your line, Dean."

DEAN (after a beat): "No."

The new writers gave Florence the heave-ho, so Flo McMichaels adopted a new character: cigarette girl Condolea Hockenhaven, who carried a torch for Dean. Vocally, Condolea was Florence with a Brooklyn accent; and sadly, just as unfunny:

CONDOLEA: (swooning) "Ahh, Deanie!"

JERRY: "I'm leavin'!"

DEAN: "Aw, Jerry, please don't!"

CONDOLEA: "Oh, Deanie, why can't we be alone? Why must your little boy always hang around? Oh, Deanie, hold me tight! Let me look in your big brown eyes. *(Reconsidering)* Or are they blue? Or are they grey?"

DEAN: "They're chartreuse."

On the 26th, *Variety* reported that NBC "this week set three different teams of scripters to work in lining up program ideas" for a Martin & Lewis TV series. "As soon as the best is selected, [a] kinescope will be lensed for pitching to clients and ad agencies." This was not on the strength of the revived radio show, but rather "good reaction to their 'Texaco' guestint *(sic)*…convinced the web that the team should be handed their own TV program as rapidly as possible." It was a roll of the dice that both Greshler and Hal Wallis would stifle; with more picture work looming, the team wouldn't return to NBC-TV until the following April.

After only four weeks, the network decided to move the show to Monday, 10:00pm—the radio equivalent of Siberia. The change took effect with the broadcast of November 7, and Lewis made no secret of his feelings with a small addition to his opening line: "Gee, Dean, I sure wish we didn't have to go to the club tonight. I'd rather just stay here in the room and read a book, or listen to our *Martin & Lewis* program being

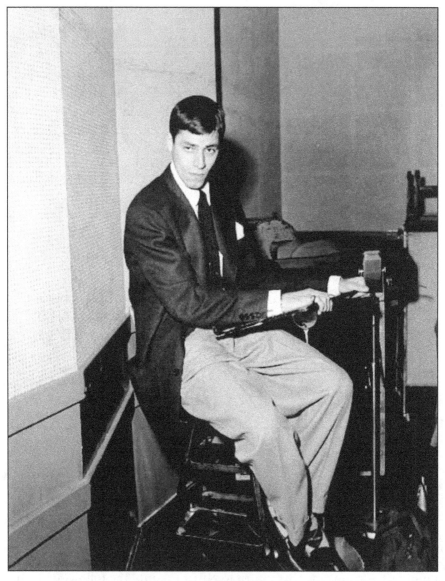

Photo courtesy of Kayley Thompson.

released at a more inconvenient time." The boys had to know that their adolescent fans would not be tuning in, guaranteeing a sharp drop in an already mediocre Hooper rating.

Eventually the nightclub idea was dropped; when that happened, guest stars disappeared as well. Martin, Lewis, McMichaels and Leonard pretty much fended for themselves. Condolea Hockenhaven vanished, and McMichaels became Daisy Esther Van Loop, established as quiet, mousy, extremely skinny ("When I was born, I weighed twelve pounds! And I've been losing weight ever since!") and in love with Jerry. For the first few weeks, Geraldine Kaye played Mrs. Gloria Van Loop, eager to marry off her daughter. Daisy Esther bore no vocal resemblance to Florence, and the comedy was usually at her expense:

DAISY ESTHER: "Mother, don't beg Jerry. It's his loss if he doesn't realize that I'm a combination Jane Russell, Betty Grable, Lana Turner and Rita Hayworth. Deep down inside of me, I'm a burning, yearning fire just waiting to explode!"

JERRY: "Are you for real?"

When the team was committed to a December stint at the Chez Paree nightclub, the show moved to Chicago for a few weeks, transcribing from a studio that echoed like an empty mausoleum. The highlight of this batch was probably the show of December 19, in which Dean and Jerry crash a big society party, only to be discovered and thrown out. Up to this point, low (and forced) comedy is the focus, but the mood changes as the two head back to their hotel. The sights and sounds of Christmas fill their senses, and Dean sings a lovely version of "Silent Night" with lyrics in both English and Italian.

While working in the Windy City, they could hardly avoid its more notorious denizens. The "wise guys" were always drawn to entertainers, especially those of Italian descent, like Dean; eager to do them favors—with an unspoken obligation that they'd respond in kind, of course. Writer Charley Issacs once recalled how, during this visit, a local mobster told Sheldon Leonard that his cronies "really like you. They think you take off real good on 'em." Said Issacs, "Sheldon swelled up like he'd just got an Academy Award."

No one else associated with the show had any reason to swell with pride, except possibly the stars—but that was due to their mass acceptance by both critics and audiences in *My Friend Irma*. All agreed that the team stole the film from the stars of the *Irma* radio show, but it wasn't translating into an audience for their own program. If anything, the film reinforced the belief that Martin & Lewis should be seen and not just heard, which meant NBC would continue to hemorrhage $10,000 per week. Worse, their contract was coming up for renewal, and the network was angling for exclusive television rights—which Abby Greshler was loathe to grant.

As the series limped toward its 39th week, NBC had spent about $750,000 in the promotion and production of *The Martin & Lewis Show*. The network's position was that, since the program had not sold, they'd be more likely to recoup this huge investment by locking up the team for a TV series in 1950—and it would be nice if they could accomplish this without a salary hike. Greshler begged to differ and, true to form, CBS swooped in to make an offer. Horrified at the thought of all that money lost to their predatory rival, NBC quickly came to terms with the agent, gaining exclusivity in exchange for cash.

The immediate impact was that *The Martin & Lewis Show* would be discontinued at the end of January. With literally nothing to lose, the boys played fast and loose with the material of their last five weeks of shows. The writers followed their lead, giving Dean a chance to use a bogus Italian accent in every show and Jerry to play around with dialects of all kinds, the weirder the better. Dean also started taking his crooning less seriously, which was nothing new for anyone who'd heard him in nightclubs. While covering "Rock-a-bye Your Baby With a Dixie Melody" during the broadcast of January 2, 1950, Martin imitates Al Jolson (who introduced the song years before), sings with his faux "Italiano" dialect, and screws around with the lyrics ("and Old Black Joe, what a schmoe!"). Suddenly the end result was becoming equal to the talent involved. Unfortunately, nobody—not even *Variety*—was bothering to tune in.

The Martin & Lewis Show departed for good after the broadcast of January 30th, 1950. Ironically, it was probably the funniest program of the whole series. Jerry is waiting for Dean outside of Schwab's drugstore, when a woman approaches and asks him to mind her baby while she shops. Jerry agrees, reluctantly, and then he and Dean find themselves stuck when the mother fails to return. In order to lull the baby to sleep, Jerry tells the story of "Jack and the Beanstalk," with himself as Jack and Dean as a very Italian giant:

DEAN: "I gotta mind to swallow you up in-a one go!"

JERRY: "Why are you talking in an Italian accent?"

DEAN: "I get-a more laughs this way!"

Having failed to locate the mother on foot, the boys take the baby down to a TV station. The station manager agrees to let them broadcast their plea, provided they cover for a fighter and manager that failed to show up for an interview show. The boys agree, and launch into one of their more verbal nightclub routines, with Jerry as a punch-drunk boxer and Dean as an interviewer:

JERRY: "I've had—ahhh—I've had sisteen fights."

DEAN: "Sis-teen?"

JERRY: "Yeah, sisteen! You know, fawteen, fitteen, sisteen!"

With that, it was all over. There was no grand farewell; announcer Rod O'Connor simply informed listeners that *Dangerous Assignment* would be heard in the timeslot the following week. By then, Dean and Jerry had started work on a sequel to *My Friend Irma*, and anticipated their future on NBC television.

* * * * *

RADIO EPISODE GUIDE I: *"THE MARTIN & LEWIS SHOW"*

NBC; SUSTAINED

FEATURING: *Flo McMichaels*: Florence (through September 6, 1949), Condolea Hockenhaven (October 7, 1949 through November 28, 1949), Daisy Esther Van Loop (from December 5, 1949), various one-shot characters; *Sheldon Leonard*: Soapie Leonard (from July 26, 1949); *Geraldine Kaye*: Mrs. Gloria Van Loop (from December 5, 1949).

ANNOUNCERS: *Mike Roy* (through April 24, 1949), *Ed Herlihy, Wayne Howell* (New York City), *Ben Alexander* (Hollywood), *Charles Mountain* (Chicago).

MUSIC: *Dick Stabile and His Orchestra.* **THEME SONG:** "The Money Song"

WRITTEN BY: *Ray Allen, Dick McKnight, Norman Sullivan, Chet Castellaw, Leon Fry* (through September 6, 1949); *Charley Isaacs, Hal Goodman, Ben Starr, Jack Douglas* (as of October 7, 1949).

PRODUCED & DIRECTED BY: *Robert L. Redd*

SCHEDULED: *Sunday, 6:30 - 7:00 pm* (April 3 through June 12, 1949); *Tuesday 9:00 - 9:30 pm* (June 21 through September 6, 1949); *Friday, 8:30 - 9:00 pm* (October 4 – 28, 1949); *Monday, 10:00 - 10:30 pm* (from November 7, 1949).

AUDITION SHOW (recorded December 21, 1948).

GUEST: *Lucille Ball.* **ALSO:** *Frank Nelson* as Abby (Dean & Jerry's agent)

DEAN SINGS: "You Won't Be Satisfied (Until You Break My Heart)"

PLOT: Dean and Jerry are nervous about starting their own radio series, and their state of mind isn't helped when Florence, the maid for their building, complains that their apartment isn't dirty. By the time they arrive at the studio, Jerry is so tense that he becomes convinced Dean doesn't want to work with him, so he walks off the show. As Dean tries to rehearse, Lucille Ball arrives to defend Jerry. Later, the three sing "The Money Song."

NOTES: Although edited for broadcast, this audition never aired. Both the edited version and a 37-minute unedited version are in circulation. On the unedited tape, Dean sings "You Was" in a duet with Eileen Woods. "The Money Song" was the team's first release for Capitol Records.

1) AIRDATE: April 3, 1949.

GUEST: *Bob Hope.* **ALSO:** *Eleanor Audley, The Martingales*

DEAN SINGS: "Bye-Bye Blackbird," "Ta-Ra, Ta-La-Ra"

PLOT: Dean and Jerry are nervous about starting their own radio series. When they arrive at the studio, Bob Hope welcomes them to the NBC roster.

NOTES: This program uses basically the same script as the Audition show; the first half is nearly identical, and several gags turn up in the second half, despite some changes in the narrative. A 42-minute unedited version is in circulation; the edited broadcast version is unavailable.

2) AIRDATE: April 10, 1949.

GUEST: *William Bendix.*

DEAN SINGS: "You Won't Be Satisfied (Until You Break My Heart)," "Far Away Places"

PLOT: The boys are in need of a guest for their second show, but can only manage to hire Florence as their secretary. William Bendix agrees to appear if Dean and Jerry will convince his producer to cast him as the romantic lead in his next picture.

3) AIRDATE: April 17, 1949.

GUEST: *George Marshall* **ALSO:** *Frank Nelson* as a Make-up Artist, *Georgia LaVerne* as a Starlet.

DEAN SINGS: "Cruising Down the River," "The Money Song" (with Jerry and Georgia LaVerne)

PLOT: Dean and Jerry are auditioning for Hal Wallis Productions, under the direction of George Marshall. While waiting, they wander around the Paramount lot and then barge into Marshall's office.

NOTES: George Marshall directed *My Friend Irma*, still in production when this show was transcribed.

4) AIRDATE: April 24, 1949.

GUEST: *Dick Powell.*

DEAN SINGS: "April Showers," "Mammy"

PLOT: Dick Powell plugs his new series *Richard Diamond: Private Eye,* which would make its premiere on NBC immediately after this program.

5) AIRDATE: May 1, 1949.

GUEST: *Madeleine Carroll.*

DEAN SINGS: "Sunflower," "I'd Rather Be a Dreamer"

PLOT: Dean and Jerry discuss springtime and romance in New York. In a sketch with Madeleine Carroll, they dramatize "some of the problems of young love in the Spring."

NOTE: Beginning with this broadcast, the show originates from New York City.

6) AIRDATE: May 8, 1949.

GUEST: *Peter Lorre.*

DEAN SINGS: "Someone Like You," "Again"

PLOT: The boys meet with a potential sponsor, who tells them he wants a mystery show. So, Dean and Jerry try to sign Peter Lorre, who tells them he wants to be a disk jockey! The three sing a mock hillbilly tune, "Drop Dead, Little Darlin.'"

7) AIRDATE: May 15, 1949.

GUEST: *Burl Ives.*

DEAN SINGS: "How it Lies," "I Don't See Me in Your Eyes Anymore"

PLOT: Dean and Jerry need to make a new record for Capitol, and their agent tells them to consider a few folk songs. They ask Burl Ives for some pointers on the genre.

NOTE: Ives sings "Lavender Blue (Dilly, Dilly)." This episode circulates in a rehearsal version recorded on May 13, 1949.

8) AIRDATE: May 22, 1949.

GUEST: *Arthur Treacher.*

DEAN SINGS: "Candy Kisses," "Three Wishes"

PLOT: The boys are to be interviewed by a lady reporter from *Vogue* magazine, but they've been evicted. Florence helps Dean and Jerry persuade Arthur Treacher to loan them his apartment - and to pose as their butler!

NOTE: This episode circulates in a rehearsal version recorded on May 20, 1949.

9) AIRDATE: May 29, 1949.

GUEST: *John Garfield.*

DEAN SINGS: "I Can't Give You Anything But Love"

PLOT: Dean wants Jerry to get in shape, so they go to a gym where they meet John Garfield. After one of Garfield's punches knocks him out, Jerry imagines he's a championship fighter.

NOTE: This episode circulates in a rehearsal version recorded on May 27, 1949.

10) AIRDATE: June 5, 1949.

GUEST: *Henry Fonda.*

DEAN SINGS: "I Can't Give You Anything But Love," "A - You're Adorable"

PLOT: Dean and Jerry see Henry Fonda on Broadway in *Mister Roberts*. Jerry decides he wants to be a dramatic actor, and returns to ask Fonda for a part in the play. The three perform a sketch where Fonda and Jerry are a pair of backwoods hicks wooing the same girl, during which they sing "Drop Dead, Little Darlin."

11) AIRDATE: June 12, 1949.

GUEST: *Marilyn Maxwell.*

DEAN SINGS: "Toot, Toot, Tootsie," "Sault Ste. Marie"

PLOT: On the basis of having seen her in the audience at the Copacabana, Jerry has fallen in love with Marilyn Maxwell. Dean asks Marilyn if she'll pretend to be in love with Jerry, in order to scare him... but the plan backfires.

12) AIRDATE: June 21, 1949.

GUEST: *Tony Martin.*

DEAN SINGS: "Take Your Girlie To The Movies," "Some Enchanted Evening"

PLOT: A member of Tony Martin's fan club files suit against Dean to stop him from using the name 'Martin.' The boys try appealing directly to Tony, but end up making things worse. In court, the two crooners square off with a duet on "Anything You Can Do" from *Annie Get Your Gun.*

13) AIRDATE: June 28, 1949.

GUESTS: *John Carradine, Leonard Dale.*

DEAN SINGS: "Candy Kisses," "You're So Understanding"

PLOT: John Carradine invites Dean to see him on stage, and asks Jerry to baby-sit his brilliant nephew Leonard. Dean believes Leonard, who has been raised in an atmosphere of culture and higher learning, will have a good influence on Jerry... but the opposite occurs.

14) AIRDATE: July 5, 1949.

GUEST: *Ralph Bellamy.*

DEAN SINGS: "Swanee," "Ghost Riders in the Sky"

PLOT: The head of New York's Paramount Theater will book Dean and Jerry, provided they have an entirely new act. At the same time, they receive a letter from Ralph Bellamy who has written an act for them. The "act" is actually a song, "When My Honeybee Starts Buzzing Around, I Always Get the Hives." The boys write a play around the song, and invite Bellamy to appear in it.

15) AIRDATE: July 12, 1949.

GUEST: *Charlie Ruggles.* ALSO: *Art Carney* as a Drunk

DEAN SINGS: "How it Lies," "Kentucky Babe"

PLOT: The team is due back in Hollywood in a week, and Jerry would like to make the trip by car. Unfortunately, the boys don't own one, so they check newspaper ads for persons looking for passengers. The second ad they answer turns out to have been placed by Charlie Ruggles.

NOTE: This was the final show to originate from New York City.

16) AIRDATE: July 19, 1949.

GUEST: *Vincent Price.*

DEAN SINGS: "April Showers"

PLOT: No further details on this episode were available.

NOTE: With this show, the series returned to Hollywood.

17) AIRDATE: July 26, 1949.

GUEST: *Frances Langford.* ALSO: *Frank Nelson* as Mr. Johnson

DEAN SINGS: "Someday You'll Want Me to Want You," "September Song"

PLOT: Capitol wants Dean to record with Frances Langford. Jerry, naturally, thinks this means the end of their partnership. Soapie Leonard, the boys' new neighbor, convinces Jerry to team up with a girl singer and make his own records – and he happens to have the perfect singer in mind: Florence. When that doesn't work out, Dean invites Jerry and Ms. Langford to sing "When Frances Dances With Me," which becomes a sketch: Jerry takes Frances to a dance, where Dean attempts to muscle in.

NOTE: Ms. Langford sings "Broadway Rhythm (It's Got Me)."

18) AIRDATE: August 2, 1949.

GUEST: *Hopalong Cassidy (William Boyd).*

DEAN SINGS: "Has Anybody Seen My Gal?" "Again"

PLOT: Dean and Jerry can't agree on where to spend their vacation. Soapie offers them a camping trip in the high Sierras for $100. Jerry forgets to bring matches, so Soapie takes their car to get some. The boys try to make the best of it, until Hopalong Cassidy accuses them of being cattle rustlers.

19) AIRDATE: August 9, 1949.

GUEST: *Burt Lancaster.*

DEAN SINGS: "Darktown Strutter's Ball," "I Don't See Me in Your Eyes Anymore."

PLOT: The boys worry about how they're going to pay their many bills. Soapie offers them a chance to "make a couple hundred bucks" by working at a circus. When Soapie expects them to cheat customers at the ticket counter, they turn instead to Burt Lancaster, who is brushing up on his acrobatic skills.

NOTE: Lancaster began his career as a circus acrobat.

20) AIRDATE: August 16, 1949.

GUEST: *Victor Moore.*

DEAN SINGS: "Where Are You," "Just For Fun"

PLOT: Soapie suggests that the boys buy their own nightclub, and will sell them an ideal building for $4,000. However, the loan company insists that they need a co-signer, so they ask Victor Moore. At first, Moore refuses, claiming he has no interest in nightclubs. He agrees to reconsider when Dean and Jerry invite him to their next show at Ciro's and promise to set him up with a French Can-Can dancer… who turns out to be Florence!

21) AIRDATE: August 23, 1949.

GUEST: *Billie Burke.*

DEAN SINGS: "Let's Take an Old-Fashioned Walk," "Some Enchanted Evening"

PLOT: Dean and Jerry inspect their new nightclub building, and discover it to be an old car repair garage. Worse, they soon learn that the land it's on is owned by Billie Burke, who wants to use it to build a shelter for homeless men. To change her mind, Jerry and Soapie pretend to be a couple of skid row bums who try to convince Miss Burke that they prefer living on the street.

22) AIRDATE: August 30, 1949.

GUEST: *Jane Russell.*

DEAN SINGS: "There's Yes! Yes! In Your Eyes," "A Room Full of Roses"

PLOT: In the midst of preparing the nightclub for a gala opening, an over-stressed Florence quits, forcing the boys to advertise for a new secretary. At the same time, a movie producer encourages Jane Russell to apply for the job, as preparation for her next role. She does so under a false name and with make-up designed to hide her identity.

23) AIRDATE: September 6, 1949.

GUEST: *Cesar Romero.*

DEAN SINGS: "Lora Belle Lee," "You're Breaking My Heart"

PLOT: No further details on this episode were available.

24) AIRDATE: October 7, 1949.

GUEST: *Gloria Blondell*

DEAN SINGS: "Someday You'll Want Me to Want You," "That Lucky Old Sun"

PLOT: It's almost opening night at the boys' new nightclub, and the boys are getting nervous. Dean wonders if they'll have the showbiz staying power of Al Jolson, which leads to a parody of the film "The Jolson Story," depicting Dean and Jerry's lives and career.

25) AIRDATE: October 14, 1949.

GUEST: *Dorothy Kirsten.* **ALSO:** *Hans Conried* as Prof. Rover Von Bagel.

DEAN SINGS: "Toot, Toot, Tootsie," "Let's Take an Old-Fashioned Walk" (duet with Dorothy Kirsten)

PLOT: Jerry invites Dorothy Kirsten, an opera singer, to perform in their nightclub. Her manager, Prof. Von Bagel, is against the idea, but she agrees to do it. The three perform an opera by Jerry entitled "Il Trovatore Goes to a Nightclub," or "How to Get Huckled For a Buck."

NOTE: Ms. Kirsten sings "Love is Where You Find It."

26) AIRDATE: October 21, 1949.

GUEST: *George Jessel.*

DEAN SINGS: "Darktown Strutter's Ball," "Just For Fun"

PLOT: The boys are worried that they won't get another picture opportunity. Jerry sees a notice in the paper that Darryl Zanuck is looking for comedians, so they head over to 20th Century-Fox, hoping George Jessel will help set them up. In turn, Jessel, whose producing job is in jeopardy, wants to appear at their nightclub, auditioning with impersonations of Al Jolson and Eddie Cantor.

27) AIRDATE: October 28, 1949.

GUEST: *Shirley Mitchell* **ALSO:** *Joseph Kearns* as the Ticket Seller.

DEAN SINGS: "I Can't Give You Anything But Love," "A Dreamer's Holiday"

PLOT: While the team is appearing in New York City, their producer Hal Wallis sends a telegram that he's coming to discuss their next picture, and makes a request: "Get tickets for *South Pacific*." A cabbie takes them to the waterfront where they find Soapie scalping tickets. Unfortunately, the place is raided and the boys are arrested. In the end, it turns out the telegram had a typo: it should have read "Got tickets for *South Pacific*."

28) AIRDATE: November 7, 1949.

DEAN SINGS: "Everywhere You Go," "Georgia on My Mind"

PLOT: While preparing to go to their nightclub, the boys look out the window and see a man being shot in the back. They try to tell the manager, the police and a reporter, but no one believes them. The police dump them in a sanitarium, where Soapie works as the treasurer ("And they think *I'm* crazy!") The head of the sanitarium decides Dean and Jerry are not bedbugs like the rest of the patients, and throws them out.

29) AIRDATE: November 14, 1949.

DEAN SINGS: "Ain't She Sweet," "Younger Than Springtime"

PLOT: As Dean and Jerry try to figure out why they haven't been able to save money, Soapie – who's been listening through the keyhole as usual – proposes that they invest $5,000 in a professional football team. They approach a finance company, which will only lend the money if the boys play on the team.

30) **AIRDATE:** November 21, 1949.

DEAN SINGS: "Goody-Good-Good To Me," "A Man Wrote a Song"

PLOT: No further details on this episode were available.

31) **AIRDATE:** November 28, 1949.

DEAN SINGS: "Just One of Those Things," "There's No Tomorrow"

PLOT: Dean receives a letter from the Child Welfare Board, accusing him of having his son, "professionally known as Jerry Lewis," working in their nightclub after 10:00 pm. The Board has Jerry take a mental test to prove he's a man. He fails, and is sent to elementary school. Dean and Soapie promise to help, but create more problems when they each bring a woman and child to the classroom claiming to be Jerry's wife and son.

32) **AIRDATE:** December 5, 1949.

DEAN SINGS: "Jingle Bells," "Don't Cry, Joe"

PLOT: On their day off from performing, Dean and Jerry do some sightseeing – and find that Soapie is in town. He offers to become their agent, and tells them he's already secured a job for them at a swanky hotel – as bug exterminators. They talk the manager into hiring them to perform, and they present a play written by Jerry: "Love in Darkest Africa."

NOTES: This was the first show to originate from Chicago, where the team was appearing at the Chez Paree nightclub.

AIRDATE: December 12, 1949. – PRE-EMPTED

33) **AIRDATE:** December 19, 1949.

DEAN SINGS: "Santa Claus is Coming to Town," "White Christmas," "Silent Night/ Notte Silenz"

PLOT: A telegram alerts Dean that Harry Cohn of Columbia Pictures expects to see the team at the Mayor's Christmas Ball, but they're not invited. Soapie gets them an invitation, but they must pretend to be Count Minestrone and Sir Yorkshire. After they are discovered and ejected, they walk down the street and enjoy the sights and sounds of Christmas.

34) AIRDATE: December 26, 1949.

DEAN SINGS: "Winter Wonderland," "Dancing in the Dark"

PLOT: No further details on this episode were available.

35) AIRDATE: January 2, 1950.

ALSO: *Paul Lipson* as "Hole-in-the-Head" Finnegan

DEAN SINGS: "Sometimes I'm Happy," "Rock-a-Bye Your Baby with a Dixie Melody"

JERRY SINGS: "Are You For Real?"

PLOT: Jerry believes the police are after him, but won't tell Dean why. Soapie recommends that Jerry hide out with his friend "Hole-in-the-Head" Finnegan, "until the heat is off." Jerry agrees, and when Dean arrives shortly after, Finnegan tries to recruit them to pull a bank job.

36) AIRDATE: January 9, 1950.

DEAN SINGS: "I Found a Million Dollar Baby," "I Can Dream, Can't I?"

PLOT: Jerry is having trouble falling asleep. When he finally does, he dreams of a fairy godfather (with a voice suspiciously like Soapie), who grants him three wishes. Jerry wishes to be President of the United States (with Dean as his secretary), a great lover (with Dean – imitating Cary Grant – as his valet), and finally Christopher Columbus (with Dean as a very Italian first mate).

37) AIRDATE: January 16, 1950.

DEAN SINGS: "Someday You'll Want Me to Want You," "There's No Tomorrow"

PLOT: The boys are shopping at a drugstore when a fortune telling scale convinces Jerry that he's very sick. Dean is skeptical, but Soapie convinces them that it's life threatening, so Jerry goes to the hospital, where he drives the doctor to distraction.

NOTE: This was the final show to originate from Chicago.

38) AIRDATE: January 23, 1950.

DEAN SINGS: "My Blue Heaven," "You're Wonderful"

PLOT: The team is due to meet with Hal Wallis to sign a contract for *My Friend Irma Goes West*. Unfortunately, Jerry believes he will bring bad luck, because he neglected to pick up a pin on the sidewalk. Soapie tells Jerry to see his fortune-teller friend, "Second-Sight Sal." When that doesn't work out, Dean suggests they go hunting for a rabbit's foot.

NOTE: This and the following show were recorded in Hollywood.

39) AIRDATE: January 30, 1950.

ALSO: *Frank Nelson* as the TV Station Manager

DEAN SINGS: "Bibbidy, Bobbidy, Boo," "Marta"

PLOT: While waiting for Dean outside of Schwab's drug store, a woman asks Jerry to mind her baby. When the mother doesn't return, Dean wants to call the police, but the druggist offers to review the charge accounts of his women customers that day, and gives the boys the addresses. When that doesn't pan out, they decide to put the baby on television and ask the mother to come down. The station manager agrees, only if the boys will appear in place of a fighter and manager who didn't show up.

NBC Publicity photo for *The Colgate Comedy Hour*, 1950.

3

1950–51:
THE COLGATE COMEDY HOUR, SEASON ONE

DEAN: "We'll only break up when Jerry dies."

JERRY: "This may be soon. My oxygen tank was due at 7 a.m., but it hasn't arrived."

– Dispelling break-up rumors to columnist
Gene Handshaker, August 1950

THE DAY AFTER THE FINAL *Martin & Lewis Show* aired, the boys began work on *My Friend Irma Goes West* (1950). Their contract with Wallis called for seven films in 5 years, and forbade them any outside work during the period each film was in production. Once *Irma* #2 wrapped in late March, the two were off to Chicago for another prolonged stay at the Chez Paree. On April 11, they returned to NBC radio with a guest shot on *Next, Dave Garroway;* four days later they appeared on the *NBC Saturday Night Revue,* the network's two-hour television variety extravaganza. The show, which had debuted in January, was intended to entice theatergoers to remain home and enjoy a different Broadway-worthy review every week. The first half-hour originated from Chicago and starred comedian Jack Carter; the remaining 90 minutes came from New York City and was hosted by various luminaries, but its chief draw was the comedy cast led by Sid Caesar and Imogene Coca. In the fall, Carter's portion would be dropped and the remainder retitled *Your Show of Shows.*

"The [Chicago] show hit its fastest pace to date, mainly because of Dean Martin and Jerry Lewis," wrote *Variety*. "Zanies made their comedics pay off for the greatest jackpot ever registered for this show. They indicate that they can be tremendous in this medium and in their own NBC show." Vivian Blaine was also a guest on the segment and, well aware of the team that seized top of the bill from her at the Copacabana two years earlier, saw to it that she'd not be ignored: "Her initial appearance in a low-cut gown constituted a gasper. There was considerable apprehension when she hopped about energetically and took low bows."

After the Chez Paree, it was back to Manhattan and the Copa, this time as headliners from the get-go. Since New York City was also the capital of television, they made three appearances, beginning with one of the earliest editions of *Broadway Open House*, NBC's first stab at late-night television, which had premiered on Memorial Day. The show aired Monday through Friday for an hour beginning at 11:15 pm. There was no permanent host, but not for lack of trying. Pat Weaver, the network's VP in Charge of Television Programming, had originally targeted comedian Jan Murray, but Murray's agent convinced him to accept a CBS show titled *Songs for Sale*, which was set for prime time. Weaver then tapped an unorthodox comedian named Don "Creesh" Hornsby, who'd scored on a West Coast show, but he had the misfortune to contract infantile paralysis and die the weekend before the premiere.

Weaver was forced to substitute whoever was available just to get the show on the air. Martin & Lewis took a shot at it and, *Variety* noted "put on a laugh-laden show which depended exclusively on them…. [They] worked no differently than they do at the Copa. It's an act that has the appearance of improvisation, but since they're essentially a colorful and zany duo, anything went. For example, they put in a couple of plugs for an imported car, which had the appearance of plugging the auto so that they could get free samples for themselves (same has been obtained since). It wasn't orthodox tele, but it was funny coming from them." In fact, the cars had been promised to the boys as payment for their appearance. Within a few weeks, both Jerry Lester and Morey Amsterdam would be assigned the hosting chore, three and two nights per week respectively.

Next, Dean and Jerry did their "punch drunk" routine (later to be immortalized in *Sailor Beware*) during a two-and-a-half hour telethon for Cerebral Palsy on June 10. Milton Berle was the host. Three days later, they turned up on Berle's season finale for *Texaco Star Theater*, television's number one program. Several books and articles, dating back to 1951, assert the team ran Berle ragged during this appearance: interrupting, out-mugging and outdancing him, essentially taking over his show and closing with a close-up of Jerry shouting, "Milton Berle night…. BIG DEAL!" However, there's no evidence of this in the surviving kinescope. The duo performs one of their regular routines, where an exasperated Dean orders Jerry to "turn in your equipment" and leave the stage. At this point, Berle chastises Martin for mistreating his partner and orders Dean to turn in *his* equipment. They have some fun with applying pies and seltzer to the host in a sketch where they play his new gag writers, while the sponsor

Martin & Lewis flank Jack Carter on NBC's *Saturday Night Revue*, April 1950.

Seen here in *At War With the Army* (1950), Jerry and Dean also did their impressions
of Barry Fitzgerald and Bing Crosby on Texaco Star Theater.

(*Robert Alda*) is decidedly unimpressed. Later they return with their impressions of Bing Crosby and Barry Fitzgerald in *Going My Way* (1944), another routine that would be preserved on film (*At War With the Army*). The finale involves a celebratory cake for Milton's second successful year; Jerry leads the cast around pretending to destroy the sets and equipment ("If you're not here in this studio, nobody else will use it!"). Madness, yes, but the sum total is nowhere near the shambles of legend.

The Copa gig ended at the close of June, and Martin & Lewis went back to Hollywood to make *At War With the Army* (1951). This was an independent production for a new concern, York Productions, the ownership of which was divided by three: Dean, Jerry and their agent Abby Greshler, the latter credited on screen as executive producer. Two weeks into filming, the powerful Music Corporation of America (MCA) agency signed the team away from Greshler. MCA was willing to cede commissions to Greshler until the two years remaining on his contract with the team were up, as they'd done when they wrested Frank Sinatra out from under General Artists Corporation. But that wasn't good enough for the feisty agent, and the end result involved sanctions from the American Guild of Variety Artists and a firestorm of suits and countersuits that took years to settle. These, however, amounted to little more than petty grievances, as MCA flexed enough muscle to put Martin & Lewis into the top money bracket starting with their NBC contract. Greshler had agreed to $25,000 per show; MCA forced the network back to the table and emerged with $25,000 for the first show, then $75,000 each for the next four, with further negotiations to follow for the remainder.

* * * * *

SIDEBAR: Here Comes Colgate

The *NBC Saturday Night Revue* had captured the evening for the network, just as they owned Tuesday night with *Texaco Star Theater*. Now they were targeting Wednesday. Pat Weaver conceived what *Variety* termed a "top-name variety show" with four hosts that would alternate each week. Vaudeville and radio stalwarts Eddie Cantor and Fred Allen were already confirmed, and NBC was negotiating with Nash-Kelvinator to sponsor...until the end of June, when the Colgate-Palmolive-Peet Company inked a deal for three Sunday nights per month in the 8:00-9:00 pm time slot, directly opposite *Toast of the Town* on CBS. Colgate was willing to spend $60,000 per week, far and away the highest budget ever allocated for one TV show.

Energized by the idea of taking on Ed Sullivan, NBC immediately shifted Cantor and Allen to the Colgate program, and turned their attention to finding hosts for the other weeks. Within a few days, the web signed Ed Wynn, whose half-hour CBS show had been cancelled for want of a sponsor, and began negotiating with Jimmy Durante. As for Wednesday night, *Variety* speculated it "will be filled by a show starring Dean Martin and Jerry Lewis, which Buick might sponsor."

Lewis, though, had no intention of submitting Martin and he to the rigors of a weekly hour, knowing the medium's voracious appetite for material; in any event, their contract with Wallis made it impossible. For its part, Colgate hadn't forgotten wanting to put the team on TV the previous year. In short order, they agreed that Martin & Lewis would host every second week (Cantor and Allen hosting the first and third, respectively) whenever they were available, with "up-and-coming young talent" taking over the hour when they were not. Frigidaire signed to sponsor every fourth Sunday with its own rotating host lineup: ex-vaudevillian Bobby Clark (one-time half of Clark and McCullough) and Bob Hope. Wynn and Durante, along with Danny Thomas and Jack Carson, were placed on the Wednesday night program under the sponsorship of Motorola and titled *Four Star Revue* (later modified to *All Star Revue*). The Sunday night show, consisting entirely of comedian hosts, was called *The Colgate Comedy Hour*, and simply *The Comedy Hour* for Frigidaire's week.

Colgate producer Ernest Glucksman has hit it off with Jerry, while Dean looks on in mock dismay, September 1950.

Performing "It's the Talk of the Town" on *Colgate*, September 17, 1950.
Photo courtesy of Kayley Thompson.

* * * * *

During the summer, Danny Thomas accepted some unsolicited comedy material from a pair of aspiring writers, who had been working as door-to-door baby photographers, named Ed Simmons and Norman Lear. Thomas performed their material at Ciro's on Sunset Boulevard, which went over big among a celebrity-studded audience. Also present was David Susskind, then an agent for MCA who also happened to be Lear's first cousin. Susskind asked Lear if he and his partner had ever written any television. "Sure," said Lear, untruthfully, whereupon Susskind, who needed to get back to New York within a few days, asked them to write a couple of sketches and drop them at his hotel.

"We had never written a television show before," Lear recalled for the Archive of American Television. Neither he nor Simmons even owned a set; they'd gather at the home of Lear's Uncle Al to watch Milton Berle and the like. "I was [renting] a little room behind another house, which was owned by an extra—a woman—and the guy she was living with was an actor." Lear borrowed a television script from the couple in order to learn the proper formatting, and he and Simmons churned out two sketches and brought them to the hotel. Susskind took them to New York for the *Ford Star Revue*, another NBC variety show.

Normally hosted by Kay Kyser and his merry band of "students," this *Revue* was continuing into the summer with musical comedy star Jack Haley as master of ceremonies. The first broadcast was roundly panned by critics; the *Long Island Star-Journal's* John Lester for one labeled it "very poor...inexpertly handled and generally spiritless." Aware of their need for fresh material, Susskind convinced the producers to give Simmons and Lear a chance. The upshot: by the end of the 12-week run, Haley was pulling bigger ratings than had Kyser and would replace the venerable bandleader permanently the following January.

Coincidentally, Jerry caught one of the shows, and enthusiastically called MCA: "I just saw a sketch on the Haley show that would have been perfect for Dean and me. Find out who wrote it. I want him to work for me." MCA, of course, knew exactly who wrote it. Luckily, Haley's show was ending just as Martin & Lewis' was beginning, so Simmons and Lear only had to double on both for a couple of weeks. Eventually they'd prove themselves worthy of an exclusive contract with the team.

Placed in overall charge of the Martin & Lewis programs was Ernest D. Glucksman, an old hand from the Catskills who'd been working in television since 1945. He flew to California in August for a meeting with the team and their handlers at MCA's Beverly Hills office. It was, he'd recall later, "my first trip to Hollywood [and] my first 3,000-mile plane trip. I practically smoked myself to death en route, the butterflies were playing football in my stomach. Tired, unshaven and unkempt, I envisioned a comfortable hotel room and a hot shower.

"But before these could be realized, I was whisked away, looking like a tramp, to MCA's luxurious headquarters. The quiet elegance of the surroundings seemed to shout at me. I found myself attending a script conference with the drone of the airplane motor still penetrating my ears. The conference sounded like a tower of Babel. In the midst of this confusion, all hell broke loose when two human dynamos, Jerry Lewis and Dean Martin, entered the room." The pair engaged in what by now had become their standard routine in such surroundings: disrupting conversations, snipping neckties with scissors, pouring glasses of water only to throw them in someone's face, and endless jokes at everyone else's expense.

"Although their shenanigans were funny," said Glucksman, "I was preoccupied with the thought, 'What will I tell the boys in New York when I report to them tomorrow?' I was bewildered, ignored and frustrated. I wondered, 'Is this how they format a show in Hollywood?'" The only tangible outcome of the meeting was that Glucksman was encouraged to hire gagman Harry Crane as an extra writer. Desperate, he "cornered Jerry and asked if I could see him at his home that evening.

"Secretly, I wondered whether or not I would accomplish anything [but] to my surprise, I found him a completely different personality. At

Newspaper ad for the team's first *Colgate Comedy Hour*, September 17, 1950.

home, he was the well-organized clear-thinking business executive, who had indexed and categorized all his show business routines and experiences. Jerry briefed me on how Dean and he liked to rehearse. I was indoctrinated on how they approached their work and I spent five hours in his library reading up on the boys." As Glucksman was leaving, Lewis made an additional request: "Remember, Ernie, when you talk to the writers, I want you to be sure to remind them that Dean and I are *two* comics, not a comic and a straight man." When Glucksman returned to New York the following morning, "I had no format to submit but I did have a working knowledge of Dean Martin and Jerry Lewis." Ernie adapted so well that he'd work for Jerry for years, eventually producing many of Lewis's solo feature films and all of his TV programs through 1963.

Of necessity, the broadcasts had to originate from New York. The creative process for the Colgate shows was as follows: a week of read-through and preliminary rehearsals at a neutral location such as a hotel, rented office or apartment; and a second week of full-on rehearsals at the International Theater located at 5 Columbus Circle, from which the show would air. Performance time was, of course, 8:00 pm Sunday. Immediately after its conclusion, Lewis, Glucksman and the writers would sit down and hash out ideas for the next one.

* * * * *

THE COLGATE COMEDY HOUR: Dean Martin & Jerry Lewis Show #1.

Airdate: September 17, 1950; NBC-TV.
Guest Star: Marilyn Maxwell
With: Leonard Barr. The Honeydreamers
Cast: J.C. McCord, Frank Gallop, William McCutcheon, Jean Carsons
Writers: Harry Crane, Ed Simmons & Norman Lear
Musical Direction: Dick Stabile
Choreography: Lee Sherman
NBC Production Supervisor: Sam Fuller
Television Director: Kingman T. Moore
Producer & Director: Ernest D. Glucksman.

OPENING: The boys arrive as party guests at a wealthy home where dress is formal; Dean and Jerry are in top hat and tails. One of the female guests requests an autograph. Jerry is handed a pen and attempts to sign but the ink isn't running. He shakes the pen, which ejects ink onto the shirt of a large man. The fellow's wife gets into an argument with Jerry; when he refuses to pay for a new shirt, she flips him onto the floor. Dean attacks her and soon a full-scale melee breaks out.

The curtain closes and the team engages in a brief bit where they are German spies. Dean hands Jerry a slip of paper, then says "Someone's coming," whereupon Jerry eats the paper. Jerry tells Dean that it's time to sing the song "for the Führer and the Fatherland!" They both break into "Babalu." Dean tells Jerry, "Ah, shut up. You make me do crazy things," and tells him to introduce his song.

DEAN SOLO #1: "I'm Gonna Sit Right Down and Write Myself a Letter"

BYPLAY: Dean explains that he and Jerry will "give you our impression of a man and woman trying to reconcile." Dean sings "It's the Talk of the Town," while Jerry, wearing a woman's floral hat, interrupts each line with a humorous comment, to wit:

DEAN (singing): "Don't let foolish pride keep you from my side…"

JERRY: "Coax me: send me hal-a-vah!"

SKETCH #1: Announcer Frank Gallop takes us to the dressing rooms of Dean Martin (large and tastefully decorated) and Jerry Lewis (small and looking like an abandoned warehouse). Jerry gripes about this inequity but Dean ignores him and orders him around. Complaining that it's too hot, Dean wants to have NBC send up a fan, but Jerry tells him he has one in his suitcase. "This couldn't cool off a cup of coffee," says Dean when he sees how tiny it is, but once Jerry turns it on, they're blown across the room. When attempting to place a phone call from his room, Jerry can't figure out why it rings when he *lifts* the receiver. Annoyed by the constant ringing, Dean tells him to pull the cord out; they both pull and pull until an operator comes through the wall. Soon after, other cast members arrive in Dean's room to rehearse. Dean tells Jerry to put the lights up, but he accidentally turns the fan back on and everyone is blown about. Finally, a representative from NBC offers Jerry a new room on the second floor, and we discover why this room is so small: it's a freight elevator.

Dean thinks he's seeing double when confronted by 16-year-old Sammy Petrillo and Jerry. Publicity for *The Colgate Comedy Hour* of November 10, 1950.

GUEST ACT #1: An unbilled dance troupe comes on while The Honey-dreamers vocalize, then Jerry introduces Marilyn Maxwell, who sings "I Love the Guy."

DEAN SOLO #2: "La Vie En Rose"

GUEST ACT #2: Dean introduces "one of the greatest eccentric dancers in the country...my uncle, Leonard Barr," who dances to "Darktown Strutter's Ball."

SKETCH #2: Outside of a movie theater, the manager (*Martin*) and ticket girl (*Maxwell*) await customers, but no one shows, even when the manager repeatedly lowers the admission price. It's so deserted that Wembley, the usher from the balcony (*William McCutcheon*), goes mad from having "not seen a human face in six months." The ticket girl spots a potential customer and poses seductively outside the box office. A young boy, Melvin (*Lewis*), bouncing a basketball is coerced by her and the manager into buying a ticket, which prompts a flock of newspapermen to cover the momentous event. Melvin gripes that he just wants to go home and watch television, but every time he says that word, the manager hits him over the head. Another usher forces the boy to purchase popcorn. Melvin's scared to enter the dark theater alone, so he and the manager watch the film together and react in pantomime to the happenings on screen.

FINALE: Dressed as an early 20ᵗʰ century policeman, Dean sets the scene of 5ᵗʰ Avenue in "the era of Diamond Jim Brady and Lillian Russell." The Honeydreamers sing "Take Me Back to New York Town." As the scene switches to a seedy barroom, Dean narrates, in song, the saga of "Frankie and Johnny," with Jerry as the philandering Johnny and Marilyn Maxwell as Frankie.

ANALYSIS AND REVIEWS: The best word to sum up Martin & Lewis' first starring TV show (discounting their one-time stint on the loosey-goosey *Broadway Open House*) is "nervous."

Dean's nerves cause him to twice muff the lyrics on his opening song. He breaks up during the "Talk of the Town" routine, which was one of their stage bits. He trips over his tongue when introducing his uncle. For the finale, someone had the bright idea of pasting his narration into a copy of the *Police Gazette*; while on camera, he reads the lines straight through without looking up. It's no wonder he'd fall so deeply in love with cue cards. Jerry comes across a bit more self-assured than his partner, but even he's more subdued than usual.

Some of the writing was also uncertain. The bit where the two impersonate Nazi spies barely gets a chuckle, perhaps because the war ended only five years before. Thankfully it's quickly dropped and they move on to more familiar material: arguing with each other as they'd done on *Texaco Star Theater* and presumably other shows. The camerawork, too, lacked a certain finesse that would come with time; shots are often too tight, with some of the action lost, and with one partner or the other moving out of frame. Clearly Glucksman was still getting used to his charges. Nor were the commercials immune: the pitchwoman for Ajax cleanser stutters at one point.

For a first effort, though, there were plenty of highlights. Both sketches were well constructed and funny. The memorable bit with Jerry's fan would be repeated in a future show, and having a switchboard girl emerge at the end of the telephone cord ("Usually my customers *dial* for the operator!") was an inspired visual gag that was cited by reviewers the next morning. For the theater sketch, Dean and Jerry's comedy of reaction while they're viewing the off-screen movie (Dean shoving popcorn into Jerry's mouth throughout) is brilliant and doesn't overstay its welcome. Although they'd been at it for less than three months, Simmons and Lear had already mastered how to write for television. In both routines and elsewhere, Dean's lines and reactions to Jerry were a little too harsh in spots, too close to "generic straight man" material, but this would be easily fixed going forward.

The "Frankie and Johnny" production number was the least-successful piece, with Jerry—despite wearing a garish outfit—getting lost in the shuffle. The focus, naturally, is on Ms. Maxwell as Frankie and the camera stays on her most of the time. Meanwhile, Lewis has little to do but prance around with her and the other dancers on an especially cramped stage. His partner is crooning the song off-camera, emerging only at the very end to take Frankie into custody. The problem was solved for future shows by simply limiting such special material to the supporting acts.

There was some behind-the-scenes tension. The show ran eight minutes over in rehearsal and last-minute cuts had to be made. On the opening credit crawl, the name of at least one guest performer was blocked out with tape. Meanwhile, although billed with his partner Virginia Estes, dancer Leonard Barr performed alone and for less than 80 seconds. According to Harry Crane, Barr & Estes were to be cut entirely, but Martin objected: "He's got everybody from Steubenville watching. It'll break his heart. If you cut that, I don't do the show." "He stuck to it," said Crane. (Barr also turned up as a newsman in the movie theater sketch.) As it is, the show ends abruptly, with a cutaway to a "Next Week: FRED ALLEN" billboard just as Dean and Jerry emerge from behind the curtain for a bow.

Newspaper critics were delighted. "What we have in the Martin and Lewis show is a full hour of utter lunacy, wild and frenzied slapstick that comes just short of wrecking the whole damn studio itself," wrote the *New York Morning Telegraph*'s critic Leo Mishkin. His colleague at the *Times*, Jack Gould, agreed: "It may be a long time before the National Broadcasting Company is quite the same again. A pair of mad zanies of the first rank, [Martin & Lewis] rollicked through sixty minutes of slapstick and horseplay that for the most part were swell nonsense." The AP's critic simply said, "The whole result was hilarious."

In its review, *Variety* made some suggestions that, as evidenced by future shows, were heeded: "What few attempts were made to vest the show with heavy-budgeted production mountings were purely incidental and, for that matter, unnecessary.... [The] sequencing might have been shuffled for more effective balancing, since the first half gave the Lewis antics an almost whirlwind pace, in contrast to some second-half lapses." Nevertheless, wrote 'Rose,' "For the moment, there's little doubt that the Martin and Lewis show gave evidence, as with Cantor last week, of video's maturity in the realm of comedy."

The boys proved themselves where it really mattered: their Audience Research Bureau (ARB, later Arbitron) rating – a four-city telephone survey conducted in New York, Washington D.C., Cleveland and Chicago – came in at 35.6, with *Toast of the Town* trailing at 23.3. "Since the Sullivan show had consistently been one of the ratings leaders last season," *Variety* reported, "it was believed impossible that the new NBC package would cut into his standing so soon." But the broadcast had done even better than the prior week's premiere, leading *Variety* to conclude, "Radio's long-established 'habit' factor, which presumably was responsible for many listeners tuning into the same show week after week, may not be marked in television...the difference in ratings between [*Colgate* and *Toast*] is apparently growing."

* * * * *

SIDEBAR: *The COMPO Controversy*

The day of the broadcast, the *Motion Picture Herald* had named Martin & Lewis the "Stars of Tomorrow," based on its annual exhibitor's poll. The next morning, the exhibitors wanted to truss them to a pole and administer forty lashes. The independent trade magazine *Harrison's Reports* ("Devoted chiefly to the interests of the exhibitors") spelled out all the details:

"A perfect example of 'biting the hand that feeds you' was displayed last Sunday night on television by comedians Dean Martin and Jerry Lewis in a comedy skit that belittled and ridiculed the motion picture industry in a way that was nothing short of vicious....

"As a result of this objectionable skit, Arthur L. Mayer, executive vice-president of COMPO [the Council of Motion Picture Organizations] has sent a vigorous protest to Frank Folsom, president of the Radio Corporation of America, parent company of NBC. Mayer wired Folsom as follows:

Duke Mitchell and Sammy Petrillo in *Bela Lugosi Meets a Brooklyn Gorilla* (1952).
Dean and Jerry they're not.

"'This organization, representing all branches of the motion picture industry, strongly protests attack on our business…. In depicting motion picture theatres as places shunned by public, both producers of show and [NBC] have done serious damage to this industry. We cannot believe that you as responsible head of Radio Corporation of America condone such irresponsible attacks and we ask that you take steps immediately to see that this scene is not repeated on other stations.'" In other words, COMPO wanted the skit removed from the kinescope before it was to run in those markets that weren't able to air the live broadcast. The scheduled date for the kinescope airing was October 1, two weeks later.

"Another protest came from Harry Brandt, president of the Independent Theatre Owners Association, how, in behalf of his organization, [sent a telegram] to Hal Wallis, producer of the 'My Friend Irma' pictures, in which Martin and Lewis are featured: 'Theatre owners in the New York area are outraged…. By virtue of your contract with them, we ask you to take whatever disciplinary action you can to curb their future antics in tearing down the good public relations that we are building up through

COMPO."' Wallis also received a brace of telegrams and letters from individual exhibitors.

"Another who was quick to comment on the ill-advised Martin and Lewis skit was Abram F. Myers, National Allied [Theatre]'s general counsel and chairman of the board…. 'Martin and Lewis are said to be good comedians but certainly they are not indispensable to the motion picture business and they and their kind should be told in no uncertain way that if they use a rival medium of entertainment to injure the motion picture business, they cannot hereafter expect to appear in the films.'

"There is little one could add to what has already been said about this matter by Messrs. Mayer, Brandt and Myers," concluded *Harrison's*, "except to say that Martin and Lewis would do well to come through with profuse apologies to the industry and with assurances that in their future appearances on radio or television they will exercise greater care in the choice of material that has any connection with the motion picture business."

So spoke the movie industry, but those on the television side had their say as well. "Production execs on the TV program," wrote *Variety*, "claimed they could see nothing out of line in the sketch. They admitted ribbing the film biz but said it was nothing more malicious that the Washington's Gridiron Club's annual ribbing of President Truman. In addition, they pointed out that the film industry has not been averse to kidding video from time to time." *Variety's* critic, incidentally, had thought the sketch was "a fabulous idea."

Broadcasting-Telecasting magazine couldn't resist its own editorializing. Its "Static and Snow" columnist Awfrey Quincy wrote, "Hollywood is all steamed up because Dean Martin and Jerry Lewis poked fun at film business. Coming from an industry which more than any other has capitalized the art of poking fun at everyone and everything, especially broadcasting, that strikes us as the height of ludicrousness." One of the recipients of COMPO's letter was J. Harold Ryan, then interim president of the National Association of Broadcasters and a member of the U.S. Chamber of Commerce Committee on Advertising, who sent *Broadcasting-Telecasting* a copy of his response to Arthur L. Mayer:

"I wonder if your memory is not rather short in this connection. Do you not recall 'The Hucksters' which MGM made in 1947 and which was a picture that not only held up to ridicule the advertising agencies and broadcasters, but also impugned the personal morality of people engaged in these occupations?

"I agree with you that it is poor business for one industry in this great country of ours to ridicule or make light of another. At the same time I am very mindful of His saying, 'He that is without sin among you, let him cast the first stone.'" In printing this, *Broadcasting-Telecasting* couldn't resist adding, "We're listening (and looking), Mr. Mayer."

Throughout the brouhaha, RCA and NBC executives kept mum, even when COMPO members made such threats as boycotting Colgate products and seeking out RCA's competitors in theater sound equipment. The kinescope aired intact as scheduled and, *Variety* reported, "While it was expected that [NBC and RCA] would do nothing in reply until after the kine had been transmitted, it is now reported that they will not answer at all. They are said to believe that the skit was staged in good, clean fun and that the protests don't merit the dignity of an answer."

By then, Dean and Jerry—at Wallis' urging—had formally apologized in a letter of their own: "We have read in the trade press and have received copies of exhibitors' telegrams complaining about our appearance Sunday evening, September 17, in the TV sketch of attendance at a movie theatre. Odd as it may seem, it never occurred to us that this material would be construed as injurious to the industry. Had we thought so, we never would have performed it.

"As you know, we are relatively new to motion pictures and are equally new to television and radio. Our principal experience has been in the intimate atmosphere of night clubs and personal appearances where satire is always accepted in good fun and without complaint. We now realize, however, that such is not always the case with respect to radio, television or movies which reach vast audiences.

"We regret, exceedingly, this incident and wish to assure the exhibitors that it will not happen again."

The team wrote the letter in the midst of a two-week personal appearance tour, during which, as a token of goodwill, they gave a free show for a convention of Allied Theater owners in Pittsburgh. "It would be like walking into the lion's den, and Martin and Lewis knew that," wrote Harold V. Cohen for the city's *TV Digest*. "But they did, and in five minutes theater owners who but a moment before were eager to strangle them were eating out of the boys' hands." This special audience gave them a standing ovation and all was quickly forgiven.

Once the tour ended, it was back to New York for their next *Colgate* go-round.

* * * * *

THE COLGATE COMEDY HOUR: Dean Martin & Jerry Lewis Show #2.

Airdate: October 15, 1950; NBC-TV.
With: Kitty Kallen, The Skylarks, The Honorable Ralph Villani (Mayor of Newark NJ), The Honorable Walter Sterling (Mayor of Steubenville OH).
Announcer: Don Pardo
Writers: Ed Simmons & Norman Lear
Musical Direction: Dick Stabile
Musical Numbers Staged by: Lee Sherman
NBC Production Supervisor: Sam Fuller
Television Director: Kingman T. Moore
Producer & Director: Ernest D. Glucksman.

OPENING: At the train station in Steubenville, a welcoming committee awaits the disembarking of Martin & Lewis. They'll be officially greeted by dignitaries from both Steubenville and Newark, including their real-life Mayors. A marching band heralds their arrival as they are wheeled in on a luggage cart by three porters. Once on the podium, each dignitary tells anecdotes about how much trouble Dean and Jerry caused during their youth. This spurs similar memories from other greeters and soon they're hurling trash at the boys and running them out of town.

DEAN SOLO #1: "I'll Always Love You"

SKETCH #1: At Martin's Gymnasium, Dean is putting members through their paces when Jerry arrives, looking to build up his physique. After he puts on gym trunks, Jerry tries to do chin-ups but can't lift himself. Pointing at the bar, Dean tells him, "This doesn't come down. You go up!" They give up and try calisthenics instead, but Jerry has his own interesting variations on the exercises, and keeps forgetting to stop when Dean blows the whistle. Called away for a moment, Dean has Jerry take over, handing him the whistle. Jerry leads the class in a run-in-place, but forgets that they won't stop until he blows the whistle, which Dean eventually does even though Jerry is bouncing around with it. Finally, Jerry tries boxing with Dean; he's a bit more successful at this and they both end up punch-drunk after two rounds.

GUEST ACT #1: Dressed in a jacket and bow tie but still wearing gym shorts, Jerry introduces Kitty Kallen, who sings "I'm Sitting On Top of the World" and "Ukulele Lady."

SKETCH #2: Inside the headquarters of Murder, Incorporated, Scar (*Martin*) tries to make a tough guy out of Myron (*Lewis*). They take target practice together and Scar even gives Myron an appropriate nickname: "Ratface." Scar orders Ratface to break down a "punk" (*Bill McCutcheon*), but fails miserably. As Scar takes the punk to see "The Big Guy," a very tall, elegantly dressed woman enters and Ratface attempts to make time with her. Scar returns and informs Ratface that the girl is The Big Guy's moll. They try to get her out, but it's too late: The Big Guy, who's less than four feet tall, has arrived. He and Scar take care of Ratface by using him for target practice.

GUEST ACT #2: The Skylarks sing "Vaudeville is Back" and "Danny Boy."

DEAN SOLO #2: Dean sings "C'est Si Bon" as The Skylarks counterpoint with "I Get a Kick Out of You."

FINALE: Jerry leads "the chore" (*DEAN:* "You mean the 'choi-or-ree'") through an interesting arrangement as Dean sings "Once in a While." He then directs pianist Lou Brown during Dean's "Eye-tralian" rendition of "Oh, Marie," taking the second chorus himself.

ANALYSIS AND REVIEWS: Up to the week before the broadcast, Martin, Lewis and Glucksman were trying to book Sophie Tucker as a special guest, but despite increasing the monetary reward her manager balked. Consequently, the show ran a little short, even after two numbers apiece from each supporting act and nearly 15 minutes of Martin & Lewis' stage shtick. Curiously, a piece of special material for The Skylarks, "Millie the Filly," although credited at the end of the show, was cut for reasons that aren't clear (*Variety's* reviewer noted some "last minute 'auxiliary cast' deletions" without explaining the whys). It would turn up during the team's next broadcast.

All-in-all, a valuable lesson was learned: special guest stars weren't necessary when these two maniacs were hosting. The show rolls along at a healthy pace; as with the previous entry, the comedy sketches don't seem padded in any fashion. The musical breaks are also swiftly and smartly handled, especially Ms. Kallen's rendition of "Ukulele Lady," for which she's accompanied by hula dancers.

The opening at the train station followed the template established by the first show: introduce Martin & Lewis within a dignified setting and let nature take its course. The gymnasium sketch was the first in another recurring theme: Dean the subject matter expert attempts to train Jerry the helpless schnook, to little or no avail. Notably, Simmons and Lear gave Dean more than ordinary straight lines. When Jerry emerges from the locker room in his trunks, Dean looks him over: "This is all of it, huh? None of this is in the locker, this is the whole thing?" The physicality of the bit enhances the comedy, even breaking them up during the part where Dean has to latch onto a bouncing Jerry in order to grab and blow the whistle.

The "Murder, Incorporated" sketch isn't as interesting, if only because it's not as visual (although the contrast in size between Jerry and "The Big Guy's" moll is nicely handled, and of course "The Big Guy" him-

Rehearsing for *The Big Show*, December 17, 1950: From left-to-right: Jerry, Dean, Bob Hope, Meredith Willson, Louis Armstrong, Frankie Laine, hostess Tallulah Bankhead, Deborah Kerr. Photo courtesy of Martin Grams, Jr.

self is a little person). Makeup and costuming garner some laughs but the crux of the comedy is verbal (*Moll:* "Where's 'The Scar?'" *Jerry:* "On his face!"); the routine could have been done on radio with few alterations.

Jerry gets a couple of moments to shine alone. Before introducing Dean's first song, he tells the home audience, "We'd like you to relax, and I'd like to come right into your living room and join you folks," while walking straight up to the camera until he's just nose and a mouth. The studio audience (who could see the end result on monitors) screams with laughter, and eventually Lewis learned he could just lead the cameramen around instead of vice-versa. Director Arthur Penn, who began his career assisting Kingman Moore on the *Comedy Hour*, remembered that Dean and Jerry were "using the medium as contemporaries of television in a way the [other hosts] were not. For example, everybody was terribly concerned that you not show the other cameras. Jerry would come tearing out of the frame and make the cameras follow him and photograph each other."

Dean is much more relaxed than in the first show. Both of his solos come off without a hitch, and the introduction of "I'll Always Love You" even garners some adolescent screaming; the tune being his biggest seller to date. His second number, "C'est Si Bon" combined with "I Get a Kick Out of You" by The Skylarks, is a delight and might qualify as video's first mash-up. He comports himself well in both sketches, and as noted, his lines are funnier and even a bit warmer. As for the finale, it's lifted straight out of their nightclub work, so he knows it well.

Even so, his partner wasn't above injecting a few surprises. A moment that stops the show comes during "Oh, Marie," when Dean is holding a nearly-operatic note. Spontaneously, Jerry walks over to him, sticks both index fingers in his mouth and pulls in opposite directions. The whole theater roars with laughter while Jerry collapses onto the piano in mock hysterics; even the musicians are howling. Dean grabs Jerry (by latching onto his *eye*!) and drags him off the piano, then resumes the song, but tests his mouth by squeezing it while he sings. This sends Jerry into genuine laughter, which continues when Dean tells him, "This wasn't in the script, buddy!"

With three minutes remaining, the boys ad-lib, thank the respective mayors (who, somewhat surprisingly, had no lines) for appearing, laugh at themselves and fall all over each other. Here's where their personal affection comes across most clearly. Dean, who couldn't resist smiling at the earlier assault on his mouth, is visibly amused by his partner's quick mind. "Brush your teeth with Ajax!" sings Lewis, to Martin's delight. Getting a time signal, Dean says, "One minute!" Jerry responds, "Oh, we can kill that in an hour!" and Dean laughs aloud, which in turn causes Jerry to laugh and collapse onto Dean's shoulder.

Variety loved the result: "The zanies whammed over an hour of entertainment that, if anything, had more punch and hilarity than their leadoff stanza. It was strictly bigtime comedy video, clinching once and for all the certainty that TV, when superior talent meets up with superior material and both combine to play for the camera and the home viewer, can pay off in entertainment value on a par with any other show biz medium…. Wisely, producer-director Ernie Glucksman bypassed the elaborate production furbelows usually identified with these major top-budgeted shows…. Rather, the accent was on the comedy duo. It was Martin and Lewis' show and they made the most of every minute."

* * * * *

THE COLGATE COMEDY HOUR: Dean Martin & Jerry Lewis Show #3.

Airdate: November 12, 1950; NBC-TV.
With: Kitty Kallen, Jack Cassidy, The Skylarks
Cast: Leonard Barr, Sid De May & Sally Moore, Bill McCutcheon, Joyce Randolph, Sammy Petrillo
Announcer: Don Pardo
Writers: Ed Simmons & Norman Lear
Musical Direction: Dick Stabile
Musical Numbers Staged by: Lee Sherman
NBC Production Supervisor: Sam Fuller
Television Director: Kingman T. Moore
Producer & Director: Ernest D. Glucksman.

OPENING: Based on the attendees' demeanor, the Morticians' Jamboree for 1950 appears to be a solemn occasion. Nevertheless, the undertakers have hired Martin & Lewis to entertain them. The boys try their best, but when yet another joke falls flat, Jerry says, "Ugh, I wish I was dead," and suddenly their morbid audience rises and heads toward them with ghoulish glee. The two literally run for their lives.

DEAN SOLO #1: "The Glory of Love"

SKETCH #1: Jerry, a "wallflower," arrives at Martin's Dance Academy. Dean tries pairing him with Elizabeth (a live girl), but he can't even walk up to her properly. Instead, Dean has him practice with "Gwendolyn," a life-size rag doll, which also doesn't work out, especially when he twirls her onto the floor in a heap. Jerry wishes to learn the "Rhumb-er" but he's too stiff, so Dean has his Uncle Leonard (*Barr*) demonstrate how to loosen up. Jerry tries it, but now he's too loose. Two professional adagio dancers (*Sid De May & Sally Moore*) arrive and demonstrate their skill. Dean wants Jerry to try it with him, so Jerry passes Sally to Dean, but when Dean passes her back, Jerry runs. Dean spins Sally around and Jerry tries to latch on, but fails—and the three collapse into a heap.

GUEST ACTS: In song, Jack Cassidy tells the story of "Millie the Filly," during which The Skylarks sing "Derby Day." Jerry introduces Kitty Kallen, who sings "I Can't Give You Anything But Love" and "Please Take Me Home."

Dean, Jerry and Mickey Bloom rehearse a sketch for *The Colgate Comedy Hour*,
February 4, 1951. Photo courtesy of Kayley Thompson.

SKETCH #2: A couple (*Lewis* and *Joyce Randolph*) leave their baby in the care of a sitter and go out for the evening. However, the sitter has a boyfriend (*Martin*), who enters through a window and settles in for a little cuddling. Just then the baby (also *Lewis*) starts crying and throwing toys out of his playpen. He escapes the pen and startles both sitter and boyfriend by his size. The "baby" wants to play games, but boyfriend orders him to go back to sleep. The sitter goes to the kitchen for some milk, while boyfriend tries to bribe him with a dollar. The kid agrees, but wants to be kissed "the way my mommy kisses me." He grabs the sitter in a passionate embrace, kisses her, and offers to raise her pay. The boyfriend pulls him away and orders "baby" to drink his milk. Sobbing, the kid sips the milk, but keeps spitting it out in a tantrum. He wants to play charades, but his clues ("Twenty-six syllables?") only frustrate the boyfriend, who throws him back in his playpen. Finally his parents come home, and both father and son (the latter now played by *Sammy Petrillo*) harass the boyfriend.

JERRY SOLO: Jerry comes out to introduce Dean's song, but he shows the band members headed from the pit to the bandstand behind the curtain, accusing NBC of wanting "you should think it's another orchestra... Don't think this network gives away nothin' for nothin'!"

DEAN SOLO #2: "Be Honest With Me"

FINALE: Dean is to sing "San Fernando Valley;" and wants Jerry to play drums, but Dick Stabile says he's required to have a drummer from the musician's union standing by. When Jerry makes a mistake, both Dean and the union drummer let him know it and they argue. After the song is done, Dean angrily orders Jerry off the stage. He then begins "Singin' in the Rain" but Jerry returns to at first spritz him with water, then progresses to a tumbler and finally a pitcher. Soaked, Dean orders Jerry to sing the same song, and he's quickly doused by Dean. Sopping wet now, Jerry shampoos his hair. Dean takes aim with a bucketful, Jerry ducks and Dick Stabile gets drenched.

ANALYSIS AND REVIEWS: A rousing hour, Martin & Lewis' *Colgate* format was beginning to solidify. Both supporting acts are presented back-to-back for the first time; this placing would continue going forward. The acts appear in between each of the two major sketches, and as with the prior show, the conclusion features the boys doing one of their nightclub routines. In this instance, "San Fernando Valley" is performed. It isn't all that different from the performance on *Welcome Aboard* two years earlier, and they'd certainly done it on stage in the interim... and yet members of the band are seen laughing at Jerry's reactions and his and Dean's comments. If anything, it's evidence that, at this juncture, the team wasn't capable of a perfunctory performance.

The dancing academy sketch plows some of the same ground as the prior month's gymnasium opus and also includes a little of what *Variety* would call "nance" humor. The timid Jerry doesn't want to be a wallflower at parties anymore: "If you teach me how to dance, then I'll go to a new party sometime next week, and I'll have all the girls, boy wow!" Dean offers to let Jerry dance with the lovely Elizabeth, and Jerry's all for it, ready to pounce. "You don't walk over like that!" Dean exclaims. "I want to see you walk very nicely." His torso thrust forward, Jerry walks stiff-legged toward the girl, but Dean calls him back. "No, no, no! Some of you didn't get there. I want you to walk over relaxed." Jerry clomps over like his knees are about to give way, so Dean pulls him back. "Walk over like a man!" Jerry puffs up his chest, extends his elbows, curls his hands into fists and begins stomping toward Elizabeth. "NO!" shouts Dean. Frustrated, Jerry tells him, "Whattaya want? I know maybe *one* other way how to walk!" "Lemme see that," says Dean, so a limp-wristed Jerry extends one arm effeminately and, hips swishing, approaches Elizabeth, lisping "Would you dance with me?" Apart from this, the sketch has little going for it; as if to compensate, guest performers are brought in. Leonard Barr's eccentric steps are basically the same as he did on the premiere, except he's given even less time. (Barr would turn up as an extra—usually during the opening—on every show the rest of the season.) De May & Moore's adagio is equally brief. When Dean fails to toss Sally Moore to a retreating Jerry, he yanks her back and the audience gasps, thinking the poor girl's arm is about to be dislocated.

After the fairly clever "Millie the Filly" production number and bubbly Kitty Kallen's two songs, the boys return with the "baby" sketch, which features its own sex-related joke. Dean leaves the room to assist the baby sitter in the kitchen. Alone, Jerry decides to watch TV. He gazes intently at the screen and lets out a "WOW!" His eyes bug out, he whistles, he crosses and uncrosses his leg, he writhes on the couch. When they return, the babysitter and Dean smile at his reactions, and Dean asks,

"You watching Hopalong Cassidy?" Still staring, Jerry answers, "No, Faye Emerson!"[1]

The other highlight is the repetitive "milk" gag: four times Jerry cries at being forced to drink, gradually his sobs subside and he raises the glass to his lips. Just as he's drinking, Dean says something like, "Milk is good for you!" "I DON'T CARE!" screams Jerry, as milk comes out of his mouth onto his pajamas, and he cries again. It's not technically a "spit-take," because he doesn't spray it; he lets it fall out of his mouth all over himself. A cutaway shows even Dean is amused, while the actress playing the sitter tries hard not to break up. The studio audience literally screams with laughter.

Once again, *Variety* loved it: "Dean Martin & Jerry Lewis, in their third show, gave further proof that low comedy pays off with high laugh results. Zanies continue to prove that their antic style is as potent on video as it's been in theatres, cafes and films." However, their critic seemed to think Sammy Petrillo's presence went beyond one visual gag: "For this show, they drew upon…Petrillo, who is an amazing double for Lewis, both visually and vocally. Petrillo was used to excellent advantage in a baby-sitter scene, with Petrillo enacting the infant. Bit also involved some clever staging since it originally might have represented a quick change by Lewis." Of course, that was the actuality: through a quick change and the positioning of the playpen, Lewis essayed the baby throughout the body of the sketch, with Petrillo cropping up only when "Daddy" Jerry was on screen. Also, Petrillo was never heard; the voice of the "baby," even after "Daddy" returned, was a pre-recorded Lewis. Finally, when they share the screen, it's clear that Lewis and Petrillo bear little resemblance to each other: Petrillo's head is longer and his ears are larger. He's a very good mimic of Lewis' facial expression, nothing more.

Another review came in the form of a memo to Jerry from Hal Wallis' producing partner Joseph Hazen. As Lewis' biographer Shawn Levy dryly put it, "Coming from one of the producers of *My Friend Irma Goes West*, it's remarkable reading." Hazen summed up the show as "all right for a couple of broken-down, has-been vaudevillians; it is certainly not worthy of Martin and Lewis…. I think the frightful slapstick ending of the show, where you pour water over Dean while he is singing 'Singin' in the Rain,' and Dean throws water over you, is a far cry from any kind of creative performance which requires your unique kind of talent and ability." Hazen, of course, missed the point entirely: it's not the slapstick but the fact that both

---

1.   It's one of the team's few topical gags: Ms. Emerson was an early TV hostess whose ample cleavage was frequently on display via a plunging neckline.

men are clearly enjoying it and each other that brings it to life. (While taking their final bow on a now dangerously slippery floor, Dean actually holds onto Jerry and advises him to take care, lest he hurt himself. Jerry then circumvents the problem by taking a calculated fall.) Conversely, the soon-to-be predictable "types" that Wallis and Hazen would force upon Martin and Lewis over the years have none of the spontaneous joy found in their early TV work.

In any event, the show performed where it mattered most, setting a new ARB audience record for the series with a rating of 39.5, once more outdrawing Sullivan's *Toast of the Town* by a 3-to-2 margin.

✳ ✳ ✳ ✳ ✳

SIDEBAR: *Sammy Petrillo*

The similarities between Jerry Lewis and the barely 16-year-old boy playing his son were more than facial. Born October 1934 in the Bronx, Sam Patrello was the son of a veteran Catskills trouper that performed under the name Skelly Petrillo. His mother was also in showbiz, eventually serving as Alice Faye's double.

Sometime in mid-1950, the boy got a "freebie haircut" from a trade school student that couldn't help laughing at the result. "I said, 'Whattaya laughing at?'" he recalled in a 1992 interview, "and he said, 'You look just like that Jerry Lewis!' And I said, 'Get outta here!' And everywhere I walked, people laughed and asked me if I was Jerry Lewis; it was unbelievable." A few days later, after the boy saw *My Friend Irma Goes West*, he decided they were right. He made his way over to the hotel where Milton Berle rehearsed and brashly presented himself. Berle's agent escorted the kid to where Martin & Lewis rehearsed, and soon after he was playing Jerry Lewis' "baby" at the conclusion of a sketch on a network TV show. As had his doppelganger, Sammy took his father's stage surname as his own.

Petrillo made a few more gag appearances: one on Eddie Cantor's next *Colgate*, and a bit on Berle's show (where *TV-Radio Life's* critic opined "the chap out-Lewised Lewis"). Jerry had MCA sign him, but no further work was forthcoming, and both Sammy and his father came to believe Lewis was stifling the lad's progress. Given the comedian's lifelong battle with insecurity, coupled with write-ups like *Variety's* and *TV-Radio Life's*, this was likely true. Regardless, since Petrillo was a minor, his dad had little trouble dissolving the MCA contract.

Dean and Polly Bergen rehearse "You and Your Beautiful Eyes," for the *Comedy Hour*, February 4, 1951. Photo courtesy of Kayley Thompson.

Petrillo didn't make a real public splash until early 1952 when he teamed with a curly-haired Italian crooner named Dominick "Duke" Mitchell (original family name Micelli). At the start, a Martin & Lewis impersonation was only one facet of their nightclub act; Mitchell would sing in the style of other popular recording artists and Petrillo would mimic various film stars and cartoon characters. By that point, though, Martin & Lewis were the sacred cash cows of Hollywood, so when fast-buck producer Jack Broder signed Mitchell & Petrillo for a film, he wanted only one thing: a Dean & Jerry reproduction. To ensure some known box office value, Bela Lugosi was engaged as the heavy. Even taking into account his films with Edward D. Wood, Jr., this picture would be the low point of Lugosi's career.

As soon as "Bela Lugosi Meets the Gorilla Man" was announced in the trade press, Hal Wallis was making noise about a lawsuit. He'd wait until he'd seen the finished picture, he told Louella Parsons, but assured her readers, "If we feel [Mitchell & Petrillo] are doing an imitation, we'll stop them." Lewis, too, confided in Parsons that he and Martin would sue if any of their shtick turned up in the film, adding, "I met Sammy when he was just a punk kid of 16 and we had him on one of our TV shows as a gag. He looked like me and so he went and hired a partner and had him cut his hair just like Dean's. You can't create something and have people swipe it right out from under your nose without doing something about it."

Once everyone saw *Bela Lugosi Meets a Brooklyn Gorilla*, as the film was ultimately titled, they knew it would likely bomb, and threats dissipated. "It is unlikely that many picture-goers will find it a good entertainment," wrote the critic for *Harrison's Reports*, adding, "At the theatre where this picture was previewed, many people walked out when Duke Mitchell, imitating Dean Martin, started to sing. Even most of the youngsters in the audience did not like it. Sammy Petrillo, who imitates Jerry Lewis, looks and behaves remarkably like him, but the ability to provoke sustained laughter is lacking."

Variety's reviewer agreed, aptly predicting the film was "destined for a quick demise.... [Mitchell & Petrillo] bear an uncanny resemblance to M&L in style and technique, but they impress as a third-rate road company of the comedy stars." Of Petrillo, wrote the critic, "He's got Lewis' manner down pat, including the maniacal laugh and the occasional Yiddish inflection. Also alike are haircut, facial contortions and gestures. It's all good for a five minute nitery turn, but wears in the 74-minute pic." *Variety* actually advised exhibitors that playing up the lawsuit controversy was the only way they'd lure customers.

After their film died (Broder sold it to TV within a year), Mitchell & Petrillo soldiered on in Vegas and assorted venues, but there was never another picture offer, and they split in 1954. They tried re-teaming a year later, when it looked like the genuine article might not work together again, but shortly thereafter gave up for good. Petrillo continued alone in clubs and on TV, turned to writing and producing, worked in some quick exploitation pictures over the years, and eventually ran a comedy club in Pittsburgh, giving breaks to such future stars as Richard Pryor and Dennis Miller. He passed away from colon cancer in August 2009, at age 74.

* * * * *

BETWIXT AND BETWEEN

As Jerry had announced on their last show, he and Dean did a two week tour that consisted of appearances in Cleveland for four days and Chicago for a week. After that, they reported back to Wallis for their fourth picture, *That's My Boy* (1951). During its production they managed to swing a guest appearance on NBC's ambitious attempt to lure radio listeners away from CBS: *The Big Show*. A 90-minute extravaganza of music and variety, hosted by "the glamorous, unpredictable Tallulah Bankhead," *The Big Show* was a big-budget expenditure at a time when advertising people were wondering just how long it would be until all their broadcast dollars were earmarked for television. No one advertiser could handle it, so it was sliced into three 30-minute segments, and the time sold to Ford Motors, Chesterfield cigarettes, Anacin headache tablets and RCA (NBC's parent company) home entertainment. NBC's Pat Weaver dubbed this multi-sponsor approach "Operation: Tandem."

The broadcast, which survives and circulates, isn't especially memorable. The boys come on during the second half-hour and, as usual, Jerry's broad antics catch the studio audience's fancy: "Okay, thank you very much, that's very sweet of you, Tallulah Bonkers, we're very happy to be here. You've been on for over a half-hour already; wash up, get your money and get outta here!" Dean sings "La Vie En Rose," tries to explain Tallulah's stage career to his confused partner, and engages in a brief bit where he and Jerry offer to purchase or trade jokes with fellow guest Bob Hope. During the final third, after Tallulah, Deborah Kerr and Dorothy McGuire perform a dramatic scene from "The Women," Dean, Jerry and Bob present their own version: "The Fellahs." On a positive note, Jerry and especially Dean sound much more comfortable than they did on their own show, but the material just isn't there. The joke exchange routine is not funny at all, and "The Fellahs" is pointless.

That's My Boy wrapped on January 10, *At War With the Army* officially opened a week later, and the team returned to NBC and *The Comedy Hour*, which had undergone some changes. Fred Allen, after four attempts, hadn't worked out to Colgate's satisfaction; the show lost audience to Sullivan each week he was on. Allen, a brilliant acerbic wit who'd had the number one radio show only a few years earlier, would never fully feel at home as a television personality, faring better as a guest on others' shows or as a *What's My Line?* panelist. NBC and Colgate would have to regularly fill one week per month on an ad-hoc basis; two whenever Martin & Lewis were tied up making a picture. They did it by turning to the tried-and-true of showbiz: Abbott & Costello, Spike Jones, singer Tony Martin; and relative newcom-

Rehearsing a little "old-time vaudeville" soft shoe for the finale of the February 4
Comedy Hour. Photo courtesy of Kayley Thompson.

ers such as Jerry Lester (who brought along his *Broadway Open House* crew
and had Fred Allen as a guest) and Phil Silvers (who would have Martin &
Lewis as *his* guests).

* * * * *

THE COLGATE COMEDY HOUR: Dean Martin & Jerry Lewis Show #4.

Airdate: February 4, 1951; NBC-TV.
Guest Star: Polly Bergen
With: Bob Fosse & Mary Ann Niles, Frank Gallop, Mickey Bloom
Announcer: Don Pardo
Writers: Ed Simmons & Norman Lear (uncredited)
Musical Direction: Dick Stabile
Settings: Theodore Cooper
NBC Production Supervisor: Sam Fuller
Television Director: Kingman T. Moore
Producer & Director: Ernest D. Glucksman.

OPENING: At her wedding reception, the bride welcomes everyone and announces that her "old high school sweetheart" Dean Martin will be attending, "and he's bringing his little friend Jerry Lewis." The two arrive and before long Jerry's into everything: he kisses the bride passionately, stuffs his mouth with food (tossing some of it to other guests) and looks over the presents. Told it's time to toast the bride, Jerry removes her shoe and Dean pours champagne in it. The wedding guests chase them out.

DEAN SOLO #1: "Tonda Wonda Hoy"

SKETCH #1: At the Elite Drive-In Movie (Now Playing: "The Murder of Mary Worth"), Dean and his date are discussing how comfortable it is. They honk for the ticket vendor (*Lewis*), who warns them not to blow the horn during the picture. When Dean asks for two tickets, Jerry checks the car thoroughly for no other passengers. "Two dollars," Jerry tells him, whereupon Dean pulls out a wad of bills and hands over at least a dozen. "You forgot the tax," says Jerry, which earns him a slap. Dean and his date try to enjoy the picture, but Jerry the usher escorts other customers through the car, Jerry the service man checks the oil, and Jerry the vendor loudly sells refreshments. When the screen goes out, Jerry acts out the rest of the movie in time with the soundtrack.

GUEST ACTS: Jerry introduces Bob Fosse and Mary Ann Niles, who dance an elaborate tap routine with an Egyptian theme. Dean introduces Polly Bergen, who sings "But Not For Me."

SKETCH #2: We take a trip back in time to when Martin & Lewis were just beginning their careers, "on the lowest rung" of the showbiz ladder. Dean has checked into a shabby hotel room, and has smuggled Jerry in his suitcase. They're both exhausted from a two-day bus trip and want nothing more than sleep, but the walls are paper thin. They overhear a couple arguing on one side of their room; on the other, a trumpeter (*Mickey Bloom*) is practicing. The boys end up reacting to the music, alternately dancing and wrestling with each other. As they are straightening up the bedsheets to "The Blue Danube," the musician switches to "The Sabre Dance" and Jerry tears the bed apart. Dean tosses him back into the suitcase and they leave.

JERRY SOLO: "When you're working in television or the movies," explains Jerry, "you always have somebody saying, 'Hey, mention the product that I make.'" He and Dean have so many friends, that he pulls out a list and reads off a number of products and services so "it'll be over!"

DEAN SOLO #2: Polly Bergen joins him for "You and Your Beautiful Eyes."

FINALE: Jerry conducts the orchestra for Dean's rendition of "It's Magic." Five minutes remain, so they each do some impressions and an old-time vaudeville dance to "Swanee River."

ANALYSIS AND REVIEWS: For some reason, Simmons and Lear don't appear on the opening credit crawl; instead the listed writers are Arnold Horwitt, Snag Werris and George Axelrod, who were actually the scribes for Jerry Lester's *Colgate* show of January 14. Nothing was guaranteed to go right when television was live.

If any exhibitors shuddered at the start of the Drive-In sketch, they were quickly reassured. "We're gonna love this," says Dean. "We don't have to fight for seats, no crowds." The lines are clearly intended as another mea culpa for the theater sketch in their first show. As for the Drive-In, no aspersions are cast on the business per se, except perhaps toward the quality of its ushers. It's all an excuse for Jerry to behave badly, which he does extremely well, and to pantomime the finale of the movie, which he does even better.

The second sketch begins with a terrific visual gag. Dean and a bellhop arrive in the seedy room with the luggage: a case for a bass viol and

A little backstage clowning with host Phil Silvers during the team's guest appearance on the May 6, 1951 *Comedy Hour*. Photo courtesy of Kayley Thompson.

a small hand-held suitcase. As soon as the bellhop leaves, Jerry begins crying for Dean to let him out. Of course, we think he's in the large instrument case… but when Dean opens it, it's empty. He then goes over to the suitcase, which has been placed on a table; when he opens *that*, Jerry's head pops out, followed shortly by the rest. The balance is a swell combination of slapstick and mime, as they try to bed down for the night but keep getting caught up in the music of the lone trumpeter.

Jerry's brief spot is intriguing, in that it illustrates how naïve he was when it came to the television business. Plugs—the "product placement" of broadcasting—had been around since radio: a writer and/or star would be offered a gratuity in exchange for mentioning a specific product or brand name during a show. Gratuities would vary, but usually involved the product being promoted. CBS producer Oscar Katz recalled that Cy Howard, the writer-creator of *My Friend Irma*, "had a garage full of appliances from all the plugs. He set his brother up in the appliance business with them."

Usually, it was tossed off with a joke. Jack Carter told author Jeff Kisseloff, "There were a million jokes. 'Some guy stole my wife's Diner's Club card. I didn't go to the police. He was spending less money than she was.'" In this instance, Jerry simply reels off the names, only occasionally throwing in a joke: "Fisk tires. They're very good. *Collier's* magazine has a story on Dean and I, February 10th issue. It's quite clever." Then he brings up Hal Wallis for their movies, and Colgate for (he looks off-stage) "Oh yeah, television!" Next comes Hadacol tonic, Bucknell shirts (who licensed a Martin & Lewis brand), Miami's Casablanca Hotel "where Dean and I stay…. They've got no rooms, no food. You sit outside and wait for Humphrey Bogart." Finally, Cadillac, which Jerry claims they'd been plugging for four years. "Fine car. Yesterday, they came through. We got a hubcap."

Another writer, Everett Greenbaum, remembered the bit, and told Kisseloff, "The Jerry Lewis writers…put all the things into one paragraph. They ruined it for everybody, because after that it became illegal." It didn't happen overnight, but most sponsors clamped down on the practice, including Colgate… not that it would stop Lewis, because nothing ever could.

Dean does a lovely job on both sides of his latest single, blending especially nicely with Polly Bergen on the second. The tunes, of course, were from *At War With the Army*. Near the close, Dean asks Dick Stabile to lead the band on "It's Magic," but Jerry gripes that he should be allowed to do it, and so turns in another musical shambles. At one point, Dean loses his starting note and Jerry tries to help him find it, eventually attempting to sing the verse himself. Dean stops him by doing exactly what Jerry did to him two shows ago: puts fingers in Jerry's mouth and pulls (albeit not as forcefully). Shortly afterwards, a lost-looking Dino sings, "I forgot the words." "You forgot the woids?" asks Jerry. "What else?" Dean answers him. "Better lock up when you're through," his partner replies, pretending to walk off the stage.

Told they have five minutes left, Jerry says, "Like the other show, we'll have to ad-lib, but no dirty jokes." "No," agrees Dean. "Everything clean, like the product we're working for." Jerry, in his mock-serious voice, says, "Yes! Colgate! And I am a satisfied user, and I say Colgate is the best dentifrice on the market; not because they are having us on their show, but because they told us to say it!" Whether this soothed the feelings of any Colgate-Palmolive-Peet executives over the plugs segment is open to conjecture, but the studio audience loved it.

"There probably isn't another comedy team today with such uninhibited zanyism and the talent to carry it off so successfully," raved *Variety*. "As in the previous shows, it was the final segment which drew the biggest payoff. Basically, it was a reprise of material they had used before, such as Lewis taking over the baton from Dick Stabile to lead the orch as Martin sang. They impersonated an oldtime vaude act and displayed their versatility with a sparkling terp turn to close the show. Opener, too, was sock...."

The reviewer added a surprising caveat: "With the success of their straight comedy, incidentally, it seems needless for the duo to play so much on their racial backgrounds, something which might not sit too well with a number of their viewers." What little "racial" material in the show was brief in length: after the wedding party opener, Jerry is still chewing away on the food he'd stuffed in his mouth, but comes to a realization: "Dean! I'm eating *ham*!" During the hotel room bit, Jerry asks Dean, "Are you sleepy?" His reply: "No, I'm Italian."

The broadcast set a new rating record with ARB, a whopping 45.9. With *Toast of the Town* having pulled 23.9, Martin & Lewis were drawing nearly twice as many homes as Ed Sullivan.

Back in Hollywood, the boys returned the following Sunday to *The Big Show*, and another lackluster outing. Jerry resumed harassing hostess Tallulah, Dean sang "Tonda Wonda Hoy" and fellow guest Groucho Marx doubled with Jerry on a sketch that had them debating whether they should double-date with Tallulah and guest Joan Davis... and vice-versa. None of the four parties are enthused about the idea, but the ladies figure they can imagine they're with Clark Gable and Gregory Peck. Jerry has a similar idea:

JERRY: When I go out with a girl I don't like, or Dean Martin... I close one eye and I think of Lana Turner and Rita Hayworth.

GROUCHO: What do you do with the other eye?

JERRY: I'm driving! Dad gave me the car, you know! Now I'm thinking of Lana Turner. Come in, Lana. Come in, Lana. Come in. Roger.

GROUCHO: Rita. Over!

JERRY: How're you making out, Grouch? Are you thinking?

GROUCHO: Yes, I'm thinking.

JERRY: What're you thinking?

GROUCHO: I'm thinking that at this advanced stage of my career, I have to play straight man to Jerry Lewis!

The pairing continues later in the show when Groucho does a take-off on Tallulah's dramatic reading of Dorothy Parker's "A Telephone Call." Dean's also in this sketch, barely; apart from his song, he had nothing worthwhile to do throughout the show, and knew it:

JERRY: (answering a phone) Hello, Martin & Lewis, cleaners and dyers: Martin's cleaning and I'm dyin'. Lewis speaking; Martin can't talk.

DEAN: How can I talk? They don't give me any lines. *(Laughs sardonically)*

JERRY: Don't you worry, Deanie boy; I'm gettin' laughs for the both of us. *(Silence)* Ahhhhhhh, laughs he says. Oh, it *hoits* me!

"MEL-vin???" Scene from *The Colgate Comedy Hour*, May 20, 1951.

With that done, they reported to Hal Wallis for another picture, *The Stooge* (1953). Although the team would plug the film and its songs in upcoming broadcasts, Wallis, for reasons that were never explained at the time, would delay its release for nearly two years.

* * * * *

THE COLGATE COMEDY HOUR: Dean Martin & Jerry Lewis Show #5.

Airdate: April 29, 1951; NBC-TV, from Chicago.
With: Helen O'Connell, Fosse & Niles, Ladd Lyon
Cast: Danny Arnold
Announcer: Mike Wallace
Writers: Ed Simmons & Norman Lear
Musical Direction: Dick Stabile
Musical Numbers Staged by: Lee Sherman
NBC Production Supervisor: Sam Fuller
Television Director: Kingman T. Moore
Producer & Director: Ernest D. Glucksman.

OPENING: The "Cure for the Common Cold" Committee has gathered for an important event. The chairwoman announces to the assembly that the cure has been found, thanks to the work of two professors from the University of Vienna. She introduces Profs. Martin & Lewis, who enter clad in fur coats, wool hats and ear muffs. They describe how they identified cold germs and produce a test tube containing 337,000 of them. In describing the cure process, Jerry breaks the tube, to the dismay of the attendees. Jerry cries out, "Don't get excited: we have the cure right here!" He and Dean pull fly swatters out of their coats and proceed to swat the table and the committee members, until they're thrown out.

DEAN SOLO #1: "Would I Love You"

SKETCH #1: On the golf course, Dean gets a new caddy, Melvin (*Lewis*), who has difficulty carrying the golf bag. Melvin argues over the club Dean is using, mistakes another player's ball for Dean's, laughs when Dean's ball winds up in a sand trap, and refuses to allow Dean to cheat on the number of strokes. Dean's girlfriend, Phyllis, shows up and tries to encourage

Melvin to play the game himself. When that doesn't pan out, Dean offers to do a trick: he'll hit a golf ball that's teed up on Melvin's mouth, but the poor caddy keeps inhaling the ball. Finally, the club strikes Melvin on the face, and he winds up punch drunk but eager to try again.

GUEST ACTS: Jerry introduces Fosse & Niles. With their company, they dance to "Steppin' Out (With My Baby)." Dean introduces Helen O'Connell, who sings a medley of "All of Me" and "Green Eyes." As an "encore," she sings the Halo shampoo jingle, after which she and Mike Wallace pitch the product.

SKETCH #2: A librarian (*Martin*) insists on absolute quiet, which becomes a challenge when a young boy (*Lewis*) enters singing "Abba Dabba Honeymoon." He tries to get Martin's attention while remaining silent, even resorting to semaphore, but finally has to whistle. The boy wants to return a few books, which turn out to be a massive amount, despite the relatively small size of his satchel. "You sure read a lot," exclaims the librarian, but the boy says he uses them as tunnels for his electric trains. Unfortunately, he doesn't have his library card, and asks if he can call his friend Herbie to borrow his. When Martin agrees, the boy shouts "HERBIE!!!" and is quickly advised to use the telephone. Desperate to keep him quiet, the librarian offers the boy a job, but he's too loud even when keeping others quiet, and when checking out a customer (*Danny Arnold*), he enthusiastically stamps ink all over him. Martin orders the boy to leave, but the lad won't go until he gets the book he came for, which is on the upper-most shelf. With the help of janitor Humphrey (*Ladd Lyon*), the boy is perched on a chair, with its legs situated on four Champagne bottles atop a table. The boy is too scared to move, so Martin leaves him there as the library closes for the day.

JERRY SOLO: Jerry lip-synchs (somewhat) to his recording of "Never Been Kissed."

DEAN SOLO #2: "I Wonder Who's Kissing Her Now"

FINALE: Jerry reads a wire thanking the team for agreeing to appear at the Italian Welfare Night of Stars at the Chicago Stadium on May 12. With two minutes remaining, Dean and Jerry demonstrate their prowess on the trombone and trumpet respectively, playing "The Sabre Dance."

ANALYSIS AND REVIEWS: In Chicago for an engagement at the Chez Paree (which is plugged behind the bandstand at the show's finale), "the funniest twosome extant," in *Variety's* words, took over the facilities of WNBQ for a wild hour. After the opening bit, Lewis—growing more confident with each appearance—spent some time disrupting the cameramen while introducing Martin's first song. He might have reasoned based on previous shows that there'd be extra time left at the end, so he could freely stretch at the start, but he and his partner wound up with only two minutes for their closing nightclub routine. No matter: the studio audience enjoyed his inability to stand still.

In kicking off Dean's entrance in the golf sketch, the pro asks, "Where've you been?" "Oh, I've been in court," Dean flippantly replies, which earns him a hearty laugh from the orchestra pit. It was true: some of the many managers and agents with whom Martin had signed percentages of his earnings before the teaming were now suing him for substantial settlements; concurrently, his first wife (and mother of his four children) sought additional alimony. Bigger laughs come when Dean inadvertently knocks the prop grass mats askew, and strikes the backdrop while taking his backswing. "You just hit the trees," Jerry helpfully points out. "They should've planted 'em farther away!" says Dean, who readjusts his tee shot. At one point a trained dog was to interrupt the game. "Hound, however, refused to obey signals," noted *Variety's* reviewer, who concluded the comics "were as funny without the canine help."

(*New York Post* TV critic Rex Lardner actually went to the trouble of tracking down "who this dog was and what it was supposed to do" for his column. "A man at NBC told me it was an anti-trick dog…a dog that does just the opposite of what you order it. If you tell him to sit up, he lies down. If you tell him to go away, he stays. 'What a dog!' Lewis was supposed to have exclaimed proudly at the conclusion of the anti-tricks. 'I trained him myself. The dog's name is Selma. Selma got confused,' the man at NBC said.")

The most memorable part of the sketch, however, is Jerry's character name. It was first used in the movie theater sketch on their debut show: "My name is Melvin," to which Dean simply replied, "Yeah, I figured it would be." Here, Dean asks his caddy's name, and when Jerry responds "Melvin," Dean's reaction is to face the audience and repeat, "*Melvin?*" Dean's girlfriend does the same when they're introduced, prompting Melvin to ask, "What is this bit? You met me, you said 'Melvin… *MEL-vin?*' Then she says, 'Hello, Mel… *MEL-vin?*'" Inevitably Melvin himself questions the sound of his name. Later, in the library, Dean calls Jerry "Mel-vin," followed by the same reaction, but Jerry smacks him, "No, that's the other sketch!"

Fosse and Niles' jazzed-up depiction of Irving Berlin's "Steppin' Out" is beautifully crafted, taking full advantage of the TV camera. It starts on the street of a busy thoroughfare, as various feet pass those of one man awaiting his date; the perspective is from the knees down. She arrives and they engage in a little playful footsie, then the scene shifts to a nightclub setting, with close-ups of smoking patrons, followed by the crux of the dance, which ends as it began, closing in on the pair's feet. Unlike similar acts on prior variety shows, this isn't a reproduction of a stage routine: it is a *television* performance. By contrast, Helen O'Connell's medley, while pleasant, comes across as ordinary. It's necessarily performed in front of the curtain (known as performing "in one") as the rest of the stage needed to be redressed for the next sketch, but after the lively and telegenic dance number, it's a letdown. Worse, O'Connell "encores" with a pitch for the sponsor's shampoo, and even duets on the jingle with a young Mike Wallace who, as a singer, is a very fine future journalist.

The library sketch, like the one at the dance academy, incorporates a specialty act, in this instance acrobat Ladd Lyon, playing the janitor Humphrey ("*Humph*-rey?" say Dean and Jerry simultaneously, trying to keep the laughs going). On stage Ladd would perform this routine, which involves balancing on a chair with its legs set upon four empty bottles, with a pre-planted "volunteer" from the audience. Said *Variety*, "Lewis took the place of the plant, but this part was integrated so adeptly into the sketch that it didn't appear to be an independent bit." It's fascinating to watch: as Ladd stands on one side of the rig, Dean stands on the other, clearly nervous about what might happen to his partner. As for Jerry, whether genuinely scared or not, he remembers to play it funny. "Humphrey" sets up a second chair upon which Jerry is supposed to recline; he and Dean wiggle it into place, which frightens Jerry even more. "Don't shake it! Oh, no, no, *don't* shake it!" As Dean laughs, Jerry pours it on. "Laugh, but don't shake it! Oh, please don't shake it! No, *don't* shake it! I don't care if you laugh, but *don't* shake it!!"

This is followed by Jerry lip-synching to his Capitol record "Never Been Kissed." Some audience members express delight when he announces it, but the performance is spiritless. In order to get laughs, Jerry stops mouthing the words at times: he yawns, catches his breath, or simply looks away. The problem is we never hear the studio audience reaction, as the sound is completely tuned to the record. Lewis clearly learned a lesson here: when reprising his "dummy act" for future shows, he'd synch to others' records (as he'd done in his solo days) and audience laughter would be audible.

"Dean Martin and Jerry Lewis have probably reached the topmost level of their development. At this point, it's probable that this team can

Jerry, Dean and Bill McCutcheon in the "Rocky's Gang" sketch, *Colgate Comedy Hour*, June 24, 1951.

do no wrong," enthused *Variety*. "Sunday's program was in keeping with the zany levels they established earlier this season.... The lads tandemmed (*sic*) in a couple of exceedingly funny sketches."

Making his Colgate debut as Jerry's fellow caddy and an unfortunate library patron, Danny Arnold (née Arnold Daniel Rothman) had an interesting background. "Danny says he never had much of a family," reads a 1952 United Press article. "He was born in Brooklyn, and worked on the vaudeville stage at the age of 6." In fact, Arnold was born in the Bronx to two Russian immigrants, Abraham and Esther Rothman. His father, a pharmacist, died suddenly when Danny was less than 2 years old. He and his mother remained in the Bronx by rooming with her brother, Martin (Max) Colker; Esther eventually became a nurse.

Arnold doesn't verifiably turn up in showbiz until 1947, when, through his friendship with Charles Chaplin, Jr., he became the manager and café performance partner of Charles' mother, Lita Grey Chaplin. He and Lita even made a movie together: an exploitation pic called *The Devil's Sleep* (1948), which took on both amphetamine ("diet pill") abuse as well as juvenile delinquency. The result, for which Arnold is credited as Associate Director, is the usual tawdry combination of sensationalism, cheesecake and very bad acting. Arnold and the ex-Mrs. Chaplin made personal appearances with the film, and gossip columnists occasionally reported on their engagement and impending marriage into 1950, after which the relationship fizzled.

By then, Arnold was in Hollywood and under contract to Warner Bros., for which he appeared in two films: *Breakthrough* (1950) with John Agar and *Inside the Walls of Folsom Prison* (1951), the latter best remembered as Johnny Cash's inspiration for the iconic "Folsom Prison Blues." During off-hours, Arnold and other young actors formed a softball club, which one afternoon took on a new first baseman: Jerry Lewis.

William Campbell, another Warner contract player who appeared in both pictures, was also on the team. "I'll never forget it, every time Jerry would raise an eyebrow, Danny would fall on the base pads in hysterics. When we got back in the car to go home, I said, 'Jesus, Danny, what is this insanity? What was all that laughing about? I didn't think it was funny at all! Am I missing something?' He said, 'You may not have been laughing, but guess where I'm going tonight?' I said, 'Where?' He said, 'I'm going over to Jerry's for dinner.'"

Arnold admitted as much at the time: "Jerry was clowning and I laughed at him. He knew a good audience when he heard one. After the game, he asked me to come over to his house and have some fun. The next day he called and asked me to have lunch at Paramount with him." The two became fast friends and off-stage collaborators. Their backgrounds, while not as sharply comparable as Jerry's had been with Sammy Petrillo, were near enough. Lewis was also likely impressed with Arnold's connection, however tenuous, to his idol, Charlie Chaplin.

Arnold remembered, "After a while, I was over there almost every day. He played jokes on me, like telling the studio cop I was an autograph hound and having me tossed over the fence." It turned out to be an audition for the type of slapstick punishment Lewis was itching to inflict on screen. Since he and Dean were "two comics," Jerry reasoned, *somebody* needed to be a stooge.

"One day I got a phone call from Chicago," continued Arnold. "It was Jerry. He said to come…and he'd get me enough work on his television show to pay my expenses. I went, and the upshot was I went on to New York with [him and Dean] and stayed with them on tour for five-and-a-half months." From this point Arnold would turn up on their every *Colgate* show through the 1952-53 season; for a time his very appearance signaled that Lewis was about to heap slapstick abuse. In 1952, Arnold would co-author the screenplay for the team's next independent production, *The Caddy* (1953), eventually transitioning to the *Colgate* writing staff.

As announced, Dean and Jerry appeared on the following week's show as guests of Phil Silvers. Dean sang "Someday, You'll Want Me to Want You," and they reprised the "Oh, Marie" routine from their second show, with a new touch: as Jerry sings his verse he thrusts the microphone stand toward the floor. Dean dives for it, but Jerry has the mic cord in hand and pulls it back safely, leaving his partner sprawled on the ground. They also interacted with the host; Jerry calls him "Phil," but he and Dean insist Jerry address him as "Mr. Silvers." Eventually the conversation has them asking Silvers for his middle name. "Melvin," he says, immediately followed by all three turning to the camera and repeating: "*MEL-vin?*" to the audience's delight. After one week, "*MEL-vin?*" was on its way to becoming a national catch-phrase—much to the dismay of the nation's real-life Melvins.

When the show wrapped, the boys dashed straight to the Copacabana for their opening performance at the club. They were scheduled for three shows each evening. Silvers was staying at the Hotel 14, just above the Copa. Leonard Lyons, in his *New York Post* nitery column "The Lyons Den," documented the evening's denouement: "At 2:30 a.m., in the midst

Rehearsing "follow the leader" for the second sketch of the June 24 *Comedy Hour*.

of the noisiest Martin & Lewis routine, Silvers suddenly appeared from upstairs. He wore a robe over his pajamas. He stumped to the nightclub floor, said: 'Shhh, less noise please. I'm trying to get some sleep,' then returned to his room upstairs."

* * * * *

THE COLGATE COMEDY HOUR: Dean Martin & Jerry Lewis Show #6.

Airdate: May 20, 1951; NBC-TV.
With: Jane Morgan, Fosse & Niles
Cast: Danny Arnold, Frances Weintraub
Writers: Ed Simmons & Norman Lear
Musical Direction: Dick Stabile
Settings: Theodore Cooper
NBC Production Supervisor: Sam Fuller
Television Director: Kingman T. Moore
Producer & Director: Ernest D. Glucksman.

OPENING: To the strains of "By the Beautiful Sea," we are at the beach about to witness the "Miss Sea Nymph of 1951" bathing beauty contest, which Martin & Lewis are judging. The ladies parade before the judges' stand, where Jerry decides, "I *like* it! I *like* it!" After examining the five lovely ladies, Jerry announces that the winner is "Miss Greenpoint," who wasn't in the lineup. "Miss Greenpoint" – homely, scarred and minus one tooth – emerges and accepts the prize, adding, "And thanks a lot, Uncle Jerry!" The boys are consequently chased from the beach.

DEAN SOLO #1: "With My Eyes Wide Open, I'm Dreaming"

SKETCH #1: Dr. Martin is making the rounds in a hospital recovery room and asks his nurse if the new orderly (*Lewis*) has arrived. Practically on cue, he loudly pops into the room and creates havoc with Mr. Miller, a patient in traction. Dr. Martin orders him to lift Miller so he can adjust the bedsheets, but Jerry twice drops Miller on top of the doctor. Martin decides to examine the orderly, and attempts to take his temperature, check his reflexes and examine his throat, all less than successfully. The doctor explains his responsibilities, but the orderly is more interested in learning how to make time with the nurse. When a fellow orderly (*Danny Arnold*) enters with a cut finger, Jerry sprinkles iodine over both him and his wound, then body-wraps him in a bandage. Dr. Martin decides Jerry needs a sedative, but Jerry drinks from the wrong bottle, and now imagines he's a monkey. The doctor lures him from the room with a banana.

GUEST ACTS: Jerry introduces Fosse & Niles, who dance to "Get Happy." Dean introduces Jane Morgan, who sings "Say 'Ça Va'"

SKETCH #2: Dean Martin is expecting his fiancée and her parents, and has engaged a new butler, Dudley (*Lewis*), who turns out to have zero experience. The evening doesn't go well: when ironing, Dudley burns a hole through one of Dean's shirts (and the ironing board); he can't tie Dean's bowtie without falling on him, or jumping on his back and doing it from behind. The guests arrive, and Dudley makes a shambles out of serving martinis, seating the guests for dinner, and bringing out the food; at all times haranguing Dean's future mother-in-law. When trying to carve a turkey, it falls on the floor and Dudley has to use a vise to keep it in place. Finally, he and Dean attempt to break the wishbone, which sends Dudley sprawling across the table. Dean's seen enough, and throws Dudley out of the house...through a window!

JERRY SOLO: Jerry shows off some of the props from the show, explaining that they're not real. The fake carving (actually a piece of paper) on the prop tree that said "Dean Loves Jeanne" during his partner's first solo now reads "Jerry Loves Patti." He peels off the paper to show the original, saying "They want people should think it's a different tree!"

DEAN SOLO #2: "Ever True, Evermore"

FINALE: Dean sings "There's No Tomorrow" while Jerry conducts the band. With five minutes remaining, Jerry wants to do a number with Dean, who suggests "You're Just In Love" from *Call Me Madam*. Unfortunately, Jerry can't synch up the counterpoint melody to what Dean's singing, even when they switch parts. Finally, Jerry asks for a different song and they duet on "My Heart Cries For You."

ANALYSIS AND REVIEWS: "Dean Martin and Jerry Lewis did it again... topping if possible their previous yockful (*sic*) sessions on the series," said *Variety*, without exaggeration. Not even an obvious cold virus could keep Lewis from creating sheer havoc, with enthusiastic assistance from his partner. His voice sounds ragged and he's seen coughing at times, but he's just as loud – and funny – as ever. Remarkably, the team was still doing three shows nightly at the Copacabana during this and their remaining *Colgate* shows, which were followed by a personal appearance tour. It wouldn't be long before Lewis' body rebelled against his workaholic nature.

This show marks the air debut of Jerry's "I *like* it! I *like* it!" which for him became another catch-phrase and even a record release, courtesy of tunesmiths Mack David and Jerry Livingston. He uses it no less than five times during the hour. He also gets a surprise after pulling back a curtain while introducing Dean's first song: Eddie Cantor is patiently standing there, waiting for next week when it's his turn to host.

The level of mayhem seen in the "disorderly orderly" sketch borders on surreal. Although Dean is ostensibly the straight man doctor, he's just as unpredictable in his own sly way. He decides to examine the new orderly, telling him to take off his clothes. Jerry objects: "Here! I don't even know you!" The doctor insists, so Lewis goes into a striptease, while Martin sings "A Pretty Girl is Like a Melody." Dean puts the thermometer in Jerry's mouth; he chews it up and swallows. Harpo Marx did the same in *A Day at the Races* (1937), but Martin & Lewis make the gag their own. (*DEAN:* "You're not supposed to eat those things!" *JERRY:* "I *like* it! I *like* it!") Finally, Dean tries looking at Jerry's throat, ordering him to say "Ahh," then "Bee," then "Dow". "Ahhhh! Beeee! Dowww!" Jerry repeats, which leads to both singing "Ahh bee dow to get you in a taxi, honey…" and dancing a Charleston to "Darktown Strutters Ball."

Once again, Fosse & Niles present a piece that can only work on television: it begins with the appearance—thanks to a neat bit of double-exposure—that they are dancing on the skin of a kettle drum being played by a giant pair of hands. Jane Morgan fares better than had Helen O'Connell in the prior show, mainly because the International Theater was equipped with a small second stage that permits her to have a scenic backdrop; that, and her song is more interesting, plus she isn't tasked with delivering a commercial.

The second sketch was a slapstick gem. In no time at all, the new valet greets his boss by sprinkling starch in his face. This is followed by a moment the audience has been waiting for:

DEAN: What's your name?

JERRY: My name is Dudley, sir!

DEAN: (*smiling*) Dudley.

JERRY: (*laughs and points at the audience*) They all thought I was gonna say 'Melvin!'

BOTH: MEL-vin?!?

Dean asks Dudley if he's ever served before. "Have I ever *served* before? I worked for the Morgans, the Astors, the Rockefellers, the Birds and the Cleans, and you have the nerve to ask me have I ever *served* before? Ha, ha, ha, ha, ha, ha, ha…" "Have you?" asks Dean. "Well, no!"

When Dean's fiancée and future in-laws arrive, things really get wild. Dudley refers to the mother as "the old lady," tosses olives into their martini glasses, gets "shot" when Dean opens a bottle of champagne (Lewis leans on Martin with such force that they both fall to the floor, Lewis on top), announces dinner by saying "Hurry up, we're all gonna eat now," spills a tub of coleslaw on the floor yet serves it anyway, and twice knocks the turkey onto the floor, placing his foot upon it when Dean reaches for it ("Get your filthy hands off it!"). Throughout all this the studio audience positively shrieks with laughter.

While struggling to fit the bird into the vise, Jerry turns to the crew: "You got too big a turkey!" In the ensuing mayhem, the wishbone falls out and he and Dean have to look for it. The actress playing the fiancée sees the prop and while Dean retrieves it, Jerry turns to the camera: "If we didn't find the wishbone, you people would be tuned in 'til 11:30! This is no joke, if we didn't find the wishbone. You see the sweat dripping down now? This is not spit: we're working!"

Despite all the havoc, planned and unplanned, the show finished ahead of schedule, leaving the two to perform additional night club material. Martin & Lewis had a reputation for never doing a routine the same way twice; watching the reactions of Dick Stabile's band, who laugh whenever they're not playing, it's entirely possible. "So kiss me," sings Dean during "There's No Tomorrow," and Jerry complies, right on his lips. He does this in all three TV performances that have been preserved, but on this one, he enacts a mock swoon, collapsing atop the piano, and proceeds to direct the orchestra while in a reclining position with his legs crossed.

Although raving about the show, *Variety's* critic added a warning: "If any criticism is due, it's that the team should be careful of too-often repetition of their favorite routines. That skit in which Lewis leads the orch while Martin sings had just a shade less lustre this stanza than previously, simply because it's been seen too often in the past." The *Brooklyn Eagle's* Bob Lanigan had similar feelings about the team overall: "Jerry's sketches on their other shows may have been funnier, but these Wackeroos from Wayback were never more destructive than they were last

Rehearsing "That Old Gang of Mine" for the finale of the June 24 *Comedy Hour*.
Photo courtesy of Kayley Thompson.

Sunday night.... As much as I enjoy the antics of this zaniest team in show business, and as much as TV needs them (which is plenty, brother!), I wish for the sake of all concerned that henceforth they will be seen less often.... Jerry has a more mobile puss than Rubber-Face Gallagher, and Dean is no slug-a-bed in the ad-lib department, but there is a saturation point in facial expressions, and ad-libbing at its best can be heard by tuning in Groucho Marx."

* * * * *

THE COLGATE COMEDY HOUR: *Dean Martin & Jerry Lewis Show #7.*

Airdate: June 3, 1951; NBC-TV.
With: The Demarco Sisters, The Johnny Conrad Dancers, Sonny King, Tommy Farrell, Danny Arnold

Writers: Ed Simmons & Norman Lear
Settings: Theodore Cooper
Musical Direction: Dick Stabile
NBC Production Supervisor: Sam Fuller
Television Director: Kingman T. Moore
Producer & Director: Ernest D. Glucksman.

OPENING: The members of the Washington Kennel Club have gathered for their annual dog show, where 30 dogs will be judged by "those internationally known dog lovers, Dean Martin and Jerry Lewis!" The first entry is Pierre, a French Poodle, but they're not impressed. Its owner insists, "Pierre has a wonderful pedigree!" "We don't care how you do his nails, Lady," Jerry responds, and tries speaking French to him. Getting no response, he decides Pierre is just a mutt. As the club members revolt, the remaining dogs burst upon the scene and the boys get chased away. After Dean tells Jerry to introduce his song, he starts to leave, but is called back. Jerry explains that Dean's birthday is June 7, "and for the kind of money I make with him, I love him." He asks the audience to join him in wishing Dean a happy birthday.

DEAN SOLO #1: "Too Young"

SKETCH #1: At Martin's School of the Theatre, the owner is having his students recite Shakespeare when Melvin (*Lewis*) arrives, "to loin, maybe, a couple things about acting." Martin wants to see what he did in the sixth grade:

> MELVIN: "Four score and seven years ago, our forefathers brought forth to this continent, *seltzer!*"

> DEAN: No, the thing goes like this: "Four score and seven years ago, our forefathers brought forth to this continent, *pizza!*"

Another student (*Danny Arnold*) wants to do his scene, but Martin advises him to first put on his costume and some makeup. Melvin asks to do a scene "with a girl in a neg-la-gee," so Martin brings out the lovely Elsie. He tries directing Melvin to walk toward her; suggesting several approaches, none of which are pleasing. The three try a "jealous husband" scene, but no matter which role he plays—boyfriend, husband or wife—

Melvin gets beaten up. The other student returns, asking Martin whether his makeup is correct. Martin believes so, but Melvin disagrees and proceeds to cover the poor fellow's face with pancake, greasepaint and powder. Finally Martin and Melvin try a Shakespearian dueling scene, which ends with Martin chasing Melvin out of the theater (and past the studio audience).

GUEST ACTS: Jerry introduces Johnny Conrad and his dancers, assisted by Rosette Shaw. Dean wonders if Eddie Cantor is still backstage (from the previous show); he pulls back the curtain to reveal actor Tony Curtis. Dean explains that it's Tony's birthday and plugs his new picture, *The Prince Who Was a Thief*. Then Dean introduces the DeMarco Sisters (who were appearing with the team at the Copacabana), who sing "I'm Late" from *Alice in Wonderland*.

SKETCH #2: A traveling salesman (*Martin*) is staying at a farmer's house while his car's being repaired. This farmer doesn't have a daughter, however; he has a son, Chester (*Lewis*). The salesman doesn't take much to Chester, but is very interested in his girlfriend Bertie, and the feeling is mutual. Chester tries distracting the now-amorous couple by putting on some dance music, but when they start kissing, he revolts. The farmer tells Mr. Martin he needs to sleep in Chester's room; when he enters, Chester's taking a bath in a wooden tub. Emerging from the tub, Chester shows off his physique. "Aww, how'd it happen?" asks Martin. While Chester resumes his bath, Martin discovers that the boy doesn't know what soap is. Martin tries to scrub Chester and gets pulled into the tub himself. Martin grabs an oar, and he and Chester begin rowing offstage.

JERRY SOLO: Speaking while getting dressed behind a partition, Lewis mentions three magazines in which he and Dean appear, then talks about their "making fun" of the name 'Melvin.' He says they've heard that kids with the name have been teased and abused, and holds up a photo of an impressive naval vessel. "Fellas, any time anybody says 'Melvin' and kids you about it, tell them: are they named after the U.S.S. Destroyer Melvin of the United States Navy." After a quick plug for Mixmaster, he introduces Dean's song.

DEAN SOLO #2: "Isle of Capri"

Newspaper ad for the team's legendary July 1951 appearance at Manhattan's
Paramount Theater.

FINALE: When Dean grabs him by the lapel of his tuxedo, Jerry gets
upset. He asks Dean how many tuxes he's owned in the five years they've
been teamed. Dean estimates about three per year, and asks Jerry, "How
many've you had?" "Thirty-nine!" gripes Jerry, who proceeds to cut up
Dean's suit with scissors. When Dean does the same to Jerry, Dick Stabile
complains that they're being "idiotic." They reply by tearing apart his suit,
suspenders and shirt.

ANALYSIS AND REVIEWS: Performing two shows back-to-back (each show having two weeks of rehearsal) in addition to their nightly duties at the Copa (once again plugged during the broadcast) took a visible toll in this segment. Neither of Dean's song performances went flawlessly: he starts the first one (possibly too early) and has to request that the choir come in; for the second, he asks for the words; cue cards becoming by now a permanent fixture. During the conclusion of their duel, Dean has to remind Jerry to drop his sword.

Having learned of the unpleasant consequences for some of their young audience, the "*MEL-vin?*" running gag is brought to a neat close during the Acting School sketch. When Martin hears the name, he immediately orders in a number of students (among them producer-director Glucksman and writers Simmons and Lear) and has them line up behind him and Lewis. Martin asks for his name again, Lewis says "Melvin," and everyone turns toward the camera to deliver the punch line. As the audience applauds, the extras jog offstage. The sketch also repeats the "show me how you walk" routine, performed exactly as in the dance academy last November.

The Cuban-flavored dance performed by Johnny Conrad and his troupe begins strong with a pair of conga drums accompanied by the superimposed head of vocalist Rosette Shaw, but the crux of it is a straight stage performance that fails to impress as much as the telegenic jazz of Bob Fosse and Mary Ann Niles. By contrast, the five DeMarco Sisters do a terrific job on "I'm Late," incorporating Martin & Lewis in the lyrics, which implies they performed this number each night ahead of the team's entrance at the Copa. In between, Tony Curtis' brief wordless appearance backfires on Dean: the audience is audibly disappointed that Curtis is given nothing to do, especially after Martin abruptly pulls the curtain shut while they're still applauding for his birthday, and then mangles the title of the movie he's supposed to plug.

Dean and Jerry "Down on the Farm" likewise revives a bit from a previous show. In this case, "*Don't* shake it!" from the library becomes "*Don't* kiss her!" as Dean and "Bertie" (dressed like *Li'l Abner's* Daisy Mae) get too familiar for "Chester's" liking. There's also a shocking moment when Jerry emerges from the tub; he's wearing pants, but they're wet and clingy, and even in a grainy kinescope it's obvious he isn't wearing a jockstrap. Lewis quickly and discreetly adjusts his outerwear in front, but his backside is also clearly displayed through the material, much to the glee of some and discomfort of others in the studio audience.

With only a few minutes left after Dean's second song, the boys cut up each other's tuxedos and practically stripped Dick Stabile for a slapstick melee that, *Variety* noted, got "a resounding boff at the finish," and possibly earned them another Joe Hazen memo.

The trade publication asserted the team "proved beyond cavil that they are the zaniest act in and out of video," but also noted that "during the last half-hour, they got bogged down in sub-par material and poor timing, and raced to beat the clock." The reviewer wasn't impressed with the "Down on the Farm" sketch, considering the bathtub conclusion to be its "saving grace," but on the whole it was another rave, with special shout-outs to Glucksman, Kingman Moore and Sam Fuller "for top effort in their departments." According to ARB, this was the second-highest rated show of the week (behind only the venerable *Texaco Star Theater*), scoring a solid 43.2 with 5,370,000 homes reached.

* * * * *

THE COLGATE COMEDY HOUR: Dean Martin & Jerry Lewis Show #8.

Airdate: June 24, 1951; NBC-TV.
With: Janis Paige, The Johnny Conrad Dancers, Danny Arnold
Cast: Adele Newton, Bill McCutcheon
Writers: Ed Simmons & Norman Lear
Musical Direction: Dick Stabile
Settings: Theodore Cooper
NBC Production Supervisor: Sam Fuller
Television Director: Kingman T. Moore
Producer & Director: Ernest D. Glucksman.

OPENING: At LaGuardia Air Field, a crowd awaits the disembarking of Martin & Lewis. At that moment, singer Tony Martin and boxer Joe Louis exit the plane to thunderous cheers. Behind them are Dean and Jerry, who are a little put out that the other two are getting all the attention. After the curtain closes, Dean orders Tony off the stage, but the latter refuses. Dean asks Jerry, "See what you can do with him," indicating Joe Louis. Jerry tries punching Louis in the arm a few times, but Louis simply says, "I *like* it! I *like* it!" Louis, though, is wearing a boxing glove and with a mere tap on the chin, Jerry is knocked for a loop.

DEAN SOLO #1: Dean sings "Pennies From Heaven" to child actress Adele Newton.

SKETCH #1: At the Gramercy Club, a quiet gathering place for society gentlemen, chief valet Dean awaits the replacement he'll be training before taking his vacation. Suddenly he sees a young man (*Lewis*) dusting off tables, chairs and guests while singing "Abba Dabba Honeymoon." Dean tries to teach him to work quietly, without much success. Various members are assaulted by the overeager valet, but in trying to lift a corpulent gout patient, the fellow falls on him, injuring his back. Dean takes advantage of this, and hypnotizes the gout patient to pick up the troublemaker and drop him through a billiard table.

GUEST ACTS: After a plug for *That's My Boy* ("We'd like you to look for it at your neighborhood mortician"), Jerry introduces Johnny Conrad and his Dancers presenting "The Blues Jump." Dean introduces Janis Paige, who sings "Get Out Those Old Records" and segues into "Don't Take That Black Bottom Away," complete with a ukulele solo.

SKETCH #2: Rocky (*Martin*) is the tough kid of the neighborhood and he keeps his gang (*Danny Arnold and Bill McCutcheon*) in line. A new kid, Harvey (*Lewis*), has moved in and wants to join, but his "Little Lord Fauntleroy" clothing and manner make him an ill-fit. He fails to impress them when, after fighting with Rocky, he runs for his mother. They call him "sissy," so he tries to win them back with a dime for ice cream. Danny takes it and buys two cones; Rocky gets one and tells Harvey to take the other away from Danny. Harvey smacks Danny around, but when Danny tries for revenge, Rocky gets it in the face with a cone. Harvey's mother wants her reluctant son to drink his milk and enlists Rocky's help. Harvey's big sister comes outside; Rocky wants to be introduced, so Harvey tries to teach him how to approach her. Finally, they all play "follow the leader." With Harvey in front, they go out into the theater and encourage audience members to follow.

DEAN SOLO #2: "Walking My Baby Back Home"

FINALE: Dean and Jerry argue about which of them will sing next, so Dick Stabile settles it: he'll play a number on his saxophone. As he plays, the boys harass him as Dean plays trombone and Jerry attempts to play trumpet. They untie Stabile's tie, mess his hair, hang an umbrella on his arm, place a derby on his head, roll up his pant legs, stick a handkerchief in his ear and even lick the sweat from his face, yet he plays on. After this, Dean wants to sing "That Old Gang of Mine" for the "old people," which brings Jerry to tears. They close it out with a Charleston.

ANALYSIS AND REVIEWS: Three shows in fairly rapid succession proved too formidable for Simmons and Lear, so a lot of bits were repeated, not all for great effect. The Rocky's Gang sketch in particular consisted of three repeated routines, two of which were used in the last show. Luckily this was the finale for the season, so the writers would have a few months to recharge.

The use of "Martin and Louis" at the introduction was inspired. "I've been wanting to meet you," Tony says to Dean, both having conveniently set aside their abysmal radio encounter of two years earlier, while Jerry and Dean burst into laughter at Joe Louis' "I *like* it! I *like* it!"

Putting Jerry the valet (whose character isn't named at all) into a gentlemen's club results only in a pale shadow of the valet scene from the previous May. In its review, *Variety* also pointed this out, concluding, "Repetition didn't do the team much good as similar effort on fresher idea (*sic*) would have paid bigger dividends." To be fair, there are attempts at originality, such as having an insulted member exit while loudly complaining, which continues when he's offstage, leaving Dean and Jerry to quietly react. Finally Dean, pistol in hand, exits and we hear two gunshots. But it falls mostly flat; neither Jerry nor Dean offers any sort of comic reaction to the long, loud tirade. The only laugh comes at the tail end of the bit, when the fellow resumes griping even after being shot.

Johnny Conrad and His Dancers perform their routine to an uptempo medley of "Blues in the Night" and "Birth of the Blues," but it's again a stage-bound piece that utilizes a single backdrop. Janis Paige, however, brings her spot to life with some lively music, including a nod to the 1920s that includes a bit of dance and light comedy, the latter of which doesn't register with the studio audience, presumably because they're tuned to the wavelength of Martin & Lewis.

The "Rocky's Gang" sketch is just a framework (albeit a lively one) for the reprisal of some popular bits. Jerry pummels Danny Arnold, who stands and takes the punishment. Watching Dean eat his ice cream cone, Jerry pleads with him, "*Don't* lick it! If it's my ice cream, then *don't* lick it! You can hold it and keep it for a while, but *DON'T* lick it!" Dean forces

Jerry to drink his milk; Jerry reacts exactly as he did in the baby sitter sketch. When the older sister arrives, the "let me see how you walk" routine is reprised, except it's now Jerry who tries to teach Dean. The payoff is exactly the same, however: the only other way Dean knows how to walk is effeminately. And it closes, as did the acting school sketch of the last show, among the theater audience; most of whom appear delighted to be involved in the proceedings. Repeated bits or no, the sketch went over big then and still registers today.

The finale, with Dick Stabile taking punishment while playing a hot jazz number, was another slice from the team's nightclub and personal appearance life, while the closing number, "That Old Gang of Mine," is possibly the oldest Martin & Lewis routine to be preserved; they were known to have performed it during their first year together.

* * * * *

In 1975, *NBC's Saturday Night* (later known as *Saturday Night Live*) debuted. Almost immediately it was hailed as cutting-edge; a radical departure from "old show-biz," with accent on youth culture both musically and comically. In reality, just like the *Colgate Comedy Hour* with Martin & Lewis, *Saturday Night* reflected the mores and tastes of its day within a comedy-and-music structure; it was the attitudes of the audience that had changed, not the form.

When Martin & Lewis were on, *The Colgate Comedy Hour* was the *SNL* of its day; the must-see TV for high school and college youth. Viewing these first season broadcasts, you see the same things you'd see on *SNL* twenty-five years later: catch-phrases, recurring characters and situations, new musical talent providing a respite from the sketches and, occasionally, comedians breaking the fourth wall or breaking each other up; you even hear the distinctive voice of announcer Don Pardo. The two worlds briefly collided when Jerry hosted *SNL* in 1983; in the opening sketch, he even told Joe Piscopo, made up to be Dean, "*Don't* lick it!" By then, Lewis was an elder statesman of comedy and his co-stars, particularly Eddie Murphy, were the young irrepressible studs he and Martin had been three decades earlier.

To be sure, there's plenty of old-time slapstick in these programs, as was expected in the wake of Uncle Miltie, but it's served with a twist of intimacy that still stands alone in team comedy. In every show, the two will grapple, wrestle, tackle, grab or pull on each other, insert fingers in each other's mouths or nostrils, hug and even kiss. In their classic two-reelers, Stan Laurel & Oliver Hardy would often bed down together for the night, yet neither initiated as much intimate contact as Martin & Lewis did while just standing in front of Dick Stabile's band.

The Colgate Comedy Hour's first year was an unqualified success, forcing CBS to dramatically raise Ed Sullivan's talent budget for *Toast of the Town*. As for Martin & Lewis, it had unquestionably turned them into audience favorites. From here on in, their personal appearances would shatter box office records and, in many cases, create pandemonium in the streets. (The Paramount Theatre appearance plugged by Jerry at the close of their final broadcast turned into two weeks of newsworthy, traffic-halting bedlam, as the team gave free "shows" from their dressing room window in order to lure ticket buyers out of their seats so new ones could get in.) Their movies would rake in millions. NBC and Colgate even agreed to more money for less work: their new contract called for five shows per season, for $200,000 per show, or $1 million a year.

The network, of course, preferred more Martin & Lewis, not less, so a deal was worked out to give them a weekly half-hour on radio under the "Operation: Tandem" umbrella, which permitted NBC to pay them a handsome $10,000 per week for 30 weeks. With Simmons and Lear's help, they'd finally pull off what had been deemed impossible: a successful radio series.

4

1951–52:

RETURNING TO RADIO
AND COLGATE SEASON TWO

DEAN: "Ladies and Gentlemen, I must apologize for my partner....."

JERRY: "Now he's apologizing for me! Mother was right; she said this could only end in grief. I've thrown away the best years of my life!" (*Mock crying*)

DEAN: "Oh come, Jerry, no! Don't cry; we're still partners! You know I love you!"

JERRY: "I hate myself for needing you so much!" (*Continues crying*)

DEAN: "Oh, don't feel that way, Jer. Why, deep inside, you're like a brother to me. I admire you. I respect you. I love you."

JERRY: (*effeminate voice*) "Shall we pick out the furniture?"

> *– Dialogue from THE DEAN MARTIN & JERRY LEWIS SHOW, October 12, 1951*

WITH THE START OF THE 1951-52 TV SEASON, two events shaped the future of *The Colgate Comedy Hour*. First, its sponsor agreed to purchase every Sunday. Second and more significantly, AT&T's transcontinental coaxial cable was finally up and running. As of September 30,

no longer would Hollywood-based stars have to travel to New York City or Chicago to appear on live TV. They wouldn't even have to work late; if a show like *Colgate* started at 8 p.m. EST, they could perform between 5 and 6 o'clock, and still get home in time to tuck the kiddies into bed. For Dean and Jerry (and Bud and Lou, Eddie, and the rest), it was a sweet arrangement. To accommodate its stars, NBC and Colgate leased the El Capitan Theater at 1735 N. Vine Street, at the legendary intersection of Hollywood and Vine.

Another upside was that the western half of the US didn't have to wait two weeks for a kinescope. The downside, though, was that they'd be watching the show just before or during dinner. For now, this seemed a small sacrifice to make, but as the concept of "prime time" became more entrenched and subsequently valuable, the particulars would change again.

Martin & Lewis and Cantor were still the linchpins of the *Colgate* hour. Abbott & Costello were no less in demand at Universal-International studios than their younger counterparts were at Paramount; they, too, only made five appearances. Newcomer Donald O'Connor joined the team for seven shows and proved nearly as popular as Dean and Jerry. The former Frigidaire man, Bob Hope, took three under Colgate's banner, and *All Star Revue's* Danny Thomas hosted two. Vocalists Ezio Pinza and Tony Martin each took a turn. Other weeks were handled by one-offs starring Jackie Gleason, Jack Carson, Herb Shriner, Ben Blue and a relative newcomer named Jack Paar. Just as he had the previous season, it was trouper Cantor who carried the heaviest load, with twelve.

The three months Martin & Lewis spent after their last *Colgate* show weren't entirely restful. After two weeks of bedlam at the Paramount Theater in early July, the duo went on to engagements in Detroit and Chicago for more of the same. Finally, on August 2 Lewis collapsed from exhaustion and they were forced to cancel the Minneapolis engagement that was to have concluded the tour. The week the cable became operational, Martin & Lewis started work on *Sailor Beware* (1952) for Wallis, which meant they wouldn't be available for several weeks beyond *Colgate's* second season premiere. Ever-disdainful of the team's forays on free TV, Wallis kept an iron grip on their days booked for his soundstages. Luckily the home audience could enjoy a weekly dose, albeit a partial one, of Dean and Jerry: their new starring radio show debuted on October 5.

This time, sponsors weren't a problem. As part of NBC's "Operation: Tandem" experiment, Chesterfield cigarettes and Anacin tablets, which had jointly sponsored two-thirds of *The Big Show* the previous season, signed on and were joined four weeks later by American Chicle, the makers of Dentyne and Chiclets gum. The format was similar to the program Bing Crosby was doing on CBS (also bankrolled by Chesterfield): Dean, introduced as the Master of Ceremonies, would sing three songs during the course of the half-hour. After the first, he'd introduce Jerry and they would engage in a little byplay (as Bing would usually do with his announcer, Ken Carpenter). Sometimes their conversation would be replaced by a mock interview where Jerry would portray an eccentric character; at other times Jerry would sing one of his own Capitol recordings. After his second song, Dean would introduce the guest star, whom Jerry would also meet, which would lead into a sketch. Finally, after one final song from Dean, the boys would sign off, reminding listeners that they "appear on radio through the courtesy of Hal Wallis Productions."

The result was a laugh-fest, although it helped to be a regular *Colgate* viewer. Simmons and Lear brought gags, catch-phrases and even entire sketches with them from television, and sometimes vice-versa. The November 9 show includes a joke used in the team's very first *Comedy Hour* (*Jerry*: "I have to get home before my mother... I'm wearing her sneakers"), and an exchange with Dean about Jerry's character's name ("Marvin Marvin Mintz") would turn up on their December 30 TV show. The broadcast of January 18, 1952, with guest Frank Sinatra, uses the premise of the "Rocky's Gang" sketch from their *Colgate* season finale the previous June; although most of the jokes are new, the "*Don't* lick it" bit is the highlight. The following week's sketch, set in Dr. Dean Martin's dentist office, uses "Say 'Ahh-Bee-Doww'" from the May 20, 1951 *Comedy Hour*.

For the movie satire on the premiere broadcast, "A Streetcar Named Max," Dean played Stanley the motorman, guest Dinah Shore portrayed Blanche, a passenger, and Jerry was Max, the streetcar. The premise was simple: Stanley is wooing Blanche, but Max loves her, too. The resulting interplay was similar to that used in most *Colgate* sketches; many listeners no doubt closed their eyes and "saw" Jerry's expressions as he delivered his lines:

JERRY: "Hey, he's putting his arm around her! (*Shouting*) Take your filthy hands off her!"

DINAH: "Who was that?"

JERRY: (*quietly*) "It's me, Max."

DEAN: "Max?!? But you're a streetcar!"

JERRY: "No, *you're* a streetcar!"

DINAH: "Hey, Stanley...the streetcar talks!"

JERRY: "Why not, I'm entitled!"

DINAH: (laughing) "You know somethin'? He's cute!"

DEAN: "Cute? Why that big tub of steel!"

JERRY: "Yeah? Well, you should see me when I diet. People think I'm a Nash Airflyte!"

DEAN: "Ah, go on and get back on the track before I strip your gears!"

JERRY: "Here, don't you get familiar!"

DINAH: "Hey, Stanley, let him stay!"

JERRY: (sounding like Bogart) "Now you're talkin', baby! How's about a kiss?"

DINAH: "Gee, I don't know. I never kissed a streetcar before!"

JERRY: "Aww, come on. It's no different than kissin' a truck!"

DEAN: "Now listen, Max. You shouldn't be talkin' like that. You're a streetcar, and…"

JERRY: (laughing) No, *you're* a streetcar!

DEAN: "You shouldn't be messin' around with girls. Why even look at 'em? Why think of kissin' 'em? Why must you torture yourself this way?"

JERRY: "I *like* it! I *like* it!"

The situation grows ever more ludicrous as Max proposes marriage to Blanche ("I can see us now, just the two of us. And in a year, a little hot rod!"). The studio audience audibly enjoys not only the lunacy of the lines, but the reactions of the performers. Poor Dinah Shore fights to keep it together, but loses the battle by the time she has to tell Dean,

"Please, you're speaking of the streetcar I love!" Worse for her, she accidentally sings one of Jerry's lines in the musical finale, a take-off of "The Trolley Song." As for the home audience, they enjoyed it enough to write letters requesting a repeat performance, which took place (with guest Virginia Mayo) on the April 11, 1952 broadcast.

Whether they liked the show or not, the trade press critics all made the same point: Dean and Jerry are at their funniest when seen. *Variety* was impressed, calling it "one of the most hilarious 30 minutes in radio. In their initial attempt in '49…Martin & Lewis were a dismal flop. But that was before TV…. Today the 'sound only' M&L presentation permits for a visualization of their antics. The listener can fill in the rest…. Too, M&L are getting a better writing assist this time up, geared strictly to their individual comedic talents. Last Friday's premiere was, for the most part, a well-paced show…. Martin, incidentally, does a glib emcee job."

On the other hand, *Billboard's* Joe Martin opined, "Just as it was last season (*sic*), the Martin and Lewis radio show was pretty much of a dud. There's no getting away with the fact that these two guys are basically visual entertainers…. The studio audience yocked it up plenty, but too often at times when the radio audience was wondering what Jerry Lewis was doing to get those laughs. Martin's [crooning] was good enough; Jerry Lewis' vocal tricks were cute enough and some of the lines were okay, too…. Miss Shore's piping on 'My Heart Belongs to Daddy' was listenable, her banter with the comedy team was smooth and Martin even turned out to be an affable emcee. So how come it wasn't a good radio show? The only conclusion is—ya gotta see 'em."

The reviewer for *TV-Radio Life* made pretty much the same complaint, and also possessed something of a short memory: "Those visual comics, Martin and Lewis, have bowed on their second radio series. As much as we like the zany pair on television, let's face it: they are not audio artists…. [The team] claimed that this would be a pleasant, easy-going show. That statement is good enough for us. However, we suggest they try a situation comedy script to help keep their ebullient enthusiasm in check."

Like its predecessor, *The Dean Martin & Jerry Lewis Show* was transcribed ahead of time, and could even be recorded on location when the boys were doing other work. One episode was taped at Ft. Benning, in front of an audience of servicemen, where they were shooting scenes for *Jumping Jacks* (1952), while two others were recorded at a San Francisco theater during a four week personal appearance tour.

A careful listen to the surviving recordings reveals a *lot* of editing, even though, as with the premiere, mistakes were often deliberately left in. Circulating among old-time radio hobbyists is a 65-minute unedited tape of the November 9 show, which is remarkable listening not only for the material that was left out of the broadcast version, but also as a mirror of Dean and Jerry's working relationship at the time. They were at the peak

"Dean Martin's a Scream" insisted Lewis in an article for this 1951 novelty magazine.

of their popularity and knew it, while still enjoying the novelty of making all that money just for having fun together. Throughout the recording Jerry takes charge and Dean willingly follows, although his second wife, Jeanne, was expecting their first child. Thrice Dean is heard asking Jerry to hurry up because "she could be having the baby now." The impending delivery clearly had an impact this evening, because Dean makes several mistakes. The biggest, and funniest, is stumbling over the introduction to his third song; when he finally gets it right, he starts singing the lyrics to the second.

The finale of the closing sketch involved Dean, Jerry and guest Danny Thomas singing special lyrics to the tune of "Betty Co-Ed." When the tape begins, Jerry and Dick Stabile discuss rehearsing the number, while Dean gripes that his microphone isn't turned on. Once the mics are fixed, Jerry asks if he wants to rehearse. Dean responds, "No, why rehearse? We're gonna do the whole show again at 10." Stabile argues, "I'd like to go over this, so I'll know what's going on," and the two turn on him:

DEAN: Don't talk to me… don't talk!

JERRY: Don't start carping or you'll wind up going back to Sicily! (*Audience howls*) And you'll deserve it, too! He used to work at a grape factory, steppin' on grapes, but they fired him.

DEAN: Why?

JERRY: They caught him sitting down on the job!

DEAN: All right, you want to rehearse this 'Betty Co-Ed' thing, or do you just want to make this a rumor?

DICK STABILE: No, why don't you just take the start?

DEAN: I don't know what I'd do without him, but I'd rather.

JERRY: Yeah. I'd shake hands with ya, but I see you're busy!

DEAN: Jerry, you shouldn't be… (*drowned out by audience laughter*) Well, there goes NBC's license!

JERRY: You wanna rehearse it once? Run it down quickly, 'Betty Co-Ed?' Uh, Dean, run it down with him...you know better the music than him.

DEAN: (interrupting) I don't want anything... I don't know music!

JERRY: (laughing) Well, if you don't we'd better not even start this show! (*Laughing, turns to the audience*) We're having loads of fun. I wish you'd join us!

Later, while Dean is speaking with their guest, Jerry enters wanting to know who it is. When Jerry trips over the word "amuse," Dean hops on it and the two start ad-libbing. On the air, it went like this:

DEAN: "Jerry, this is Danny Thomas, the comedian!"

JERRY: "Oh, goody! Do you think he'll a-muse me?"

DEAN: You were going to say 'abuse me,' weren't you?

JERRY: My subconscious mind was woiking. I don't like how well you two are working together!

In the studio:
DEAN: You were going to say 'abuse me,' weren't you?

JERRY: My subconscious mind was woiking.

DEAN: "Jerry, this is Danny Thomas, the comedian!"

DANNY: (reads Jerry's line) "Oh, goody! Do you think he'll amuse me?"

DEAN: (laughs)

JERRY: Well, good night! (*Starts to leave, then returns*) I don't like how well you two are working together!

DEAN: "Jerry, this is Danny Thomas, the comedian!"

JERRY: Oh, goody! Is he abusive?

DEAN: Jerry, this is the abusive Danny Thomas! Let's get this line in here!

The sketch is a take-off on Groucho Marx's quiz show, *You Bet Your Life*, with Dean as "Groucho Martin" and Jerry and Danny as contestants. After two or three flubs, Dean cries out, "I can't even talk in my *own* voice, you got me doin' this," tries his line again, then starts reciting Groucho's expedition monologue from *Animal Crackers* (1930): "After four days on the water and three on the boat…we finally penetrated into the interior of Africa. We took some pictures of the native girls, but they weren't developed…" "Here!" interrupts Jerry while the audience howls, then adds, "We're going back next year!" They swing back into the sketch, and when they get to the jackpot question ("If E is to X what L is to F, what is the sum total of the third equation?"), the chime rings before Danny can get his answer out. "I'm time, your sorry is up!" says Dean, and the audience explodes as all three (and presumably the band) fall apart with laughter. The blown line and audience reaction were kept in the broadcast, but not the follow up. Danny laughingly makes a crack about how the producer is now bald-headed, then it's Jerry's turn:

JERRY: Are you sure you put your contact lenses in? 'I'm time, your sorry is up?!?'

DEAN: (*justifying his nervousness*) My wife is havin' a baby!

JERRY: Throw me down the stairs, my hat! Throw the baby over the fence, some milk!

DEAN: (*as Groucho*) "Well, I'm sorry, your time is up. Thank you, Mr. Bacciagalupe" (*trips over his tongue saying the name*).

DANNY: (*laughing*) You're Italian! How come you can't say that?

DEAN: This is written in Spanish!

At last they get to the "Betty Co-Ed" piece, which—since it wasn't rehearsed—takes several attempts. When the first one falls apart, Thomas observes, "Wouldn't this be priceless on film?" As the audience applauds in agreement, he adds, "You ladies and gentlemen are not here at a great performance, but you're certainly here at a *rare* one!" The director is heard asking for Danny and Jerry to repeat their line "What do we know about quiz shows?" which leads into the song. The two huddle to discuss the timing, and Dean asks, "When are you two picking out the furniture?"

JERRY: (*lisping*) I saw a lemon oak set for the dining room…

DEAN: Jerry! I had an uncle that acted that way. Now he's my aunt! (*To the laughing audience*) I'm funny when you get to know me; I'm funny!

They never do get the song right all the way through; the final version was assembled from three different takes. To cap it off, Jeanne Martin wouldn't have the baby for another 10 days, so the following week's taping may not have gone much better for her nervous husband.

Despite the early criticism, the series built an audience, and when *Variety* tuned in the February 15, 1952 broadcast, they gave an unqualified thumbs-up: "The Dean Martin-Jerry Lewis NBC radio show is still rolling at a solid clip, with a clever scripting job by Ed Simmons and Norman Lear supplying click material for this stanza…. [The] piece de resistance was a quickie takeoff on the stage-film hit *Born Yesterday*, with William Holden guesting in the intellectual's role and Lewis making like the dumb blonde. It was a cute bit carried by Lewis' well-timed handling of the string of gags. Martin and Lewis also scored with their reprise duet of "Little Man, You've Had a Busy Day." The rest of the comedy byplay was in this team's standard payoff groove. Martin's solo vocalling (*sic*) of a brace of standards and pop hits was, as usual, highly listenable."

Readers of *Radio-TV Mirror* magazine voted Dean and Jerry's show their favorite radio comedy program of the season; the honor was announced on the team's April 11 broadcast. The season wrapped two weeks later, after 30 transcribed performances that survive and circulate among collectors and, despite being audio only, do a more capable job of imparting genuine Martin & Lewis madness than many of their movies.

* * * * *

JERRY: "Dean is more than a straight man. He also has a great sense of comedy. In some of our routines he gets at least half the laughs. Sometimes in night clubs we switch the act entirely, and he does my lines and I do his."

– *To columnist Bob Thomas, February 1951*

Martin's cry of "I'm funny" to a studio audience could easily be taken as a harbinger of the conflict to come. In later years Norman Lear would recall, during more than one interview, "as long ago as when we were rehearsing our first [*Colgate*] show at the Paramount Caterers that Jerry, who was supposed to be the 'funny one,' couldn't stand it if Dean got any laughs. Dean could be insanely funny with a line. Any morning that Dean would come in and start being funny with the lines or do funny things, Jerry would wind up in the corner on the floor someplace with a belly-ache. And a doctor would have to come. This was always true. Whenever Dean was very funny, strange physical things happened to Jerry." Alan "Bud" Yorkin, who joined the *Comedy Hour* staff during its second season, also recalled more than once, "Dean would ad-lib an exceptionally funny line at Monday's rehearsal, and everybody around would fall on the floor, laughing. We'd never hear it again until we went on the air on Sunday. Then Jerry would do *Dean's* ad-lib, before Dean could, and get the screams from the audience. This happened on a number of occasions. It was unbelievable how he could pull that on his own partner."

While Lewis' insatiable lust for adoration is well-documented, including by himself, the fact is the hard evidence—the *Colgate* hours themselves—contradicts both Lear and Yorkin. Martin ad-libs at least once in nearly all the early broadcasts and Lewis' usual reaction is to laugh and attempt to top him. Before the first season was done, Simmons and Lear were giving Martin his own jokes, with Lewis' blessing. As for Yorkin's observation, it omits the possibility that Lewis *asked* his partner between Monday and Sunday if he could have the line, perhaps intuitively feeling he could do more with it. All members of teams expect such give-and-take, yet even if this wasn't the case, Martin was no fool; burned once or twice, he would have learned to keep his sense of humor in check until airtime.

Moreover, although naturally funny when at ease, Dean was rarely "insanely" comic on the air. For one thing, Jerry completely overpowered him in that department and always had the audience on his side; for another, Dean wasn't yet the assured performer he'd become. His self-deprecating comment "I can't even talk in my *own* voice" wasn't mere levity, it betrayed a deeper anxiety. He'd dropped out of high school and would be a married father before he learned to speak without defaulting to 'dese,' 'dem' and 'dose.' His daughter Deana wrote that her mother "worked tirelessly teaching him proper pronunciation and diction." "I could barely hold a conversation," her father confessed to her about those days. "At times it was embarrassing." Whether reading or reciting dialogue, it took several years before the memory of that embarrassment faded. There are times in the early *Colgate* shows, most especially when introducing supporting acts, that Dean appears stiff and self-conscious. On TV *and* radio, he occasionally delivers a laugh line that fails to get a reaction from the audience, only because he pales in comparison to the assured Jerry.

Lewis summed up his partner's job as "a heavy load. He was the straight man. There were times they didn't even mention his name in a review." In the trade press, Martin would get a nod for the "fine warbling" of his songs that would usually be buried under kudo after kudo crediting Lewis for every ounce of comedy. Every so often, though, an astute journalist caught on to the dynamic. "Those who think that he is 'only a straight man' to Lewis' clowning betray an appalling ignorance of the strategy of comedy," wrote Leo Rosten for *LOOK* in early 1952. "Martin uses superb timing, an off-beat style and a dry, droll humor all his own."

"Few people realize it," asserted their *Colgate* producer Ernie Glucksman, "but Dean sets up 60 per cent of Jerry's gags and he functions like a colored spotlight to heighten Jerry's crazy humor." Their first show of the new season proved both Glucksman and Rosten correct.

THE COLGATE COMEDY HOUR: Dean Martin & Jerry Lewis Show #9.

Airdate: November 3, 1951; NBC-TV.
With: Dorothy Dandridge, Bob & Eddie Mayo
Cast: Danny Arnold, Jimmy Wallington, Donald MacBride, Marion Marshall
Writers: Ed Simmons & Norman Lear
Musical Direction: Dick Stabile
Art Direction: Furth Ullman
NBC Production Supervisor: Sam Fuller

Television Director: Kingman T. Moore
Producer & Director: Ernest D. Glucksman.

OPENING: The Institute of Archeology is displaying an assembled dinosaur skeleton provided by Dr. Sills. However, the director says there is some dispute as to the figure's authenticity and explains that two experts will conduct an independent examination. The experts are Martin & Lewis, and as they examine it, the dinosaur collapses. As usual, they're chased away.

DEAN SOLO #1: "Solitaire"

SKETCH #1: Jimmy Wallington sets the scene for a look back at the start of the team's career. "They haven't worked in weeks, they haven't eaten in days." At Murray's Booking Agency, the boys arrive and attempt to impress the secretary (*Marion Marshall*), but there's nothing available for them. As they're about to leave, she pulls out her lunch; desperate for food, the two grab her sandwich and drive her from the room. At that moment, they overhear Murray (*Donald MacBride*) receive a call requesting a ventriloquist act. Dean volunteers himself with Jerry as his dummy. Jerry's not happy with the arrangement, especially when Murray invites Dean to join him for lunch. It takes a while, but eventually Murray suspects that Martin's "dummy" might be a real human being. To prove him wrong, Dean rips off Jerry's arm!

GUEST ACTS: Dean introduces Bob and Eddie Mayo, who perform a specialty dance, "Tunisian Ball." Jerry introduces Dorothy Dandridge, who sings "Blow Out the Candle."

SKETCH #2: At the State Prison, the warden and guard discuss the behavior of "two vicious killers." The warden has been sent a special investigator named Plummer to impersonate a convict and gather information. An unimpressive specimen, Plummer (*Lewis*) is placed in the cell with the two intimidating toughs (*Martin* and *Danny Arnold*). They push him around and even eject him through the cell bars, but he returns, always trying to be friendly. When midnight rolls around, another prisoner breaks through the floor with a knife and package. Plummer runs off to warn the warden, but the two toughs follow him. The box is opened and a candled cake is removed as everyone sings "Happy Birthday" to the relieved warden.

Six Steps in Two Weeks to a *Colgate Comedy Hour*: Week One, Step One: A read-through of the script. Photo courtesy of ABCDVDVIDEO

Week One, Step Two: Preliminary rehearsals. Photo courtesy of ABCDVDVIDEO

Week One, Step Three: Conferring with the producer. Photo courtesy of ABCDVDVIDEO

Week Two, Step Four: Costume Fittings. Photo courtesy of ABCDVDVIDEO

Week Two, Step Five: Full stage rehearsals. Photo courtesy of ABCDVDVIDEO

Week Two, Step Six: Camera blocking. Photo courtesy of ABCDVDVIDEO

JERRY SOLO: Dean introduces Salvatore Innskeep (*Lewis*), who "sings" "Be My Love" by lip-synching to Mario Lanza's recording.

DEAN SOLO #2: "Bella Bimba"

FINALE: The boys repeat "Oh, Marie" by special request. (*Dean:* "Well, who requested this?" *Jerry:* "Your mother!")

ANALYSIS AND REVIEWS: The team's second season bow is one of the highlights of their TV career. Everything works: the sketches are clever and last just as long as they should; Dean and Jerry are relaxed and openly enjoying themselves and each other; the supporting acts are top notch. Although the boys could hardly be said to have rested well over the summer, they show no strain or weariness as was evident at times toward the end of the prior season. Certainly Simmons and Lear had recharged *their* batteries, despite the extra load of scripting the radio show.

The "Ventriloquist" sketch proceeds smoothly, and even though the onus is on Dean to manhandle his "dummy" partner, Jerry certainly takes his share of punishment; having his face slapped and hair pulled, and falling to the floor at regular intervals. The closing, when Dean tears off Jerry's fake arm, had repercussions later: six-year-old Gary Lewis was watching at home and, suitably traumatized by the gag, refused to speak to "Uncle Dean" for several weeks.

With their "Tunisian Ball," Bob and Eddie Mayo bring a full dance troupe, a little stage smoke and a lot of flash to what is essentially an extended tap routine. The trappings of a native worship ceremony, one that even depicts a moment of human sacrifice where a young white woman is carried and dropped into an open pit, lift the performance out of the routine. The young Dorothy Dandridge, in her television debut, scores with a surprisingly suggestive number, enhanced by her beauty and bare shouldered gown.

The "Prison Spy" sketch harkens back to previous shows: Jerry wants to be liked by his cellmates even though he's there to uncover what is set up as an escape plan. He gets to slap Danny Arnold around and sit on him a couple of times, but he also gets yanked a lot by Dean. He tries to impress them with a tough-guy growl; to this Dean responds by pulling Jerry's lower lip forward and tipping his cigarette ashes on it. Whether or not the gag was planned, judging from Lewis' reaction, a burning ash ended up in his mouth. Martin also floors both his partner and Arnold with an ad-lib during the following exchange, where they try to discover if the new cellmate is a stool pigeon:

DANNY: "Wait, I'll find out. Hey you! You ever packed a 'G' on your hip when you copped a heist?"

JERRY: "Did I... wha'???"

DEAN: Did you ever take it on the lam with a shamus who had the croaker beside the creek?

A smiling Arnold turns his head away from the camera before breaking up, but Lewis openly laughs aloud at his partner, before turning toward the audience: "He ad-libbed; I don't know *where* I am now!"

Introduced by Dean as having "a fine operatic voice," an eccentrically costumed Jerry serves up a taste of his pre-teaming record act, mouthing and gesticulating outrageously to Mario Lanza's million seller of the previous year, "Be My Love," and the audience just falls apart with laughter. It's a cinch that, had he been received like this at the shady night clubs where he'd started out, there probably wouldn't have been a Martin & Lewis. Which is not to say that Lewis isn't funny here; his rubbery face is remarkably expressive even in the extreme. The number permits him to build his shtick to a hilarious crescendo and is just the right length to keep from becoming tedious. But the screaming laughs are out of proportion to the bit's simplicity, and it's because the audience had fallen in love with Jerry Lewis long before the show even went on the air.

Dean carries off "Bella Bimba" beautifully, although it contains one less verse than the version he sang on their radio premiere. The reprise of "Oh, Marie," although lacking the mouth-pulling assault on Dean from the year before, does include the thrown mic stand bit used in their guest shot with Phil Silvers, and again it stops the show. Pianist Lou Brown gets into the act as well; Jerry twice yells at him to "Play regular!" and Dean asks, since he has both black and white keys, why he's "playing in the cracks." When Martin holds a note, though, Brown gets his revenge, yelling "Sing regular!" Jerry gets another surprise from Dean. In the midst of the song, he starts gyrating as the drummer gets sidetracked on the tom-tom. Observing Dean's disapproving look, Jerry falls into his arms with a mock sob. Dean hugs him as usual and then, suddenly inspired, licks the side of Jerry's face. Jerry snaps to attention and looks at Dean with a mixture of incredulity and admiration, then pulls out a handkerchief, wipes off his cheek and cries, "*DON'T* lick it!"

Variety, as usual, had a glowing, if somewhat verbose, critique: "Considering the hit-and-miss quality of the *Colgate* showcase to date, the M&L duo's return – with some of their zaniest material to date – provided a sorely needed shot in the arm for Colgate in the competitive rating sweepstakes…. If, as the current hue and cry would have one believe, the major clowns are going around in a repetitive groove, and the sameness of material and faces has already created a TV crisis, these ominous overtones haven't, at least as yet, caught up with the Martin & Lewis comedics. Even their 10-minute repeat as a closer of their now trademarked buffoonery at the piano and mike, backed by Dick Stabile's orch (*sic*) remains one of the top hilarities in TV's comedy catalog."

Since it was telecast live rather than delayed kinescope, *Variety*'s West Coast-based sister publication *Daily Variety* published its own review: "What you expect from Dean Martin and Jerry Lewis you generally get. There's rarely a letdown in their madcap antics and yesterday's first from Hollywood was a whopper that set a dizzy pace for others in the *Colgate Comedy Hour* rotation to follow…. Theirs is comedy as ultra-zany as ever came across the channels." The critic also gave plaudits to Glucksman, Kingman Moore, and the cameramen: "Trying to keep the comics in frame must be akin to kodaking (*sic*) a frightened deer. They're never in one place, but the lensmen seem always to come out on top."

Again, the ARB survey put them well ahead of *Toast of the Town* and, according to *Television Digest*, outdrew even their movies: "Dean Martin & Jerry Lewis reported to have enjoyed [an] NBC-TV audience of 28,960,000 November 4, whereas their average film plays to around 20,000,000; American Research Bureau says their audience is [the] largest for any regularly scheduled program, giving Milton Berle [a] higher rating but fewer viewers-per-set." It's unknown how Hal Wallis (or Berle, for that matter) responded to that blurb, but the producer immediately put the team back into service stripes for their next picture, *Jumping Jacks*, which began production on December 3. Only the weeklong break between Christmas and New Year's enabled Dean and Jerry to tackle their next *Colgate* assignment before filming wrapped in late January 1952.

* * * * *

THE COLGATE COMEDY HOUR: Dean Martin & Jerry Lewis Show #10.

Airdate: December 30, 1951; NBC-TV.
With: Eve Young, Ray Malone and His Dancers
Cast: Danny Arnold, Mike Mazurki, Margaret Dumont
Announcer: Hal Sawyer
Writers: Ed Simmons & Norman Lear
Musical Direction: Dick Stabile
Choreography: Ray Malone
NBC Production Supervisor: Sam Fuller
Television Director: Kingman T. Moore
Producer & Director: Ernest D. Glucksman.

OPENING: The teacher at Birdwheel Public School (*Margaret Dumont*) has made a holiday celebration of the kids' week, and she has a special surprise. "I've invited some very famous men to pay us a visit, and I know they're great favorites of yours!" When she introduces Martin & Lewis, the children are disappointed. The boys try to entertain with jokes and dancing, but get no reaction from the kids, until one of them arm wrestles Jerry to the ground and another bites Dean on the arm. Finally the children chase them away.

DEAN SOLO #1: "Kentucky Babe"

SKETCH #1: Dean is a lifeguard for the Rick Hotel at Miami Beach, and he's awaiting his new apprentice. Marvin M. Mertz (*Lewis*; the M. also stands for Marvin) arrives and proves to be less than experienced. He can't swim and he's not very impressive when trying to enforce a "no ball playing" rule opposite a tough guy (*Mike Mazurki*). On the other hand, his father packed a very sizeable lunch for him and Dean to enjoy. While eating, though, they hear a cry for help. A drowning man (*Danny Arnold*) is brought in and Dean shows Marvin how to administer artificial respiration. When Marvin tries it, he gets a face full of sprayed water. Eventually he takes on too much and Dean has to administer it to him...whereupon Dean gets a spray of water in *his* face.

GUEST ACTS: After a quick plug for *Sailor Beware*, Jerry introduces Eve Young and Ray Malone and his Dancers. Ms. Young sings "Hello, Young

Lovers" among a garden setting; while other couples pair off, she is alone. When she finishes singing, Malone enters; she kisses him and he goes into a strenuous dance with the others. Ms. Young sings a reprise as she and Malone pair up.

SKETCH #2: Dean confides to Danny that he has a problem: he's been working with "the little monster" so often for so long that everyone he meets is Jerry Lewis. When he goes home, he sees Jerry in the bookcase and in his liquor cabinet. He calls Dr. Howser begging for help. Meanwhile, Dean's blonde wife Jeanne tries to comfort him, but she looks and sounds like Jerry Lewis. Dean tries to shake it off, but eventually chases her away, as Dr. Howser (*Lewis* again) arrives to diagnose the patient. When Dean can't get a word in, he strangles the doctor. Deciding he needs to shave, dress and go out, he heads to the washroom, looks in the mirror and sees Jerry's reflection. When the real Jerry arrives to rehearse, Dean, now thoroughly crazy, threatens to kill him. He begins talking to the camera, saying, "You at home, *you're* Jerry Lewis!" When he hears his dog, Rex, barking, he feels relieved and calls for him, only to discover Rex now looks and behaves like Jerry in a dog costume.

JERRY SOLO: Jerry uses television to make an appeal on behalf of his family: they'd like to find his Uncle Louie, who has been missing for many years. He shows them a photograph and asks if anyone knows of or has seen his uncle to please call. Immediately a pageboy brings out a phone; the caller says he'll tell Jerry where to find his uncle for $20,000. Jerry agrees, and when the caller tells him, he hangs up the phone and rushes over to a camera, where Louie is the cameraman.

DEAN SOLO #2: "Night Train to Memphis"

FINALE: Dean wants to sing "Bella Bimba," but Jerry's "accompaniment" on trumpet drowns out the song. He summons Jerry and tells him they're through, saying: "Hand in your equipment." Jerry has to hand over his cuff links, tie, tap shoes and trumpet. Jerry begs and Dean allows him one last toot on the horn before taking it. Ordered to leave, Jerry sadly walks away. When Dean tries to sing again, Dick Stabile comes scolds Dean for mistreating "that sweet little kid." As Dean expresses remorse, Jerry enters riding a kid's scooter. He tells Dean that he knew he'd be wanted because, as they both sing, "A good man nowadays is hard to find!"

Jerry takes a moment to read a telegram from the Chicago chapter of the Muscular Dystrophy Association, thanking the team for making an appeal on behalf of their cause. Jerry explains that there is no cure for muscular dystrophy and asks for donations "to help children who may die any day." Dean adds, "There's supposed to be at least 40 million people watching this show. Could you imagine if every person would send in one penny, what would happen?" Jerry answers, "It would be wonderful and would help a lot of children."

ANALYSIS AND REVIEWS: A crackerjack combination of writing and performance resulted in another first-rate *Comedy Hour*. The "Lifeguard" scene is very funny, while "Everybody is Jerry Lewis" is probably the cleverest sketch they ever performed. The integrated song and dance in between the sketches makes for a nice, out-of-the-ordinary respite. Only a lackluster final routine, the "Turn in Your Equipment" bit they did on *Texaco Star Theater* a year-and-a-half earlier, keeps this show from equaling their prior broadcast in every way.

The opening scene in the classroom has the added pleasure of Margaret Dumont's presence. The comedienne, long associated with the Marx Brothers, actually worked with nearly all the classic movie comedians, but this would be her only round with Martin & Lewis. Still, it's made memorable when she is the only one laughing helplessly at their antics, until they tell her to "Shut up!" and Jerry adds, "Get out of here, you're drunk!" to Dean's amusement.

Martin's rendition of "Kentucky Babe" is one of his best solos in the entire series. Accompanied by The Ebonaires, the exact same arrangement was repeated on the June 5, 1955 *Comedy Hour*, yet for some curious reason, he never recorded it, at least not for release.

The beach, with Lewis as apprentice lifeguard, is an inspired setting for the traditional 'solid pro mentors hopeless newcomer' routine. By-now standard lines and gags turn up, including a dissertation on Lewis' character name, Marvin Marvin Mertz (*Dean*: "Which would you rather be called, Marvin or Marvin?" *Jerry*: "My friends call me Sidney!") and the small container that holds impossibly large quantities, in this case, Marvin's box lunch. In the scene where Jerry can't get the attention of the husky ball-tossing visitor (*Mike Mazurki*), even when getting in his face and pounding on his chest, Dean walks over and politely asks him to play somewhere else, and the big fellow meekly agrees. "What is he, one of your *Italian* friends?" asks Jerry, which of course breaks Dean up. Bug-eyed, Jerry advises the audience, "We didn't rehearse *that!*"

Jerry's plug for *Sailor Beware* ends with a laugh when he looks into the camera, asking, "Did you hear, Mr. Wallis, the way we said it nice? You'll give us the money now, like you promised?" The mini-musical, combining Eve Young's vocal with a routine by Ray Malone and his Dancers, made for a nice change of pace. The "plot" is slight: at a formal gathering, surrounded by "young lovers," Young's dance card is empty, while Malone plays a shy suitor who dances up the courage to approach her.

The second sketch begins with a special effects gag that could only be appreciated on the monitors: Jerry's face is superimposed over Danny Arnold's, scaring Dean away. After that, though, it's a workout for Lewis: he appears behind the bookcase; seconds later inside the liquor cabinet. He dresses as Jeanne Martin (blonde wig and cotton robe), then as Doctor Howser (hat, jacket and ascot), then rushes back into the Jeanne costume, then strips to his undershirt for the shaving scene, then dresses as himself, then into a dog costume. These constant changes keep Dean alone for much of the time, and he can't resist getting silly: while picking up the phone, he talks to himself, "Call the doctor. Dial any number, just call the doctor." As he strangles Dr. Howser, the bit is staged so that Jerry is replaced by a dummy. While Jerry screams off stage, Dean twists the "doctor's" legs: "I'll wrap you in knots, that's what I'll do! Hurry up and get dressed! How long can I keep wrapping? Hurry up!"

It's the shaving scene that makes the sketch. It starts out as a "mirror routine," wherein two people face each other and move in concert as though each was a reflection of the other. It's a turn as old as vaudeville itself, performed in film by pioneers such as Max Linder and Charlie Chaplin, up to the Marx Brothers, the Three Stooges and beyond. For Martin & Lewis, though, the bit lasts about 45 seconds before they break character: as Dean is applying shaving cream, Jerry tells him, "Not so fast." "Okay," says Dean, at which they both break up. With the first swipe of the razor they're back in sync, then Dean takes a different position, so he maneuvers Jerry's arm. Giggling now, Dean swipes the razor again, but instead of using the sink, he flicks the shaving cream on his partner's shirt. Smiling, Jerry looks at it, swipes his own face and flicks his razor at Dean, who's still giggling. The two comport themselves like a pair of mischievous schoolboys even as Jerry continues to give Dean directions ("Shave some more." "Wipe it off your face"). Dean's still laughing as he exits the bathroom to dress, telling the audience, "We should never do a long bit." It probably *seemed* long to Martin, whose reactions were the centerpiece throughout, but actually ran less than 11 minutes. The Lifeguard sketch was over a minute longer.

The most significant portion of the finale is the appeal on behalf of the Muscular Dystrophy Association, the team's first. The battle against this disease (actually a group of diseases that cause the voluntary muscles to deteriorate), would soon become synonymous with Martin & Lewis, and then Lewis alone. Bud Yorkin, the show's new stage manager, had a young nephew who'd succumbed to the disease; knowing through his sister's involvement how desperately the fledging organization (founded only the year before) needed help, he asked Lewis to make time for a plug at the end of the show. "Jerry had never heard of muscular dystrophy," recalled Yorkin. "[He] wanted to know how you pronounced it, and how it was spelled."

Lewis would often credit his sons for inspiring some of his outlandish behavior when on stage; that a disease could physically afflict a child to the point of death deeply touched his hyper-emotional nature. For his part, Yorkin had already observed Lewis' love of attention and flattery, hence the receipt of MDA's telegram. Arrangements were made to add further appeals to the team's radio series, beginning with the broadcast of January 11, 1952.

On January 17, NBC issued a press release stating, "To date, more than 10,000 individual contributions, averaging more than $1 apiece, have been mailed to organization headquarters in New York as a result of the one appeal.... The pair will continue to ask for donations on both radio and TV until sufficient funds are raised to cope with the muscular dystrophy." Along with contributions, columnist Inez Gerhard noted, "There were scores of letters from dystrophic victims who never knew there was a Muscular Dystrophy association." At the end of the month, Martin and Lewis were invited by Justice William O. Douglas to become national co-chairmen of the MDA's entertainment division, which they accepted.

At the close of their March 28 radio broadcast, after nearly three months of weekly appeals, Jerry answered the question on the minds of most fans: "Our friends have asked us to explain why we have made muscular dystrophy 'our charity,' so to speak. Well, Dean and I first leaped to the aid of MDA when we learned that here is perhaps the only major fatal disease that has never had a champion. There is no cure for muscular dystrophy now. If you have it, you die. But with the start of this campaign, the priceless gift of hope is now the possession of every sufferer of this dread disease. Dean and I are proud and happy that we were able to start this ball rolling, and we hope you will work along with us. If our scientists get the opportunity to continue their research, millions of future sufferers will have the opportunity to continue their lives."

* * * * *

THE COLGATE COMEDY HOUR: Dean Martin & Jerry Lewis Show #11.

Airdate: February 10, 1952; NBC-TV.
With: Ray Malone, Jill Jarmon, Danny Arnold, Sheldon Leonard, Mike Mazurki, Marilyn Borden, Rosalyn Borden, Maurice Cass
Announcer: Hal Sawyer
Writers: Ed Simmons & Norman Lear
Musical Direction: Dick Stabile
Choreography: Ray Malone
NBC Production Supervisor: Sam Fuller
Television Director: Kingman T. Moore
Producer & Director: Ernest D. Glucksman.

OPENING: The racketeer members of Mayhem, Incorporated have gathered for their annual "Dillinger Award" dinner meeting. When one hoodlum opposes starting the meeting, the chairman (*Sheldon Leonard*) shoots him, declaring, "The decision is now unanimous." He explains that "a couple of famous entertainers" will make the award presentation. Martin & Lewis enter, and Jerry's immediately alarmed by the dead body in the front row. They refuse to perform, so the gangsters start shooting. Jerry threatens them with a grenade, but when Dean asks where he got it, Jerry shows him an empty hand, saying, "I was only fooling." They both get chased away.

Jerry tells Dean, "I'm going to introduce your song, Max, so fly away." Dean professes not to understand him, so Jerry explains, "I called you Max and I told you to fly away because Maxfly is the name of a golf ball and the sponsor doesn't want us to make any more plugs." Dean adds, "We need the golf balls!" and Jerry concludes, "We both play golf, so send them to the house right away. Oh, I can just see the sponsor sitting at home now, squeezing all of the Colgate toothpaste out of the tube, and he's *screaming* something *awful!*"

DEAN SOLO #1: "When You're Smiling"

SKETCH #1: Danny Arnold explains that viewers have sent in thousands of requests wanting to know about the private lives of Martin & Lewis, so we're taken to their homes. Dean, who lives in a palatial estate reclines poolside in his luxurious backyard, while Jerry, who lives next door, occupies what he calls "an upholstered sewer." Dean has a distinguished butler in tails (*Maurice Cass*) and a young female assistant who lovingly welcomes every chore. Jerry employs a grubby-looking guy (*Mike Mazurki*) and a frowsy gum-chewing broad, neither of whom likes him. Unhappy with the disparity of their lifestyles, Jerry insists that a 70-30 split "ain't halfies! Let's go back to the 65-35!" Dean is expecting NBC's Pat Weaver; when he arrives, Dean brings him over to meet Jerry. At that moment, Jerry is painting a chair and he proceeds to mistake Weaver's cane for a chair leg and paints it up to the man's glove. Realizing his mistake, he falls into Dean's arms crying. As Weaver negotiates with Dean, Jerry repeatedly comes into the yard to eavesdrop. "Will you go fly a kite?" Dean demands, and so Jerry does just that, returning with kite in the air. Weaver wants to try it and takes the kite from Jerry, who begs him: "*Don't* fly it! You can look at it all day…but *DON'T* fly it!" Sobbing, Weaver gives the kite back to Jerry and departs. So does Jerry, as the kite lifts him into the air.

GUEST ACTS: After being lowered to the stage ("They kept me up there all through the *commoicial!*"), Jerry introduces Ray Malone and his dancers presenting "The Samba Mambo." Dean speaks about the team's upcoming personal appearance tour and a telethon they're doing in New York City the following month, concluding with a plug for their Friday night radio series. Then he introduces Jill Jarmon, who sings "I Don't Stand a Ghost of a Chance with You."

SKETCH #2: At Dean's soda fountain, service is a mite slow because he's waiting for a new assistant from the employment agency. Jerry arrives and Dean tries to train him on how to serve ice cream and wait on customers. He does neither well, scooping the ice cream with his hands and spilling a milk shake all over the counter (and Dean's lap). A customer (*Danny Arnold*) asks for French ice cream, and gets a multi-scoop serving with fruit and whipped cream toppings (*Jerry:* "We use Reddi-Wip… and Golden Meadow ice cream. The writers get $80"). When the customer asks if he can take some home, however, Jerry scoops it into his jacket pockets and onto his head, along with the whipped cream. Another customer demands a giant malted, which is served in a three-foot tall glass and mixed with an outboard motor (that fails to start). The appalled customer leaves, and Dean insists that Jerry drink it. He does, tumbling into the glass while energetically sipping from a straw.

JERRY SOLO: Supported by The Borden Twins, Jerry sings "Cuanto Le Gusta."

FINALE: With less than two minutes remaining, Dean explains that they had to whittle the show down from 90 minutes to 60, "and I don't think we made it." Jerry apologizes, but takes a few seconds to request more donations for MDA.

ANALYSIS AND REVIEWS: For sheer laugh quantity, this installment hits the bullseye. Even minus their usual concluding byplay, Martin & Lewis are in top form throughout, visibly enjoying each other and the havoc they're creating.

The "Home Life" of Martin & Lewis revisits the premise of unequal treatment from their first show, with the added benefit that neither is taking it too seriously. Hapless Jerry gets abused by his "staff," although his face plays it for comic sympathy, he can't resist going for a belly laugh. "She's overacting, this kid," he says after his female aide slaps his face. Dean rolls along nicely, laughing at his partner's ad-libs and kicking in a few *bon mots* of his own, such as "I'll be back in a flash, Gordon!" Both of them break up when Jerry tries to shake money out of his "piggy bank," which happens to be a genuine pig. He's supposed to get angry when Jerry accidentally paints his jacket, but doesn't have it in him: "Don't be 'sorry' to me, you... you...." "Don't say it, it might be dirty," says Jerry, which cracks Dean up. The unbilled actor playing Pat Weaver (*Variety's* reviewer credited Danny Arnold, but it isn't him) adds to the fun with his childish reaction when Jerry wants his kite back.

Ray Malone's segment begins with close-ups of feet dancing, similar to a previous Fosse & Niles number, and turns into a jazz tap performance with Latin overtones that is energetic and enjoyable. Jill Jarmon does a pleasant if unmemorable job on her song; it's easy to see why she didn't make a career of it. She quickly abandoned singing for acting, changed her name's spelling to Jil Jarmyn, and for the next dozen years appeared on several TV sitcoms and dramas, and in such double-bill fare as *Swamp Women* (1956) and *Tarzan's Fight for Life* (1958).

The Soda Fountain sketch is a slapstick gem, with the boys having as much fun here as they did shaving together in the last show. When Jerry picks up the ice cream by hand, Dean scolds him:

DEAN: No, you don't do it that way, Zelma! Look, you get your-self a scoop, right?

JERRY: What did you call me?

DEAN: Zelma!

BOTH: (*singing*) Zel-ma that you love me tonight!

Preparing Dean's strawberry milkshake from scratch takes some time, so Jerry starts singing "Strawberry Milkshake, for the man!" which he segues into a version of "The Party" from Gordon Jenkins' concept album *Manhattan Tower*: "Strawberry milkshake / Put in the cream / Put in your ashtray / Turn out the lights / 'Cause we're havin' a milkshake / And the people are nice." When he gets to the last line, he collapses with laughter, which in turns amuses Dean. As soon as he recovers, Jerry cries, "Dean! I ad-libbed! Don't you *love* me?" and kisses his partner on the lips.

When the always-abused Danny Arnold walks in as a customer, we *know* what's going to happen, but that doesn't lessen the laughs. When he asks that his sundae be made with French ice cream, immediately Dean and Jerry turn to each other and sing "La Marseillaise," after which Dean adds, "When we get lost, we get lost!" John Crosby, the *New York Herald-Tribune's* long-time radio and TV critic, had this scene especially in mind when he wrote an appreciation of the team a few weeks later: "The special appeal of Martin & Lewis has pretty well defied everyone's analysis though everyone, God knows, has tried…. My own theory is that Martin and Lewis have added a new and irresistible element to the classic traditions of slapstick—namely, charm. The boys seem to be having more fun than the customers even when they are dripping wet, which is most of the time. They are indulging in the sort of monkeyshines I suppose all of us would like to get away with but don't dare.

"At one point in their last appearance… Lewis, in the role of a soda jerk, was decorating a customer's face and hair with strawberry ice cream.

'Don't tell me that's enough,' he told Martin, 'because I'm having fun.' So he continued daubing for several more minutes, enjoying himself hugely. Martin, who was only watching this mayhem—which is not nearly so much as committing it—seemed to be having a fine time, too." Indeed, Dean starts giggling from the moment Jerry tucks the first scoopful into Danny's jacket and is laughing out loud by the time his partner is applying the whipped cream. Their shared glee is in part due to the fact that the ice cream has started melting under the lights. Of course, Danny gets revenge by smashing his sundae into Jerry's face like a pie; Dean enjoys that as well, laughing as he says, "You can't go around waiting on customers like that!"

Crosby's piece continued, "Their shenanigans are not much different from any of the other comedians that came out of the borscht circuit, but they are nicer people, and there seems to be a good deal more to both of them. Martin, for instance, is more than an ordinary straight man—a singer, a comedian in his own right, and very much a person. Lewis has more bounce and more tricks, it seems to me, than a half dozen Abbotts and Costellos, and in addition is considerably more sophisticated: 'I'm the unhappiest person that ever was a mortal.'

"The team has been widely admired for their timing, but I set little store by this. Frankly, they don't seem to bother with timing exactly; they just know when enough is enough and pass on to other things. Anyway, they're terribly, terribly funny." John Lester, TV critic for the *Long Island Star-Journal*, said simply, "They were a riot. These two hit some kind of a high in comedy every time they [appear] but were super-hilarious last night."

Daily Variety's reviewer asserted, "Martin and Lewis would never have attained their present eminence in teevee if it weren't for the boys at the typewriters, who dream up and put into words the daffy dillies that set the maddening pace for them. Worthy the accolade to crown their efforts are Ed Simmons and Norman Lear. It's their wild imaginings that have raised M&L to the peerage of their particular type of comedy. There is generally a freshness and inventive genius to the wild orgies created for their subjects and they're rarely let down."

Although their sister publication labeled it "hilarious fun," *Variety* was less impressed. "It's about time the two comics started disciplining themselves to stick a little more closely to a prepared script. That ad-libbed confusion ties in with their brand of comedics but it can also lead to a state of diminishing returns. Confusion showed at its best (or worst) in the final sketch.... It was unadulterated slapstick and, while it drew plenty of fullscale yocks, it was overdone. Withal, M&L gave the impression that much of their material, about 50% of which must have been ad-libbed, would go socko at the Copa but was just a little too broad for top TV." The Copacabana reference was ironic; back in 1946, a *Variety* reviewer covering the team at the Havana-Madrid opined that their shtick "probably wouldn't go in the more sedate niteries."

They were wrong both times: Martin & Lewis were "socko" *everywhere.*

* * * * *

BETWIXT AND BETWEEN: THE NEW YORK HEART HOSPITAL TELETHON

As Dean noted on the show, Martin & Lewis were scheduled to host a telethon in New York City to raise funds to build the first New York Cardiac Hospital. The program began at midnight on Friday evening, March 14 and continued for 16½ hours, airing over NBC's flagship station, WNBT-4. It wasn't a network broadcast but might as well have been, given all the attention it received. In the days leading up to the broadcast, NBC issued two press releases plugging the show and the "stars from every corner of the entertainment world" that were participating.

It was no exaggeration; the talent lineup was stunning. From television: Morey Amsterdam, Milton Berle, Sid Caesar, Faye Emerson, Jackie Gleason, Jerry Lester, Dagmar, Dave Garroway. From Broadway: Yul Brynner, Ezio Pinza, Vivian Blaine, Phil Silvers. From motion pictures: Mickey Rooney, Celeste Holm, Gabby Hayes, Ralph Bellamy. Vocalists and musicians: Frank Sinatra, Mel Torme, Sarah Vaughan, Perry Como, Harry Belafonte, Cab Calloway, Connee Boswell, Eddie Fisher, Nat "King" Cole, Helen O'Connell, Skitch Henderson, Ella Fitzgerald, Gene Krupa. Plus dozens of other notables, and time enough for Dean's uncle Leonard Barr and Jerry's dad Danny Lewis, who also presented Jerry with a cake for his 26th birthday. Local merchants and businesses donated over $50,000 in merchandise that was auctioned during the broadcast.

NBC even issued a bulletin through the AP while the show was on the air; Saturday morning papers carried the news that $400,000 had been pledged during the show's first seven hours. Even if most cities couldn't tune in, the goodwill engendered for the team knew no boundaries.

Attempting a mirror routine, they can't resist breaking each other up. Scene from
The Colgate Comedy Hour, December 30, 1951.

Locally, of course, the reaction was off-the-charts, with the *New York
Times'* Jack Gould leading the pack in effusive praise, calling the show "a
unique example of concentrated Americana in the television age," and
noting, "In the metropolitan area, there was almost a mass hypnosis in
watching the entertainment world's most successful act of the moment
stay on its feet night and day. Tired as they were, the two performers never once were curt or abrupt as they accepted pledges over the telephone
or received cash donations from an endless succession of children in the
studio audience…. Within the framework of their amusing slapstick art
and their relish for the non-sequitur, they gave an astonishing demonstration of patience, understanding and personal dignity." *Variety* concurred:
"The buffooning Lewis and the singing straightman Martin responded to
any kind of donation, whether a quarter or a few Gs.

"Beginning at midnight Friday, it took over an hour for the show to
warm up, but after that it seemed to ride smoothly at anchor." Unfortunately, the only surviving kinescope footage comes from the first hour.
Introduced by their old *Scout About Town* booster Barry Gray, the team

enters, and Jerry immediately says that a portion of the pledges will be donated to MDA, which in less than three months had become their official cause. Dean sings "My Heart Has Found a Home Now," written especially for the show by Dick Stabile. They each light up Chesterfields (no small irony there, given the amount of smoking-related heart disease the hospital would treat over the years) and plug their radio series.

They immediately get on the phones for a few minutes, and then introduce Jackie Gleason, who also answers a few calls. At this point, most of the callers just want to speak to Martin & Lewis (mostly the latter), and don't actually pledge. Vivian Blaine, at the time appearing on Broadway in *Guys and Dolls*, comes on to perform "Singin' in the Rain," after which she, too, takes some calls. Phil Silvers comes on and, to his credit, makes a plea for serious pledges, then interacts with Dean and Jerry. Silvers introduces Rose Marie, who sings "My Blue Heaven" and also gets on the phones.

Barry Gray returns to speak about heart disease, explaining that in the 47 minutes the show has been on, 55 people have succumbed. Gray introduces Harry Hirschfeld, columnist for the *New York Mirror*, who is one of the founders of the hospital committee, to talk about the goal of the telethon. The kinescope ends as Hirschfeld is speaking.

It's a pity the final hour wasn't preserved instead, as *Variety's* Leonard Traube noted "the closing was the smash. At about 15 minutes before the finale, Lewis started to reel off a list of thank you credits, getting down even to the coffee pots. As if to show he wasn't exhausted when by all medical authority (plus his 'built') he should have been, he and Martin worked themselves up to a sizzling Charleston. Then Lewis bowed to the tooters – 'want to thank the musician's union for their low wages.' With about four minutes to go, they went into their 'dust-off' dance, crawling offstage. With time still left, they returned to man the phones, but got right up and proceeded to operate seltzer bottles, turning the siphon on Ernie Glucksman and others as if to show that slapstickery was still their trademark, or maybe to establish that their energies were not wholly spent."

When all was said and done, $1,148,419 was pledged, the tally coming one half-hour after the show ended. "When the mail money is counted," Traube wrote, "the figure should be considerably upped; less, of course, the uncollectables and phony pledges." Over a year later, Barry Gray would assert that the latter were considerable. Writing about the show, and Milton Berle's two prior telethons for Damon Runyon's cancer fund, Gray exclaimed, "In all cases the difference between what was pledged and what was collected sounded like hugely dissimilar amounts. For there was always the manufacturer of sleazy, shoddy lingerie who wanted a free television plug and would phone one of the stars appearing, and in full view of millions offer three of his products free if someone would bid $100. The ad he received was worth an incalculable sum. The bidder who called to get his name mentioned in the same announcement sometimes did not come through, and the end result was [that the] stars, TV network, and charitable organization were left holding the bag." The end result was that 35%, or roughly $400,000, of the phone pledges was actually collected, while mailed checks brought the total to a respectable, if still disappointing, $800,000.

Those who stayed awake watching the marathon broadcast, were no doubt saying, as Jack Gould did in his review, "Thank heaven for Sunday morning and late sleeps." Meanwhile, the show's two principal stars flew back to Hollywood to rehearse their next *Colgate* hour, which was to air seven days later.

* * * * *

THE COLGATE COMEDY HOUR: Dean Martin & Jerry Lewis Show #12.

Airdate: March 23, 1952; NBC-TV.
Guest Star: Danny Lewis
With: Tommy Wonder, Margaret Banks, Danny Arnold, Elizabeth Root
Cast: Gail Bonney, Peter Votrian, Harvey Dunn, Ruth Saville, Sarah Bacon, Linda Williams, Evelyn Lovequist
Announcer: Hal Sawyer
Writers: Ed Simmons & Norman Lear
Musical Direction: Dick Stabile
NBC Production Supervisor: Sam Fuller
Television Director: Kingman T. Moore
Producer & Director: Ernest D. Glucksman.

OPENING: At a meeting of the Birdwheel School Parent-Teacher Association, the chairwoman (*Gail Bonney*) introduces "the two young men who have captured the hearts of our children." Martin & Lewis enter and the parents start griping. A mother sobs that her child has a haircut just like Jerry's, "but she's a girl!" A father complains that his two boys destroy the house and put ice cream in his hair. A father (*Danny Arnold*), brings his son (*Peter Votrian*) forward, and all he does is cross his eyes and talk like Jerry. When dad tries to shake him out of it, the kid goes, "No, *don't* shake me! You can hug me and squeeze me, but *don't* shake me!" The furious parents chase them away, and Dean tells Jerry that he's responsible for it all. Jerry says, "All right, I don't wanna be in trouble with you, then I'll start singing." Dean replies, "No, I *like* it, I *like* it that way. *Don't* sing it!"

DEAN SOLO #1: "You Made Me Love You," which he sings to a photograph. At the end, we see the photo is Jerry in costume for *Sailor Beware*.

SKETCH #1: At Martin's photography studio, two lovely models have arrived. They ask Dean to close the window shade while they dress, but he tells them there's no need, as they're on the 63rd floor. As they start to disrobe behind the changing screen, Sylvester, a window washer (*Lewis*), drops down, starts to scrub and reacts to what he sees. Dean brings him in and demands an apology, telling him, "You were peeping, Tom!" Sylvester punishes himself with slaps on the face, soap on the tongue and a little arm twisting. "I punished myself good, boy" he tells Dean, adding, "Those writers have got to go!" After Sylvester's fired by his boss (*Danny Arnold*), Dean offers him a job as a model, dressing him in a nightshirt and cap, and posing him with a cup of "Ovaltone," a drink that helps you sleep. To demonstrate what he wants, Dean drinks some and Sylvester copies him, but the beverage is potent and they both fall asleep, Sylvester collapsing on top of the photographer.

GUEST ACTS: After plugging an article about the team in the April 22 issue of *LOOK*, and making an appeal on behalf of the Red Cross, Jerry introduces Tommy Wonder and Margaret Banks, who dance to "Organ Grinder's Swing." Dean introduces Danny Lewis (calling him his "partner-in-law"), who sings a specialty song about Jerry: "That's My Boy," which incorporates a parody of Jolson's "Sonny Boy."

SKETCH #2: It is spring training time in Sweetwater, Florida, and the pennant-winning New York Bruisers are getting in shape for baseball. Their coach, Leo Roacher (*Martin*) is at the Roney Birdie Hotel for a meeting with the Rookie of the Year, Willie Lomond (*Lewis*). Roacher's wife (*Evelyn Lovequist*) doesn't want the new player to know he has "vision like an umpire," so she removes his thick eyeglasses. When Lomond arrives, he too removes his glasses; consequently, neither man can see too well, and the meeting quickly goes awry. During batting practice, Lomond keeps missing the ball but hitting Roacher. When eating lunch, Roacher spreads jam on Lomond's arm and pours coffee in his lap. Finally, each mistakes the other for Mrs. Roacher and they dance through a wall and out of the hotel room.

JERRY SOLO: Danny Arnold tells the audience that last week was Jerry's birthday and asks that they greet him with belated birthday wishes. He introduces Jerry, who thanks them and explains how deeply appreciative he is to everyone involved with the show, particularly the crew. He's interrupted by a technician (*Norman Lear*) who tells him they're suddenly off the air. Jerry gets furious, slaps the man and demands to know how this happened. Danny runs out to say they're back on, and Jerry's nice again. Then another crew member (*Ed Simmons*) tells him they're off again, and Jerry pummels him until Danny tells him they're back on. This keeps happening until finally Jerry's screaming "I DON'T CARE!" and they carry him off stage.

DEAN SOLO #2: "Rainbow, 'Round My Shoulder"

FINALE: Jerry wants to be treated normally, but Dean says he isn't normal, which Jerry proves by doing a crazy dance. With one minute left, Jerry says hello to a 9-year-old boy in Rhode Island who has muscular dystrophy, and asks for additional contributions, explaining, "It's our charity because it's had no help."

ANALYSIS AND REVIEWS: After an all-night telethon the previous weekend, immediately followed by a week of rehearsal for this show, Dean and Jerry must have been feeling pretty punchy. They take a lot of liberties with the material; the ad-libs fly and the two repeatedly break each other up.

The PTA opening is an inspired reworking of the "Steubenville welcoming committee" from the first season. In the earlier show, Dean and Jerry were lambasted for the damage they did *as* children; here, they're taken to task for the damage they do *to* children. Young Peter J. Votrian does a marvelous job playing Danny Arnold's impaired offspring, whose vocabulary is now a series of Lewis catch-phrases.

Rehearsing the first sketch of the February 10, 1952 *Comedy Hour*.
Photo courtesy of Kayley Thompson.

In no other show does the team take as much liberty with material as they do in the photography studio sketch, either because they've forgotten the order of their lines or ad-libbed new ones. Almost as soon as they're on screen together, they mess up:

JERRY: I should be punished. I am sorry…

DEAN: Yes, you must punish yourself, Sylvester!

JERRY: I certainly will, sir. How'd you know my name?

DEAN: (*laughing*) Oh, just lucky, I guess!

JERRY: (*to the audience*) From the rehearsal, he knew my name!

After that, Jerry mentions that photography is his hobby and loosely incorporates a plug for Revere cameras (*Jerry;* "When're you gonna send

them like you said?") When superintendent Danny Arnold fires Sylvester, it turns into a variation of "Turn in your equipment" ("Your squee-
gee! Your sponge!"), complete with stingers from Stabile's orchestra. With
each item he tries to talk the boss out of it; at one point Dean asks him,
"You don't want to do the regular routine?" "Nah, it's stale already, I'm
tired of it," Jerry responds.

The kicker, though, comes with the ad for "Ovaltone." When Dean
pours it from a pitcher, the stuff *looks* rancid; assuming it was made from
milk, the drink was left under the lights too long and has begun to curdle.
Dean bursts out laughing as Jerry says, "Oh boy. It looks like gangrene!"
It's in the script that Jerry's facial reaction shouldn't be the "satisfied smile"
that Dean's requested, so he sips and makes a face, but then turns to Dean:
"If you think I'm kidding, you're crazy! Wait'll you taste it!" After Jerry's
second taste, Dean is supposed to demonstrate what he wants. "Show
me, won't you? This I gotta see!" Dean sips and practically gags, as Jerry breaks up and turns to the camera: "Who's the prop man, a broken
chemist?" They begin yawning to signal that the drink is working, but
every time each takes a sip, the other laughs at his predicament. Finally,
Jerry exclaims, "They spend three hundred thousand for a program, they
couldn't put Coke in here!" which earns a round of applause.

The dance performed by Tommy Wonder and Margaret Banks is unremarkable; as if in recognition of this, Ms. Banks flares her skirt above
her waist several times, exposing not only the entirety of her bare legs
but also "a generous showing of femme underpinning," as *Daily Variety*
tactfully put it. Admittedly the result is no more revealing than the bathing suits of the day, but it's still a surprise and one wonders if she was this
energetic during rehearsals.

By all accounts, Danny Lewis would never win a "Father of the Year"
award. He put his career ahead of everything else for most of his life, and
he and his wife Rae were not given to showering effusive expressions of
love upon their offspring. Ed Simmons noted, "They were small-time
people, two-bit people. They weren't anything remotely resembling a
Jewish mother and father." The couple began in the business together;
he'd sing, she'd play piano, in the lowest cafés and vaudeville houses and
over small radio stations as far back as 1927. But Lewis the elder's specialty was songs in the Al Jolson style, and the big time already had the
real thing. By the early '30s and the coming of crooners, mainstream audiences had wearied of Jolson and not even the small-time wanted a pale
imitation. So Danny's career was the Catskills in the summer, Miami in

the winter, and catch-as-catch-can in between, with young Jerome either left behind with relatives or shunted along like an excess piece of luggage.

When *The Jolson Story* (1946) rekindled America's love for the venerable entertainer, Danny resurrected his career, appearing in 1947 at a few small theaters, moving on to Philadelphia's Latin Casino and Manhattan's Glass Hat; both now well acquainted with his famous son. By the summer of '51, he was booked at the Paramount with the team's *That's My Boy*, which had been arranged by Jerry, as was the *Colgate* appearance.

According to Simmons, Dean was "annoyed" that Danny was appearing, although not, as the writer assumed, because of nepotism or his partner's controlling nature. He could hardly object to either, having made an issue out of his uncle's appearance the previous season. After nearly six years alongside Jerry, he well knew how deeply his partner craved parental acceptance and approval, to little avail. He also felt that Danny was merely a Jolson derivative with an unremarkable voice and – worst of all – was performing a piece of specialty material, written by Eli Bass and Bobby Cole, that was about his admiration of Jerry. At rehearsal, Simmons recalled, "Dean was smoking and looking at Danny with such disgust. And Dean flicked his cigarette to the ground and said, 'That's it. Next show I'll put my mother on. She'll make a dress.'"

Dean's introduction, thankfully, was cordial if not terribly enthusiastic. Viewed today, the most notable aspect of Danny's performance is how much he resembles the older Jerry Lewis, the one who'd sing his heart out during MDA Telethons. His voice is more cultured than his son's, but it's near enough to be comparable. As for the song, it's not terribly clever and gets middling laughs from the audience.

For the baseball player sketch, Dean's character "Leo Roacher" is based on New York Giants manager Leo Durocher, whose team had won the National League pennant the previous season. Durocher was married to actress Laraine Day, who would appear on Martin & Lewis' radio show the following year and was every bit as glamorous as Evelyn Lovequist, playing Mrs. Roacher, is here. Apart from that, it's essentially a one-joke idea that, like most of Simmons and Lear's work, doesn't overstay its welcome, although *Variety* disagreed. Noting the team's recent telethon and devotion to muscular dystrophy, the reviewer wrote, "With such sensitivity about human ailments of greater and lesser degree, it is surprising that they indulged in that myopia marathon.... Nearsightedness is an obvious joke, like a banana peel or the snowball on the stovepipe hat, but they made it an elongated affair."

It was also surprising to see the writers make hay out of Jerry's own megalomaniacal tendencies. The abuse he heaps upon Simmons and Lear looks shockingly rough considering neither is a professional actor, yet by all accounts, everything was sweetness and light between them at the time. "We had a real romance going," Norman Lear recalled for Arthur Marx. "Eddie and I and Dean and Jerry were like four fraternity brothers. We were all around the same age, and we had fun together. As a matter of fact, when we had to be in California without our wives, Eddie and I stayed in Jerry's home. We were in twin beds [in the guest bedroom] and Jerry would jump from one bed to the other. We'd have pillow fights and free-for-alls. When we had to go on the road with them and we checked into a hotel, Jerry would take the fire hoses off the walls in the hotel corridors and we'd have water fights. Of course, we'd pay for the damage later. But we were really like a bunch of fraternity boys."

Daily Variety's critic was quick to credit the two scripters: "Jerry Lewis can wring as many laughs from a facial distortion as most comics do with a raucous line, but the main asset is having such writers as Norman Lear and Ed Simmons turning out the material. They know their

"Zelma that you love me tonight!" Scene from *The Colgate Comedy Hour*, February 10, 1952.

subjects and the wide range of M&L antics, and rarely does a routine or piece of funny business fail to come off.... Nothing is rational with the daffiness boys, and that apparently is the way the lookers would have it." The more discerning *Variety*, along with criticizing the ballplayer routine, took exception to "the hottest act in show business today waxing so overly generous in their 'we-love-everybody' plugs" for Revere cameras, *LOOK* magazine, as well as the hotel and restaurant frequented by the team during a recent appearance in Boston. "Judgement on plugging everybody is something that Colgate-Palmolive-Peet should control."

But as Jerry pointed out on the previous broadcast, Colgate had been trying to do just that and neither he nor Dean cared. They were bringing more eyes to NBC on Sunday nights than any of Colgate's other hosts. And, as the network well knew, they no longer needed TV; their movies were reaping millions at the box office, with their latest, *Sailor Beware*, the biggest moneymaker to date. They were even taking on Wallis, refusing to do his remake of an old Bob Hope picture, *The Ghost Breakers* (1940), and forcing him to hire Simmons and Lear for rewrites. They also got him to revise their contract a year ahead of time; it, too, was now worth one million per year.

There was no controlling "the daffiness boys."

* * * * *

THE COLGATE COMEDY HOUR: Dean Martin & Jerry Lewis Show #13.

Airdate: April 27, 1952; NBC-TV.
With: Kitty Kallen, The Four Step Brothers, Danny Arnold, Harvey Wheelwick
Cast: Jack George, Harvey Dunn, Jack Fisher, Peter Votrian, Lee Erickson
Announcer: Hal Sawyer
Writers: Ed Simmons & Norman Lear
Musical Direction: Dick Stabile
NBC Production Supervisor: Sam Fuller
Television Director: Kingman T. Moore
Associate Television Director: Arthur Penn
Producer & Director: Ernest D. Glucksman.

OPENING: It's the Annual Convention of Librarians, and although the atmosphere is quiet, their president (*Jack George*) is anticipating a wonderful celebration. They've even hired Martin & Lewis to entertain, but every time Jerry opens his mouth they 'shush' him. Since they're not silencing Dean, he offers to sing "three or four thousand songs," but Jerry explains he has to leave for an appointment. His wristwatch sets off an alarm that gets louder and louder, so the librarians chase them out.

DEAN SOLO #1: "One For My Baby (and One More for the Road)"

SKETCH #1: Auditions are under way for "The Birdwheel Frolics of 1952," for which Josh Martin (*Martin*) is the producer. He and the casting director (*Danny Arnold*) discuss a guy that Martin threw out four times yesterday. The poor fellow (*Lewis*) returns and attempts to sing "the Johnnie Ray number," and gets tossed by Martin. He returns as part of a dancing act with two little boys (*Peter Votrian and Lee Erickson*) and gets tossed, but not before Martin tells him he needs a leading man who's "a cross between Marlon Brando and The Continental." He returns in a torn t-shirt and suspenders, and proceeds to romance an unseen woman, unsuccessfully. He tries posing as an agent, but Martin catches on, and finally gives him a chance as a dancer. When he's called to the phone, Martin tells Jerry to lead the chorus girls, explaining that if he wants them to stop, he should blow the whistle. Jerry has them do a Charleston, but forgets to blow the whistle, and Martin gets rid of him once and for all by throwing him down an elevator shaft.

GUEST ACTS: Dean introduces Kitty Kallen, who sings "How About You?" When it's over, Dean asks if she'd sing a quick duet of "Three Blind Mice" with him, but Jerry overhears and wants to participate. Kitty and Dean start the song as a round, but when Jerry comes in, he's too slow. Kitty leaves the stage in horror, and Dean begins strangling Jerry.

SKETCH #2: We take a trip back in time to the boys' early vaudeville days, as they're sailing to Europe for their first overseas engagement. However, only Dean has passage, so Jerry has stowed away... in a golf bag! Once he's emerged, Jerry complains, but suddenly begins choking; Dean reaches into his mouth and removes two golf balls and a club. Almost immediately, Jerry has to hide again, as the captain (*Danny Arnold*) arrives, tells Dean there are stowaways aboard and searches the cabin.

The captain is called to the deck because of an approaching storm, and Dean figures he and Jerry can eat the captain's lunch. They do, but the ship rocks and tosses in the storm, and Jerry gets nauseous.

DEAN SOLO #2: "Oh, Marie"

FINALE: Dean introduces the Four Step Brothers and asks if he can dance with them. Again, Jerry barges in demanding to be included, so the six start out together with a soft-shoe tap. The Step Brothers object because they want to dance some swing, and each one demonstrates what they mean. Once each of the four have had a turn, Dean and Jerry take solo spots themselves, before all six dance off the stage.

ANALYSIS AND REVIEWS: Some new ideas and familiar gags and phrases combined for "a boffo session best slanted to showcase the varied talents of this versatile pair," as *Daily Variety* put it. If the end result wasn't as inspired as their previous four entries, you couldn't tell it by the studio audience reaction.

The show marked the start of a new running gag: the fake credit, in this case "Harvey Wheelwick." Jerry had been incorporating "birds" and "wheels" into songs and dialogue almost since the beginning of the series ("I hear music and there's no one there / I hear birdies and their wheels are bare"). There would be more variations in the credits come the following season. The "Librarian's Convention" opening is rather flat, with the only real laugh coming at the very end, when Jerry's wristwatch sets off an alarm that grows in intensity to a ludicrous degree. The joke would have worked just as well on their radio program. The overriding theme of the "Birdwheel Frolics" sketch is Jerry's desperate need to be the center of attention, even to the point of pushing cute children behind him when he intrudes on their act. It concludes with a reworking of the whistle bit in last season's gymnastic sketch, but it's at the midpoint that the proceedings come to life.

The idea of marrying a parody of Marlon Brando's *Streetcar Named Desire* characterization with one of *The Continental* was certainly brilliant... at the time. For those who have forgotten or never knew, *The Continental* was a short-lived phenomenon, the brainchild of actor Renzo Cesana. The concept was that the elegantly-garbed "Continental," complete with ascot and smoking jacket, would seductively romance a woman, only "she" would be the viewer. Cesana had actually introduced the character on radio, where it flopped, but then he talked Los Angeles station KTLA into taking it on. "I knew right away it was a big [bleep]in' idea," recalled Alvin 'Bud' Cole, a KTLA producer, for Jeff Kisseloff's *The Box*. "The secret to the show was the illusion. The woman at home thinks when he opens that door and says, 'Come in, darling,' and the camera goes in, and he lights her cigarette and hands her champagne, that broad is sittin' at home thinking that he's with her.... Durante, Berle, every one of them [either] did him or had him on as a guest."

Using his "punch drunk" voice, Jerry romances the camera and offers "her" a stein of beer. Before passing her a cigarette, he works in a plug for Chesterfield by holding up the pack. A muscular, clawed hand takes the cigarette. "You've been goin' to the gym, ain't ya!" he says, before breaking up. After he lights her up, the smoke nearly obscures the picture. "Baby, your dress is on fire!" he tells her; finally Dean's seen enough and yanks Jerry out of the set, to audience applause. *The Continental* had made such a big splash locally that CBS took it on in January 1952, but scheduled it at 11:00 p.m., when its target audience – the bored American housewife – was unlikely to be tuned in. It went off the air just as Lewis was readying his parody. Amazingly, the concept would be spoofed by Christopher Walken on *Saturday Night Live* during the 1990s, to an audience with little-to-no knowledge of the original.

The effervescent Kitty Kallen, who would tour with the boys later in the year, makes her third *Comedy Hour* appearance and scores nicely with "How About You?" The attempt at a round of "Three Blind Mice" with Dean and Jerry is another example of cross-pollination from the radio series, as they did the same routine with Ann Sheridan at the close of their season finale, which had aired two days before.

The "stowaway" scene begins as an exact replica of the previous year's boardinghouse sketch, with Jerry hiding in a much-too-small container. The bit where Dean retrieves his golf balls and club from Jerry's mouth is not framed too effectively, but gets a round of applause anyway. Aside from that, not much happens until the ship starts tossing as they eat. Even here, there's a surprising lack of versatility while Jerry builds toward full-on seasickness, and it takes the slapstick of the rocking boat, with he and Dean rolling around on the floor, to garner any laughs.

Jerry sacrifices his solo spot so that he and Dean can spend some time with the Four Step Brothers, a quartet of dancers who combine swing with jive and a touch of gymnastics in their routines. It's a welcome change of pace from the more staid dance routines of earlier shows,

Brooklyn's Bedford Stores use the *NY Cardiac Hospital Telethon* to sell RCA TV sets, March 1952.

Flanked by Jerry and Dean, Mel Torme encourages viewers to pledge toward the Cardiac Hospital.

and moving it to the finale, so Martin & Lewis can participate, is another inspired decision.

By this point in the season, Colgate and/or their ad agency had insisted that it air in prime time in the west as well as the rest of the country. The show was still performed live at 5:00 p.m. Hollywood time, but it was now possible to have a kinescope ready for airing two hours later (called a "hot kine" in the trade). "Kine quality was not particularly good, however," opined *Daily Variety*, "and it's to be hoped Colgate decides to either resume live for the Coast or film the show next season." Apart from that, their reviewer loved the show, especially the "Birdwheel Frolics" sketch: "Lewis delivered a takeoff to end all takeoffs, when he caricatured a combo Marlon Brando-The Continental type.... [The] routine is excellent, with Lewis' imitations of the two close enough to provide real yocks."

Newspaper critic John Lester agreed: "Jerry hit the high spot with his 'continental' burlesque in which he had them tumbling out on top of each other for several minutes. Not chuckles, either, but big yaks, real howls…. The closing bit, with the famous Step brothers, possibly the finest and most exciting act of its kind, was the perfect wrap-up for the hour, the kind of a close that left the viewer wanting more, all on the basis of a real demonstration of versatility and talent." Overall, Lester concluded, the show "was a honey, one of the best the boys have ever turned in and one that indicated they're heading in a good direction for the future. The slapstick and roughhouse were still very much in evidence but both were used as hilarious devices rather than for their own sake, as they have been several times in the past."

Calling it "their most successful season in TV," 'Rose' of the weekly *Variety* proclaimed, "Unlike other comics who exhaust their stocks-in-trade by overdoses of video, M&L have achieved that rare talent of easing their way through variations of old and familiar business, yet managing to [give] it a continuing spark of freshness and comicality. They wear well on TV, and it's a cinch that, come the '52-'53 Colgate cycle, they'll be as welcome as they were for their second semester last [fall]."

* * * * *

The *Colgate* season was finished, and the team was in the midst of shooting the *Ghost Breakers* remake, now titled *Scared Stiff* (1953), when they made a guest TV appearance that was a milestone in more ways than one.

Vincent X. Flaherty, sportswriter for the *Los Angeles Examiner*, conceived the idea of a telethon to help fund the U.S. team's trip to Helsinki, Finland for the summer Olympics. In May, he discussed the idea with Bob Hope and Bing Crosby, then shooting their sixth picture together, *Road to Bali* (1952) (in which Martin & Lewis made a memorable cameo); each agreed to co-host. Hope was under contract to NBC, Crosby to CBS, so both networks agreed to take on the program, which would also be Crosby's television debut, a long-awaited event in itself.

In keeping with the political atmosphere of the day, the fundraiser was framed as the means to make certain the team would outperform the Soviets, who would be making their Olympic debut. "Russia has been training 20,000 athletes for five years to make one big splash in Helsinki," Flaherty wrote. Crosby, who'd been rejecting TV for years, said, "This is one time I couldn't refuse. I think every American should get behind our Olympic team and send our athletes across at full strength. We've got to show up the Reds." Hope added, "Old Joe Stalin thinks he's going to show up our soft capitalistic America. We've got to cut him down to size."

Avery Brundage, president of the U.S. Olympic Committee, de-emphasized the politics in his statement: "This is a most wonderful thing. It assures us of being able to send our strongest group of athletes to the Olympic games. The Olympic Committee will be eternally grateful to Bob Hope and Bing Crosby."

The telethon, originating from the El Capitan, went on the weekend of June 21-22, beginning at 11:00 p.m. East Coast time, and aired for 14½ hours over a reported 68 stations. Some four hours into the show, while reading pledges, Crosby tells Hope, "There's a couple of mustangs in the wings. If we don't get them on pretty soon...." "Oh, yes, we've got to get these boys on," says Hope, "and they're very wonderful for coming over here to help us: Martin & Lewis!"

With that, a two-man whirlwind comes leaping on stage. As Dean cordially shakes Bing's hand, Jerry jumps upon Hope and smothers him with kisses. Dean literally has to pull his partner off of Hope, who angrily smacks him with the pledge papers he'd been reading. Having witnessed this assault, Crosby quickly departs. "All right," says Lewis, "it's time for the old-timers to sit down!" "Yeah, the younger generation is here," agrees Dean, as Jerry calls for some "wake-up music." The two dance a

Martin and Lewis read pledges on the air. Photo courtesy of Kayley Thompson.

Charleston for about seven seconds; Dean tells the band to stop playing, as Jerry calls for Bing:

JERRY: Uh, Bing? Bing Croughsby? Bing Crisby? Here, fellow! Boy! Young man! Here, innkeeper, find that boy! (*Turning toward Hope*) Bob?

DEAN: Mr. Hope?

JERRY: Robert? Where's Bing Croughsby? Here, fine lad! Up there! Walk him around for an hour!

BOB: (*swats Jerry again with his papers*) Stop talking about my father that way!

JERRY: Bing! Bing! Fine lad! Here, boy!

BOB: (*joining in*) Boy! Here, boy! (*grabs microphone*)

JERRY: Good boy, here! (*Barks like a dog*)

BOB: (*to Dean*) When…. Listen…. When did they cut…. Hey, listen….

JERRY: Bing! (*faces the band*) All together: (*leads them as a choir and sings*) Bing Crosby! / Bing Crosby!

BOB: (*taps Dean to get his attention*) When did they cut the strings off him?

JERRY: (*to Hope*) I'll be singing yet, Bob! (*resumes calling*) Bing!

BOB: He's hiding, and I don't blame him!

DEAN: He's in Helsinki right about now.

Crosby never does return; he'd later say he "ran like a bandit" to off-stage safety in fear that Lewis would yank off his toupee. Having delivered his joke, Hope turns the show over to Martin & Lewis and departs.

"In this battle of the comics," wrote Frank Krutnik in his book *Inventing Jerry Lewis*, "Lewis' nonstop, rapid-fire shape shifting is a dazzling wonder. Even Martin seems perpetually astonished at how far his partner is prepared to go to get a laugh, and through much of Lewis' performative skirmish with Hope he stands with a hand in his pocket, doing very little apart from just being there. But he does what little he does extremely well—and his being there is crucial. Lewis needs Martin's presence to legitimate his actions, and the audience needs him too, as an alibi and pretext for enjoying Lewis' bewitching excess."

Bewitching or not, the excess displayed here eclipses anything Lewis had ever done on television. Under the pretext of introducing Dean's song, Jerry begins addressing the cameras. The light on one of them has apparently gone out, and Lewis looks from camera-to-camera: "Which camera is on? None of them!" The cameras are switching back and forth, as happened on a couple of *Colgate* shows, but miffed at Crosby's snub, Jerry's not in the mood to play that game. "Let's not fool with the child star," he warns them, only half in jest. He continues dragging out the introduction ("We didn't know we were going to be here until four weeks ago, so naturally we're unprepared and we'll only be able to do two or three hours!"), while Dean stands and waits. Tired of that, he heads to the microphone to hurry Jerry along, when something loudly falls to the floor off-camera. Jerry hops right on it: "Here, pick up your teeth!" Dean tries his own joke; "Bing just fell off his wallet again," but nobody laughs. "Fell off the wallet again," Jerry says as if critiquing the joke, then resumes his own ad-hoc monologue. Eventually he introduces the song, and as the band starts playing, he walks straight into the camera.

Dean begins "When You're Smiling," but he's barely into it when Jerry takes over a camera and pushes it right up to Dean's nose. "Am I comin' in clear?" Dean asks, but it isn't an issue for the viewers, as the director never cuts to Jerry's camera. He continues the song but the interruption has rattled him; he seems to lose his place, and turns to Dick Stabile, who at that moment appears to be listening to direction from an earpiece. "You followin' me, Dick?" Dean asks, but Stabile doesn't respond. He asks again, and finally Stabile turns, smiles and makes an "OK" sign. But Dean's lost now, and sings "When you're cryin'" instead of "Keep on smiling," and turns again to his conductor. "What song is this?" He sings the wrong line again, and faces Stabile again, "You sure you got the right music?" By now he's getting laughs, so he points to the band, asking "Do those boys know each other?" He starts the second chorus with a Jolson

Camera blocking for the photography studio sketch, *Colgate Comedy Hour* of March 23, 1952.

imitation and takes a long pause. "Sing it!" Jerry calls out, to which Dean calls back, "I'm singin', already!" The song ends, Dean takes a curtsey, then it cuts to Jerry whistling and encouraging the audience applause. He looks into the camera, smiles, crosses his eyes and sticks his tongue out, then walks back to his partner.

"I've never heard you sing better, believe you me," says Jerry. "That was one time you sang beautifully. No, I'm not kidding, at all?" Perhaps tiring of his partner's energy, Dean pulls him up short: "If you had one more head, you could have a wonderful rock garden. You could start it all together." Jerry laughs and places his hands alongside Dean's face, setting up a gag they'd done twice before on *Colgate*; peering toward Dean as if looking into a Mutoscope, he laughs again and turns to the audience: "Dirty pictures!"

They segue into a stage routine they'd not yet performed on television, where Jerry imitates Ezio Pinza (who had appeared earlier) singing "Some Enchanted Evening" from *South Pacific*. Before it begins, though, they take the opportunity to plug their regular sponsor: Dean starts the Ajax Cleanser jingle, Jerry immediately joins in, and after singing the last line ("Floats the dirt right down the drain"), they raspberry each other and wipe their faces. Jerry then starts the Halo Shampoo jingle and, while singing, lifts his hands. Dean, knowing what Jerry's up to, shakes his head 'No' repeatedly, but Jerry tries for it anyway: as the tune ends, he reaches up to "shampoo" Dean's hair, but Dean manages to dodge him. Then the routine starts.

Jerry sings, "Some enchanted eve-en-ing / You vill meet a strange-UHHH!" Dean screams and ducks beneath Jerry's mouth, asking him, "What've you been eating, Fab?" There's no laugh, so Jerry resumes the song, but Dean interrupts, trying again: "Fab?" "They heard you; it wasn't funny," says Jerry. As Jerry sings, "Then fly to her side," Dean softly hums and lowers his hand from Jerry's torso to his waist. They stop, look down at Dean's hand; they look up, Jerry's eyes are crossed with a puzzled expression. Jerry returns Dean's hand to his torso, singing, "And make her your own." This time Dean hums with a growl and lowers his hand again. Once more they stop, but now Jerry's smiling: "I *like* it! I *like* it!"

When the routine ends, Dean makes a plea for contributions. He mentions being from Ohio like Bob Hope, and Jerry encourages him to say hello to all the guys in Steubenville. "Dum-dum, Ape Head (note: these

"It looks like gangrene!" says Lewis as Martin breaks up. Scene from
The Colgate Comedy Hour, March 23, 1952.

were *not* made-up names), all you guys, send in that money there!" Jerry pulls out a list of *his* friends "seated at Lindy's," reeling off names like Jack Carter, Henny Youngman, Jan Murray, Jerry Lester, Leonard Barr, Charles & Lillian Brown (owners of Brown's Hotel in the Catskills, which will feature prominently in this tale anon), Ray Malone, Bob and Eddie Mayo, and others. "These are performers who make thousands of dollars a week," concludes Jerry, "and between all of them they sent seven dollars."

Having spotted Hope at the phone bank, Lewis dashes over; Hope and three female flight attendants are taking pledge calls. He turns to the latter: "All right, you girls have gotta take off; we've got the plane leaving at 7:30!" He picks up a receiver: "Hello, Fred? Is the weather clear?" He turns back to the stewardesses: "I've got seven-twenty-two going out; there's thirteen passengers, and they're all *nauseous!*" Dean, who's actually at the microphone, tries speaking, but Jerry's off again; he sprints past his partner to an array of lilies upon the stage. He plucks one off, lays down in front of the flowers, places the lily on his chest, saying "Oh, promise me that someday..." then stretches out like a corpse. "Don't do that again, you scared me!" says Dean as Jerry launches into another Charleston.

Instead of joining him, Dean tells Jerry to go into the audience and collect money. This is the first recorded instance of a bit that would become a staple on the Lewis-hosted telethons for MDA. As Jerry heads into the seats and prods the audience for cash, Dean reads the telephone numbers. The numbers he gives out don't match those appearing on screen, plus he's mispronouncing words: "For the Long Beach a-REE-a, call...." When he's through, he invites Bob Hope back to the microphone. As Bob says, "I think he's going into business for himself," the camera cuts to Jerry, now in the back rows, still collecting. "How much you got, Jer?" asks Bob. "I don't know; I'm keepin' it for myself!" is Jerry's response.

As Hope resumes reading pledges (Hal Wallis and Joe Hazen pledged $250), Lewis has moved over to the telephone volunteers and is collecting from them. He yells, "Bob, hold it down a minute! We may not ask you on again!" He calls loudly for Dean, who returns to the microphone saying, "I'm here." Pointing to one of the operators, Jerry says, "One of your paisanos wants to share a pizza with you!" He answers a phone, listens a few seconds and says, "I'm sorry, lady, I'm married!" and hangs up.

Lewis returns to the stage, and Hope tells him to "stay right here; the caretaker will be here soon." Instead, he goes over to the band, puts on Stabile's headset so that the earpiece is covering his left eye, and leads the musicians in a rendition of "Old Folks at Home," which gets faster as it goes along. When he's done with that, he returns to the phones, picking one up: "Hello, room service? Send up a...." He pauses. "Hello? You think I'm terrific? It's a dead line." By now Martin has joined him, and Lewis hands him a receiver. Dean listens a second, and says, "What're you asking me for, lady? Ask your old man!" Then he and Jerry each pick up a receiver and ad-lib a conversation with each other.

They return to the stage, where they're told there's a station break in three-and-a-half minutes. Jerry addresses the audience: "There's no question about it, you've been a very dull crowd." Then he turns to a camera and reminds viewers that they're getting Hope and Crosby for free, adding: "Send in the money or we'll have to put on a test pattern. I'll eat one of the lenses and you'll never see us again." With that, he walks straight into the camera, blacking out the picture for a second. Once more, he tries for a Charleston, and then stops to plug *Jumping Jacks*: "We're participating in this deal, so go see it!"

They were supposed to have been on for ten minutes; they stayed for nearly a half-hour. When the networks finally cut away for the station break, Martin and Stabile literally carried Lewis offstage. Once they'd left the building, Crosby returned, asking Hope, "Is 'Operation Pandemonium' over? I sat it out in the bomb shelter."

More than "perpetually astonished," Martin was genuinely disturbed by Lewis' wildness. He knew his primary task was to reel in his partner from the brink of insanity; here, each time he tries, Lewis snaps the line. You can almost see the thoughts turning in Martin's head: "Is *this* what it's going to be like? Is he going to constantly overwhelm me?" The answer wouldn't be long in coming. As for Lewis, when it came out that Crosby hid in fear of losing his hairpiece, he was furious. "I was so offended by it, for the next eight years, I never talked to Crosby, and our dressing rooms were right adjacent to one another at Paramount," he told Bob Costas in 1993. "That he didn't know me well enough to know I would never do such a thing." Maybe... or maybe not; in a 1952 radio interview over WCCO, Minnesota, host Cedric Adams told Lewis, "It looked at one time as if you were about to pull off Crosby's toupee, is that right?" Lewis' response might have been in jest, but sounds belligerent: "If he stood there, I'd have pulled it off!"

When the program ended, a total of $1,020,000 had been pledged; but when it came time for the U.S. team to sail, "did the $1,000,000 flow into the Olympic Fund treasury? Ha and ha ha!" wrote sports columnist Lou O'Neill. "Vincent X. Flaherty... is authority for the statement that

Rehearsing the Baseball Player sketch for the March 23 *Comedy Hour*.

less than 11% of the pledges have come through with the actual cash. This is a new high in welshing…. Even discounting the usual number of drunks and others who tried to be cute by 'contributing' in other persons' names, the returns have been abysmal." Dick Ferris, an executive with the Amateur Athletic Union (AAU) announced, "The reported $1,020,000 killed our fund campaign all over the country. People read that Hope and Crosby had raised more than a million, so they figured the job was done." Another sports writer, Dick Walsh, noted, "At the moment the American Olympic committee is still one half-million dollars short and if the deficit

Jerry's father, Danny Lewis, may have performed, but Dean's dad, Guy Crocetti, was also present for the team's March 23, 1952 *Comedy Hour.*

is not made up, the athletes will be asked to pay as much of their own expenses as they can afford and the committee will have to go in hock for the rest."

Ed Sullivan—still a syndicated columnist first, TV host second—further stirred the pot: "The FCC, in the interest of the public, the networks and the performers, should determine (1) how much of the money reportedly raided by telethons actually has been translated into cash; (2) refuse permission for other telethons unless the sponsors can prove an immediate public need; (3) compel networks to inform the freight-carrying public how much money is raised (not pledged, because pledges demonstrably are phony).

"Just how phony these pledges are has been suspected but never confirmed until the AAU disclosed the deception.... Other telethons have been luckier. Nobody ever has compelled a public audit. If a telethon is a flop, if the announced total bears no resemblance to the comparatively small sum actually realized, the networks, understandably, don't want potential advertisers to feel the network lacks pulling power or sales appeal.

TV had better grow out of the hush-hush, top secret stage and emulate the sincerity of newspapers, which list contributions in their annual drives for funds to care for under-privileged children and similar causes…. It is high time the public, which pays the way, is permitted look into the cash register they are asked to fill."

Then Sullivan dropped a bombshell: "Just how unnecessary this particular telethon was is indicated by the complete record. I asked the AAU what they'd do, since the Hope-Crosby telethon had raised only $100,000. 'Oh we have enough money,' I was advised. 'Our college groups, our track meets, our boxing finals, and ordinary contributors raised enough to take care of it.' Somewhat startled, I asked how much that represented and was told, 'Well, $850,000 covers the Summer Olympics and Winter Olympics. We have that in hand.'"

News of this sort eventually led to repercussions not only from the FCC and the public, but primarily from talent unions, which itself led to problems for Martin & Lewis when they planned their own extravaganza, this time entirely for the benefit of muscular dystrophy, the following year.

Whatever the truth in the matter, the U.S. Olympic team sailed, competed, and came home with more medals than did the Soviets, although it was close. The final tally: United States – 40 Gold, 19 Silver, 17 Bronze (total: 76); Soviet Union – 22 Gold, 30 Silver, 19 Bronze (total: 71). No other nation's total came close.

Nobody blamed Hope & Crosby for the fallout surrounding the telethon, although in later years, Hope—benignly or not—would claim they were collecting for Cerebral Palsy, an apolitical charity. Certainly no one faulted Martin & Lewis for participating, and had the show not lasted over half-a-day, they might have walked away with *all* the glory. In a story headlined "Martin and Lewis Wow Late Viewers on Telethon," Merrill Panitt, TV critic for the *Philadelphia Inquirer*, bemoaned the fact that Philly's NBC and CBS outlets both "decided to close up shop" at 3 am. "Those lucky enough to catch the show on WDEL-TV (the Wilmington station stayed on all night) saw Jerry Lewis toss aside what few inhibitions he has on his regular TV appearances. Lewis just took over and if it hadn't been for a station break… he'd still be on, and the audience still would be in stitches. He tried to get Crosby and Hope to stay at the microphone and trade wisecracks, but Crosby vanished. After a minute of wrestling with Lewis for the mike, Hope took off too. It was smart showmanship on their part because the studio audience by then was all for Lewis, and any attempt to out-gag him would have been suicidal."

Even when serving as a theater full of stooges, audiences certainly were "all for Lewis" and whether they believed him crucial or not, didn't mind Martin either. The team was named the #2 box office attraction for 1951, and their current release, *Sailor Beware*, would gross more than any of their previous four. Every time they went out on a four-week personal appearance tour, they'd return a quarter-million dollars richer. Their radio show had won an audience award. Their *Comedy Hour* appearances continued to clobber the competition. They'd even received their own comic book that spring: *The Adventures of Dean Martin & Jerry Lewis* debuted on the stands in late May (cover date: July 1952), published by D.C. Comics, the owners of Superman and Batman.

Movies, theater, radio, television and print: by 1952, Dean Martin & Jerry Lewis were the kings of all media, with no end in sight to their reign.

* * * * *

RADIO EPISODE GUIDE II: *"THE DEAN MARTIN & JERRY LEWIS SHOW"*

NBC "Operation Tandem" for Chesterfield cigarettes, Anacin tablets and Chiclets, Dentyne and Beeman's Pepsin gum.

ANNOUNCER: *Jimmy Wallington*
MUSIC: *Dick Stabile and His Orchestra.* **THEME SONG:** "I'll Always Love You"
WRITTEN BY: *Ed Simmons and Norman Lear*
PRODUCED & DIRECTED BY: *Dick Mack*
SCHEDULED: *Friday, 8:30 - 9:00 p.m.*

1) **AIRDATE:** October 5, 1951.

GUESTS: Dinah Shore, The Skylarks.

DEAN SINGS: "Bella Bimba," "Shanghai," "If You Were the Only Girl in the World"

DINAH SHORE SINGS: "My Heart Belongs to Daddy"

BYPLAY: Dean interviews Beautiful Ben (*Jerry*), one of the country's top wrestlers.

SKETCH: "A Streetcar Named Max," a parody of *A Streetcar Named Desire*. Jerry portrays the title role.

2) AIRDATE: October 12, 1951.

GUEST: George Raft. **ALSO:** Carole Richards (Vocalist)

DEAN SINGS: "Meanderin'," "I Ran All the Way Home," "I Don't Know Why (I Just Do)"

As a myopic manager and player, Dean and Jerry dance with each other instead of with Evelyn Lovequist.

DEAN AND CAROLE SING: "That Old Soft Shoe"

BYPLAY: Dean interviews Zelda Glick (*Jerry*), the President of the Dean Martin fan club.

SKETCH: A gangster version of Martin & Lewis's movie "That's My Boy." Title: "That's My Boy?"

3) AIRDATE: October 19, 1951.

GUEST: Bing Crosby. **ALSO:** Carole Richards (Vocalist)

DEAN SINGS: "I Wish I Was," "I'll String Along With You"

DEAN AND BING SING: "Sam's Song"

BYPLAY: Dean sings "Little Man, You've Had a Busy Day," while Jerry plays the child being put to bed.

SKETCH: Dean and Jerry portray Bing's brothers Bob and Everett respectively (Everett was Bing's business manager). The sketch parodies the relationships between the Crosby brothers.

4) AIRDATE: October 26, 1951.

GUEST: Arlene Dahl.

DEAN SINGS: "In the Cool, Cool, Cool of the Evening," "Solitaire," "I Don't Stand a Ghost of a Chance"

BYPLAY: Dean interviews Dr. Noel Dabney (*Jerry*), a 13-year-old genius.

SKETCH: Jerry and Arlene are Mr. and Mrs. Tarzan; Dean is a reporter who exposes Tarzan as a fraud. At the end Jerry sings "I'm Nobody's Tarzan Now."

5) AIRDATE: November 2, 1951.

GUEST: Denise Darcel.

DEAN SINGS: "Walking My Baby Back Home," "Hangin' Around," "Just One More Chance"

BYPLAY: Dean interviews Merwyn M. Mertz (*Jerry*), the senior class valedictorian and handsomest man on campus.

SKETCH: A sketch about how organized gambling has impacted college football. Gangster "Dino Martini" and his moll (*Denise*) try to get All-American Bronco Felcowski (*Jerry*) to throw a game.

NOTE: The program was recorded at a Los Angeles university campus (not specified during the show).

6) AIRDATE: November 9, 1951.

GUEST: Danny Thomas. **ALSO:** Bonnie Bishop (Vocalist)

DEAN SINGS: "Whispering," "What'll I Do?"

DEAN AND BONNIE SING: "While You Danced"

BYPLAY: Dean sings "It's the Talk of the Town," while attempting to reconcile with his wife (*Jerry*), a routine they performed on *The Colgate Comedy Hour* of September 17, 1950.

SKETCH: Satire of *You Bet Your Life*, titled "No, You Bet *Your* Life!" Dean as "Groucho Martin" and Jimmy Wallington as "George Feminine." Danny and Jerry are the contestants.

7) AIRDATE: November 16, 1951.

GUEST: Shelley Winters

Jerry takes command on the *Olympic Telethon*, much to Dean's surprise.

DEAN SINGS: "Night Train to Memphis," "Blue Smoke," "If I Could Be With You"

BYPLAY: Dean interviews Konrad von Krunch (*Jerry*), world-renowned connoisseur of fine foods.

SKETCH: A parody of Ms. Winter's film "A Place in the Sun," entitled "A Spot in the Shade." Dean and Shelley plot to kill Jerry by drowning him.

8) AIRDATE: November 23, 1951.

GUEST: Dennis Morgan.

DEAN SINGS: "I Wonder Who's Kissing Her Now?" "I Won't Cry Anymore," "Pennies From Heaven"

JERRY SINGS: "Lay Something on the Bar (Besides Your Elbow)"

SKETCH: Dean, Jerry and Dennis perform in an investigative drama as would be sponsored by the United States Mint: "Just Plain Bills."

9) AIRDATE: November 30, 1951.

GUEST: Jane Wyman

DEAN SINGS: "My Blue Heaven," "Rock-a-Bye Your Baby (With a Dixie Melody)"

JANE WYMAN SINGS: "I Love That Feeling."

BYPLAY: A return visit by Dr. Noel Dabney (*Jerry*), the 13-year-old genius.

SKETCH: Touring movie stars Marie Lamarr (*Jane*) and Gregory Grant (*Dean*) are stuck in Arkansas when their car breaks down and seek help from a farm boy (*Jerry*).

10) AIRDATE: December 7, 1951.

GUEST: Joan Davis

DEAN SINGS: "Who's Sorry Now?" "Never Before," "You've Got Me Crying Again"

BYPLAY: The boys portray a traffic cop (*Dean*) citing a woman driver (*Jerry*).

SKETCH: An "original operatic melodrama" entitled "The Curse of an Aching Heartburn."

11) AIRDATE: December 14, 1951.

GUEST: Jane Russell

DEAN SINGS: "In the Cool, Cool, Cool of the Evening," "A Kiss to Build a Dream On," "If I Knew Then What I Know Now"

JERRY SINGS: "I Love Girls"

SKETCH: The stars present their own version of Jane Russell's *The Outlaw*, entitled "The In-Law." (*Jerry:* "Sheriff, you'll never take me alive!" *Dean:* "Okay, then I'll take you the way you are.")

12) AIRDATE: December 21, 1951.

GUEST: Helen O'Connell

DEAN SINGS: "Jingle Bells," "White Christmas," "It's Easy to Remember"

DEAN AND HELEN O'CONNELL SING: "How Do You Like Your Eggs in the Morning?"

BYPLAY: Dean interviews 2nd Lieutenant Lyman T. Muldoon (*Jerry*), three-time winner of the Good Conduct medal.

SKETCH: Helen is Jerry's babysitter, and Dean is her boyfriend. Based on the sketch used on *The Colgate Comedy Hour* of November 12, 1950.

NOTE: This show was taped at Ft. Benning in Georgia, where the team was filming scenes for *Jumping Jacks*.

13) AIRDATE: December 28, 1951.

GUEST: Dale Evans

DEAN SINGS: "The Sailor's Polka," "Blue Smoke," "With My Eyes Open, I'm Dreaming"

DALE EVANS SINGS: "T is for Texas"

A spring 1952 advertisement for DC Comics' newest title: *The Adventures of Dean Martin and Jerry Lewis.* After the team split, the comic book would become *The Adventures of Jerry Lewis* and last until May of 1971.

BYPLAY: Dean interviews the top insurance salesman of 1951, Mr. R. J. Wick (*Jerry*).

SKETCH: In a western scene, Dean portrays Dale's husband, Roy Rogers—and Jerry is his horse, Trigger!

14) AIRDATE: January 4, 1952.

GUEST: Mona Freeman

DEAN SINGS: "Meanderin'," "Never Before," "I'll String Along With You"

BYPLAY: Dean sings "Only a Bird in a Gilded Cage," as Jerry comments between lines.

SKETCH: A true-life drama of the frozen north: "Nanook the Schnook." (*Dean:* "Nanook, ya schnook, do you mind if I rub noses with your wife?" *Jerry:* "Sure. No skin off my nose!")

15) AIRDATE: January 11, 1952.

GUEST: Hans Conried. **ALSO:** Marion Marshall

DEAN SINGS: "Oh Boy! Oh Boy! Oh Boy! Oh Boy! Oh Boy!" "As You Are," "June in January"

JERRY SINGS: "I've Had a Very Merry Christmas"

SKETCH: Conried impersonates a British film star, John Newton. Together, he and the boys perform a satire of "Oliver Twist," with Jerry as Oliver, Hans as Fagin and Dean as the Artful Dodger.

NOTE: Marion Marshall and Dean request donations for the March of Dimes in the middle of the show. This show also included Jerry's first radio appeal for contributions to MDA.

16) AIRDATE: January 18, 1952.

GUEST: Frank Sinatra. **ALSO:** Carole Richards (Vocalist)

DEAN SINGS: "Bella Bimba," "The Little White Cloud that Cried," "Out in the Cold Again"

DEAN AND CAROLE RICHARDS SING: "That Old Soft Shoe"

FRANK SINATRA SINGS: "I've Got a Crush on You"

BYPLAY #1: Dean sings "These Foolish Things" and Jerry plays the woman that left him behind.

BYPLAY #2: Dean interviews the famous marriage expert, Dr. Konrad von Krunch (*Jerry*).

SKETCH: Dean, Jerry and Frank (aka "Muscles") imagine if they'd known each other at childhood. At the close they sing a parody of "School Days." Loosely based on the sketch used on *The Colgate Comedy Hour* of June 24, 1951. Later, the three try singing "Row, Row, Row Your Boat" as a round, but Jerry louses up the timing.

NOTES: This special episode ran for 45 minutes, with the final quarter-hour sponsored by Buick, which would debut their 1952 model the following day.

17) AIRDATE: January 25, 1952.

GUEST: Alexis Smith

DEAN SINGS: "Aw, C'mon," "Anytime," "That Old Feeling"

BYPLAY: The boys present a soap opera: "Just Plain Balderdash." Dean plays Max and Jerry plays Natalie, and they talk about their problems.

SKETCH: "A stirring drama dedicated to that stalwart guardian of our oral health: the American Dentist." Dr. Dean Martin is the "painless dentist," Alexis is the nurse and Jerry the patient, who has a tooth stuck in his forehead.

18) AIRDATE: February 1, 1952.

GUEST: Gordon MacRae. **ALSO:** Carole Richards

DEAN AND CAROLE RICHARDS SING: "I Love the Way You Say Goodnight"

DEAN SINGS: "It Might as Well Be Spring"

GORDON MACRAE SINGS: "Baby Doll"

BYPLAY: Dean interviews the healthiest man in America, Dr. Byron J. Bicep (*Jerry*).

SKETCH: Another segment of "No, You Bet *Your* Life," with Dean as "Groucho Martin." The contestants are Gordon MacRae and the president of the Nelson Eddy ("Nelson *Eddy*?!?") Fan Club (*Jerry*).

19) AIRDATE: February 8, 1952.

GUEST: Rhonda Fleming

DEAN SINGS: "Bye-Bye Blackbird," "Close to You," "Out of Nowhere"

JERRY SINGS: "North Dakota, South Dakota (Illinois and Indiana Moon)"

SKETCH: A drama about Giuseppe (*Dean*), an organ grinder; Maria (*Rhonda*), the girl who watches him from the window, and Sam (*Jerry*), his monkey.

20) AIRDATE: February 15, 1952.

GUEST: William Holden

DEAN SINGS: "Down Yonder," "Cry," "I Surrender, Dear"

BYPLAY: By request, they repeat "Little Man, You've Had a Busy Day," and repurpose the recording from the October 19, 1951 show.

SKETCH: The trio presents a version of *Born Yesterday*, with Jerry in Judy Holliday's role.

21) AIRDATE: February 22, 1952.

GUEST: Linda Darnell

DEAN SINGS: "Rainbow 'Round My Shoulder," "Until," "When You're Smiling"

BYPLAY: Another interview between Dean and renowned gourmet Konrad von Krunch (*Jerry*).

SKETCH: In the wake of Jo Stafford's hit record "Shrimp Boats (is a-Comin')," the team presents a drama that answers the question: "What's been keeping the shrimp boats?" The sketch incorporates *Mutiny on the Bounty*, allowing Dean to employ his Clark Gable impersonation as Mr. Christian. Jerry is Captain Blah and Linda is a girl caught in their shrimp net.

22) AIRDATE: February 29, 1952.

GUEST: Tony Curtis

DEAN SINGS: "San Fernando Valley," "Never Before," "Maybe It's Because I Love You Too Much"

BYPLAY: Dean tells about a crazy auto mechanic he dealt with earlier in the week; Jerry volunteers to play the mechanic.

SKETCH: An "Arabian Nights" tale about a magic lamp: "Rudolph, the Red-Nosed Genie." Tony and Dean play sons of the Sultan, and Jerry is the genie. (*Tony:* "I'll rub the lamp and get him out!" *Jerry:* "You can light the lamp, but *don't* rub it!")

23) AIRDATE: March 7, 1952.

GUEST: Corinne Calvet

DEAN SINGS: "Oh Boy! Oh Boy! Oh Boy! Oh Boy! Oh Boy!" "My Heart Has Found a Home," "We Just Couldn't Say Goodbye"

BYPLAY: Dean interviews the foremost authority on income tax, Mr. Herbert Swine (*Jerry*).

SKETCH: Martin M. Martin (*Dean*) hires a French maid (*Corinne*) to handle the feeding and care of his son, Junior (*Jerry*). (*Jerry:* "At lunch time, I eat six hardboiled eggs, a half-a-pound steak, two hamburgers, three pounds of French fries, a quart of milk and three Wilson golf clubs." *Dean:* "What? Whoever heard of eatin' a Wilson golf club?" *Jerry:* "Check with the writers. I'm just as surprised as you are!")

NOTE: Most of the show originates from an unspecified theater where the boys are appearing. Dean's songs were pre-recorded. Corinne Calvet appeared with the team in *My Friend Irma Goes West* (1950) and *Sailor Beware* (1952).

24) AIRDATE: March 14, 1952.

GUEST: Lizabeth Scott

DEAN SINGS: "I Wonder Who's Kissing Her Now?" "A Kiss to Build a Dream On," "Night Train to Memphis," "That Old Gang of Mine."

JERRY SINGS: "I Like It! I Like It!"

BYPLAY: There's no sketch; Dean and Jerry engage in repartee with their guest, and Dean sings a fourth song.

NOTE: Most of the show originates from an unspecified theater where the boys are appearing. Dean's songs were pre-recorded; Jerry's was live. Lizabeth Scott would appear with the team in *Scared Stiff* (1953).

25) AIRDATE: March 21, 1952.

GUEST: Marlene Dietrich

DEAN SINGS: "When You're Smiling," "Maybe," "Hands Across the Table"

BYPLAY: Dean interviews the most famous tree surgeon in the country, Dr. Ludwig von Krevis (*Jerry*).

SKETCH: Dean, Jerry and Marlene perform a parody of the latter's radio series *Café Istanbul*. In "Café Turkistan," Marlene plays Michelle, a dancer; Dean is Rick Martin, an American; and Jerry is Mata Jerri, a spy disguised as a clumsy waiter named Harold.

26) AIRDATE: March 28, 1952.

GUEST: Ann Sothern

DEAN SINGS: "When the Red, Red, Robin," "Please Mr. Sun," "Only Forever"

BYPLAY: Dean interviews the renowned big game hunter, Frank Bick (*Jerry*).

SKETCH: Another chapter of the popular soap opera "Just Plain Balderdash." Dean is Sidney, who is married to Sandra (*Ann*) but has fallen madly in love with Gretchen (*Jerry*).

27) AIRDATE: April 4, 1952.

GUEST: Claire Trevor

DEAN SINGS: "About a Quarter to Nine," "Pretty as a Picture," "I Kiss Your Hand, Madame"

BYPLAY: Dean again interviews the noted 13-year-old genius, Noel Dabney (*Jerry*).

SKETCH: A look at "the manly art of self-defense," titled "A Dressing Room Named Perspire." Jerry is "Killer Levitch," Claire is Billy, his sparring partner, and Dean is Rocky, his manager. Billy and Rocky have fixed the upcoming fight, but Killer refuses to go along with it.

28) AIRDATE: April 11, 1952.

GUEST: Virginia Mayo

DEAN SINGS: "For Me and My Gal," "All I Have to Give You," "Mighty Like a Rose"

JERRY SINGS: "The Book Was So Much Better Than the Picture"

SKETCH: Based on listener requests, the sketch "A Streetcar Named Max" is performed. Virginia Mayo plays Blanche DuBois, originally portrayed by Dinah Shore in the episode of October 5, 1951.

NOTE: At the close, Betty Mills, representing *Radio-TV Mirror* magazine, announces (in a pre-recording) that readers have chosen the show as Favorite Comedy program of the year. Jerry also gives thanks to the Tall Cedars of Lebanon fraternal organization for being the first to have raised funds for MDA.

29) AIRDATE: April 18, 1952.

GUEST: Boris Karloff

DEAN SINGS: "You Must Have Been a Beautiful Baby," "The Little White Cloud That Cried," "Empty Saddles"

BYPLAY: Dean again interviews the international gourmet Konrad von Krunch.

SKETCH: "Just Plain Dracula," which is actually the story of a family of werewolves. Karloff is the father; Martin and Lewis are his sons. At the conclusion, the three sing "Ghoul Days" – a parody of "School Days."

30) AIRDATE: April 25, 1952.

GUEST: Ann Sheridan

DEAN SINGS: "The Object of My Affection," "Anytime," "Never in a Million Years"

BYPLAY #1: Dean's interview with wrestler Beautiful Ben (*Jerry*) from the first show is re-performed.

SKETCH: A satire of the *John J. Anthony Program*: "John J. Martin's court of severed relationships." Jerry and Ann are Mr. and Mrs. Max Fink. (*Dean*: "Mister Fink! I want you to hold your tongue!" *Jerry*: "I will not!" *Dean*: "Why not?" *Jerry*: "My fingers get wet!")

BYPLAY #2: Dean, Ann and Jerry try a round of "Three Blind Mice," with the same results as their attempt at "Row, Row, Row Your Boat" with Frank Sinatra. This routine would be repeated with Kitty Kallen on the April 27 *Comedy Hour*.

NOTE: At the conclusion, Jerry announces that they'll be back next season under the sole sponsorship of Chesterfield cigarettes.

Dean and Jerry with each other's hand puppets, just one sample of the Martin & Lewis merchandise available in 1952.

5

1952–53:
Colgate Season Three and the Chesterfield Radio Series

DEAN: "It was love at first sight. The kid looked up to me because I was older. Now I look up to him because he's younger."

JERRY: "Our relationships are somewhat like those between a father and his kid. The nine years make the difference. There's no love com-pair-able."

– As quoted by Leo Rosten and Hedda Hopper, respectively; 1952

WHEN DEBATING THE QUESTION "Does success bring happiness?" there's one sure answer: Not if you're Jerry Lewis. The comedian who'd started out with a routine dummy act was now one of the most beloved entertainers in America, but he was still a bundle of outward nervous energy, inwardly terrified that the bubble would burst at any second. After all, when you reach the top there's only one direction left to go.

And so, he broadened his horizons. From his first day at Paramount, Lewis took an interest in the production process. Once he had money to play with, he spent it on cameras and moviemaking equipment. For a time in 1950 he had his own camera shop on Vine Street, but the business end of the venture proved too much of a hassle and he gave it up. Instead, he turned to home movies. He'd shoot "screen tests" of friends and colleagues in 16mm sound that were mainly gag sessions, which gradually became more elaborate. In 1951, when buddy Tony Curtis griped about the sword-and-sandals pictures in which Universal kept casting him, Lewis offered to produce and direct him in a homemade comedy. The result was *Fairfax Avenue*, an overtly Jewish send-up of *Sunset Boulevard* (1950), with Curtis in the William Holden role (re-named Yakov Popowitz) and his wife Janet Leigh taking Gloria Swanson's place.

Lewis gave his $60,000 enterprise a name: Gar-Ron Productions, named for sons Gary and Ronnie. He turned it into a private club; members included Martin, Curtis, Leigh, Mona Freeman, Jeff Chandler, John Barrymore, Jr. Danny Arnold co-wrote screenplays and co-directed with Jerry, *Colgate* casting director Howard Ross handled the same for Gar-Ron, publicist Jack Keller served as a prop man. Spouses were involved as well: Mrs. Ross served as script girl and Mrs. Keller handled wardrobe. All were obligated to pay $10 per month in dues.

The club gathered three nights per week and Sundays to produce these epics. Movie parodies were the order of the day: after *Fairfax Avenue* came *Watch on the Lime*, *The Re-Enforcer*, *A Spot in the Shade* and *Come Back, Little Shiksa*. This last, a parody of *Come Back, Little Sheba* (1952, a Hal Wallis production), stars Dean in Burt Lancaster's role of the alcoholic Doc Delaney. Patti Lewis plays Doc's agreeable wife, Lola, and Janet Leigh handles the Terry Moore part, re-imagined as a brazen hussy. Everything is switched up: Lola sweetly encourages Doc's alcoholism and attraction to Leigh, who desperately wants to get intimate with the athlete Turk (*Tony Curtis*, of course), who only wants to pose for her. At one point, Doc and Lola attend an AA ("Always Alcoholic") meeting, and Doc is asked to sing. Dean boozily gives out with a song, and it's almost like watching an audition for his solo career: he's in fine voice, just a little slurry as he messes around with lyrics and time signatures, and kibitzes with his accompanists.

Never one to do things halfway, Lewis would hold premieres, complete with search lights, at his Pacific Palisades home. Family, friends and colleagues were invited, detailed programs were printed, awards would be handed out, a mock-newsreel would be produced. All of which was touted in *LOOK* and *TV Guide* as just elaborate fun, but there's no question the experience was Lewis' equivalent of film school, and soon enough he'd be taking his education into the real world.

With the season cut back to 39 weeks, Colgate had assembled its dream lineup: Martin & Lewis, Eddie Cantor, Donald O'Connor, Bob Hope and Abbott & Costello each alternating five weeks, with Cantor, O'Connor and Hope also stepping in when the two teams weren't available. In addition, the show would have its 100th installment in mid-March, and the sponsor planned an elaborate celebration to feature all seven hosts. Then Cantor suffered a heart attack mere hours after his first show on September 28, and Colgate had to scramble again. Regulars O'Connor and Hope took some of Cantor's scheduled hours when subs weren't available, and Ben Blue, along with TV newbies Judy Canova, Ray Bolger and The Ritz Brothers filled in on other weeks.

As for radio, Chesterfield's makers, Liggett & Myers, placed the team in the Tuesday, 9:00 pm time slot, which had been Bob Hope's for the previous four seasons; it also meant Hope lost Chesterfield as a sponsor. Eventually, General Foods would pick up Hope on behalf of Jello, for a daily 15 minute morning show, and a prime time series that didn't begin until the following January. Curiously, Martin & Lewis cut their first show for Chesterfield on July 29, with full production on the remaining 42 weeks commencing in September. Perhaps the sponsor wanted an audition, even though they knew well what they'd bought.

Liggett & Myers also brought their own announcer, George Fenneman, to replace Jimmy Wallington. Fenneman recalled Lewis' penchant for physical humor and his reaction to one such prank: "On the first show I was on, he grabbed me by the tie and pulled me up like he was hanging me. I laughed, because we were in front of an audience. When the show was over, I said, 'Jerry, don't ever touch me again. You can talk to me, but don't ever touch me, or so help me, I'll punch you right in the mouth in front of the audience and everyone. You can punch me back, but I'll punch first.' He never did touch me again. I think I gained some respect." Having Fenneman on board made for some humorous moments when Dean would portray "Groucho Martin" for their periodic *You Bet Your Life* parodies, especially when Dean couldn't keep from accidentally saying "Feminine" during interchanges such as these from the October 14 broadcast:

DEAN (as "Groucho Martin"): "Fenneman, supposing you tell our listeners the secret word. It's a common word; we use it every day."

GEORGE: "Ladies and gentlemen: the secret word is 'Litheon-amicdirgititis.'"

* * * * *

DEAN: "Gentlemen, it's time to get on with the questions. This is your big chance to beat the other couples. George Fenneman will remind the audience who's winning so far."

GEORGE: "The sponsor and the sponsor's wife are way ahead with eighteen million dollars."

The premiere won the team a couple of raves in the trade press. "Daku" wrote for *Variety*, "Dean Martin and Jerry Lewis rang the bell with their madcap mélange mixed up for a seasonal opener on NBC Tuesday, with [the] half-hour moving at a swift, entertaining pace, assuring the duo a front-running spot in the radio sweepstakes... Since studios aren't as sensitive to satires of their pix on radio as on TV, the team did a socko takeoff on Paramount's *The Greatest Show on Earth*, with guess-who playing the titular role in 'The Greatest Shmo (*sic*) on Earth,' and Martin as John Ringling South. Guestar (*sic*) Rosemary Clooney joined in the general buffoonery.... George Fenneman peddled the Chesterfield ciggies smoothly, and was a capable partner in some of the M&L madness."

Billboard's Bill Smith was a little more restrained, but still positive: "Dean Martin and Jerry Lewis are two guys who can sound as funny on radio as they frequently are on TV and almost always are in personal appearances.... The high squeals of indignation uttered by Jerry against Dean's placid assurances still make for high comedy. For some strange reason young Jerry's bits, of what he calls 'shtickluh,' even tho only heard via radio, take on an element that is almost visual. Martin's roller-bearing singing was as pleasant as usual... [while] Rosemary Clooney's line reading was surprisingly good. She gave plenty of heft."

In August, Simmons and Lear had been named Best Comedy Writers of 1951-52 by the National Gag Writers Institute, so it only made sense to have them continue double-duty with radio and TV. That would change after *Colgate* made its season premiere.

* * * * *

THE COLGATE COMEDY HOUR: Dean Martin & Jerry Lewis Show #14.

Airdate: September 21, 1952; NBC-TV.
Guest Star: Rosemary Clooney

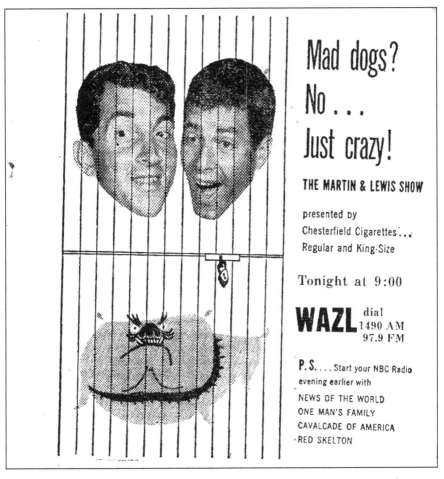

September 1952 newspaper advertisement for *The Dean Martin & Jerry Lewis Show.*

With: Danny Arnold, Sara Berner, Harvey Birdbox
Cast: Harry Lang, Elsie Baker, Joseph Waring, George Milan, Byron Kane
Announcer: Hal Sawyer
Writers: Ed Simmons & Norman Lear
Musical Direction: Dick Stabile
Production Supervisor: Edward Sobol
Executive Producer: Sam Fuller
Television Director: Alan "Bud" Yorkin
Producer & Director: Ernest D. Glucksman.

In September, Rosemary Clooney appeared on the season debuts of *The Dean Martin & Jerry Lewis Show* and *The Colgate Comedy Hour*. Photo courtesy of ABCDVDVIDEO.

OPENING: The annual Psychiatrists' Conference is in session, and for the first time, they're going to try something different: entertainment. They've hired Martin & Lewis, but when the boys begin their act, the doctors object. They want to see Dean and Jerry perform while lying down on a couch. They try, but soon *they're* objecting. Jerry insults them, but the doctors explain that they aren't bothered because they're "well-adjusted." The boys turn this into a song, which has the psychiatrists' dancing about the stage.

DEAN SOLO #1: "You Belong to Me"

SKETCH #1: The show has received many letters asking how Martin and Lewis spent their summer vacation. We're taken to Dean's ancestral home in Italy, where the boys spent two weeks. Although the matron of the home (*Sara Berner*) loves Dean, she's not too crazy about his friend "Jerky Lewis," especially when he wants to stomp grapes. Dean tries teaching him about Italian food and culture, but he's not catching on quick. Jerry feels something in his shoe and when he looks inside, he pulls out several sharp objects, each larger than the one before. Jerry's mother calls long distance but before Jerry can talk to her, the operator objects to his voice. Dean tells him to speak quietly and to use hand gestures; when Jerry does this, the operator's hand comes through the phone to return the gestures. Dean's uncle Salvatore (*Harry Lang*) drops by just as Jerry brings out an Italian sandwich large enough for the three of them to partake, which they do. The sandwich is so heavy, Jerry can do pull ups and hang by his legs. Then Dean gives him some wine to drink, and Jerry gets sloshed. Now determined to press some grapes, he climbs into one of the tubs and pulls Dean in with him.

GUEST ACTS: Dean introduces Rosemary Clooney, who sings "Half as Much" and "Botch-a-Me."

SKETCH #2: It is Dean's wedding day, and he's nervous, of course, especially about leaving all the gifts unattended during the ceremony. His future mother-in-law (*Elsie Baker*) tells him not to fret as she's hired a detective to guard them, from an agency that guarantees absolute discretion. Just then, sirens are heard, a car crashes, and Sherlock Fink (*Lewis*) arrives, complete with stalker cap and pipe. He immediately grabs the woman that hired him, calls her "Slippery Sadie" and threatens to take her in (*Dean:* "In one hour, this is going to be my mother-in-law." *Jerry:* "In two hours, you'll be sorry I didn't take her in!"). Dean reminds him he needs to be inconspicuous, and takes him to the gift room. Mother complains that it's hot; Fink says he has a portable fan. When he turns it on, everything and everyone is blown across the room. Cleaning up the mess, Fink is surprised to see that a man in a cap and mask (*Danny Arnold*) has entered the room and is putting merchandise into a sack. He claims to be "Aunt Elsie's boy" and that he needs to return the presents because they're too small; Fink helps him collect them. When Dean enters, the crook asks Fink, "How do you know he isn't a burglar?" As the three laugh about that, the thief pulls a gun, clobbers Fink with it, and departs through a window. Dean's butler (*Byron Kane*) tells him the wedding's about to begin, so Dean orders Fink to finish cleaning up, "and then you GO!" Fink looks about for a vacuum cleaner; he finds one and discovers that it's made by the same company that made his fan. When Fink enters the room where the wedding ceremony has just concluded, everyone is blown about.

JERRY SOLO: Explaining that he and Dean don't believe in putting their children on television like other entertainers, Jerry admits to having a young nephew, Arnold, who is talented. He brings Arnold out; the child stands stone still with a stoic expression. Jerry coaxes him to talk, sing and dance, all to no avail. As Jerry gets carried away with his own dancing, the kid walks off stage and his uncle is forced to follow.

DEAN SOLO #2: "Hominy Grits"

FINALE: Clad in a bow tie and snazzy cap, Jerry's a cool cat prepared to bop. He tries to help Dean "get with it," but the crooner's a little too square, as Jerry silently informs the audience with his fingers. Jerry demonstrates how to scat sing, but Dean fails at this too. He asks if Dean can play a horn. Dean picks up a trombone, while Jerry leads the band in an introduction that is so intense (and long), that he collapses when it's over. Finally, Jerry gets a trumpet and the two try their hand at playing "Where or When."

ANALYSIS AND REVIEWS: With almost every multi-season comedy-variety show, there comes a point when format turns into formula. For Martin & Lewis' show, the point begins here. Formula is not merely the overuse of familiar tropes and individual gags, it's also reflected in the attitude of the stars, and here, for the first time, the duo are less invested in putting over a good performance, Dean's two solos being an exception.

It's not as though they were frazzled. Apart from taping the audition for the new Chesterfield series on July 29, immediately followed with two weeks at the Chez Paree, they'd done nothing since wrapping *Scared Stiff* in mid-July. Yet both of them seem wearied by the sameness of the whole business. Lewis compensates by overacting, while Martin doesn't even try to compensate. For example, during the Italy sketch Jerry begins climbing onto and straddling the sandwich; there's a metal bar tucked inside, which Dean and Harry Lang have to hold in place. The expression on Dean's face during this bit is clearly annoyance; he looks toward where the band is usually seated until the finale as if to say, "Didn't I tell you he'd get carried away?" Later on, Jerry mixes up the order of his shtick in the Wedding Gifts sketch and resorts to checking a cue card, after which he turns to the camera and says, in earnest, "I told 'em we shouldn't open the season," as if the mess was NBC's fault.

The little toy fan that creates a hurricane returns from their very first show and the more recurrent gag of pulling impossibly large objects out of a small container are revisited. During the latter, Jerry ad-libs a commentary about how much each object had hurt his foot, but it soon changes to his asking the prop man hiding underneath if he has any more items. There's even an attempt to create a new catch-phrase: "Who's he callin' a fink?" Jerry-as-Sherlock says it each time Dean addresses him by his last name, and when the mother-in-law-to-be also calls him Fink, he and Dean both say it; in all cases looking straight into the camera.

The joke credit begun last season continues with "Harvey Birdbox." There's no dancing act this time around, so Rosemary Clooney gets two songs; a nice cover of Hank Williams' "Half as Much" and her hit "Botch-a-Me" (which was originally spelled *"Baciami,"* Italian for "Kiss Me"). An NBC press release stated that choreographer Bill Skipper was slated to appear; for undisclosed reasons he did not.

To illustrate how lackluster the material was, the show-stopping moment is a failed gag. In the Wedding Gifts sketch, Dean tells Sherlock Fink to take off his coat so he'll be less conspicuous. When he does, the camera zooms in on Fink's T-shirt, which reads "Police Athletic League." When the gag garners little more than chuckles, Dean asks if it's spelled correctly. Jerry reads it to make sure and says "Yeah," so Dean concludes, "Well, then it must be the joke." Jerry breaks up at this, but when the audience applauds, he takes offense and walks toward them: "What, are you happy because the joke wasn't funny?" Dean pulls him back, but he's not done: "What, do you think we gotta come up with them all the time?" Again, Dean pulls him back, but Jerry keeps pushing forward: "Ain't we entitled to louse one up here and there?" and then, to Dean, "I'll smack 'em all in the mouth!" As Dean tries to reignite the sketch, Jerry makes one more comment: "They got in for *nothin'*!"

Neither of the *Varietys* was impressed with the broadcast. "Mediocre material plus an apparent lack of rehearsal and preparation resulted in a [not so good] opening for the *Colgate Comedy Hour* season last night," read *Daily Variety's* review. "Muffing lines, missing cues and seeking to capitalize on such slovenliness for laughs, M&L were far from their best…. Even Lewis' great flair for slapstick couldn't overcome almost a complete lack of laughable material." The critic for the weekly version concurred: "There was nothing the boys did here that they hadn't done before – but with a difference. That M&L are 'repeat artists,' with the ability to pyramid their laughs and popularity with each successive reprise of the same trademarked zanyisms, have been more of a virtue than a detriment in their fabulous career – but only when they're generating that spark and when they're getting an even adequate assist from their writers. Last Sunday, neither the spark nor the script assist were in evidence."

The Hollywood Reporter's critic was appalled, renaming the show "'The Low Comedy Hour.' When they have to fall back on such crude devices as slobbering over an out-sized sandwich, wrestling around in a tub full of crushed grapes, and blowing the furniture around with an overly powerful fan—then they've either slipped badly or figure they can take these shows in their stride." Bob Lanigan of the *Brooklyn Eagle* held much the same opinion. "These clowns (Dean is one, too, y'know) were up to all their old tricks, and that was where their show faulted. They needed a few new tricks. They had a long period of time in which to prepare for this opener, but to me, it looked as though they chorused throughout their rehearsals: 'Oh, the people love us, so we can give them anything, and they'll still love us.'" Only the *Long Island Star-Journal's* John Lester, probably their biggest booster on the amusement pages, raved, albeit with a caveat about the script: "The hour they were on was a crazy, madcap, riotous one. When their material is good, the boys deliver it and score soundly. When it's weak, they kid it or cover for it in some nonsense manner that's equally funny or nearly so, and this amounts to as nearly perfect a formula as one is likely to find anywhere." Maybe, but it's still a *formula.*

Lester was the exception, as *Billboard* pointed out three weeks' later: "Dean Martin and Jerry Lewis, along with their TV writers Ed Simmons and Norman Lear, are bending all efforts to make their next Colgate comedy show a bell-ringer. Reason for the concerted drive to hit the peak is to make up for their last show, generally conceded to have been a dud. Criticism of the last show by the press in general as having been one of their worst TV appearances has sparked the activity." The article went on to say that Simmons and Lear flew to Dallas where the team was in the middle of an engagement at the Texas State Fair.

Unmentioned in the article was that Lewis also had NBC release the pair from scripting their radio series, bringing in two new writers for that task: Arthur Phillips, a veteran screen and radio comedy scribe, and Austin 'Rocky' Kalish, formerly a songwriter. If anyone doubted that television was their bigger priority, despite the fact that the team's radio visits were weekly, the change in writers, which took effect on their December 9 broadcast, settled the matter.

* * * * *

THE COLGATE COMEDY HOUR: *Dean Martin & Jerry Lewis Show #15.*

Airdate: November 30, 1952; NBC-TV.
Guest Star: Kitty Kallen
With: Robert Strauss, Danny Arnold, Peppy Mano, Goldcup and Bird
Cast: Rose Plumer, Max Palmer, John Shawley, Byron Kane, Joseph Leon, Steve Keldrick
Announcer: Hal Sawyer
Writers: Ed Simmons & Norman Lear
Musical Direction: Dick Stabile
Production Supervisor: Edward Sobol
Executive Producer: Sam Fuller
Television Director: Alan "Bud" Yorkin
Producer & Director: Ernest D. Glucksman.

OPENING: Reporters from across the country have gathered at a top secret meeting held by NBC, to introduce their latest development: life-sized television. A network spokesman explains that Martin & Lewis are working in a nearby studio to help with the demonstration. An enormous screen is unveiled and tunes in the team, who begin to entertain. While they're dancing, Dean and Jerry enter the meeting and demand to know who the imposters are on screen. The two Martins and Lewises interact with each other belligerently, until the live Jerry throws a punch at the pair on screen, knocking them both down. A couple of burly assistants rush to their rescue and threaten the two partners at the meeting. After walking off camera, the assistants enter the demonstration room and toss Martin and Lewis out.

Before introducing Dean's song, Jerry takes a moment to introduce, "all the way from Irvington, New Jersey," his mother, who stands up, smiles, and blows him a kiss.

DEAN SOLO #1: "There Goes My Heart"

SKETCH #1: The head of a movie studio (*Danny Arnold*) and another executive are reviewing the latest Tarzan footage and discussing what might happen should their star become incapacitated. The studio head makes a decision: "We're going to start a school for Tarzans!" We move to the school where Dean is instructing a number of promising candidates, when a new, not-so-promising student (*Lewis*) enters. Dean has him change into a Tarzan costume, and puts him through a series of tests, such as swinging from a rope and attacking a dummy gorilla. Neither works out well: Jerry's swing goes nowhere except down, and the "dummy" ape keeps blocking his attack. When he tries breathing exercises with the other students, he keeps getting pinned between their chests. Still, when the studio calls because their Tarzan is ill, Dean is willing to send them his new pupil. Jerry gets over-excited and swings through a wall, whereupon he winds up bandaged and confined to a wheelchair.

GUEST ACT: After saying hello to Jerry's mother (who blows him a kiss), Dean introduces Kitty Kallen, who sings "Almost Like Being in Love" and "St. Louis Blues."

SKETCH #2: Byron Kane speaks about two types of child psychology: the "spare-the-rod-and-spoil-the-child" types who believe in corporal punishment, and the "new school" parents who learn from books that a child should not be punished for fear of inhibiting and frustrating him. Paul (*Martin*) and his wife are of the new school, yet Paul's concerned about its effect on their son Rodney (*Lewis*). He's especially concerned about the kid's chemistry set, but his mother believes as long as they follow Dr. Marvin's book, their son will be fine. Rodney, however, is a handful; he chases away his playmates when he wants to inject them with a hypodermic needle, smacks his father and breaks a vase over his mother's head. A neighbor (*Robert Strauss*) asks Paul to watch his young son for a few minutes, but warns him not to let Rodney even touch him. Rodney shows Herbie his pet termites (kept in a flask) and chemistry set, and decides to "mix something" that makes things grow. He pours some down Herbie's throat, and the child becomes an eight-foot giant, much to the fury of the boy's father ("Every week, a new suit!"). Fed up, Paul destroys Rodney's chemistry set, but also smashes the flask with the termites...and the house soon falls apart.

JERRY SOLO: After plugging an upcoming issue of *LOOK* with a cover story on the team, Jerry is asked to make an announcement on behalf of the police and FBI. Having received word that an elderly woman who has been robbing banks is at large, Jerry asks the audience to please notify their local police department if they should spot her. He holds up a photograph: it's the same woman he'd introduced earlier as his mother (*Rose*

Plumer). He glances at the photo and does a double take. "Ma?" he cries.
"If you needed money, ma, why didn't you call me, ma?" He walks toward
her and she pulls out a pistol, warning him to stay away. She runs out of
the theater firing as he chases her.

DEAN SOLO #2: "Louise"

FINALE: Dean tells the audience that Jerry will sing a song "in his own
legitimate voice." As Dean leads the orchestra, Jerry sings "Because of
You." His rendition is mostly straight, but he can't resist throwing in a
few goofy moments. The audience heartily applauds, however, and this
upsets Dean enough that he grabs a suitcase and leaves the stage. When
he comes back, the two sing a specialty song, "You'll Never Get Away"
(lyrics by Danny Arnold).

ANALYSIS AND REVIEWS: A marked improvement over the previous
show, Martin & Lewis "showed that careful planning and imagination are
going into their efforts, rather than relying completely on the spontaneous zaniness," as *Variety* aptly put it. The time and attention Lewis spent
with Simmons and Lear in Dallas clearly paid off. Even the "School for
Tarzans" sketch, which could have been merely 1950's "Body Building"
scene in new clothes, consisted of 95% new gags; only Dean's comment
about Jerry's physique ("This is the whole thing?") was copied from the
original.

The opening was especially clever, even though it contained another
attempt to sell "Who's he callin' a fink?" as a catch-phrase. Let *Variety*
describe it: "The demonstration of 'live-sized TV'... utilized rear-screen
projection to achieve the effect of Martin & Lewis doing a terp bit on a
kingsized (*sic*) teleset, with the kicker coming when the duo entered in
person to heckle themselves on the screen. It was a hilarious turn, with
perfect timing, and came off without a flaw." There was some interesting
fallout from this bit: six weeks prior to the airing, a singer-pianist named
Peter Carew debuted a new act he called "Multi-Vision" that incorporated
filmed images of himself with which he could carry on a conversation and
also would sing harmonies behind him. It's not certain if Simmons and/
or Lear could've seen it, but ten days after the *Colgate* program, Carew
placed a half-page "Open Letter to the Trade" in *Variety* that detailed the
origin and contents of his act, the venues at which he'd performed it and,
noting the broadcast date of the Martin-Lewis sketch, concluded, "when

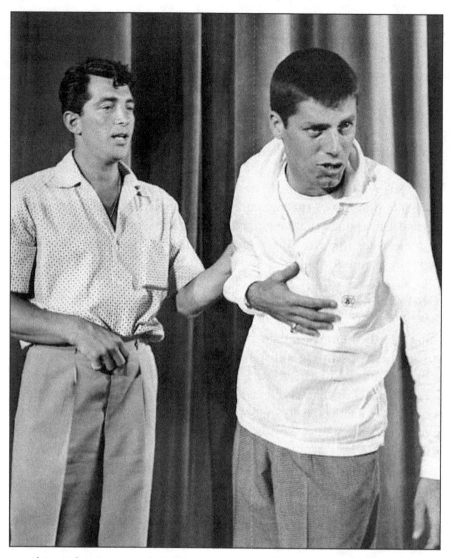

Above and opposite: Jerry's clearly calling the shots while rehearsing the finale of the September 21, 1952 *Comedy Hour*. Photos courtesy of Kayley Thompson.

you see me in various night clubs and theatres around the country—please don't accuse me of taking the idea from *them*."

The props used in the Child Psychology sketch were also considered newsworthy, hence an NBC press release: "A special set of plastic props that can be constructed in half an hour [were] used by Martin and Lewis.... Believed to be in use for the first time, the plastic is an acetate product that is very durable. For instance, if a scene calls for a piano, the plas-

tic is poured over the instrument and in ten minutes the plastic mold is cut off and an exact replica of the piano is present—hollow and extremely light." The prop piano and other items were part and parcel of the sketch's rousing conclusion, when Rodney's termites cause the furniture, shelves and finally the roof to collapse. The scene "proved a standout of inventive comedy," in the words of *Daily Variety*. As for the sketch, it's among the cleverest of the team's canon, with the terrific payoff of first Jerry then

Dean fainting upon sight of the now giant-sized Herbie. Dean also gets one of Jerry's catch-phrases: after being warned by Herbie's father that Rodney had better not even touch his son, Paul pleads: "You can look at him, speak to him... *Don't* touch him!"

Dean's two solos were fine, as always. Kitty Kallen's two were also enjoyable, although she lacked the gravitas necessary to make "St. Louis Blues" a standout. Jerry surprised the critics with his only-slightly-gagged-up rendition of "Because of You." *Variety* thought he "showed a good au naturel voice;" John Lester went further, writing, "He demonstrated he has a very good 'straight' voice, especially since one isn't expected." The close, featuring Danny Arnold's "You'll Never Get Away," was a nice change-of-pace that didn't skimp on laugh lines:

Jerry: "I count my lucky stars / each time I hear you sing / And Dean, I wouldn't trade you for / two Comos and a Bing!"

Although they'd announced their next appearance for December 28, a four-week extension was requested so they could finish up *The Caddy.* Unfortunately, during the second week of January, Jerry had an accident on the Paramount lot while riding a motor scooter Dean had given him for Christmas. He tried to go back to work after two days but it was not to be: he'd aggravated a knee injury from four years' previous and entered Cedars of Lebanon Hospital on January 13 for a cast and prolonged stay. Even then, he briefly left the hospital three days later to record the radio program that would air on the 27th; an ambulance drove him to and from NBC. Interviewed briefly at the studio, he assured reporters he would be able to go on with the *Colgate* broadcast scheduled for the 25th.

* * * * *

THE COLGATE COMEDY HOUR: Dean Martin & Jerry Lewis Show #16.

Airdate: January 25, 1953; NBC-TV.
Guest Stars: Connie Russell, Ray Malone
With: Danny Arnold, Ira Grossel, Bernie Schwartz, Peppy Willow
Cast: Ralph Stantley, Ladd Lyon, Pat Shay, Gordon B. Clarke, Ruth Saville
Announcer: Hal Sawyer
Writers: Ed Simmons & Norman Lear
Musical Direction: Dick Stabile

Production Supervisor: Edward Sobol
Executive Producer: Sam Fuller
Television Director: Alan "Bud" Yorkin
Producer & Director: Ernest D. Glucksman.

OPENING: Dean comes on stage and explains that tonight's program will be a little different. Jerry, who was released from the hospital yesterday, is at home and everyone is invited to see him. The scene dissolves to Jerry seated in his den and threading a 16mm projector, when Dean enters. Jerry explains that he's going to run scenes from their TV shows for "the gang" (who are off-camera and sound a lot like Dick Stabile and the band). Dean hopes that it begins with the airport arrival scene (from June 24, 1951); Jerry confirms his guess and runs it.

DEAN SOLO #1: "I'll String Along with You"

SKETCH #1: After plugging their DC comic book, and the "Best Comedians" award they received from *TV Forecast* magazine, *and* their radio sponsor Chesterfield, Jerry runs the kinescope of the New Valet sketch from May 20, 1951.

GUEST ACTS: Dean introduces Connie Russell and Ray Malone, who combine song and dance into a scene set behind a Broadway theater where Miss Russell is appearing. Malone is a suitor waiting with flowers at the stage door as she exits the theater with a medley of "New York (a Wonderful Town)" and "Broadway Rhythm." He's chased away by her entourage and dances alone until she appears with an encore of "Broadway Rhythm." They leave together in a taxi.

SKETCH #2: A kinescope of the Library Sketch from April 29, 1951 is run.

JERRY SOLO: A kinescope of Jerry's miming to "Be My Love" from November 3, 1951 is run.

DEAN SOLO #2: With the end of the show approaching, the band has set up in the den, and Jerry asks Dean to sing "I Don't Care if the Sun Don't Shine."

FINALE: The two sing another version of "You'll Never Get Away," during which Jerry thanks everyone for their concern while he was in the hospital.

ANALYSIS AND REVIEWS: This "Greatest Hits" show, born of necessity, is on one level a study in contrasts. Dean Martin has grown in ability and handles his emcee chores, solo songs and comedy scenes with aplomb; contrasted by clips in which he appears somewhat tentative and more than willing to be led by his capable partner. Jerry Lewis, too, has grown; even if he seemed a self-assured performer in 1951, he was intimidated by the medium's technical demands and willing to follow orders. Now he was becoming a creator, eager to take control of every aspect of the show and present himself as more than just "Melvin" or "Dudley." Forced to sit in one place, he doles out comedy in increments, yet still manages to assert himself. As the camera is fixed on Dean during his second solo, suddenly we see Jerry's "good" leg come into view and tap his foot in time

Martin & Lewis plug their radio sponsor around the time the show changed writers.

to the music, right where Dean is resting his hand. Dean, of course, shifts his arm, but opts further to stand up entirely and move away from Jerry. This is new: the partners, who up to now had appeared so indissoluble, are beginning to compete with each other.

Still, their mutual affection hasn't died, and keeps whatever tension that may have been brewing between them under wraps. They'd been a team for six-and-a-half years and each understood the other's virtues and faults. It would take a greater hurt than a foot tapping on a hand to cause a serious rift.

This time around, the fake credits included the birth names of two stars and members of Jerry's Gar-Ron club: Ira Grossel (*Jeff Chandler*) and Bernie Schwartz (*Tony Curtis*). Neither actually appeared on camera, but a gossip columnist for *Screenland and TV-Land* magazine reported the two were co-writing a sketch that would be submitted to Martin & Lewis for future consideration. Nothing ever came of it.

Daily Variety noted "This first 'reissue' in the Colgate series was good fun even for those having their second helping." The weekly *Variety* agreed: "While Martin & Lewis were on hand for some integrated live portions...it was a reprise via kine of old familiar M&L bits, as hilarious today as they were a year (*sic*) ago, save for a quality in the kine recording that suffered when stacked up against the live segments. But kine or live, Lewis' takeoff on Mario Lanza remains a gem."

John Lester's brief review echoed the trades' sentiments: "Since Jerry couldn't get around, the show consisted for the most part of film clips of previous Martin and Lewis shows, and the clips were well worth repeating. In fact, last night's *Comedy Hour*, during which the boys took things easy, was one of their best.... The principal 'live' portion of the show was contributed by dancer Ray Malone and singer Connie Russell, an excellent sequence concerning a young man's yearning for a Broadway star."

The New York Herald Tribune's John Crosby enjoyed the show enough to devote half a column to endorse the concept of reruns: "[Is there] anyone here who wouldn't rather see a good one (to say nothing of a great one) over again rather than a bad one for the first time? Evidence in support of this small, dim crusade was provided involuntarily by Martin and Lewis on their last show....

"Lewis is the closest thing to a convulsion of nature we have and this may easily be the longest interval he has ever sat down in his life, certainly in front of an audience which normally affects him like a glass of water on Alka Seltzer. Anyhow, a sitting, quiescent Lewis is not what the customers are led to expect, so the bulk of this show consisted of kinescope films of some of the best bits of their old shows.

"This turned out to be a perfectly splendid idea. Many of these bits I hadn't seen and I'll bet there were a lot of others who hadn't either. One in particular, a scene in a library... is sort of a classic of sheer insanity. The kernel of the Martin and Lewis charm (if that's the word for it, exactly) lies in their pure outrageousness. They do violence to all the inhibitions the rest of us must suffer from. If we can't muster up the courage to raise hell in a library, we can at least watch Lewis make a shambles of the place and derive an obscure vicarious comfort from it.

"Anyhow, it's nice to have Martin & Lewis back in action, even sitting down. I hope the knees come out of it as well as the Lewis personality, which emerged unscathed. Stay off scooters, though, [which are] not for $1,000,000 comedians." Thus warned, the comedian in question eventually healed up (albeit while still recording radio shows) and work resumed on *The Caddy* on February 12, the picture wrapping eleven days later.

With Phillips and Kalish turning out the radio scripts, specific movie and radio satires gradually vanished in favor of original playlets based upon the shopworn plots of old film and live drama. An exception was made on two occasions when the guest was Jack Webb, each show resulting in a *Dragnet* parody. Of course, *Dragnet* was also a Chesterfield show, so there were no complaints. Each play was given a gag title, delivered by George Fenneman, such as this from the February 24 broadcast: "It is the story of a cold-blooded newspaper editor who has no friends, but who is loved by Marilyn Monroe; entitled (*music stinger*) 'So Who Needs Friends?'" Fenneman even kidded the sponsor, such as introducing the troupe as "The Chesterfield 'Oooooooh, They're Best for Yoooooooou' Players."

Despite this, *The Dean Martin & Jerry Lewis Show* took a turn toward the conventional, with gags that were often obvious if not downright banal. However one critic, Bob Lanigan, actually preferred these jokes to the team's recent TV appearances, devoting an entire column to the subject: "It's no secret that Dean Martin and Jerry Lewis comprise the best comedy team in the theater today. You couldn't prove this statement from anything in evidence on their two 'live' shows this season, however. Both offerings were quite miserable.

"Although Martin and Lewis have been on radio regularly since September, I have only had the good fortune to hear two of their weekly half-hour programs. Both were hilarious! Both, incidentally, were funnier by far than anything they have shown on TV all season."

Rodney (Lewis) is up to something dangerous, and only his father (Martin) is aware of it in this rehearsal shot for a sketch on *The Colgate Comedy Hour*, November 30, 1952. Photo courtesy of Kayley Thompson.

Lanigan illustrated his point by printing the following exchanges, taken (and slightly misquoted) from the team's April 21 broadcast:

JERRY: I'm not puny. I go to the gym every morning. Yesterday I bent a bar.

DEAN: A STEEL bar?

JERRY: No, a Hershey bar.

DEAN: Why, Jer, anyone can do that!

JERRY: Oh yeah? With almonds?

* * * * *

JERRY: My family was very ashamed of my cousin Irvin. He got out of the Army as a Corporal.

DEAN: That's nothing to be ashamed about. Many fellows get out of the Army as Corporal.

JERRY: My cousin went in as a Colonel.

* * * * *

JERRY *(as a member of the Foreign Legion):* I don't like this cot. I won't sleep in this cot!

DEAN: There's nothing wrong with that cot! What's eatin' you, anyway?

JERRY: That's the trouble – I don't know what's eatin' me!

Lanigan continued, "Frankly, I don't know why people like Jack [Benny], Dean and Jerry, and others, refuse to utilize radio scripts that have established them as the top funnymen of our time. They, or their ill-advised counselors, seem to think that the TV audience is very different from radio's. It isn't at all. I can't remember when I've heard a Jack Benny, Amos 'n' Andy, Fred Allen or Martin and Lewis radio show that was bad. I wish I could make that statement about the TV presentations of these humorists, but I can't.

"My only suggestion to these fellows, and many others who have approached TV with the idea that it was something 'different' is—stick to your radio punning, boys, and you'll panic the people."

* * * * *

In March, Martin & Lewis went to work on their next opus for Wallis, *Money From Home* (1953). They were, however, permitted a break for their guest appearance on what today would be called "a very special *Colgate Comedy Hour*."

THE COLGATE COMEDY HOUR: #100.

Airdate: March 22, 1953; NBC-TV.
Starring: Bob Hope, Eddie Cantor, Abbott &Costello, Donald O'Connor,
Martin & Lewis
Cast: Sid Fields, Bobby Barber, Sidney Miller
Announcer: Hal Sawyer
Musical Direction: Dick Stabile
Production Supervisor: Edward Sobol
Executive Producer: Sam Fuller
Television Director: Alan "Bud" Yorkin
Producer & Director: Ernest D. Glucksman.

OPENING: At the Colgate-Palmolive-Peet factory, each product has its own office. In the main reception area, dancers perform as a manager (*Sid Fields*) goes from office to office calling for a salesman. When the dance ends, the manager loudly asks for the salesman: "I think his name is Bob Hope!" Dressed in tails and clutching an Oscar, Hope comes out of an office; the curtain closes and he delivers his monologue.

SKETCH #1: Hope introduces Eddie Cantor who, as his Maxie the Taxi character, is visiting the Lincoln Memorial. Maxie thanks Lincoln "for what you taught me about democracy," and is shocked when Lincoln's voice responds to him. Maxie asks Lincoln what he thinks of the new President; the response is, "Nice that one of our boys finally made it." Maxie doubts that he'd be able to rise to the office, but Lincoln reminds him of his own humble beginnings: "Any American has the same opportunity regardless of their origin." When Maxie mentions the great progress and inventions that have happened since his day, Lincoln wants to know, "How many schools have you?" After this vignette, Cantor sings an Irving Berlin medley: "When the Midnight Choo-Choo Leaves for Alabam," "You'd Be Surprised" and "Alexander's Ragtime Band."

SKETCH #2: Cantor introduces Bud Abbott & Lou Costello. The scene is a garage that has exercise equipment and a massage table. Abbott is trying to lose weight and Costello is his coach. They've just returned from a two-mile run, but when Bud steps on a scale, he's gained three pounds. Lying on the table, an exhausted Bud wants a rubdown, but Lou doesn't know how to do it. Luckily the "Fatless Frankie" radio program is coming on. Lou tunes it in and Bud tells him to just follow the instructions. "Fatless Frankie" (*voice of Sid Fields*) says to start by applying rubbing alcohol or witch hazel. Lou asks, "Which one should I use?" Bud replies, "Use either," so Lou gets a bottle of ether. Frankie instructs to "rub faster, faster." Costello does, and Abbott passes out from the fumes. Next, Frankie says to get a bottle of soothing skin lotion. Lou leaves the room to get the lotion, and while he's gone, a commercial about how to repaint an automobile comes on. When Lou returns, the next instruction he hears is to "check the body for rust marks and sandpaper them off." Lou sands Bud's chest and arms, spending extra time on a mole. "Next, look for dents or bulges. Take a hammer and hammer them out." Lou picks up a huge hammer and pounds on Bud's stomach. When it's time to paint, Lou starts on Bud's neck. "Give the body plenty of paint. Don't miss any crevices." Lou does just that. "As one side dries, paint the other side." Costello turns Abbott onto his stomach. "Be careful not to splash paint on the seat," says the radio, so Lou covers Bud's rear end with a towel. "Check the headlamp and test the horn." Lou lifts Bud's eyelids and pushes his nose, which honks. "Take the grease gun and give the body a good going over." A guy (*Bobby Barber*) comes in to use the arm exercise bands; the phone rings, and Lou answers. "It's for you," he says to the guy, who in turn asks Lou to hold his bands. Lou takes them, and is pulled through the garage wall, which causes the whole room to collapse.

SKETCH #3: Costello introduces Donald O'Connor, who is in the songwriting office with his partner, Sidney Miller. The two are working on a new Broadway musical to compete with *South Pacific*. Their title: *North Atlantic*. Donald keeps coming up with song ideas and tries them on Sid (accompanying on piano), who is not too enthusiastic, in part because he's starving. After arguing back and forth about their musical, they sing a verse of "Friendship." For the next verse, O'Connor imitates Lionel Barrymore and Miller does Edward G. Robinson. Next they do a verse as Ronald Colman (*O'Connor*) and Peter Lorre (*Miller*). They switch to "Too-Ra-Loo-Ra-Loo-Ral (That's an Irish Lullaby)" with O'Connor as Bing Crosby and Miller as Barry Fitzgerald. They close out "Friendship" while impersonating two Jimmys: Cagney (*Miller*) and Stewart (*O'Connor*).

FINALE: Hal Sawyer comes out to speak about a new NBC invention, but he's interrupted by Martin & Lewis, who come running from the audience and onto the stage. They complain that event though they're part of the series, Colgate "didn't invite us to come on the show." When the curtain opens to reveal Dick Stabile and his orchestra, they accuse him of being a traitor; the same with pianist Lou Brown who gets pummeled. They settle down and Jerry asks Dean to sing. In turn, Dean asks Jerry to conduct the band, but Jerry replies he just wants to watch Dean sing. Assuring his partner he can watch while conducting, Dean sings "Alone." An open-mouthed Jerry stares at him, at one point pressing his face against Dean's. The number ends with the four-note fanfare for *Dragnet*. They're told that time is running short, and Jerry calls the clock-watchers "a bunch of S.S. Troopers." Dean reminds Jerry that he needs to make an important

Robert Strauss is aghast at what Jerry's done to his son in this rehearsal shot for the November 30 *Comedy Hour*. Photo courtesy of Kayley Thompson.

announcement, and Jerry says, "Next Week is National Fire Week. We want everyone to burn everything they own!"

ANALYSIS AND REVIEWS: A lot of ballyhoo came out in preparation for this show. So did a lot of grief, behind the scenes.

NBC press releases touted the all-star lineup as a "million dollar show," during which each performer or team would be given eight minutes to strut their stuff. Network affiliates were conducting searches for "most handsome" and "most beautiful" centenarians: "More than 50 stations are already enrolled in the unique search, making on-air announcements and conducting elimination contests on their locally-owned shows." Each station was to select one winner from each category, and the seven hosts would choose the two ultimate winners. These were Maximilian von Stephany, 100, a Germany-born resident of Cincinnati, and Mrs. Ann C. J. Milne, 104, born in London, England and residing in Salt Lake City. Each was flown to Hollywood to appear on the April 5 *Comedy Hour*, hosted by Donald O'Connor.

During rehearsals, Ernie Glucksman had his hands full, according to *TV Guide*. "Hope opened the show with his usual monologue. He did not, however, read a single line. He just stood there and mumbled, not being willing to give the others the slightest clue as to what his material might be." Cantor was checking a watch throughout Hope's mumbling turn, and then "suddenly arose from his seat in the front row and hurried to the back of the theater. 'Look, look!' he whispered to [Glucksman], shoving a stopwatch into the harried gentleman's face. 'Hope's been on 11 minutes already.' The producer, who should some day hold down this country's top diplomatic post, calmed Cantor and got Hope out of there."

Abbott & Costello and Martin & Lewis had a history that went deeper than mere competition for box office dollars. Back in 1944, when Dean was a struggling solo artist, Lou Costello – arguably wartime entertainment's hottest commodity – gave him $1,000 and offered some managerial duty in exchange for 25% of his earnings. By then, Martin had already brokered away 70% of himself, but cash was cash and Costello was a name, one who hinted of a break in a future Abbott & Costello picture. In the midst of the newer team's rise, as Dean settled accounts during his "Oh, I've been in court" phase, Costello privately made noise about suing Martin for $100,000 but was eventually placated with $20,000.

Neither man would forget although Martin, never one to dwell on bad *or* good memories, tried his best. In the meantime, he and Jerry were now Bud and Lou's professional equals: each corporation owners, motion picture stars, Colgate contractees. So when Abbott & Costello got up to rehearse, they took a page out of Hope's playbook and "merely walked through their act, uttering not a single word.... Someone finally asked [Martin & Lewis], 'What's the matter with those two? They afraid you're going to steal their material?' Lewis let the question sink in and then let fly. 'What material?' he wanted to know. 'Who wants it?'

"When it came time for Martin and Lewis to run through their sketch, they tossed the script out of the window and did a merciless take-off on the Abbott & Costello routine, the latter two sitting stonily in the front row, never moving a muscle."

What was the outcome of this petty nonsense? Hope's monologue lasted eleven-and-a-half minutes as he ignored "the frantic wavings of the floor manager," Cantor had to cut a number ("There's No Business Like Show Business") from his medley, Abbott & Costello performed an uncharacteristic slapstick routine where Bud didn't move and took all the abuse, Donald O'Connor emerged unscathed (the songwriting/imper-sonation sketches with Sid Miller were usually the highlight of his *Comedy Hours*) and Martin & Lewis – because they came on last – had the least amount of time and needed to "chop an entire sequence out of" their routine. Additionally, there was to be a presentation of engraved silver trays to each act from Colgate, but that was also cut, as were the closing credits.

The show was set up so that Martin & Lewis' appearance would be a surprise; they were deliberately omitted from the opening credits, and at the close they suddenly rushed from the back of the theater complaining about not being invited. Someone, however, neglected to explain this to NBC, as they'd sent out press releases stating that all the hosts would appear, and local newspapers printed this fact the night of the show. Apparently nobody told Hope either; his monologue blithely mentioned that Martin and Lewis were among those waiting to come on and entertain. He even asserted that, offstage, Lewis was a serious, thoughtful and gentle soul, "and I should know: my dressing room is right next to his cage."

Overall, and in spite of the friction, the show was a sort of "Best of the 1953 *Comedy Hour*," and critics either liked that or they didn't. "The 100th milestone hoopla played like a benefit" for Colgate, noted *Variety's* 'Rose,' "each of the comics allotted their own segment for their familiar turns with no attempt to integrate the talent or augment the layout with production furbelows. But under the skillful director-producer auspices of Ernest D. Glucksman... it played as good as it read in a 60-minute

Jerry is released from the hospital to the custody of his partner Dean and pal Tony Curtis in January 1953. Photo courtesy of Kayley Thompson.

back-to-back comedy showcasing of Colgate's major standard-bearers." According to *Variety*, Hope "gagged and sang his way through one of his class routines;" Cantor's medley "was off the top shelf. A sock performance;" Abbott & Costello gave "a sketch in the A&C métier of comedics, designed for the duo's fans;" O'Connor "clicked anew... each succeeding stanza testifies to his mounting stature in show biz;" Martin & Lewis "capitalized on every second… The boys have been playing it smart this season, their TV appearances few and far between. On Sunday's 'benefit,' they wowed 'em."

On the flip side, the critic for *Broadcasting-Telecasting* magazine called it "something of a letdown…. This anniversary telecast, which climaxed $14 million worth of entertainment provided by Colgate-Palmolive-Peet since the series began, would have been a more notable event had the stars shelved their usual routines and worked together as a cast in a single production. As it was, the *Comedy Hour* plodded along in a disconnected slowly-paced fashion. It lacked the over-all polish expected of professional showmen."

* * * * *

THE COLGATE COMEDY HOUR: Dean Martin & Jerry Lewis Show #17.

Airdate: May 3, 1953; NBC-TV.
With: Mary McCarty, Benny Rubin, Sheldon Leonard, Danny Arnold, Fay McKenzie, Sol Seeltime, Wheel Bird & Wheel
Cast: Phil Tead, Frank Nelson, Jack Kruschen, Donald Lawton
Announcer: Hal Sawyer
Writers: Ed Simmons & Norman Lear
Musical Direction: Dick Stabile
Production Supervisor: Edward Sobol
Executive Producer: Sam Fuller
Television Director: Alan "Bud" Yorkin
Producer & Director: Ernest D. Glucksman.

OPENING: It's time for "Guess The Guests," hosted by Sidney Swirl (*Frank Nelson*)! Panelists cover their eyes and try to guess the identity of the mystery celebrity. When Dean and Jerry enter, the panelists have no idea who they are, even though they are not disguising their voices, and even after they ask the panelists to look at them. Frustrated by the lack of recognition, the two tear up the set and are thrown out.

DEAN SOLO #1: "Your Cheatin' Heart"

SKETCH #1: The boys have just taken out an insurance policy that, as the agent (*Phil Tead*) explains, is worth one million dollars to each partner should anything happen to the other. As the realization of what this means kicks in (accompanied by the "Dum-de-Dum-Dum" of the *Dragnet* theme), Dean and Jerry suddenly become very suspicious of each other. At home, Dean's wife (*Fay McKenzie*) scolds him for his attitude, assuring him just before she goes out to shop that "Jerry loves and trusts you." Meanwhile, Jerry is crawling toward Dean's front door, avoiding windows. He finally works up the courage to enter, but things don't get easier. When they hug, they frisk each other. The plumber (*Sheldon Leonard*) calls about a clogged drain, but Jerry answers and thinks it's his partner's murder scheme. He hides Dean's hunting rifle in his pant leg but it goes off when they rehearse a dance routine. After a few more painful misunderstandings, the agent shows up: he forgot to get their signatures on the policy. They tear it up, throw him out the window and embrace.

GUEST ACT: Dean introduces Mary McCarty who sings "Who Cares?" and "Flaming Youth," the latter from her Broadway revue *Small Wonder* (1948). The number includes a silent movie parody and a chorus line dancing to "Ain't She Sweet?"

SKETCH #2: Danny Arnold explains he's been reading the *Tales of the Arabian Nights,* and confesses he finds the character of the whipping boy the most fascinating: when the Caliph's son has misbehaved, it is the whipping boy who must endure the punishment. We're taken to the castle of a mighty Caliph (*Benny Rubin*), whose son, Abdul (*Martin*) has done so much wrong that the whipping boys keep dying from the punishment. When the guards capture a thief (*Lewis*), Abdul makes him the new whipping boy. The Caliph learns his son has taken the keys to the harem (*Dean:* "Let me tell you, pop, you got a nice batch of chicks back there"), so the whipping boy is smacked and pushed to the ground. Then Abdul summons the concubines and kisses them, for which the boy is slapped. When it's time to worship before the statue of the god Mufti, the disrespectful son forces his father to deny food for the boy. Finally alone, the whipping boy worships the god statue but accidentally breaks it. He takes the statue's place and when father and son return, he advices the Caliph to punish Abdul directly. The Caliph immediately complies and "Mufti" enthusiastically joins in.

Marilyn Monroe is the guest star on the team's radio show of February 24, 1953.

JERRY SOLO: After plugging the team's upcoming tour dates and trip to Europe in the summer, Jerry tells the audience that the editors of *Parent's Guide* magazine have voted to give him an award. He invites the editor-in-chief, Mr. Fred Thompson, to the stage. Mr. Thompson presents him with an award, the first in the magazine's history. The inscription reads, "To Jerry Lewis, in consideration of the vast influence he holds over the minds and mores of American children, in appreciation of the superior comedic talent with which he has brought joy to their hearts, and in recognition of the example he sets before them, *Parent's Guide* magazine is proud to tender this award." As Jerry expresses his gratitude, the trophy starts ticking. As the noise gets louder, he becomes more nervous. He goes into the audience to give it back, but Mr. Thompson (*Donald Lawton*) runs away from him. As Jerry chases him up the aisle, the award explodes.

DEAN SOLO #2: "When the Red, Red Robin Comes Bob-Bob-Bobbin' Along"

FINALE: Jerry asks Dean if he can sing "Red, Red Robin" himself. Dean says okay, but to clear it with Dick Stabile. When Jerry can't get a straight "yes or no" answer, he goes crazy.

ANALYSIS AND REVIEWS: *Variety* called this Martin & Lewis hour "a notch below their usual form," and it's a fair assessment. The downside includes a slow, unfunny opening (based on the "Mystery Guest" segment of *What's My Line?*), a fairly straightforward first sketch and an uninspired closing. On the plus side, "The New Whipping Boy" is a gem, neither sketch is overly formulaic (despite the return of *"Don't* kiss her!" during the Whipping Boy scene), the ad-libs are choice and the rapport between the boys is still in high gear. Certainly the two hadn't had as much fun on camera since the second season.

Dean especially seems to be enjoying the "Whipping Boy" sketch, giggling at his partner's solicitations, such as: "Oh, father of a bird, sister of a wheel." After being given the whipping boy job, Jerry says, "Oh, thank you, father of a new nose," and Dean bursts into laughter as Jerry exits, also laughing. Dean immediately forgets what he's supposed to do, and has to be cued by the stage director. "You threw me off!" he calls to the offstage Jerry, who can be heard laughing. Dean also visibly enjoys his partner's reactions to being smacked or knocked about. At one point, after Benny Rubin pushes him to the ground, Jerry turns to Dean: "Isn't he overacting a little bit, this fellah?" Later, after he's slapped by a concubine, he asks, "Who wrote this sketch, the Nuremburg jury?"

The earlier Insurance Policy scene offers the twist of Dean and Jerry mistrusting each other for the sake of a million dollar payout. Had it been performed just a year later, it might've been tinged with bitterness, but here the jokes are only jokes. The two stick fairly closely to the script, which wasn't exactly loaded with laugh potential; two ad-libs getting bigger laughs than the material. Dean, listening in on the conversation between Jerry and the plumber, says, "Oy vey," causing his partner to break up. A few minutes later, having lost his place, Dean says, "Which one of us can think of the line?" Jerry laughs and turns to the camera: "There'll be a test pattern in three minutes!" and Dean breaks up.

Comedienne Mary McCarty was a television veteran, having entered the medium as a regular on *The Admiral Broadway Review* in 1949, the series that brought Sid Caesar and Imogene Coca together. Unfortunately, as John Lester's review put it, "She has appeared to better advantage at other times." She opens with "Who Cares?" but abruptly stops after about a minute: "Ah, who cares? Let's do the next song." It's meant to be a joke, but no one laughs. Her specialty piece from *Small Wonder* is a fine production but the audience is silent, save for a few meagre laughs during her silent film reenactment. McCarty, like Janis Paige before her, was at a distinct disadvantage when trying to put over comedy on a Martin & Lewis show.

"The maddening pace set this season by Jerry Lewis and Dean Martin tapered off into milder lunacies last night," wrote 'Helm' of *Daily Variety*. "The laughs were there and abundantly but the explosive howls that generally attend their wild melees lacked sustained drive.... The skits fashioned by Ed Simmons and Norman Lear were more dialogic than violent, which may have accounted for the sub-normal receptiveness of the theatre audience." Conversely, 'Chan' of the weekly *Variety* placed the blame upon the stars: "The team didn't expend its customary quota of energy, which perhaps explains the noticeable lag in several spots of the show." The critic thoroughly enjoyed the Whipping Boy sketch, claiming it "should become a classic in the Martin & Lewis repertoire."

Even John Lester, usually good for a rave when his peers say otherwise, had some reservations: "They had a little trouble getting started on this show and seemed to be working uphill for most of the hour. By the time the curtain was ready to fall, though, they had the audience

Martin & Lewis rehearse for the finale of Colgate's 100th *Comedy Hour* in March 1953.
Note the cane in Jerry's hand; he was still trying to ease the burden on his knee.
Photo courtesy of Kayley Thompson.

as thoroughly as ever.... Dean and Jerry were up to their old wackiness last night and if you've seen one of their shows you've seen them all. Their tremendous drawing power lies in the fact that, even though you've seen them before, their freshness, brashness and charm win you all over again."

* * * * *

THE COLGATE COMEDY HOUR: *Dean Martin & Jerry Lewis Show #18.*

Airdate: May 31, 1953; NBC-TV. From New York City
Guest Stars: Patti Lewis, The Four Step Brothers
With: Danny Arnold, Sue Bird, Sylvia Seep
Cast: Jimmy Little, Marcia Walters, Christopher Walken
Announcer: Don Pardo
Writers: Ed Simmons & Norman Lear
Special Material: Danny Arnold
Musical Direction: Dick Stabile
Executive Producer: Sam Fuller
Television Director: Alan "Bud" Yorkin
Producer & Director: Ernest D. Glucksman.

OPENING: The manager of a big city hotel is very excited because "two of the biggest Hollywood stars" will be staying there. Sure enough, Tony Curtis and Janet Leigh enter the lobby and they're swarmed with autograph requests. While this is going on, Dean and Jerry enter expecting a reception, but they're ignored. Jerry encourages Dean to order Tony off the stage, but Dean can only think about Tony's swashbuckling pictures and greets him warmly. Dean tells Jerry to order Janet off the stage, but she grabs and kisses him, which prompts an "I *like* it! I *like* it!"

DEAN SOLO #1: "Love Me, Love Me"

SKETCH #1: At the Penny Arcade, a mother awaits her husband (*Martin*) and their son, Rodney (*Lewis*). The husband arrives, having left Rodney at the shooting gallery. He shows his wife two bullet holes in his hat, and hopes the kid will wind up being a target. Instead, we hear shooting and a policeman rushes out to investigate. Rodney enters with a pistol pointed at the cop's head, but when he sees his parents, he lets the cop go. Eventually Mommy takes the gun away and orders Daddy to play games with Rodney. Rodney begs Daddy for money, first for a racy Mutoscope, "Models in the Sun," then for an arm wrestling device that overpowers him. Daddy wants to try the claw machine to get a fancy cigarette lighter; Rodney breaks into the machine and uses his arm as the claw. Finally, after the proprietor warns him not to tilt it, Rodney tries a pinball machine. Rodney's play is violent, but whenever Daddy tries to show him the gentle method, the pinball tilts. Rodney tries it once more, pulling the handle back about six feet; when he lets go, the machine crashes through the wall. Rodney agrees to go home, but Daddy wants him to try one more game: the "Electricity is Life" shock machine. Rodney gets a major jolt and can't break free; Daddy plans to leave him there, but taps his son on the shoulder and is himself stuck by the current.

GUEST ACT: Dean introduces Patti Lewis, who sings a duet with her husband: "If You Loved Me Truly," followed by a solo: "My Daddy, My Hero, My Love."

SKETCH #2: Aboard a commercial airliner, the pilot (*Martin*) is warned by his co-pilot (*Danny Arnold*) about the new steward, Herbie (*Lewis*).

While Dean and Tony Curtis look on, Jerry tries to order Janet Leigh off the stage...

... and gets this result. Rehearsal shots for *The Colgate Comedy Hour*, May 30, 1953.
Photos courtesy of Kayley Thompson.

Dean wants to see him, but he's in the cabin trying to wake a sleeping passenger with his fists. When the passenger awakens, Herbie asks him if he wants a pillow, which he takes from another passenger. Dean comes out and tells Herbie to address the passengers quietly with the microphone. This doesn't work out too well, as the flight details he gives are all wrong. Herbie brings the pilots' dinner into the cockpit where he tries his hand at being the navigator; this puts the plane on course for Fujiyama. He tries hiding from the pilot by disguising as a passenger, but it doesn't work.

Patti and Jerry Lewis sing "If You Truly Loved Me." Photo courtesy of Kayley Thompson.

Dean tells him to serve the champagne, but Herbie can't open the bottle. Dean takes over and gets the cork out, whereupon they both get sprayed.

JERRY SOLO: Jerry plugs the July 5-11 issue of *TV Guide* with a cover story on him and Dean. He also explains how between the two of them, they have seven children with one on the way ("Jeanne's gonna have another baby"), and tells the audience how much pleasure they get from children. A small boy in the audience begins to heckle Jerry ("You're giving me a headache!"), who gradually begins to lose his temper. Finally, Jerry comes into the audience and starts to rough up the boy, but Dean comes out: "What are you doin' to my kid?" Dean picks up the boy and heads to the wings, his apologetic partner in pursuit.

DEAN SOLO #2: "I Don't Care if the Sun Don't Shine"

FINALE: Dean and Jerry sing a verse and chorus of "You'll Never Get Away" that incorporates a little fancy footwork, and use the second verse to introduce the Four Step Brothers. As they did on their final show from the prior season, the boys accompany the Steps' strenuous routine.

ANALYSIS AND REVIEWS: Since Dean, Jerry and Patti were leaving for Europe the next day (where the team was to perform in Glasgow and at the London Palladium), their final Colgate turn originated from New York's International Theater, where it all began. Based on the screams when the boys made their appearance (and when Jerry headed into the seating area), the audience included a fair quota of teenage fans.

The opening with Tony Curtis (who also received screams) and Janet Leigh is, of course, a reworking of the "Martin and Louis" scene from two years' previous. It's fun, but might have been more effective had the original not been repeated just two shows ago.

Before the season began, Jerry likened his love for Dean as that of a son toward a father. Now, for the second time in five shows, he was playing Dean's rambunctious child, and from the looks of his performance here, the "son" was getting a little rebellious. Thrice, the script calls for Rodney to shower his daddy with effusive praise ("What a terrific daddy you are, boy!"); each time he gets more violent about it. The first time, he wraps his arm around Dean's neck and jumps up and down, forcing him to the ground. The second time, he does the neck grab and jumping, then follows it up by slamming his head against Dean's stomach. The third time, after the neck grab, the proprietor gives his leg a boost and he leaps onto Dean's back, again sending him to the ground. There's payback near the end when Daddy, yelling "Oh, what a good kid!" gives Rodney the same treatment, but the roughhouse takes its toll: when he's done, a clearly winded Dean tells Jerry, "I'm gettin' old for this kind of stuff!" As a side note, a boy who twice beats the arm wrestling machine to Jerry's none, is 10-year-old Christopher Walken.

Dean gives Jerry's wife a more enthusiastic introduction than he did for Jerry's dad. Of course, the former Patti Palmer was a professional vocalist who, unlike Danny Lewis, had a taste of the big time working and recording with Jimmy Dorsey's orchestra in the early '40s. Her duet with her husband is cute, but her solo, "My Daddy, My Hero, My Love," is mawkish in the extreme. Reportedly she'd recorded it in secret as a gift for Jerry's 27th birthday; her sentimental husband loved it, of course, and promptly arranged for a performance on *Colgate*.

The "New Steward" sketch is the latest in the cycle where Lewis plays idiot novice off of Martin's cool professional. In this edition, Jerry considerably ups the violence quota: checking on a mother with her baby, Jerry grabs the infant and hurls it back into her lap; that it's obviously a doll only slightly lessens the cruelty. (Later in the sketch, he'd drive the point

Rehearsing the Arcade sketch for the May 30, 1953 *Comedy Hour*.
Photo courtesy of Kayley Thompson.

home by grabbing the doll and smacking its head against the wall.) Then he takes the seatbelt of an elderly female passenger, extends it as far as it will go and releases it so it snaps against the woman's stomach. That elicits an "Ow!" from several women in the audience. Leonard Barr, making a return as a sleeping passenger, gets the worst of this brazen behavior as Jerry repeatedly pounds his chest to wake him; wisely, Barr is wearing a chest protector under his shirt. Dean's not immune either; thrice Jerry grabs his necktie and yanks it above his head (the very gag that irked George Fenneman), adding a piquant shout of "Jesse James!" to reinforce the "hanging." There's no real conclusion to the bit; he and Martin go to the galley to get champagne, but have trouble opening the bottle. When the cork finally gives way, they are both sprayed with the stuff. Playoff and fadeout. Since they were using the imagery of a genuine airline (United) in the set-up, perhaps a more obvious conclusion of flight trouble was rejected by higher-ups for fear of litigation.

The conclusion with the Four Step Brothers basically repeated the prior year's season finale, with an added comedy touch where Jerry initiates the steps and everyone (including Dean) mimics what he's doing.

Since the show originated from New York, only *Variety* reviewed the show, and they called it "one of their worst.... The script was incredible and even the [well-known] M&L antics couldn't get it off the ground. The penny arcade sketch was full of trivia and visual clichés, excepting Lewis' live fingers in the digger machine bit. As for the plane doings with Martin as pilot and his pard as steward—and that very unfunny champagne fizzing finish—it would hardly rate an amateur night slotting."

Variety also took exception to Patti Lewis' appearance, having apparently forgotten she was once Patti Palmer: "The theory of relativity went much beyond Einstein's conception when the masterminds put Mrs. Jerry Lewis into a singing bit with her husband and then [a solo]. There was no reason why she rated a bigtime teleshow other than this trick of nepotism. The duo could be flirting with their rating.... The hour [only] woke up via the high kinetic hoofing and challenges of the Four Step Bros, who were joined by the stars for a creditable bowout."

Although their radio series wouldn't end until July 14, Martin & Lewis had actually wrapped up production by May 8; they'd spent the prior three months transcribing two or three shows per week in order to meet the quota and still make their trip to the U.K. For their penultimate show, the writers worked up a version of the old chestnut that had been composed by Harry M. Woods in 1927: "Side By Side." The result was a

Rehearsing the Arcade sketch conclusion for the May 30, 1953 *Comedy Hour*.
Photo courtesy of Kayley Thompson.

good-natured ribbing of Dean and Jerry's partnership and a promise that it, and their friendship, would continue:

> DEAN: *Oh, the dollars we've earned have been many*
> JERRY: *But the relatives take every penny*
> DEAN: *But we'll still be chums*
> JERRY: *Supporting those bums*
> BOTH: *SIDE BY SIDE!*
>
> DEAN: *I sing and let Jerry be funny*
> JERRY: *But why do you keep all the money?*

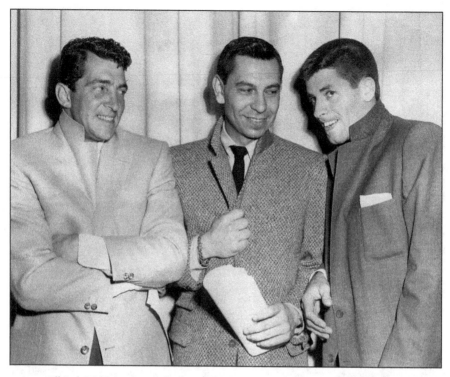

All Jack Webb wants are the facts; all he gets are the gags when he appears on Dean and Jerry's radio show.

DEAN: Well, I drink champagne
JERRY: And I just drink rain
BOTH: SIP BY SIP!

DEAN: Though we've had to struggle
JERRY: For every hard-earned cent
DEAN: I live in a mansion
JERRY: And I live in a tent!

DEAN: I've got twenty servants on my staff
JERRY: And he pays them all out of my half
DEAN: But I travel the road
JERRY: And I share his load
BOTH: SIDE BY SIDE!

* * * * *

In 1951, Mack Sennett was asked to name his "top ten" among movie clowns. In a list that included W.C. Fields, Buster Keaton, Mabel Normand and Red Skelton, only Charlie Chaplin ranked higher than Dean Martin & Jerry Lewis, of whom Sennett exclaimed, "Their talents have written a whole new chapter in motion picture history." In 1952, according to columnist Richard L. Coe, Chaplin himself said that Lewis' scenes in *Sailor Beware* "marked him as today's greatest comic." Now, in 1953, Lewis was striving for something greater, "determined to stick to the Chaplinesque character that he tried for the first time in *The Stooge*," wrote columnist Erskine Johnson. "It will be a lovable, wistful Jerry, with a minimum of pratfalls, mugging and seltzer water from now on out."

Despite the abundance of slapstick in their TV appearances, Lewis insisted he was "thinking about the future." He told Johnson, "The public may take the pie in the face for two years. But they'll take a beloved schnook character for 30 years. True humor comes out of real situations. You can't force comedy. I can't argue with the public or Mr. Wallis that with a pie in the face you get laughs. But I say that you can get as much laughter with pathos and heart. Maybe it's a losing battle I'm fighting. But I'm going to fight. It's just as funny to be the little schnook that everybody loves as a guy with water squirting out of his arms."

Lewis geared up for his "fight," little realizing that his main opponent would be his own partner. For Dean Martin was also "thinking about the future," and didn't much like where it was headed.

* * * * *

RADIO EPISODE GUIDE III: *"THE DEAN MARTIN & JERRY LEWIS SHOW"*

NBC for Chesterfield cigarettes.

ANNOUNCER: *George Fenneman*

MUSIC: *Dick Stabile and His Orchestra.*

OPENING THEME SONG: "Tony's Bop"

CLOSING THEME SONG: "I'll Always Love You"

WRITTEN BY: *Ed Simmons, Norman Lear* (through December 2, 1952); *Arthur Phillips, Austin "Rocky" Kalish* (from December 9, 1952)

PRODUCED & DIRECTED BY: *Dick Mack*

SCHEDULED: *Tuesday, 9:00 – 9:30 pm*

NOTE: Broadcast dates marked with an asterisk, as of this writing, are not in circulation.

1) RECORD DATE: July 29, 1952
AIRDATE: September 16, 1952.

GUEST: Rosemary Clooney

DEAN SINGS: "Hominy Grits," "Once in a While"

ROSEMARY CLOONEY SINGS: "Botch-a-me."

SKETCH: "The Greatest Shmoe on Earth" – a story of a circus that satirizes DeMille's *The Greatest Show on Earth*. Dean plays John Ringling South, Rosemary is Henny, the bareback rider, and Jerry is looking for a circus job. South hires him to replace "The Great Birdwheel," their star high-diver who recently perished.

NOTE: Although not billed on the air, Jack Douglas is credited on the script as co-writer of this episode.

2) RECORD DATE: September 4, 1952
AIRDATE: September 23, 1952.

GUEST: Jeff Chandler

DEAN SINGS: "Pretty Baby," "Wish You Were Here," "Riding Down the Canyon"

BYPLAY: Dean interviews Florence Dank (*Jerry*), the world's greatest channel-swimmer.

SKETCH: A western saga of the three James brothers: Jesse (*Dean*), Frank (*Jeff*)…and Harry (*Jerry*).

3) RECORD DATE: September 13, 1952
AIRDATE: September 30, 1952.

GUEST: Jimmy Stewart

DEAN SINGS: "Walkin' My Baby Back Home," "You Belong to Me"

JERRY SINGS: "I Can't Carry a Tune"

SKETCH: Dean, Jerry and Jimmy "present their version of a breakfast variety show" as broadcast over a prison radio station.

4) RECORD DATE: September 15, 1952
AIRDATE: October 7, 1952.

GUEST: Jane Wyman

DEAN SINGS: "My Baby Just Cares for Me," "Second Chance," "I've Found a Million-Dollar Baby"

BYPLAY: Dean interviews Harvey Goober (*Jerry*), the world's greatest designer of automobiles.

SKETCH: A satire of *Gone With the Wind*, in which Jerry plays a wounded soldier "in a Union suit."

5) RECORD DATE: September 22, 1952
AIRDATE: October 14, 1952.

GUEST: Hoagy Carmichael

DEAN SINGS: "Sometimes I'm Happy," "Half As Much," "Two Sleepy People"

BYPLAY: Dean interviews Clyde Cranston (*Jerry*), the world's greatest authority on etiquette.

SKETCH: Another episode of "No, You Bet *Your* Life" with "Groucho Martin."

6) RECORD DATE: September 25, 1952
AIRDATE: October 21, 1952*.

GUEST: Ann Sheridan

DEAN SINGS: "I'm An Old Cowhand," "Here I'll Stay," "I Only Have Eyes For You"

JERRY SINGS: "I Hang Your Picture Upside Down"

SKETCH: Another episode of that take-off on daytime serials, "Just Plain Balderdash."

7) RECORD DATE: September 27, 1952
AIRDATE: October 28, 1952*.

GUEST: Joan Davis

DEAN SINGS: "I Wonder Who's Kissing Her Now," "I'll Always Love You," "Oh, Marie"

BYPLAY: Dean interviews Hans Von Obendorffer (*Jerry*), the world's greatest physician.

SKETCH: An "insulting routine" entitled "Men Made Up to Take Out," in which Miss Davis visits the Martin Escort Service in search of a man.

Leslie Caron, Dean, Marilyn Monroe and *Redbook*'s Wade Nichols appear to enjoy Jerry's clowning when the magazine bestows its awards during the February 17, 1953 *Dean Martin & Jerry Lewis Show.*

8) RECORD DATE: September 29, 1952
AIRDATE: November 11, 1952*.

GUEST: Dorothy Lamour

DEAN SINGS: "Quarter to Nine," "Somewhere Along the Way," "June in January"

JERRY SINGS: "Strictly For the Birds"

SKETCH: A "regular and king-size version" of the Robinson Crusoe story entitled "Robinson Crusoe and His Electric Footprint."

9) RECORD DATE: November 7, 1952
AIRDATE: November 18, 1952*.

GUEST: William Holden. **ALSO:** Shirley Mitchell as Nancy (Holden's secretary).

DEAN SINGS: "For Me and My Gal," "I Know a Dream When I See One," "If You Were the Only Girl"

SKETCH: A story of "the constant war that our gentlemen of the press have been waging against the insidious rulers of organized crime." Its title: "Blossom Time." "Flash" Holden and "Scoop" Lewis take on the toughest gangster in town: "Scarface" Martin.

NOTE: In addition to Simmons and Lear, this episode was written by Hugh Wedlock and Howard Snyder. An outtake recording circulates of Dean clowning around while introducing and performing the third song.

10) RECORD DATE: November 14, 1952
AIRDATE: November 25, 1952*.

GUEST: George Jessel

DEAN SINGS: "Glow Worm," "Because You're Mine," "Deep Purple"

SKETCH: A satire of *Dragnet*, with Jerry as Sgt. Joe Saturday. Dean and Jessel play a delicatessen owner and singing waiter, respectively.

11) RECORD DATE: November 18, 1952
AIRDATE: December 2, 1952*.

GUEST: Ann Blythe

DEAN SINGS: "My Lady Loves to Dance," "Two to Tango," "I'm Yours"

JERRY SINGS: "They Go Wild, Simply Wild About Me"

SKETCH: Satire of "the one-word psychological dramas that have been popular on film," entitled "Pooped."

12) RECORD DATE: December 5, 1952
AIRDATE: December 9, 1952*.

GUEST: Linda Darnell

DEAN SINGS: "Louise," "Why Don't You Believe Me," "It's Beginning to Look a Lot Like Christmas"

BYPLAY: Dean interviews the world's foremost authority on how to achieve success, Prof. Otto Von Fritzendorfen-huffenheimergangen-fritzenfeltenklaber-drindensmorgendern-florf, Jr. (*Jerry*).

SKETCH: A take-off on *Cinderella*, with Jerry starring as "Cinderfeller," Dean as his evil step-brother Cinderseymour, and Linda Darnell as both the Fairy Godmother and the Princess.

13) RECORD DATE: December 9, 1952
AIRDATE: December 16, 1952*.

GUEST: Ginger Rogers

DEAN SINGS: "I Feel Like a Feather in the Breeze," "To See You Is To Love You," "Silver Bells."

SKETCH: A South American expedition of the "International Explorer's Club" to find the missing Professor Pierre Henri Francois Lafayette Jacques de Rochemont Duval.

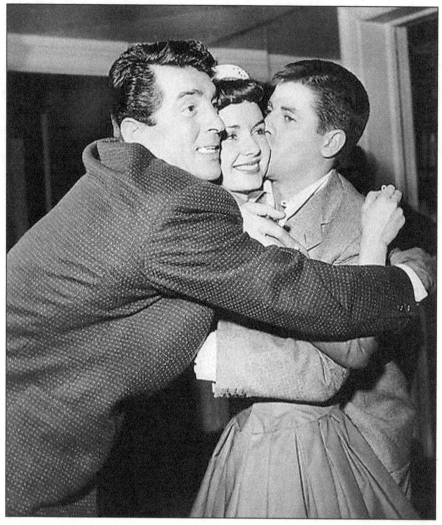

For guesting on their May 26, 1953 broadcast, Debbie Reynolds is about to be smothered by the attentions of Martin & Lewis.

14) RECORD DATE: December 12, 1952
AIRDATE: December 23, 1952*.

GUEST: Tony Martin

DEAN SINGS: "Who's Your Little Whosis?" "Silent Night"

DEAN AND TONY MARTIN: "Nothin'"

SKETCH: A "soon to be forgotten saga of piracy on the high seas" that "takes place aboard the pirate ship, the S.S. Christine… formerly the S.S. George." (*Jerry:* "This is a Buoy that turned into a Galley.")

15) RECORD DATE: December 19, 1952
AIRDATE: December 30, 1952*.

GUEST: Esther Williams

DEAN SINGS: "Don't Let the Stars Get in Your Eyes," "Kiss," "Heart and Soul."

JERRY SINGS: "I Had a Very Merry Christmas"

SKETCH: "A tale of two hermits of the desert, men who lived all their lives without women," entitled "Every Night Canasta." Dean and Jerry portray hermits who are meeting a mail-order bride.

16) RECORD DATE: December 23, 1952
AIRDATE: January 6, 1953*.

GUEST: Victor Mature

DEAN SINGS: "If I Could Be With You," "What Could Be More Beautiful?" "You Were Meant For Me."

SKETCH: "A drama of the Lost Souls in the French Penal Colony on Devil's Island…outcasts of society who share the same cell together, year after year," entitled: "Pass the Airwick."

17) RECORD DATE: January 2, 1953
AIRDATE: January 13, 1953.

GUEST: Jack Webb

DEAN SINGS: "Is You Is or Is You Ain't My Baby," "I Went to Your Wedding," "Everything Happens to Me."

SKETCH: A spoof of *Dragnet* that incorporates the story of *Goldilocks*, entitled "Hairnet."

18) RECORD DATE: January 12, 1953
AIRDATE: January 20, 1953*.

GUEST: Janet Leigh

DEAN SINGS: "Just One of Those Things," "Keep It a Secret," "There Must Be a Way"

SKETCH: "The Life of King Henry VIII," with Miss Leigh as "Princess Janet of Leigh."

19) RECORD DATE: January 16, 1953
AIRDATE: January 27, 1953*.

GUEST: Tony Curtis

DEAN SINGS: "Sweet Georgia Brown," "Kiss," "Can't We Talk it Over?"

SKETCH: "A dramatic story of the submarine service. A tale of those courageous men who each day sink beneath the ocean waters, entitled… 'Glub, Glub.'"

20) RECORD DATE: January 27, 1953   **AIRDATE:** February 3, 1953*.

GUEST: Terry Moore

DEAN SINGS: "Do You Ever Think of Me?" "Congratulations to Someone," "The Very Thought of You."

SKETCH: "A soon-to-be-forgotten play of organized crime" headquartered in a barber shop: "Come Back, Little Shaver."

21) RECORD DATE: February 2, 1953
AIRDATE: February 10, 1953*.

GUEST: George Jessel

DEAN SINGS: "Bye-Bye Blues," "I Miss You So," "The One in My Arms."

GEORGE JESSEL SINGS: "Toot, Toot, Tootsie Goodbye."

SKETCH: "The story of men who traveled west by wagon train; men who, though sick to their stomach, pushed their way through the Indian country, entitled… "Tums Along the Mohawk." At the close of the sketch, Jerry's toes are shot off by Indians, and all three sing "Foot, Foot, Footsie, Goodbye."

Marlene Dietrich appears on the team's penultimate radio program.

22) RECORD DATE: February 3, 1953
AIRDATE: February 17, 1953*.

GUEST: Donna Reed

DEAN SINGS: "I Want to Be Happy," "Because You're Mine," "I'm Yours."

SKETCH: An updated retelling of the "Rip Van Winkle" story. Jerry plays Rip, Donna Reed his wife, and Dean is their dog Bernard! (*Dean:* "I brought along a bottle of booze." *Jerry:* "Bernard—you're a saint!")

NOTE: An unedited portion from the first third of this show circulates, where Jerry tells Dean about a visit to the dentist.

23) RECORD DATE: February 17, 1953
AIRDATE: February 24, 1953.

GUEST: Marilyn Monroe

DEAN SINGS: "You'd Be Surprised," "Little Did We Know," "How Deep is the Ocean"

SKETCH: Jerry portrays the "cold-blooded newspaper editor who has no friends, but who is loved by Marilyn Monroe." Marilyn is a reporter and Dean plays the paper's publisher.

NOTE: The final 10 minutes of the show is the presentation of the annual REDBOOK AWARDS to Outstanding Young Hollywood Personalities for their contributions to the art of motion pictures. Wade Nichols, editor of *Redbook Magazine*, presents awards to:

> *Marge & Gower Champion:* Best Young Dance Team, seen in MGM's *Everything I Have is Yours.*
> *Julie Harris:* Best Young Actress, for her performance in Columbia's *The Member of the Wedding.*
> *Leslie Caron:* Best Young Foreign Actress.
> *Marilyn Monroe:* Best Young Box Office Personality.
> *Dean Martin & Jerry Lewis:* Best Young Comedy Team.

24) RECORD DATE: February 10, 1953
AIRDATE: March 3, 1953*.

GUEST: George Raft

DEAN SINGS: "No Deposit, No Return," "'Til I Waltz Again With You," "Blue Moon"

JERRY SINGS: "Never Smile at a Crocodile"

SKETCH: The story of a spy who has engaged in espionage and sabotage against the U.S., entitled "Shame on You."

25) RECORD DATE: February 6, 1953   **AIRDATE:** March 10, 1953*.

GUEST: Zsa Zsa Gabor

DEAN SINGS: "My Jealous Eyes," "Little Did We Know," "Let Me Love You Tonight."

SKETCH: "(Scream) of Nineteen-Fifty-Three," a story about a woman (*Zsa Zsa*) who contrives with her lover (*Dean*) to kill her husband (*Jerry*).

26) RECORD DATE: February 17, 1953
AIRDATE: March 17, 1953*.

GUEST: Gloria Swanson

DEAN SINGS: "It's Only a Paper Moon," "How Do You Speak to an Angel," "It's a Sin to Tell a Lie."

SKETCH: Dean plans to rent his home, and wants Jerry to pose as his butler. Gloria Swanson is the prospective tenant, who is dismayed by butler "Lewis." While at the house, Fenneman shows up to introduce tonight's play: "a sad tale about a talented trumpet player whose nose was too long," titled "Young Man with a Horn."

NOTE: Dean introduces "How Do You Speak to an Angel," as a brand new love song. The following year it would be sung by both Dean and Jerry (individually) in their film *Living It Up*.

27) RECORD DATE: February 20, 1953
AIRDATE: March 24, 1953*.

GUEST: Phil Harris

DEAN SINGS: "When My Sugar Walks Down the Street," "I Confess," "Twilight on the Trail."

JERRY SINGS: "Louise" (his song in *The Stooge* which was in release at the time.)

SKETCH: Another satire of *You Bet Your Life* "as played thousands of years ago in the Garden of Eden by Adam and Eve." Title: "You Bet Your Leaf." Once again, Dean plays "Groucho Martin."

28) RECORD DATE: February 23, 1953
AIRDATE: March 31, 1953*.

GUEST: Jack Webb

DEAN SINGS: "Love is Just Around the Corner," "Anywhere I Wander," "The Night is Young and You're So Beautiful"

SKETCH: A "peachy keen sequel to *Dragnet* entitled 'Son of *Dragnet*,'" which takes place in Colonial times, with Webb as Sgt. Thursday ("It used to be Friday, but after twenty years on the force, they gave me a day off"). When Manhattan Island is stolen from the Indians, Thursday and his two partners Crocetti and Lewis track down the thief, "Hock-Shop Harry."

29) RECORD DATE: March 3, 1953
AIRDATE: April 7, 1953.

GUEST: Mitzi Gaynor

DEAN SINGS: "Supposin'," "All That I'm Asking is Sympathy," "I Wished on the Moon"

SKETCH: A satire of *A Star is Born*, with Jerry as an alcoholic actor, Gaynor as his fabulously successful actress-wife and Dean as their agent.

30) RECORD DATE: March 6, 1953
AIRDATE: April 14, 1953.

GUEST: Linda Darnell

DEAN SINGS: "Them There Eyes," "Pretend," "I Dream of You"

SKETCH: "The stark drama of two men, cast adrift on a tiny raft in the South Pacific. For days they drift beneath the blistering sun, dying from thirst, slowly going mad, bodies emaciated with hunger – and all they have with them is Linda Darnell, entitled: 'It Should Happen to Me!'"

31) RECORD DATE: March 12, 1953
AIRDATE: April 21, 1953.

GUEST: Vic Damone

DEAN SINGS: "In the Shade of the Old Apple Tree," "Ohio"

VIC DAMONE SINGS: "Lovelight"

SKETCH: "A tale of the French Foreign Legion…men who would kill at the drop of a hat, fight at the drop of a hat, make love at the drop of a hat, entitled: 'Hat-Droppers of 1953.'"

32) RECORD DATE: March 17, 1953
AIRDATE: April 28, 1953.

GUEST: Laraine Day (actress and then-wife of Leo Durocher, manager of the NY Giants baseball club)

DEAN SINGS: "Thumbelina," "Have You Heard," "The Nearness of You"

SKETCH: The story of a hot baseball prospect from hillbilly country, who "used a King-Size Chesterfield for a bat." Title: "He Hit Them One-Fifth Longer."

33) RECORD DATE: March 20, 1953
AIRDATE: May 5, 1953.

GUEST: Anne Baxter

DEAN SINGS: "It's The Breeze," "Your Cheatin' Heart," "Moments Like This"

SKETCH: A young woman who must choose between the mad inventor she loves and "a wealthy sneak" who gives her furs, entitled "The Mink Fink."

34) RECORD DATE: March 24, 1953
AIRDATE: May 12, 1953.

GUEST: Joanne Dru

DEAN SINGS: "Wild Horses," "The Time is Now," "High Noon"

SKETCH: A take-off on the way commercials are inserted in TV dramas at the most exciting points. In this case, nearly every incision of Ms. Dru's emergency surgery is sponsored.

35) RECORD DATE: March 27, 1953
AIRDATE: May 19, 1953.

GUEST: Fred MacMurray

DEAN SINGS: "Side By Side," "If I Could Write a Book," "Alone"

SKETCH: A story of cattle-men "who welcomed the railroad" versus "very, very sad" Indians: "Blackfeet, Why Are You Blue?"

36) RECORD DATE: April 3, 1953
AIRDATE: May 26, 1953.

GUEST: Debbie Reynolds

DEAN SINGS: "Look-a My See," "A Fool Such As I," "I Only Have Eyes For You"

JERRY SINGS: "Never Smile at a Crocodile"

SKETCH: A parody of *Hansel and Gretel*, entitled "Look, Ma, No Hansel!"

37) RECORD DATE: April 7, 1953
AIRDATE: June 2, 1953.

GUEST: Jeff Chandler

DEAN SINGS: "What Can I Say After I Say I'm Sorry," "Downhearted," "Long Ago and Far Away"

SKETCH: "The Chesterfield Smoke-Signal Players" present the story of the American Indian.

38) RECORD DATE: April 10, 1953
AIRDATE: June 9, 1953.

GUEST: Phyllis Thaxter

DEAN SINGS: "Twice as Much," "A Girl Named Mary and a Boy Named Bill," "You Always Hurt the One You Love"

SKETCH: The "pitiful tale of a paroled convict, an ex-murderer, who couldn't hold a job because of his one little mistake—a man who in desperation was driven to drink—entitled (*Hiccup!*)"

39) RECORD DATE: April 24, 1953
AIRDATE: June 16, 1953.

GUEST: Joseph Cotten

DEAN SINGS: "A Quarter to Nine," "Second Star to the Right," "Say It Isn't So"

SKETCH: A satire featuring an upper-crust garrison of Her Majesty's soldiers stationed in India: "How Much is that Cobra in the Window?"

40) RECORD DATE: April 17, 1953
AIRDATE: June 23, 1953.

GUEST: Vera-Ellen

DEAN SINGS: "I'm Sittin' on Top of the World," "Outside of Heaven," "Apple Blossom Time"

SKETCH: A story of a has-been movie actor (*Jerry*) who spends all his time at the corner bar, titled "High by Noon."

41) RECORD DATE: April 21, 1953
AIRDATE: June 30, 1953*.

GUEST: Ida Lupino

DEAN SINGS: "Please Don't Talk About Me When I'm Gone," "I Miss You So," "I'll Get By"

SKETCH: Lewis portrays a private eye whose wife (*Lupino*) wants to kill him so she can run off with her sailor boyfriend (*Martin*).

42) RECORD DATE: May 5, 1953
AIRDATE: July 7, 1953.

GUEST: Marlene Dietrich

DEAN SINGS: "When the Red, Red, Robin," "Say You're Mine Again"

SKETCH: "Public Enemy Number One: Pinky Manishewitz." Miss Dietrich plays "Frivolous Sal" and Dean is the District Attorney. *Fenneman:* "It's a story that Hollywood didn't dare make..." *Jerry:* "So we did it in Glendale."

NOTE: In lieu of Dean's second song, he and Jerry sing a parody of "Side By Side," and another at the close of the sketch.

43) RECORD DATE: May 8, 1953
AIRDATE: July 14, 1953.

GUEST: Gloria Grahame.

DEAN SINGS: "If I Could Sing Like Bing," "Love Me, Love Me," "I Won't Cry Anymore"

SKETCH: Jerry's life story from birth to age 18, with Dean and Gloria as Mr. & Mrs. Lewis. Gloria also portrays Jerry's girlfriend, a bubble dancer.

The inequality of *3 Ring Circus* (1954) is captured in this page from *TV and Movie Screen* magazine. Jerry, in costume, is front and center; Dean, waiting between takes, is an afterthought.

6

1953–54:
COLGATE SEASON FOUR,
THE MDA PARTY AND
FEUD #1

DEAN: "Occasionally we disagree on how to do a particular routine, but we have a very simple way of getting around this..."

JERRY: "Yeah, we do it *his* way!"

– As quoted in SCREEN MAGAZINE, May 1953 issue

DESPITE THE CLAIM at the end of the final broadcast, *The Dean Martin and Jerry Lewis Show* didn't return for a third season on radio. Chesterfield decided to limit its audible spending to programs that it also carried on TV (*Dragnet, Arthur Godfrey*, baseball), and steered a fraction of its Martin & Lewis money toward recording Perry Como's thrice-weekly CBS-TV show and peddling the soundtrack to 500 Mutual network stations. No other sponsor was interested in covering the team's hefty price tag.

Starring on the radio had long lost its glamour for both men, but Dean would quickly miss the outlet for his music. Two or three songs each week had amounted to a sweet plug for his records. In November, during a TV special for Muscular Dystrophy, he'd make mention of their radio show, then turn to his partner and pointedly ask, "Whatever happened to that show?" It was, perhaps, the first time Dean ever questioned Jerry about a decision made on the team's behalf. It wouldn't be the last.

By now they'd been together seven years, and were comfortably seated at the top of the showbiz ladder. Their most recent release, *The Caddy*, produced by their York Corporation, was in theaters doing just as well for them as their other pictures had done for Hal Wallis, and they were in pre-production for another: *Living it Up* (1954). Their new deal with Wallis was more palatable: only one film per year, in full color and with a larger budget; *Money From Home*, their first under this contract, was about to be released in 3D.

And yet…it was at this juncture that Dean began showing signs of discontent. "The seven year itch," a phrase originally devised for a long-term skin irritation, has long since been defined as the time frame when a noticeable loss of happiness has arrived, usually within a marriage, but also in interpersonal relationships such as a job. In the case of Martin & Lewis's relationship, both marriage *and* job would be apropos, and as it turned out, evidence suggests Martin was especially susceptible to the condition. In 1948, his first marriage began its dissolution at the 7 year mark. Later, after splitting with Lewis, he focused on becoming a serious film actor; this lasted roughly from 1957-64, whereupon he grew bored and mainly indulged in uncomplicated schlock such as the Matt Helm pictures. After eight seasons of musical variety, *The Dean Martin Show* introduced the celebrity roast feature, originally taking up the second half of the weekly hour, and eventually becoming a series of monthly specials. At that point, its host needed to do little more than make brief introductions and sit back and laugh at everybody else's jokes.

In retrospect, it was a good thing Martin teamed with Lewis in 1946, as the following year would have been his seventh in show business. Had nothing progressed after that, he might've chucked the whole thing and the world would be minus one legend.

With the radio show now defunct, its writers were added to the team's *Colgate* staff. Danny Arnold also primarily moved from performing to writing. They could afford the augment: the *Comedy Hour* was now television's most expensive variety show, as the Associated Press reported: "When its 39 weeks are up next spring the sponsor will have spent an estimated $150,000 a week for the program, or about $6,000,000 for the season. That's at the rate of $2,500 a minute. [*Your*] *Show of Shows*, next highest budget show, costs more than $1,500 a minute."

All Star Revue having been canceled, Jimmy Durante moved over to the *Comedy Hour* to replace Bob Hope, and would host eight times plus guest on two others. The seemingly indestructible Eddie Cantor returned for seven. Abbott & Costello were to host six times but Lou Costello fell ill the week before their first show in November. Bud Abbott hosted alone, Martin & Lewis stepped in as special guests (which counted toward their own five episode quota) and, since the precedent had already been established, kinescope highlights of previous A&C appearances were used to fill out the hour, one of which was their "rub-down" sketch from the 100th show. Bud and Lou returned during the season's latter third to guest on one show and host three others. Donald O'Connor, who'd win the Emmy for Best Male Star on a Regular Series in February, hosted only four times this season and left the *Comedy Hour* for good the same month as his Emmy win.

In spite of all that money and hoopla, once O'Connor departed, only one other *Colgate* broadcast besides Dean and Jerry's put a major crimp in *Toast of the Town's* rating: the February 28 performance of the musical *Anything Goes*, starring Ethel Merman, Frank Sinatra and Bert Lahr. That unexpected success would put ideas in the sponsor's head, and comedy would gradually take second place to music… even when Martin & Lewis were on.

∗ ∗ ∗ ∗ ∗

THE COLGATE COMEDY HOUR: Dean Martin & Jerry Lewis Show #19.

Airdate: October 4, 1953; NBC-TV.
With The Skylarks and Sidney Sillman.
Cast: Marc Platt, Fay McKenzie, Peter Leeds, Byron Kane, Eddie Ryder, Frankie Branda, Suzanne Ames, Dona Cole, Maria English.
Special Guest Star: Burt Lancaster.
Announcer: Hal Sawyer
Writers: Ed Simmons, Norman Lear, Arthur Phillips, Austin Kalish, Danny Arnold.
Television Director: Bud Yorkin
Producer & Director: Ernest D. Glucksman.

OPENING: A crowd waits at New York Harbor for Dean and Jerry's return from Europe. The two disembark and perform a song-and-dance about their trip, which includes comic observations of Great Britain, France, Germany and Ireland. "We want to be specific, the continent's terrific," they sing, "but it sure is great to be home!"

SKETCH #1: The subject is husbands who suffer from "television-itis." Paul (*Martin*) is watching the fights on TV in his living room, much to the dismay of his wife (*Fay McKenzie*), who feels he spends too much time glued to the set. However, each time the match gets exciting, a commercial comes on, and a pitchman (always *Lewis*) grabs the wife's attention. Each pitchman shows up with a product (a device that will "de-fuzz" your TV tube) or service (dance lessons), interrupting Paul's enjoyment of the boxing match even more. When Paul misses the fight's conclusion, he destroys his set in frustration, whereupon a junkman (*Lewis* again) shows up to collect it.

DEAN SOLO #1: Jerry plugs a *LOOK* magazine article about muscular dystrophy, and introduces Dean, who sings "You're the Right One" from *The Caddy*.

SKETCH #2: Dean and Jerry have checked into the Ritz-Bird Hotel. The two are out of the bedroom (brushing their teeth with *Colgate*) when a news bulletin comes on the radio: a dangerous patient, Doc Delaney, has escaped a local hospital. He is described as alcoholic and continuously calling for his dog, Sheba. At that moment, Delaney (*Burt Lancaster*) enters the room through a window. After a few scary moments, the boys discover him and, realizing he's insane, they introduce themselves as his nephews from Scranton, and try to humor him, without much success.

JERRY SOLO: Jerry tells the audience that he and Dean like to answer requests, and that viewers have asked why they don't dance on the show more often. He explains that dancing is not what it used to be. With the help of an elderly woman, Jerry demonstrates a slow waltz of thirty years before. With a bobby-soxer, he dances the Jitterbug of ten years earlier. "Now we'll show you why people don't dance anymore." He and an elegantly gowned woman proceed to stomp back and forth across the stage to one of the Hit Parade's top tunes: the staccato theme to *Dragnet*. At the conclusion, she takes Jerry's arm over her shoulder and pulls him offstage.

DEAN SOLO #2: Dean sings "That's Amore" (also from *The Caddy*).

FINALE: Jerry conducts the band while Dean sings "There's No Tomorrow."

ANALYSIS AND REVIEWS: For the second year in a row, Martin & Lewis hosted *Colgate's* season opener with a show that was less than their best.

The mini-musical was an interesting departure from the old 'Dean-and-Jerry-destroy-something' opener; only trouble is it's neither funny nor clever. The trip itself made headlines when the team lambasted the British press for giving their opening a negative review and publicizing the booing from a small, anti-American claque. There's no mention of this in the number, for which The Skylarks portray American reporters. The boys do the same dance steps for every country they describe in song; only when Jerry dons a frilly skirt and dances the can-can does the number (and the studio audience) roar to life.

The 'Television-itis' sketch takes forever to go nowhere. Dean watches TV, Jerry does all the commercials as different pitchmen, after which he instantly arrives at Dean's home. But he never stays long, and only as Duvall the dance instructor does he engage in physical comedy with his partner. Almost none of Jerry's commercial dialogue is humorous; the few laughs mostly derive from his facial expressions. Dean's dialogue is sparse, and most of it sounds ad-libbed. Unlike 1951's "Everyone-is-Jerry" sketch, he doesn't try to make funny; each time the televised fight resumes, he repeats the same lines ("Hit him with your fist! Hit him with *his* fist!"). Also, scenes showing the match on TV are sloppy. The narration never matches the action, and whoever looped the boxing footage forgot to remove the leader, which can clearly be seen at one point. The biggest audience reaction comes on a gag the team had used time and again: big items (in this case musicians) are removed from a container too small to hold them.

The second sketch is a parody of *Come Back, Little Sheba*. In the original film, Lancaster played the alcoholic Doc Delaney and Shirley Booth played Lola, the wife who pined for their lost dog, Sheba. Booth won the Best Actress Academy Award for her performance, something Delaney doesn't let his invisible wife forget in this sketch. "Take your Oscar and get out!" he screams before ordering the boys to toss her through the window. This sketch is clever at least, but it's not terribly amusing. The biggest laugh comes when Jerry's prop suitcase malfunctions. He turns to the audience and explains how it was supposed to send his clothes flying into the air when opened, "but we ran short of money and couldn't get a spring."

Dean does his usual fine work on both solos, although the first was performed on film, for reasons unknown. "There's No Tomorrow" hadn't

Burt Lancaster with the boys on the October 4, 1953 *Colgate Comedy Hour*.
Photo courtesy of Kayley Thompson.

changed much since it appeared during the first season, except for one new gag: as the music builds to a crescendo, conductor Jerry rushes headlong into the orchestra, colliding with musicians and knocking them and their stands over. It's a show-stopping moment that rates the biggest laugh and loudest applause of the evening.

As usual, the team walked off with a resounding victory in the ratings race. Trendex gave them an audience share of 62.2, with Ed Sullivan's *Toast of the Town* a distant second: 31.8.

Variety's 'Trau' summed it all up as "A good show, but not from their top section," labeling the 'Television-itis' sketch "noisy and replete with slapstick that just didn't register effectively," and the *Sheba* takeoff as the moment when "the hilarious capers identified with the team [finally] came off." *Daily Variety*, always more cheerfully disposed toward the pair than their East Coast sister, also noted the program's weaknesses but gave Dean and Jerry the benefit of the doubt. "While some of their past shows have been faster and funnier," wrote 'Helm,' "last night's takeoff wasn't mild by any means. What slowed the tempo… were sketches that lacked inspired comedics both in word and action." The reviewer also noticed that "Ed Simmons and Norman Lear have three new helpers on the script this season but they've done better before by themselves." Little did Helm know that this would be the last *Colgate* for the two scribes.

Having completed their near-term obligation to NBC, the boys went to work on *Living It Up*, which co-starred the leading lady of Jerry's Gar-Ron films, Janet Leigh. Her memory of making the picture was that it wasn't far removed from the home movies: "They clowned around and such, but that was part of their charm… it was great fun, but it was still very professional." They had two distractions: the guest appearance on the Bud Abbott-hosted *Comedy Hour*, where they took over the final 15 minutes, and their long-awaited "telethon" for muscular dystrophy.

* * * * *

DEAN MARTIN AND JERRY LEWIS PRESENT THEIR RADIO AND TELEVISION PARTY FOR MUSCULAR DYSTROPHY

Broadcast Live from the Carthay Circle Theater in Hollywood
Airdate: November 25, 1953; ABC Radio and Television Networks
(East Coast)
(West Coast kinescope and transcription airdate: December 1, 1953)
Featuring: Eddie Cantor, The Minneapolis Letter Carriers Quartet,
Carole Richards, Walter Scharf & His Orchestra, Phil Harris, Anna
Maria Alberghetti, Jane Wyman, Danny Thomas, Sammy Cahn, Bar-

bara Bates, Spike Jones & His City Slickers, Vic Damone, Phil Silvers, Jules Styne.
Directed by Stuart D. Phelps
Produced and Directed by Ernest D. Glucksman

DESCRIPTION: Eddie Cantor introduces Dean and Jerry. They introduce William Dougherty, President of the National Association of Letter Carriers, who briefly explains the Letter Carriers' role in the campaign. Jerry introduces the Minneapolis Letter Carriers Quartet, who sing "Sentimental Journey."

Dean sings "That's Amore," and Jerry sets the stage for his trumpet solo, but is halted by Dean, who tells him it's not time for that yet. They introduce Carole Richards, who sings "Over the Rainbow." Conductor Walter Scharf leads the orchestra in a medley of songs from the Danny Kaye film *Hans Christian Andersen*, which had been released exactly one year earlier.

Jerry tries to play his trumpet solo, but is again stopped by Dean, who introduces Phil Harris. Harris sings "Minnie the Mermaid." Dean returns to sing "You Alone" (recorded by Perry Como), and dedicates it to "his kids" (there are over a dozen children on the stage with him). Jerry is jealous and asks the camera to show *his* kids, which turn out to be two chimpanzees. He then speaks in earnest about muscular dystrophy, explaining that although the exact cause hasn't been identified, the researchers are certain that, with nine million dollars they would be able to acquire enough radium to eradicate the disease. He also explains that the letter carriers will be spending their days off – including Thanksgiving Day—collecting the envelopes that have been distributed, and asks that viewers please fill them to the best of their ability.

Dean introduces Anna Maria Alberghetti, who sings an operatic number and a popular song, "Sing, Sing." Jerry conducts the band as a zany chorus for Dean's rendition of "Once in Awhile" (a routine they'd performed on their second *Colgate* show). Then Jerry brings out his trumpet once more. He is again stopped by Dean, who explains that it's time for a station break.

This is perhaps the biggest glitch in the show: Dean is told he's three minutes early for the break, so Jerry conducts as the band plays a straight version of "Gypsy." Then the pair do a quick buck & wing dance, with Jerry taking a pratfall. The picture fades for the break - but there really isn't one, so the picture returns as Dick Stabile and the band are playing "Lullaby of Broadway," intended as filler for the studio audience during the "break." When the number is over, and everyone finally realizes they're back on the air (having never really left it), Jerry—who is on camera—has to tell the director three times to switch to his partner.

When Dean finally appears, he introduces actress Jane Wyman, and the two sit down to discuss what the letter carriers are doing and precisely how the money they're collecting will be used. When the camera cuts back to Jerry, he's joined by Dean to introduce Danny Thomas—but the two are surprised by the news that there's a *real* station break coming up. Both are at a loss on how to fill the two minutes, until Dean has an idea. He reminds Jerry that they've never told a joke in their entire career, and (with a slap on the face) instructs him to do so. Jerry begins a long-winded, pointless story about attending a party in 1921 ("Mae Busch and Chester Conklin were there"), and he's cut off before finishing.

When they return, the boys resume their introduction of Danny Thomas, who does a couple of stand-up routines and concludes with "The Best Things in Life are Free." Then Dean sings "The Christmas Blues," accompanied by Sammy Cahn (who wrote the lyrics) on piano. Jerry comes on with the trumpet, but Dean informs him that he's supposed to sing instead. Jerry sings "With These Hands," then chats about the letter carriers' "mission of mercy" with actress Barbara Bates (who appeared with them in *The Caddy*).

Spike Jones and His City Slickers provide a raucous rendition of "The Poet and Peasant Overture," as well as generous plugs for their Universal-International picture, *Fireman, Save My Child*. Jerry introduces the tuxedo-clad stage crew (most of whom are cleaning up after the City Slickers). Dean introduces "another of my paisanos," Vic Damone, who sings "Wrap Your Troubles in a Dream" and "I Can Tell."

Jerry has Dean move the piano onto the stage while he introduces "one of *my* people," Phil Silvers. With Julie Styne on piano, Silvers plays Hoagy Carmichael's "Stardust" on the clarinet. His playing is impressive, which he doesn't fail to remind us ("Ladies and Gentlemen: what you just heard cost my mother and father thirty-thousand dollars!"), but halfway through he's interrupted by members of Stabile's band who play better. Silvers takes this out on Styne.

With several minutes to go, Dean sings "I Don't Care if the Sun Don't Shine," then he and Jerry do their "Talk of the Town" routine, which they'd performed on their first *Comedy Hour* (with a slight variation: instead of asking Dean to coax him with halvah, Jerry requests a pizza). They close out with "There's No Tomorrow," exactly as performed on their most recent *Colgate* program. With one minute of airtime left, Dean finally allows Jerry to play the trumpet. Credits roll as Dean thanks the audience and Jerry struggles to play "Where or When."

ANALYSIS AND REVIEWS: During the filming of *Living It Up*, Martin and Lewis prepared for their second televised fundraising event, this one entirely for the benefit of Muscular Dystrophy. Since they were making a picture, an all-day broadcast was out of the question. Instead, Lewis enlisted the aid of the National Association of Letter Carriers who would deliver, and later collect, postage-paid envelopes (embossed with the faces of Dean and Jerry) to be used for MDA donations. The deliveries and collections were to be made on the carriers' own time, and Dean and Jerry would publicize the carriers' "mission of mercy" on a radio and television special on Thanksgiving Eve (which the West Coast would see and hear via kinescope and transcription six days later). Since NBC had banned fundraising shows the previous January, the struggling ABC network offered free airtime.

Originally the show was to run for four hours and an impressive talent roster had been announced for the simulcast: Bing Crosby, Jack Benny, June Allyson, Dick Powell and Jeff Chandler, among others. At the start of November, however, the major talent unions, claiming that televised drives had become "dreadfully overdone," instituted an immediate ban of all network telethons. Columnist John Lester noted, "This has put Dean Martin and Jerry Lewis in hot water, since they've already announced a four-hour benefit for muscular dystrophy on ABC-TV...but they now come under the ban as it pertains to the networks." ABC and the team pointed out that this wasn't a traditional telethon, since there'd be no telephone pledges. They cut the broadcast to two hours, in hopes the program would be considered more of a spectacular than a telethon, but the biggest names, fearful of their unions' costly reprimands, dropped out anyway.

The few remaining performers would do their scheduled turns, but even with airtime cut in half, there was padding: the *Hans Christian Andersen* medley conducted by its composer, Walter Scharf (whom Lewis hired to score *Living It Up*), four songs from Dean and one from Jerry, and several Martin & Lewis routines. A running gag had been conceived whereby Jerry would attempt a trumpet solo, only to be put off by Dean, who insisted that the next act needed to be introduced. This bit worked for a while, until Martin was forced to postpone Lewis's trumpet in favor of Lewis's singing.

A rehearsal shot for the opening of the January 10, 1954 *Colgate Comedy Hour*.
Photo courtesy of Kayley Thompson.

In preparing for the simulcast, Dean was as supportive of his partner as always. When NBC waived the team's contract in ABC's face and said, "You can't use them. They're exclusive to us," it was Dean who told NBC in rather earthy language what they could do with themselves. But during the show itself, Martin's patter had a bit of an edge to it. Possibly the stress of doing the program while performing in a movie—and the need to work harder than expected to cover up the no-shows—left him a little frazzled. Whatever the cause, this show marked the first telltale signs that all was not well in Martin-&-Lewis-Land.

After Jerry's earnest speech about MD and the letter carriers, Dean tells him, "That was beautifully done. You talk a lot, but you talked so beautifully that time, I wanted to put my arms around you and hit you right square in the eye." Perhaps he was trying to be funny, but his face registers nothing but disgust and it kills the joke. Later, when introducing Lewis's song—a quite competent rendition of "With These Hands" —Martin offers a comment seemingly about his partner's build: "He's not thin anymore. He's put on a little weight—got it all up in his head." For his part, Jerry—calmly and in his natural voice—orders Dean to move the grand piano to the stage. When a stage hand offers to help, Jerry, pointing at his partner, says, "No, no; this fellah will do it."

Technically, the program is a farce. Apart from the glaring "station break" glitch, there are other problems. The Carthay Circle Theater appears to be quite cramped—as evidenced by the fact that the team repeatedly needs to move the piano on and off stage—and this hampers their antics. Indeed, when Spike Jones and His City Slickers finish their bit, the set looks like a tornado swept through it, even though only a couple of music stands and band chairs have been knocked over. For some inexplicable reason, just as Danny Thomas is beginning his routine, someone plants a stationary microphone in front of him, even though he was coming over the boom mic just fine. Evidently the latter needed to be somewhere else, and he's just as taken aback as we are at the interruption.

Colgate producer Ernie Glucksman staged the show as best he could, but much of his work is sabotaged by ABC's technical director, Stuart D. Phelps, who had never worked with Martin & Lewis. Camera placement is very poor, particularly in those moments when cue cards are being used. When Dean and Jane Wyman make their pitch, it's painfully obvious that the cards are either too far away or not well lit. The two strain to read and remain natural, but all pretense is lost when Martin is forced to pause and say, "I wish you'd turn the card." Phelps also appeared to have no knowledge of the team's work; favoring close-ups in semi-profile, which diluted the effectiveness of Lewis's mugging, and occasionally switching the live camera to Dean just in time to miss one of Jerry's sight gags.

As for sight gags, there are enough of them to make you wonder how the radio audience could have enjoyed the show more than intermittently. Nearly all the Martin & Lewis routines, the running gag with the trumpet and the bit where the team introduces their "kids," were visual (and, in

Dean's case, the joke went completely over the heads of the audience). The worst offender was Spike Jones, who indulged in a lengthy silent bit with his banjo player, Freddie Morgan, who comes across as a bargain-basement Harpo Marx. The business lasts nearly five minutes and must have mystified radio listeners, assuming any held out that long without turning the dial.

At least one critic enjoyed the result: Pittsburgh's Harold V. Cohen wrote in *TV Guide* that the two were "better than they've ever been…. They should do all of their shows without a script." On the flip side, *Variety's* 'Chan' didn't pull any punches: "Martin & Lewis's two-hour network stint for Muscular Dystrophy could have been a stroke of genius… (eliminating) the need for phone calls, telegrams, frenzied pitches for more dough, giveaways, and all the impediments to good showmanship that normally encumber a telethon. But they fluffed it. (The) entire production seemed to be pasted together at the last moment in a haphazard manner… the overall effect, via insufficient preparation and routining *(sic)* and poor technical setup and execution, was highly disappointing. (The) radio end of the simulcast couldn't have been too edifying either, what with long periods of silence and emphasis on sight gags and action."

All-in-all, the show was a mixed blessing, worthy of preservation if only for being the earliest surviving complete Muscular Dystrophy telecast. Whatever its failings, they assuredly had no impact on the team's reputation. The fact that the show aired from 11:00pm to 1:00am on the East Coast, and from 10:30pm to 12:30am via kinescope on the West, over a network with fewer affiliates than NBC, guaranteed they had a much smaller home audience than usual. The MDA had no complaint; when the letter carriers were done, $3,342,950 had been collected, marking the campaign a resounding success.

Still, *Variety's* harsh criticism undoubtedly stung Lewis, given his devotion to this cause. And if Dean was starting to burn with resentment at Jerry's control of the act, Chan threw a log on the fire with this comment: "There was a little too much of Martin's singing." Why four straight songs in two hours was considered "too much," when Dean had been singing three per half-hour radio show, is a mystery Chan didn't bother to explain.

Martin and Lewis went back to work on *Living It Up*, which had another four weeks to go, when reports circulated that the two were openly feuding. "Visitors to the set," read one such account, "had been telling stories of embittered sessions of name-callings and one instance outside the stage where Martin jumped up and down on Jerry's bicycle in an at-

The debut performance of one of Lewis' most popular pantomimes took place on the *Comedy Hour* of January 10, 1954.

tempt to smash it." It got to the point where Dean took on the task of quelling the rumors, claiming it was all "off-stage gagging."

"We're always insulting each other. But our insults are never in a serious vein. It's only our own particular way of showing our love and respect for one another.... To Jerry and me and to all those who really know us, the very idea of a break in our friendship, let alone a professional divorce, simply isn't in the books. Sure we quip and yell and howl and even call each other names. We'll probably continue to do so. We can't change our style of close friendship now, so let the chips fall where they may." He also took issue with claims that he was growing "disgusted" with his partner's tendency to favor performing over physical health. "I was mighty worried, that's all—not disgusted. That zany screwball means a lot to me, and not only from a financial standpoint, either. Any implication that my concern is based on money is utterly false. I happen to love the kid like a brother and I hate to see him in pain. Maybe Jerry is a little too enthusiastic about taking those falls but I for one know he is taking good care of himself."

Left unspoken was the true point of contention between them. *Living It Up* was partially owned and funded by Dean, and his character, Dr. Steve Harris—while not as out-and-out unlikable as in most of their Hal Wallis productions—is a self-serving cad, using his misdiagnosis of Jerry's Homer Flagg to score them a trip to New York City and himself a chance to woo the gorgeous blonde reporter Wally Cook (*Janet Leigh*), whose paper is funding the trip. Meanwhile, Homer develops his own crush on Wally, and even takes a serious turn at the film's love song, "How Do You Speak to an Angel," right at the moment when he discovers she prefers Steve. It's an open bid for sympathy that pits the audience against Martin and Leigh's romance until near the end, when Homer selflessly grants his blessing to the couple.

Lewis' desire for undistilled pathos was having its inevitable effect: the diminishing of Martin. Fifty years after the fact, Lewis openly admitted he was focused on his growing ego, his love of filmmaking and "the unlimited comic possibilities for the Jerry character on screen," to the point where "I was developing a certain myopia about Dean." Inevitably, his myopia carried over to the *Comedy Hour*, where his next creative decision only widened the growing breach between him and his partner.

BETWIXT AND BETWEEN: *Simmons and Lear*

DEAN: "Being busy in pictures, television, radio, night clubs and theatres makes it pretty hard to create all our own gimmicks. So we have a couple of writers—Ed Simmons and Norman Lear—who work with us in most of these mediums."

JERRY: "Who needs them?"

– As quoted in SCREEN MAGAZINE,
May 1953 issue

By the time October was nearing its close, Lewis decided the answer to his question was "We do." Thus were Simmons and Lear signed by the team to a non-exclusive pact that paid them $10,400 per script for five shows. The deal, said *Variety* in its October 28 issue, "will net them a record $52,000 while leaving them free for other scripting chores." Yet within six weeks, Lewis would change his answer to "We don't," and fire them.

What had happened in the interim? Simply that Simmons and Lear had hired a press agent to trumpet their record-breaking salary. It was a natural reaction; now that they were no longer exclusive to Martin & Lewis, they'd want to advertise in order to score additional work. And as with any commodity, what you advertise had better be more desirable than the competition. When producers with enough writing budget went looking for comedy talent, what could be more desirable than the scripters for the nation's number one comedy act?

Yet there was a dark side of which Simmons and Lear should have been aware: comedians generally don't pay writers to take the bows. In its January 13, 1954 issue, *Variety* noted "The [reason for the firing] most frequently quoted is that the comics resented an exclusive Page One story in DAILY VARIETY noting the writers' precedential deal in terms of money. Understood M&L figured that made them too important and also pointed up they needed the most expensive writers in the business to hold their rated position."

Additionally, the contract had reset the market value for the commodity. "Martin and Lewis have brought joy to the hearts of TV comedy writers for announcing that they would pay their own particular brace of writers $52,000 this season," began an editorial in the November 27, 1953 issue of *TV Guide*. That couldn't have won them a lot of admiration from their fellow comedians.

The two scribes also changed agencies, leaving MCA, which still represented their employers, and signing with William Morris; this could also have strained the working relationship. Finally, it's possible that, after more than three years of exclusively writing for Martin & Lewis for TV, radio, stage and motion pictures, Simmons & Lear were approaching burnout. Given most of the trade reviews from last season, not to mention the previous show, Lewis might well have been burned out on them. Whatever the true reasons for the firing, Simmons and Lear dutifully turned in a script for the forthcoming show, which reportedly went straight into Lewis's wastebasket, while Kalish and Phillips, augmented by Danny Arnold and Harry Crane, carried the ball.

* * * * *

Is Dean really angry? Yes, he is. The closing shot of the finale for
the January 10 *Comedy Hour*.

THE COLGATE COMEDY HOUR: Dean Martin & Jerry Lewis Show #20.

Airdate: January 10, 1954; NBC-TV.
With The Modernaires, Franklin Pangborn, Duke Art, Jr., Birdie Brick-
erbrack
Cast: Buck Young, Bobby Faye, Jane Easton, Tyler McVey, Donald
Lawton, Bob Carson, Gus Schilling, Lee Wilson, Snub Pollard, Danny
Arnold
Announcer: Hal Sawyer
Choreography: Nick Castle
Writers: Arthur Phillips, Austin Kalish, Danny Arnold, Harry Crane
Television Director: Bud Yorkin
Producer & Director: Ernest D. Glucksman

OPENING and DEAN SOLO: While being told in song to "Wait in Line,"
a crowd has gathered to see the Martin & Lewis stage show. A troupe

of singers introduces Dean, then Jerry, but only Dean comes out. Dean begins a song, "I've Got a Right to Sing the Blues," but is disturbed by an overlong horn counterpoint. Moving toward the bandstand he sees that the trumpeter is Jerry. The two argue, with Dean labeling his partner "Incorrigible." Jerry leaves and Dean sings "Pretty Baby." In a satire of Montgomery Clift's *From Here to Eternity* character, Jerry returns in an army uniform and bugle, calling himself "Pvt. Robert E. Lee Pruitt," and Dean interviews him. At the conclusion of this bit, Jerry presents Dean with a gold record for "That's Amore."

SKETCH #1: We are in Martin & Lewis's dressing room, and Dean is on the phone with his arranger, going over the music for their upcoming stint at the Copacabana. Jerry arrives with lunch and tells Dean his cousin Herbie has written a new song for him: "The Alligator Hop-Jump-Skip-and-Slide Song." Mr. Balaban (*Tyler McVey*), the head of Paramount, arrives with his wife, son and daughter, to discuss a picture deal with the team. Jerry promises to be on his best behavior. Mr. Balaban tries to discuss matters solely with Dean, but Jerry keeps interrupting and making a mess, especially when he's acting as their servant. When the food arrives it has to be served on their laps, so Jerry extends a hand towel to act as a protective cloth. However he causes it to snap back and the food is spilled all over the Balaban family. After the Balabans have departed, the theater manager (*Donald Lawton*) asks Dean and Jerry to placate the fans that are blocking traffic outside. They toss photographs, their ties and their jackets, but the fans loudly chant, "We Want Dean! We Want Jerry!" so they dive out the window.

GUEST ACTS: Having retrieved their jackets, Dean and Jerry make their way to the stage door, when they're besieged by autograph hunters. While they sign, an agent (*Gus Schilling*) approaches them with a supporting act for their Copa engagement: The Modernaires, who sing "Crazy, Man, Crazy." As they sing, the fans gathered outside begin to dance. They also sing an up-tempo version of the Halo Shampoo jingle.

DEAN SOLO #2: As he's having his shoes shined backstage, Dean sings "Easy to Remember."

SKETCH #2: With only 40 minutes until their next show, Dean and Jerry have gone to Brubaker's toy department to find a gift for Dean's son Ricci. There is a special display: a woman's face shaped with "Miracle Play

Clay" which its inventor (*Duke Art, Jr.*) is hoping to sell to the store. The floorwalker (*Franklin Pangborn*) assures him that Mr. Brubaker will be interested. Dean and Jerry arrive, and in less than 10 minutes, Jerry tries to steal a boy's licorice, knocks the floorwalker into a wading pool, creates an explosive liquid with a child's chemistry set (which lands on the floorwalker), and obliterated the clay face. A furious Mr. Art walks out, threatening to sue Martin & Lewis for ruining his sale. "We're gonna get sued again," Dean gripes, so Jerry poses as the model head and Dean as Mr. Art. The impressed Mr. Brubaker (*Danny Arnold*) wants the bust of Jerry's head for his office and appears to rip it off, much to Dean's dismay. But Jerry is intact, so Dean browbeats him again.

JERRY SOLO: Bob Carson explains that new sounds in popular music are a significant trend, and introduces Pietro del Canto (*Lewis*), who performs "for the first time on any stage a new work by Leroy Anderson." Pietro enters, sits down at a typewriter and mimes to Anderson's newly-released Decca recording of "The Typewriter."

The tension between Martin and Lewis is palpable in this candid still
from *3 Ring Circus* (1954).

FINALE: Dick Stabile introduces Dean Martin and "That's Amore," but Dean's barely through a verse when Jerry interrupts, expecting to do a number together. Dean roughly orders him off the stage. Jerry demands that he apologize or there'll be consequences. "I'll take the consequences!" says Dean. Jerry leaves; Dean resumes the song. Suddenly Jerry appears with a fistful of money and starts bribing the cameramen and boom operators to push Dean against the piano. Once Dean is trapped, Jerry hops on the piano and starts slapping him on the head. Even after Dean says, "You're overacting, Jerry!" his partner continues to box his ears and pull his hair, yelling, "Go on, sing! Sing!"

ANALYSIS AND REVIEWS: For their first show without Simmons and Lear, the team tried a new approach: tying (nearly) everything together with a theme. The opening number outside the theater leads to a facsimile of the Martin & Lewis stage show that incorporates Dean's first solo. The first sketch takes place in their dressing room between performances; it concludes with them diving out the window. When we return from the commercial, they're on the street headed back to the theater. After the Modernaires' performance of an early rock-n-roll tune, the two are just inside the theater, where Dean does his second song for the shoeshine boy. Prior to singing, he tells Jerry he wants to run to the store to get a present for Ricci, which sets up the second sketch. Only Jerry's solo and the surprisingly harsh finale are unrelated to the theme.

In a sense, the opening of this show is the old closing: after some brief clowning and a solo from Dean, Jerry comes out and the two do a nightclub routine. In this instance, the bit is brand new, although based somewhat on the type of impromptu interviews they did on radio. They'd perform it next at the Copa engagement that is repeatedly plugged during this show.

In the dressing room, and to a lesser degree the toy department, Martin is the classic straight man, with little or no patience for his partner's antics. He's still capable at breaking up when Lewis ad-libs, but he's not his usual bemused self the rest of the time: he barks orders at Lewis, grabs him and shoves him around. For his part, Jerry strives for sympathy, well-aware that he's being put-upon but following orders nevertheless. Still, the audience is primed for the ruckus that Jerry raises when serving food and drink to the Balaban family (although portrayed here by actors, Barney Balaban was the real-life head of Paramount), screaming with laughter at every slapstick indignity. No less funny is his solution when a towel dispenser malfunctions; he runs offstage, grabs a stagehand and forces the guy to hold the thing in place until the bit is over.

The highlight of the toy department is Franklin Pangborn taking a beating that Danny Arnold never would have countenanced. Pangborn was, of course, an old hand at slapstick, who'd done two-reelers under Mack Sennett's supervision. When he emerges in disarray, his face filthy and clothes shredded after an off-screen explosion, Dean can't keep from laughing, and when he subsequently lands yet again in the wading pool and flails about, even Jerry is laughing and impressed. Neither interrupts with an ad-lib, they simply step aside and admire the skill of an old pro. (Another two-reeler veteran, Snub Pollard, makes a thankless, unbilled appearance as a theater employee.)

Clad in tails and a fright wig, Lewis' rendition of "The Typewriter" is far and away the apex of his *Colgate* solo turns. "It could well become a classic of its kind," predicted *Daily Variety* and of course they were right: the piece turned into one of Lewis' most popular pantomimes; a standard in live performances up to the end of his life and even incorporated into one of his movies, *Who's Minding the Store?* (1963). This is his debut with the composition, and although he makes a few mistakes, it doesn't matter: his comic instincts and energy are enough to make even the miscues hilarious. There would be more polished performances over the decades, but he never again put it over with such zest as he does here.

Today, anyone even casually viewing the conclusion of this episode could perceive how angry Dean was at Jerry's "overacting," yet the critics never mentioned it. *Variety* called the show "a standout blending of trapping and staging that gave the madcap revelers socko support. The pacing was fast, the coordination was out of the top-drawer and the chorines were an eye-appealing assemblage of pulchritude…. There were plenty of sketches to please the M&L contingent and the boys gave their all in each."

Daily Variety's 'Kap' termed it "a seasonal high" for Colgate, adding, "Both music and comedy divisions were of sufficient caliber to keep the setsiders more than pleasantly occupied for the 60 minutes." An anonymous critic for the *Buffalo Courier-Express* opined the team "sparked a completely entertaining 'Comedy Hour.' Maybe it was because we hadn't been exposed to the Martin and Lewis brand of television mayhem for quite some time, but nevertheless the show was fast, frantic and funny."

Upon concluding the broadcast, the team headed back east for their first Copacabana engagement since 1951. It was considered such a milestone, Jerry had one of the shows filmed in 16mm sound. They opened on January 21 and three days later, while between Copa shows, appeared as the "mystery celebrities" for the real-life 'Guess the Guests,' *What's My Line*. When they sign in, they repeat the gag from the *Colgate* sketch where Jerry mangles his signature and Dean takes the chalk away from him. Once they're situated, Arlene Francis asks "Are you in pictures?" Jerry starts to answer, but is stopped by Dean, who threatens him with a fist. With a disguised voice, Dean answers "Yes." The same happens when asked if they're in television, but when Arlene asks, "Are you male?" Dean defers to Jerry, who pouts. In his own voice, Jerry says, "How're they gonna know it's us if they've got the masks on?" He keeps it up, and after the laughter dies down, Arlene says, "Well I guess I know who it is now!" "You'd *better* know who it is," Jerry replies, to which Arlene says, "If I said 'Milton Berle,' what'll you do?" After demonstrating the shtick they were doing while the panel was blindfolded, Jerry plugs their Copa appearance and *Money From Home*.

On stage and TV, all appeared normal. Offstage, the tension that had been brewing between the two partners for several months was about to spill out into the open.

* * * * *

SIDEBAR: *Martin vs. Lewis, Round One*

When "That's Amore" became Dean's first big smash at the end of 1953, it created a strain. Martin was justifiably proud of his accomplishment; it was something for which he'd been striving since before the team was born. Unfortunately, the insecurity within Lewis's psyche that had remained relatively dormant during the glory years began to flare. Maybe Dean would decide that he didn't need Jerry anymore. Maybe Dean was beginning to listen to those hangers-on who enjoyed telling each one that he'd be an even bigger star without the other. Rather than talk out his feelings, Lewis began to brood - and to assert his presence in their act, with the conclusion of the last *Comedy Hour* serving only as the most recent example.

In truth, Dean *was* growing weary of Jerry's antics overshadowing him, not to mention their hectic schedule, which left him little time to enjoy the fruits of success. He also couldn't have been pleased with the dismissal of Simmons and Lear, the writers who made sure *he* was funny, too. But his real bone of contention was their movies: the one element of their work destined for posterity. Martin clearly resented that most were cut from the same cloth: Jerry the innocent simpleton hero who carried the picture, and Dean the smooth sharpie who never seemed deserving of his partner's friendship... until the final reel when he suddenly became, in his words, "a good guy."

Another issue was festering. Lewis had always run the business side of the partnership and had been assisting their writers almost since the team began using them. All of this was fine with Martin, until Lewis began extending his involvement to other creative matters: the camera work, the casting, the directing. At NBC, he'd spend as much time on these things as he did rehearsing, while Martin sat around and waited. With *The Caddy*, he got a taste of the same in their motion picture work. In retrospect, Dean should have expected Jerry would want to graduate from elaborate home movie productions to the real thing. Up to now, he was only beginning to resent it, but with their next picture for Hal Wallis, he'd be openly disgusted as his partner's ambition left him in the dust.

Wallis and his partner Joe Hazen, along with their wives, were at the Copa and enjoyed the opening night performance from a ringside table. After the show, Wallis and Hazen met briefly with Martin and Lewis, setting up a luncheon meeting for the following day to discuss their next picture: "Big Top." The film had been in the planning stages for several weeks; the script written by Don McGuire, a friend and collaborator of Jerry's since 1951.

When Wallis asked Martin if he'd be attending, Lewis kiddingly advised his partner: "You'd better let me go with him alone. I can get more out of him." Given his growing disenchantment with the status quo, perhaps that should have thrown up a red flag for Dino. Up to now, Martin had grudgingly accepted their scripts as the nature of the business, believing neither he nor Lewis were in a position to tempt the fate of the box office. But with a friend of Jerry's as the lead writer, and with Jerry himself overseeing the results, perhaps he could expect something better this time. So Dean left the business to Jerry, who went over the script with Wallis and made several suggestions—for his own character.

On February 8, the scheduled first day of shooting, Wallis had the Clyde Beatty Circus, a fifteen-car train and eighty-five cast and crew members standing by on location in Phoenix, Arizona. All that was missing were the two stars, who refused to show up. The team's agent, Herman Citron, told Wallis bluntly that Dean refused to do the script as written— this despite the fact that it contained several of Jerry's suggestions—and Jerry wouldn't do the film against Dean's wishes.

McGuire and two of the team's *Colgate* writers, Arthur Phillips and Harry Crane, sat down and hammered out further revisions, while Martin, Lewis and Citron met with Wallis. Lewis confessed, "I am enough of a ham that when you told me this business with the elephants and the other sequences, that I could only see what wonderful things I could do..." to the point where he completely overlooked his partner's role, the conniving, slimy manager of the circus. It's not recorded whether Dean opined on how well his partner was looking out for him, but he did make his objections known about the script. Wallis later wrote, "He said that he doesn't want to play a cheat and doesn't know what he is doing in the picture."

Lewis, Phillips and Crane spent one more long night penning revisions, with Martin once again deferring to his partner. The end result wasn't much different, and Dean realized that it was endgame: with Jerry and their writers having turned in a final script, he'd have to go to work. But that didn't mean he'd have to *like* it.

Shooting for the film, eventually titled *3 Ring Circus*, began in Phoenix on February 17. Reportedly, two weeks went by before Dean was even needed for a scene, at which point some of the extras began wondering aloud about the size of his part and if he was still Jerry's partner. Young children hired for an orphanage scene would gather around Jerry; some of them didn't even know who Dean was. Lewis would later write, "It got pretty hairy. There were days when I thought Dean would ditch the whole package."

On March 3, Dean walked in on Jerry having his picture taken for publicity. He finally boiled over: "Hey, Jerry, what am I around here, a fifth wheel? If I'm not important to the act anymore, just let me know!" Reporters around the set got more from Martin: "I'm sick and tired of playing stooge to that crazy, mixed-up character!" Lewis retaliated with, "I'm fed up with my partner's sensitivity. Everything I do is wrong. Anything happens he don't *(sic)* like, he blames it on me. He hates me." The two stopped speaking and production nearly ground to a halt.

To the end of his days, Martin would excoriate *3 Ring Circus*, eventually projecting its flaws onto the team's entire cinematic canon. Here he was, once more, playing second fiddle—maybe even less—to his beloved partner, the *important* one, whom Wallis had not only permitted to select the film's writer and composer (Scharf again) but also its director, Joseph Pevney. The story had Dean singing only twice: once to caged animals, once to Jerry. This while "That's Amore" was still red hot and had just received an Oscar nomination for Best Song by the Motion Picture Academy!

This particular feud, the first to be reported, lasted eight days. On March 12, in a meeting at MCA, the pair were forcibly reminded of their various commitments and coerced into a cordial reconciliation. Lewis also, according to the *New York Journal-American's* Louis Sobol, "listened to Martin's complaint that he was 'sick and tired' of his partner's endeavor to 'run' everything, and promised from now on to let agents and others take care of things." Sobol also overheard Martin's muttered opinion of Lewis' promise: "He didn't think the agreement would last six months." Three days later, when Dean didn't appear at Jerry's birthday party—because he hadn't been invited—the gossip columnists again speculated on Martin and Lewis's rapidly diminishing future together.

A press release, signed by both, was issued on the 18th:

> *Since there seems to be an uncommonly large number of people in Hollywood and all the other parts of the country phoning reporters with daily communiques regarding the latest status of the Dean Martin-Jerry Lewis 'feud' and with the 'inside dope' as to the impending split-up of the team, we feel it our duty to give you the true facts. These are the facts, ma'am. Dum du dum dum.*
>
> *We had a disagreement. Well… it wasn't exactly a disagreement, it was a fight. It all started when Dean called me a dope. I got mad and told him to prove it and that's what we fought about. He did.*
>
> *What our 'unofficial' press agents don't know is that they are right. We are going to split up as a team. We have even picked the date. It will be on July 25, 1996, which will be our golden anniversary as a team. We figure by that time we will have enough kids between us to keep us supplied in wheel chair grease and bifocals.*
>
> *We sincerely hope we have cleared up this ridiculous situation and that everyone can get back to reading about Sheree North and her censored films.*
>
> *Warmest regards, Dean Martin-Jerry Lewis*

One week later, Dean appeared at the Hollywood Pantages to sing what was by now his signature song for the Oscar ceremony. Afterward, Bing Crosby would tell columnist Erskine Johnson, "He really put his heart into it. He sang it like the Academy members were still voting." Unfortunately voting had long been completed; the ultimate winner would be "Secret Love" from the Doris Day picture *Calamity Jane*. Perhaps what

Jerry about to drive into the camera...

Martin was actually doing was sending a message to Hollywood and Hal Wallis… and his partner.

Needless to say, the lighthearted press release didn't keep columnists at bay. Aline Mosby sought out Abbott & Costello at NBC the day of their latest *Colgate Comedy Hour*, for their take. How had they managed to just celebrate 18 years together? "It's as simple as this," Bud Abbott told her. "We lead separate lives, but we get together now and then for Christmas or birthdays. Another thing: there's no jealousy in our act. I don't profess to be the funny man, and Lou doesn't want to be the straight man." Lou Costello added, "When it's time to rehearse, we're business partners. After our TV show, I may see him at his home, or he may come to my home, but after today I probably won't see him for three weeks, until it's time for our next rehearsal."

On April 5, no less an authority than Groucho Marx felt compelled to write a personal letter: "I've been reading in columns that there is ill feeling between you boys and that there's even a likelihood that you might go your separate ways. I hope this isn't true for you are awfully good together, and show business needs you…. If there is any ill feeling

...and his partner's reaction. Scenes from the May 31, 1954 *Colgate Comedy Hour*.

or bitterness between you, it will eventually affect your work. If that feeling does exist, sit down calmly together, alone—when I say alone, I mean no agents, no family, no one but you two—sit down alone, and talk it out."

Reportedly Marx sent copies to both partners, but only Jerry replied, thanking Groucho profusely, noting "the sagacity of your words" and assuring him, "[I] have every intention of following your advice." And in fact Dean and Jerry did meet privately shortly thereafter, and things settled down.

Near the conclusion of shooting for *3 Ring Circus*, the two men spoke with writer Maurice Zolotow, of *The American Weekly*, a Sunday newspaper supplement. Dean instructed Zolotow to "write down this part word-for-word just like I say it. I know that individually, going it alone, we would not be as great as we are together." Martin further proclaimed, "When we shook hands on our partnership, I said in my heart, this is forever, 'til death do us part. It still goes! Sometimes he makes mistakes. Sometimes I make mistakes. But as long as people let us alone, the team of Martin & Lewis will go on."

For his part, Lewis told Zolotow, "The closer you are to a person, the deeper the feelings. If the feelings are hard feelings, then they're twice as hard. And if you're emotional, like Dean and I are emotional, well, you can't help flipping your lid sometimes. We yell at each other... and it gets in the papers. So from this they build up a story that we're going to bust up. Never in a million years! Get this: we're a partnership, a real partnership.

"This idea that I'm the funny guy and Dean is just a straight man is wrong. People may not notice it, but he's got as many joke lines as straight lines. I feed him as many straight lines on our television show as he feeds me. Both of us have a different style of playing comedy, but we're both essential to each other's success. Anyway," continued Lewis, "Dino means more to me than a partner in a two-act. Outside of my wonderful wife, Dean is the person I've been closest to in my whole life. We're so close that our minds think like one mind. There's a very deep and profound love between Dean and me, and our act is good only because of this feeling of closeness."

In wrapping up his article, Zolotow brought himself into it and proved exceptionally prophetic: "I would hazard a guess—and it is only a guess—that, unless there is a profound change of character to both men, the same conflicts that have exasperated them in the past will be repeated again and again.

"Sooner or later, Dean Martin and Jerry Lewis may attempt a trial separation. If, during this period, Jerry can prove to himself that he can make a superbly artistic masterpiece of comedy, and Dean can prove to himself that he can stand on his own two feet as an actor and a singer, then I doubt that the two of them ever will be united again.

"But I suspect that there is an almost chemical affinity between these two. That a mysterious catalytic reaction occurs when they are thrown together. And that this makes them a whole that is greater than the sum of its parts. If this is true, they will be compelled to come together again."

When the team came together for their next *Colgate* appearance, they would go to great lengths to showcase what Jerry termed their "very deep and profound love."

* * * * *

THE COLGATE COMEDY HOUR: Dean Martin & Jerry Lewis Show #21.

Airdate: May 2, 1954; NBC-TV.
With Dick Humphries, Gretchen Houser, The Treniers, Marvin Seed
Cast: Bob Carson, Frances Farwell, Helen Eby-Rock, Henry Slate, John Harmon, Charles Williams, Bobby Faye, Snub Pollard
Announcer: Hal Sawyer
Writers: Arthur Phillips, Harry Crane
Musical Direction: Dick Stabile
Choreography: Nick Castle
Television Director: Bud Yorkin
Producer & Director: Ernest D. Glucksman

OPENING: Martin & Lewis are returning to the 500 Club in Atlantic City for their 8th anniversary as a team, and the boardwalk is abuzz with anticipation. The boys arrive, and they dance and sing about all the places they've performed over the years, concluding, "When we got together in Atlantic City, that was a lucky day / We've seen a lot of show biz, but we found out there's no biz like working in a class café!"

SKETCH #1: The owner of the 500 Club (*Bob Carson*) tells a reporter (*Henry Slate*) how Dean and Jerry discovered each other: Dean was working as a waiter for room and board, and Jerry had just been hired as a busboy. In a flashback, Dean is getting ready for bed when Jerry arrives with his suitcase. He hangs his coat jacket in a closet and is trapped between all the other coats. After getting stuck with him, Dean extracts Jerry and tells him to go to bed, in the top bunk. Jerry keeps stepping on Dean, so they switch places. In order to hang a picture of his mother (a photo of Jerry with a blonde wig), he hammers a nail in the wall, and breaks a water pipe. He tries sealing the leak with bubble gum, which eventually explodes. While they're both out of the room, a musician leaves his accordion under the bed. Jerry plays "Lady of Spain" on the bed until a frustrated Dean removes the accordion. They put it in the closet, but Jerry knocks over a bucket of sand. He leaves to get a broom. The musician returns with a female singer (*Frances Farwell*) to practice on the piano in the room. Dean claims he's really a singer and asks for a chance. He sings "I'm in the Mood for Love" as Jerry returns and begins sweeping up the sand. Enthralled with Dean's voice, he fails to pay attention and removes

Lewis rehearses The Skylarks for the May 31, 1954 *Comedy Hour* as a barely interested Martin looks on. Photo courtesy of Kayley Thompson.

the female singer's skirt. The owner comes in and fires Jerry, who sadly leaves.

DEAN SOLO #1: Although it's their lunch break, Dean talks pianist Lou Brown into playing for him while he sings "If You Were the Only Girl." At the song's end, we see that other workers have gathered around and are applauding. The club owner comes out, orders the others back to work and fires Dean: "Singers are a dime-a-dozen. What I need is good waiters, and you're not one of them."

GUEST ACT: The owner calls for a run-through of a production number, which is an elaborate dance performed by Dick Humphries and Gretchen Houser.

SKETCH #2: We're still in the past, and Dean's working at a store that sells records and musical instruments. He's dusting up when the boss (*John Har-*

mon) tells him "the agency's sending over a new man to help out." The boss leaves for the bank, and Dean continues dusting. The "new man" is Jerry, who arrives as Dean is cleaning out the inside of a tuba. Jerry can't resist and blows into the mouthpiece, sending Dean into shock. Next, Jerry accidentally pulls a table away just as Dean is placing a pile of records on it; the disks all break. This time, Dean goes for the broom, telling Jerry "don't move a muscle." A customer (*Charles Williams*) wants to find an instrument for his son; he's looking at the horns, but Jerry tries to sell him a bass drum. Dean sees this and carries the drum away, while Jerry continues pounding it. Again, Dean tells Jerry to stay still while he leaves the room. A delivery boy (*Snub Pollard*) wheels in Dean's lunch. Once again a customer (*Helen Eby-Rock*) enters; this one wants a record and asks for suggestions. Jerry puts on a disk of classical "dinner music" and proceeds to eat Dean's lunch to it, but as the music gets more raucous, the food is destroyed. Disgusted, the woman leaves just as Dean returns. Angry at the loss of his lunch, he shoves Jerry into a phone booth which collapses around him. The owner returns and fires them both. Dean wants to know, "How can you make so many mistakes in one day?" "I think 'cause I get up early," says Jerry and Dean laughs. Deciding that Jerry is funny, Dean suggests they work together in show biz, and this leads to a duet: "We Belong Together."

DEAN SOLO #2: It's now the present day at the 500, and the owner introduces Jerry, who in turn introduces Dean because "the old pizza eater's getting a little older as the years go on, and the voice is just about gone." Dean sings "Almost Like Being in Love."

FINALE: Jerry comes out and the two introduce The Treniers, joining them in a rousing rendition of "Rockin' is Our Bizness." There's time left over after the final commercial, so the group sings "Palmolive Soap" to the music while Dean and Jerry talk about the Palmolive School Girl Beauty Contest and their upcoming 11-city tour.

ANALYSIS AND REVIEWS: Following the "storyline" format of their last broadcast, this celebratory show is a lighthearted preview of the team's return to the 500 Club scheduled for mid-July, the dates coinciding with their true 8th Anniversary. The boardwalk bench, where after their first night of "who-the-hell-cares" comedy they sat, smoked and discussed a partnership, was being moved inside the club and marked with a plaque: "On this spot in July 1946, Dean Martin and Jerry Lewis became a team."

They'd also premiere *Living It Up* there on July 16, which the city declared "Martin & Lewis Day," complete with a parade, celebratory cake and an unscheduled late show at the 500 for an invited audience. The opening number here anticipates a touch of the event's spirit, although labeling the 500 Club "a class café" does a disservice to the word "class." Some two years later, the team appeared on live television from the actual club, which looked positively seedy compared to the glittering set for this Hollywood-based show.

After the opening, we're handed pure fiction. The sketch with Martin as a waiter and Lewis a new busboy who doesn't even make it onto the floor before getting sacked, is the first bona fide TV appearance of "lovable, wistful Jerry," the Chaplinesque "little schnook." He's still capable of destruction, except it's not propagated by an unrestrained id, but rather through sheer innocence. Thankfully, he's still capable of breaking character to get a laugh; one of the show's biggest comes after Jerry hammers his nail into the water pipe behind the wall. A steady jet emerges, which he tries to plug, but can't, so he calls on "Mr. Martin" for help. Sprayed in the face, Dean cries out, "A point of order"—a topical reference to the unintended "catch phrase" of the Army-McCarthy hearings then in progress. That's funny enough, but then Martin blocks the water with his hand, and Lewis tells him, "You're laughing, but you forgot to take your watch off!" Now laughing *and* cringing, Martin switches hands and gets an ovation from the audience. Beyond that, the sketch has Lewis creating accidental chaos until he's dismissed, and concludes on a sad note as he gathers his belongings, says a quiet goodbye to Martin and departs.

After Dean's first solo, Dick Humphries and Gretchen Houser, along with a company of background dancers, perform a lively number that at least has the advantage of looking like it belongs in 1946. Then it's back to unintentional havoc with Martin in a music store and Lewis as the "new boy." He's barely there a minute when he's unknowingly disturbing the table upon which Martin expects to place an armful of 78s, which of course shatter. And the audience is with him: when Dean goes to get a broom, telling Jerry, "You stand there, real nice and stupid like you are," people can be heard groaning, shocked that Martin could be so harsh to this lovable kid. The highlight here is the "dinner music" bit, where Lewis eats in time with the various classical pieces (actually being played live by Stabile's orchestra). As with the typewriter, it's a clever piece of musical mime; *unlike* the typewriter, there's little to no subtlety to Lewis' performance.

Although the conclusion is the same, with both getting fired, this sketch doesn't end sadly but rather segues into a specialty duet written by Danny Shapiro and Hal Borne:

DEAN: We belong together; like romance and flings, horses and swings,
JERRY: Juleps and mints, lighters and flints,
BOTH: We belong together!

BOTH: We go strong together;
DEAN: Like honey and bees, pizzas and cheese
JERRY: Benches and parks, Groucho and Marx,
BOTH: We belong together!

BOTH: Delilah found romance with Sampson, her fella.
    The Dodgers are nowhere without Camp-anella!

BOTH: We belong together;
DEAN: Like judges and fines, Duncan and Hines,
JERRY: Buttons and bows, Broadway and shows,
BOTH: Like Fibber McGee and Molly; Kukla, Fran and Ollie,
Buddy, we belong together!

Intended to reassure viewers that the recent feud was a one-time occurrence, the number also incorporates a bit of soft shoe which they mostly perform hand-in-hand. The following season would see the tune employed as the closing theme for their *Comedy Hours*.

Since Jerry's solo spot was incorporated into the last sketch, he humorously introduces Dean's next number. After that come The Treniers, a bona-fide rhythm and blues combo, proclaiming "Rockin' is Our Bizness." The Treniers were known to have influenced pioneering white rockers such as Bill Haley. Aside from its value as an early rock-n-roll performance, their appearance here might have been influential in another way. Nineteen year-old Elvis Presley was a Dean Martin fan and likely watching this evening. Up to this point, he'd made a couple of private recordings of various ballads. Two months after this show, while auditioning at Sun Records in Memphis, he and two session musicians spontaneously worked up a lively rendition of "That's Alright, Mama," and literally jump-started his future. It's not a stretch to imagine Presley grooving to The Treniers and wondering if rocking might be *his* business.

Some controversy surrounds this show, in that Martin apparently knew it was going to come up short and suggested to Lewis that he sing a third song. His suggestion was dismissed; exactly how *that* went down is unknown. But the evidence is on the kinescope: after the two plug Palmolive's Most Beautiful Schoolgirl contest, list the cities of their upcoming tour, and remind viewers that Jimmy Durante will be next week's host, Dean turns to Jerry and says, "I told ya I should've sung another song; we wouldn't have had to stretch here!"

As usual, *Daily Variety's* 'Helm' loved it: "From the opening gun, M&L were off like a shot in as mad a mélange of props and gimmicks as has been seen on the tv sets in year of Sundays. The bedlam gave the lookers little respite from their maniacal madness, the comics catching their breath only during the intrusion of the filmed commercials.... They never worked harder or were more deliriously received by an audience that rocked with the gags and calloused their hands from applauding." And, as usual, *Variety* was a little bit pickier, 'Jose' writing: "It's been a long time since these zanies cavorted and consequently many would regard this as a special occasion. But on the basis of past performances by this team, it's somewhat subpar, mainly because they can do and have done better.... Probably the highlight of the session was Lewis' interpretation of 'music to eat by.' Latter was a unique bit of business."

The team's biggest booster, John Lester of the *Long Island Star-Journal*, perceived something troubling beneath the surface, and used his entire space on May 7 trying to define it: "I've bled a good deal just thinking about today's column. I've bled over it for weeks, in fact, but after watching Dean Martin and Jerry Lewis on last Sunday's [show], it seemed the time had come to write it.

"In substance it is merely that Dean and Jerry are through as a team, at least as the wildly irresponsible, madcap, loveable, hilarious team the public has known on television for the past three years. The boys may remain together physically for years—and maybe not—but the pure blending of two uninhibited comic spirits is no more. It's not only tarnished or sullied, this blending, but it's gone entirely and some lesser thing has taken its place....

"Naturally, those of us who watched Martin and Lewis from the beginning knew the indefinable something they had, in addition to their many talents, the something that lifted them above the heads of most performers, and we also knew it couldn't last forever. These things never do last forever, and all one can do is fervently hope they'll last as long as possible. In the case of Martin and Lewis, 'as long as possible' apparently meant about eight years."

Lester summed up their recent feud, up to the joint press release, and opined that "something characteristically flip, or the impromptu drenching of the reporter who inquired as to the state of affairs, all in the spirit of the boys' normally wild nonsense, would have been more to the point. Anyhow, the joint statement was followed by several public appearances intended to show that all was well, but, apparently, whatever hurts there are had gone deep, as is frequently the case with hurts between sensitive people who've long been very close.

"I thought I saw clear evidence of this Sunday; not necessarily evidence of a hurt, a chill or a strangeness between the boys, but less evidence of the wholesome warmth and refreshing familiarity that made them act and think as one person in the past. Jerry seemed more aware of this than Dean, at least he reacted to it more definitely. He worked harder, he 'pressed' more for comic effect and brought many of his laugh-provoking devices—the faces, the 'idiot' walks, the timing tricks, etc.—into play.

"As a result, we laughed, when we laughed, at devices and not at Jerry. In the past, we laughed at Jerry no matter what he did, with or without devices. There is a great difference…. If what I feel and fear really has taken place, then the chances are they'll rarely, if ever, equal their best TV shows again but will always be in danger of equaling their worst.

"I sure hope I'm wrong," Lester concluded. Unfortunately, he wasn't.

* * * * *

THE COLGATE COMEDY HOUR: Dean Martin & Jerry Lewis Show #22.

Airdate: May 30, 1954; NBC-TV.
With The Skylarks, The Nick Castle Dancers, Tom Ache-Latt, Sylvia Nift, Barney Holton, Paul Seatcover
Cast: Mary Ellen Kaye, Byron Kane, Paul Power
Announcer: Hal Sawyer
Writers: Arthur Phillips, Harry Crane
Special Lyrics: Sammy Cahn
Musical Direction: Dick Stabile

Choreography: Nick Castle
Television Director: Bud Yorkin
Producer & Director: Ernest D. Glucksman

OPENING: A group of onlookers (*The Nick Castle Dancers and The Skylarks*) are gathered outside the gates of Paramount studios wanting to know how to get into pictures. A guard opens up the gate and out steps Martin & Lewis. In song, they're asked what the secret is to movie success, and they respond by singing "That's Entertainment" – both the version from *The Band Wagon* (1953) and a special lyric that describes their own situation.

SKETCH #1: We're on the set of a hotel room and "Mr. Taurog" is directing Dean and Mary Ellen Kay in a honeymoon scene. Dean carries his bride over the threshold, and while he kisses her, a noisy bellhop (*Lewis*) bursts into the room in a motorized cart, carrying their luggage. He repeatedly honks a horn to get Dean's attention; eventually it works. Jerry congratulates Dean several times on his new marriage and takes even more opportunities to passionately kiss the bride. After unloading (badly) the luggage and golf clubs, the bellhop hints none-too-subtly for a tip. When Dean catches on, he flips a quarter, but it falls down the back of his new wife's dress. The bellhop is impressed, crying, "Dig that crazy piggy bank!" as he proceeds to reach for the quarter. Dean throws him out, but he returns with champagne, and Dean shoots the cork at his stomach. He returns again to start the phonograph, but the bride's $3,000 fur is on the turntable and gets shredded. Finally Jerry offers to dim the lights but the switch is broken, so he gets a ladder to remove the bulb. When he can't climb the ladder properly, Dean offers to do it for him. While Dean's holding onto the chandelier, a worker enters and removes the ladder. The new groom swings back and forth and is eventually hurled out the window, leaving Jerry to kiss the bride once more.

DEAN SOLO #1: In a department store, Dean's daughter asks about the record album of songs from *Living It Up*, and he explains it's his and "Uncle Jerry's" new picture. She asks him to buy her a present, and he agrees because, as he sings, "Money Burns a Hole in My Pocket"

GUEST ACTS: At the conclusion of Dean's song, a studio technician comes in and orders that the set be struck "for the production number."

The Nick Castle Dancers cavort as The Skylarks sing "A Shine on Your Shoes" from *The Band Wagon*.

SKETCH #2: Seymour (*Lewis*) is the new member of The Friendship Club, where lonely hearts gather to meet, dance and perhaps find true love. Upon joining, he's welcomed by the manager (*Martin*) and the other members. "Are you a lonely heart?" the manager asks him, to which Seymour replies, "I'm lonely all over." Dean invites him to have refreshments, but Seymour mistakes the punch bowl for a basin and washes his hands in it. The manager suggests he get acquainted with someone. Seymour approaches a female mannequin, but Dean tells him it's a dummy used for dancing lessons and encourages him to approach a real girl. Seymour says he's too shy. To break the ice, Dean gets up a game of charades, but Seymour's too anxious and shouts out guesses in a rapid fire fashion. Finally, Dean halts the game, and announces that everyone is going to the beach. However, no matter how he configures it, Dean realizes there's no room for Seymour in either car. They leave, and Seymour stays behind. He introduces himself to the mannequin, and after conversing with her (in mime), they dance.

JERRY SOLO: Paul Power introduces Roland Capehart (*Lewis*), who conducts a university glee club (*The Skylarks*) in an a capella rendition of "Danny Boy."

DEAN SOLO #2: Dean "plays guitar" and lip-synchs to his own recording of "That's What I Like."

FINALE: Dean and Jerry perform "Every Street's a Boulevard (in Old New York)" from *Living It Up* (1954).

ANALYSIS AND REVIEWS: Perhaps Lewis, after reading some of the reviews for the prior show, decided he'd better be (mostly) funny. Perhaps, too, he got ahold of John Lester's column and figured some more public reinforcing of his bond with Martin was in order. Whatever the motivation, the end result was a *Colgate Hour* that, for the most part, coupled the wild, anything-goes hilarity of the early years with the structured framework of more recent broadcasts.

Once again, there's a theme that links almost everything together, at least during the first half: it's all taking place in a motion picture studio, presumably Paramount. The opening number gives Martin & Lewis another chance to comment in song about their union, this time with special lyrics for "That's Entertainment" courtesy of Sammy Cahn. This one is the first of four he would write for them, the final two coming after a much longer, more serious breach.

In reality, these special songs only emphasized that something had changed. Once upon a time no one would have thought it necessary to *announce* that Dean and Jerry liked each other. It was obvious to anyone watching that their mutual admiration fairly leapt off the screen. Now, like the openings themselves, every gesture between them seems choreographed, with a message handed to us in lyrics:

JERRY: Take a boy, with a charm that's a joy
DEAN: And a loon, with a face like a goon
JERRY: If they jell…
BOTH: Bet the public will yell, "That's Entertainment!"

DEAN: Well I recall, I was nothin' at all
JERRY: I must confess, I was probably less
BOTH: We were fair, but now since we're a pair… That's Entertainment!

JERRY: A friend to the end, that's what Dean means to me,
DEAN: Chums come what comes, Jerry boy, we will be,
BOTH: As anybody can see,
DEAN: Our friendship just thrills us
JERRY: At times it almost kills us.

DEAN: Ah, the team that began as a dream,
JERRY: Thanks to you, is a dream that came true,
BOTH: It's not smart, but it's straight from the heart,
DEAN: It's corny, we fear
JERRY: But corn that's sincere
BOTH: Is Entertainment!

Framing the honeymoon hotel scene as a motion picture take was not only a waste of time, but detracts from the opening of the sketch; luckily it rolls along nicely from there. Once more, Jerry is the boisterous lunatic who will do anything for a laugh, and whose wild behavior is likely to stop the show. He manages both here: after dropping off the luggage and failing to get tipped for his trouble, he gets back into his motorized cart (which is emblazoned with "Brown's Hotel, Loch Sheldrake NY") and, with a wild-eyed, open-mouthed smile, plows right into the camera that's shooting him, instantly taking it out of service. The screen goes black for about two seconds until Bud Yorkin switches to Dean and Mary Ellen Kay reacting. Dean puts his hand to his head in shock, and you can clearly see him say, "Oh, Jesus!" The only reason you can't hear it is the audience is screaming with laughter.

Another laughing ovation comes after Dean's thrown out the bellboy a second time and gently touches his bride's features as they embrace:

DEAN: "Ah, whose pretty lips are those?"
MARY: "Yours, darling!"
DEAN: "And whose cute little nose is that?"
MARY: "Yours, darling!"
DEAN: "And whose gorgeous eyes are those?"
MARY: "Yours, darling!"
JERRY (opening the door): "When you come to the shiny new quarter, that's mine!"

Once Dean sings to his "daughter" and The Skylarks and Nick Castle Dancers perform their combined specialty, the movie studio framing device is dropped entirely. The "Friendship Club" sketch starts out like something from the old days as well, as timid Seymour converses with the manager. Dean asks why he wants to join the club, but keeps talking, not giving Seymour an opening to answer. However, instead of getting angry and yelling as in previous sketches, Seymour simply says, "I forgot" and makes his "poor schnook" face. Here, Jerry plays the innocent idiot, wearing nearly the same outfit as in the two sketches from the previous show. A few years later, he recalled this sketch, and his partner's reaction: "I was a poor slob who came to join a friendship club. I tried so hard to make friends, but then everybody teamed up to go out for refreshments (*sic*) and I was left alone. I ended up dancing with a manikin. Dean hated this bit. He kept saying, 'Why don't you cut out this sad stuff and just be funny?'"

Lewis reverted to being funny in his solo spot, leading The Skylarks in "Danny Boy." Evidently he was pleased enough with the result to extend and incorporate this "chorale director" routine into their next York picture, *You're Never Too Young* (1955), adding Dean to the bit as well. The finale, "Every Street's a Boulevard (in Old New York)" was their first recording as a team since "That Certain Party" in 1948. It has a lot of charm here, as it did in *Living It Up*, and they were using it in their personal appearances as well, but again, the emphasis is on choreography, not comedy.

Still and all, it was the strongest of their four starring *Comedy Hours* this season, although neither the weekly *Variety* nor its daily sister thought so. 'Gros' of the East Coast trade, never a big slapstick fan, decided the show "was better as a songfest than a comedy outing. The madcap duo tried hard in an assortment of sketches, but the yocks were few and far between. However, the show was an overall pleaser because of the many tune insertions." Gros opined that both of the *Living It Up* numbers "were sock trailers for the film," but declared "the team's tomfoolery was just okay in a sketch about a lonely hearts club and very weak in a vignette showing Martin as a newlywed and Lewis as an intrusive bellboy."

Daily Variety's 'Kap' wasn't quite so harsh, although calling it "not their best of the season, but a generally entertaining show that had some slapstick highlights...." Of the newlywed sketch, Kap noted, "Writers Artie Phillips and Harry Crane sneaked some oldies into this one, but did it so artfully that the laugh pace was maintained. Second sketch revolved around a Friendship Club which Lewis attempts to join. This gave the crew-cut comic ample opportunity for some expressive pantomime and it closed out on a note of pathos.... Highlight of this was a brief lightning satire on professional charade players."

Where it mattered most, though, the show came through: according to Trendex, the broadcast drew 62.3% of the total television audience: a new record for NBC in the competition against Ed Sullivan and, as it turned out, a lasting one, too. No future *Colgate Hour*, not even the final six Martin & Lewis shows, would better or even match this rating.

They would continue to handily top Sullivan, however, and that was fine with NBC. It was fine with Colgate, too, but the sponsor wanted stronger numbers for the weeks Dean and Jerry weren't on. CBS, preparing to launch a Hollywood-based drama series called *Climax!*, tried to woo Colgate away from the *Comedy Hour* for the new season, but the head of the company, Joe McConnell, was a former NBC president and couldn't envision making a change. Nevertheless, some cost-cutting was demanded which the network reluctantly had to accept. For the coming season, Colgate reverted to buying three Sundays out of four; NBC's Max

Liebman—whose *Your Show of Shows* was departing—would produce a 90 minute spectacular for each remaining Sunday. A press release in April promised the *Comedy Hour's* fifth season "will present a sparkling parade of comedy and variety shows. NBC will produce a number of book shows similar to the widely acclaimed production of 'Anything Goes' that was seen on the program this season, as well as the Martin and Lewis shows. In addition, 20 big-name variety shows will be produced by Ted Bates & Co., the advertising agency for Colgate-Palmolive." To that end, Colgate also bought the 14 summer Sundays ahead of the fall season and turned those over to the Bates agency as well; they came up with *The Colgate Summer Comedy Hour*, which alternated origination between New York and Hollywood.

Just prior to their Atlantic City trip, Martin and Lewis jointly appeared on CBS's *Person to Person*. Hosted by newsman Edward R. Murrow, the series consisted of live interviews with notable personalities via remote; cameras and monitors were brought into the celebrity's home or workplace, while Murrow conducted the interview from the network's New York studio. It was the nearest 1950s TV came to the star-centric culture of today.

The interview, which aired on July 2, takes place in the Lewis home. The camera follows them around and it's mostly clowning until Murrow asks Martin, "You fellows must have had some high and low points in your partnership. What would you say has been the team's greatest single success?" His response: "Well, as a single I was never a success. But I must say, in all seriousness, as a single success, to me, when Jerry and I met at the 500 Club in Atlantic City about eight years ago. We woke up one morning and we found we were a team, that's all. That's the success I think we have."

Murrow turns to Lewis, who's nervously biting his lip: "Jerry, what incident in your professional career has been the most serious, or is that a fair question?" "Well, yes, Ed, I think it's a fair question," says Lewis. "I think it's about time to more or less relax now and answer it seriously. I think the most critical time in my career was when Dean and I had more or less of a feud. But the thing that so few people realize is that Dean and I have had probably one of the greatest Damon and Pythias associations that any two men have ever had, and we were entitled to have the one beef that we did have in eight years. But it cleared the air beautifully and we like one another pretty much."

Another exchange is equally telling:

MURROW: Jerry, tell me this: Why do people laugh at you two? Did you ever sit down and figure it out?

JERRY: Well, Ed, we more or less had a science in our comedy, and we knew that Dean was the good lookin' guy and I was the goof, and it would make for a good combination. But at the same time, I think that the affection that Dean and I show in our work and the... the uh... the potenence (*sic*) involved in our performance, that so many older people feel that Dean is more or less a boss or the authority and I'm the underdog, and so many people in life go through this every day, that they can laugh and chuckle at... reality, actually.

MURROW: Dean, would you say that this applies to your boy and girl fans as well?

DEAN: Oh, I think so. I think Jerry's absolutely right.

MURROW: That they have a feeling that there is somehow a familiar relationship here that they see in actual life, is that it?

DEAN: I think that's correct.

It might seem odd that Martin, who admittedly wasn't given to deep reflection, would consider the moment when they became a team as their greatest success, especially given the volumes of scrapbooks chronicling their rise and the awards and citations on display in the Playhouse. You'd expect him to mention topping the exhibitors' polls, or the massively high ratings of their *Colgate* shows, or the mob scenes they create at personal appearances. But to the end of his days, Dean would consider teaming with Jerry as one of the greatest turning points of his career; the moment when stardom became something to be grasped and not just dreamt. Beyond that, he would let his partner do the pontificating, however awkwardly, and just smile and agree.

At the close, a puckish Murrow says, "This has been a very pleasant visit with Abbott & Costello all the way out there...." Dean laughs (as does Murrow), as Jerry jumps up from his chair: "What? What?!?" Dean says, "Sit down, Laurel." Now smiling, Jerry thinks for a few seconds and says, "Well, you're very kind, Mr. Pearson..." making Dean and the crew break up.

Eight years on, they were still wildly successful. They could still make each other laugh. They still liked one another "pretty much." That would do, for now.

An MDA fund-raising event from Autumn, 1954. Soon enough, the gloves would come off between Martin & Lewis. Photo courtesy of Kayley Thompson.

7

1954–55:
COLGATE SEASON FIVE AND FEUD #2

DEAN: "You want to know why we don't do more TV shows? In five years we've done 23 shows. Three of those were bad, but 20 were good."

JERRY: "That's right, and at that rate it will take 20 years to burn ourselves up, but if we had done 23 shows in the first year we would be through now."

– As quoted by columnist Hal Humphrey, January 1955

WHATEVER OPTIMISM NBC HAD about the *Colgate Hour* at the start of April had dissipated by the end of August. "With the fall teeoff (*sic*) approaching, NBC makes no bones that it's distressed over the Ted Bates agency's program contribution to the Colgate 'Comedy Hour' summer showcase, expressing alarm over possible 'Toast of the Town' inroads on the Sunday 8 to 9 rating unless the agency considerably hypoes the fall-winter schedule," wrote *Variety* in their September 1 issue, saying as diplomatically as possible that *The Colgate Summer Comedy Hour* was a dog and the network expected better showmanship during the regular season. "For the past several seasons, 'Colgate Comedy Hour' was strictly an NBC 'baby,' but the Bates agency wrested away 20 of the productions as a coin-saving expediency."

Ed Sullivan must have been salivating, and with good reason. The Bates agency's idea of better showmanship was to hire singer Gordon

MacRae as permanent host for their shows. Cantor, Durante, O'Connor and Abbott & Costello had been released, although the latter would guest on two of MacRae's hours toward season's end. (Durante and O'Connor alternated hosting a half-hour *Texaco Star Theater* on Saturday evenings during this season.) Sadly, NBC didn't fare much better: the "book shows" they'd promised weren't nearly as successful as *Anything Goes*. Lastly, the Max Liebman-produced "Color Spectaculars" kicked off with a musical called *Satins and Spurs*, which made television history as one of its earliest bombs. "Reactions of critics and viewers were so hostile that Betty Hutton, who had made her television debut in the show, [threatened] to retire from show business," recalled Arthur Shulman and Roger Youman in their 1966 pictorial history of TV, *How Sweet it Was*. NBC now found itself in an uphill battle to maintain interest in these monthly shows as well. Consequently, this was the year *Toast of the Town* regained dominance of the timeslot, knocking *Colgate* from #10 to #27 in the season's ratings, while climbing from #17 to #5. CBS would reward its host by changing the name of the program the following fall to *The Ed Sullivan Show*.

The last original holdovers, Martin & Lewis, were supposed to open the season on September 19, but Lewis was recuperating from viral pneumonia and ordered to stay in bed. When he was finally permitted to get up in mid-October, work began on *You're Never Too Young* (1955), a York production, and their seasonal TV bow was rescheduled for November. Then Lewis came down with jaundice. A two-week engagement at Ciro's night club turned into a Dean Martin semi-solo gig (he was occasionally assisted by other performers, including Tony Martin, Alan King and Ethel Merman) while his partner recovered. Before they knew it, it was almost Christmas and their picture still hadn't wrapped—but they owed Colgate a show.

* * * * *

THE COLGATE COMEDY HOUR: Dean Martin & Jerry Lewis Show #23.

Airdate: December 19, 1954; NBC-TV.
With Vera Miles, Milton Frome, Margery Maude, Hank Mann, Sylvia Hickle, Marvin Middlebird, The Nick Castle Dancers with Gretchen Houser and Dick Humphries, Jack Benny (as "Phil Abrams")
Announcer: George Putnam
Writers: Arthur Phillips, Harry Crane

Musical Direction: Dick Stabile
Choreography: Nick Castle
Production Design: Furth Ullman
Television Director: Bud Yorkin
Producer & Director: Ernest D. Glucksman

OPENING: We're backstage at Broadway's Belasco Theater and The Nick Castle Dancers are rehearsing for opening night of "Martin & Lewis in 'Happy Daze.'" A stagehand enters and hangs a sign that says "Show Cancelled." The dancers lament in song that "It's just before Christmas" and they're "back on relief." "Where's Dean and Jerry?" they want to know. Martin & Lewis enter and sing "Lose That Long Face" from *A Star is Born* (1954), which includes two verses of special lyrics.

SKETCH #1: At the bus station's greasy spoon, Charlie (*Martin*) is chief cook and waiter. After all the diners depart to board their bus, he gets his dinner together and sits at a table by the window. As he eats and reads his paper, a broke and hungry kid (*Lewis*) walks by, sees the meal and is soon salivating. Once Charlie notices him, the kid mimes that there's food on his face, but Charlie misses the spot, so the kid comes in and wipes it off. He asks for a job, and Charlie puts him to work as the bus to Steubenville arrives. The passengers enter and Charlie has him serve spaghetti, which is on one long bunch. The kid drapes the long spaghetti over five plates and then chops it with an axe; unfortunately he also splits a customer's jacket in two. As the customer gripes, the boarding call is heard and everyone departs without paying. Charlie explains to the kid that he's got to be fast, and another bus arrives. All customers but one (Hank Mann) agree to spaghetti. Charlie and the kid argue with the guy and the boarding call is heard. The kid grabs a rope, ties one end to the counter and runs off to fasten the other end. When he returns, he tells the passengers, "That bus ain't goin' anywhere without you, I took care of that." As he and Charlie prepare the spaghetti, the bus pulls out and drags the counter and passengers away. Frustrated, Charlie plants the kid on top of the grill and puts up a sign: "People Burgers."

DEAN SOLO #1: After plugging *3 Ring Circus*, Jerry introduces Dean, who sings "Without a Word of Warning."

GUEST ACT: Jerry thanks the firefighters for collecting donations on behalf of MDA the previous month, and then introduces The Nick Castle

Dancers with Gretchen Houser and Dick Humphries in the production number "Swing Alley."

SKETCH #2: Mr. and Mrs. Martin (*Martin, Vera Miles*) arrive at the Happy Haven for Children orphanage to adopt a little boy. Miss Adams (*Margery Maude*) greets them and introduces the boys, including a very tall one, Orville (*Lewis*). "He's been with us a long time," says Miss Adams, and Orville adds, "Twenty-nine years." Vera thinks Orville is a good choice, telling Dean, "He'd be more than a son; he'd be a companion to you." While Miss Adams and Vera gather Orville's things, the two men get acquainted, and what began as some playful punching turns into wrestling on the floor. "Look at them," says Miss Adams, 'playing like children!" Later, at the Martins' home, Miss Adams brings Orville over. As she and Vera check out the boy's bedroom, Dean comes home from work, exhausted. Orville wants to remove his galoshes, and ends up pulling him onto the floor. Asking Dean to read the funnies, Orville sits on his lap and rocks the chair, which ends up tumbling backward, injuring the new father's arm. Frustrated, Dean tells Orville he doesn't want him and tells him to go back to the orphanage, just as his wife enters the room. "I can't take this kid," he says, "I can't be a father; I like a nice, quiet house." Vera tells Orville to give Dean a book that is under the sofa cushion; he does and she asks Dean to read it. Dean reads excerpts from Alan Beck's essay, "What is a Boy." When he's through, he and Orville embrace... and trade a couple of playful punches.

JERRY SOLO: Jerry announces that it's time for his "spot in one," the moment when he gets to do a specialty alone. Unfortunately, the writers weren't able to come up with anything for him, so he sets up a folding chair and sits until his three minutes are up. He makes a few faces, whistles, yawns, moves his arms around, but is otherwise quiet. Finally he says, "I can just see Mr. Colgate now, figuring out what this is costing him!" and laughs. He looks at his watch: "That's it," picks up the chair and leaves the stage.

DEAN SOLO #2: "Mambo Italiano"

FINALE: Dean calls Jerry to the stage for the big moment. Jerry starts: "You've read about it. You've heard about it. It is now our good fortune and our privilege to make the introduction." "This is really an exciting spot," says Dean. "The first time on our show." Jerry agrees. "We'd like to present our guest star, Mr. Phil Abrams." To the strains of "Love in Bloom," Jack Benny walks out and takes center stage between Dean and Jerry. "I know what you're thinking," says Dean. "It's not him." "This is our guest star, Phil Abrams, and we're very thrilled having him with us tonight," Jerry says, adding, "It's time for the Colgate spotlight to fall on our guest star." They back away and, after a pause, Jack says, "Hmmmm." They shake his hand, and Jerry says, "Wonderful, Phil! We've never enjoyed anything more in our lives." Jack leaves the stage.

In answer to requests, the duo performs "Every Street's A Boulevard (in Old New York)" from *Living It Up*.

ANALYSIS AND REVIEWS: Hal Humphrey didn't ask Dean and Jerry which *Colgate Hours*, in their opinion, were the first two "bad" ones, but the third was definitely this show. "Martin and Lewis, making their first appearance of the 1954-55 season," wrote *Variety*, "were expected to but did not deliver a Trendex drubbing to Ed Sullivan's 'Toast of the Town' on CBS. The comedy duo racked up a 32.4, less than three pegs ahead of the 29.9 for 'Toast.' In the past, M&L have usually run roughshod over the Sullivan stanza." At first, blame was placed on some inaccurate publicity on CBS's part, with plugs for *Toast* that promised about 40 stars. "When it came to a rundown of the names," said *Variety*, "it could identify less than a dozen that would fit in that lofty marquee class," with the majority of those being in a special filmed sequence, not appearing live. Nevertheless, reviews of the *Comedy Hour* were hardly sparkling, and eventually NBC got wind from Trendex that people had tuned *out* their show in favor of Sullivan's.

For the first time in the post-Simmons and Lear era, the program made no attempt to tie everything together with a storyline. It began, as had become custom, with a production number that set a scene; in this case, the cancellation of a Broadway opening. This "theme," however, was set up solely for the Martin & Lewis duet on "Lose That Long Face" and as with last season's "That's Entertainment" there were some special team-centric lyrics:

> DEAN: *Unless you're near me to cheer me, I got the longest face in town,*
> JERRY: *I don't need a gratuity to say your charm is my annuity,*

> *DEAN: We need each other, brother,*
> *BOTH: For without each other, we would be lost,*
> *DEAN: As long as we're together, pal,*
> *JERRY: All things we'll weather, pal,*
> *BOTH: We'll part when sunshine turns to frost*
> *JERRY: With a song on your lips,*
> *DEAN: With your muggin' and quips,*
> *BOTH: We'll both get merry-like, get Dean-and-Jerry-like,*
> *We're gonna get your long face gone!*

Earlier in the song, they sang "If you cannot smile on us / Please turn the dial on us," little realizing that's exactly what would happen.

The first sketch, set in the bus station restaurant, had almost nothing going for it. Jerry, in his "poor schnook" outfit, eventually gets hired and by his incompetence louses up Dean's business. There are no clever gags, and even a mistake—upon tasting his soup, Dean is supposed to lower the price but there's no chalk on the board, so he explains the gag verbally—gets a half-hearted reaction. The funniest line in the sketch is Jerry's: after he chops the customer's coat in half, he says, "It's the first time I ever saw a suit with two pairs of jackets!" The towing away of the lunch counter is the big visual gag and gets a decent laugh, but as it dies down an ovation begins, likely fostered by a lighted "APPLAUSE" sign.

The second sketch is mawkish in the extreme. It's one thing for Jerry Lewis the comic to pretend to be a rambunctious nine-year-old child. It's quite another for him to act like a nine-year-old that admits to being an orphan for 29 years. Vera Miles' Mrs. Martin isn't a real character, only a plot device, while Jerry's Orville doesn't deliberately cause havoc, it just happens because he's a grown man who's never been around adults because he's been rejected by family after family. The audience laughs when he first appears, but once his character has been established, it's pathos—or more accurately, bathos—the rest of the way. The concluding essay, "What is a Boy," written by Alan Beck of the New England Mutual Life Insurance Company in 1949, recorded by Arthur Godfrey in 1951, is read by Dean as perfunctorily as possible, and there's no attempt to close with a laugh. Mercifully, the sketch just ends.

The rest of the show was unmemorable. "Swing Alley" was, at best, ordinary; a production number that would've looked no different had it aired five years earlier. Jerry's solo spot was, as he'd promised, nothing. The lyrics to Dean's "Mambo Italiano" are too obviously an attempt to recapture the spirit of "That's Amore." The "Special Guest Star Phil Abrams" bit was apparently conceived at the last minute and Benny's participation was, according to *Variety*, reciprocation for a cameo appearance Martin & Lewis had made on his show the previous May. Thankfully, it didn't last much longer than the one joke it was. (Benny actually fared better nearer the end when he came out for a bow, telling the boys he's going to throw

With the Four Step Brothers, who made their final appearance with Dean and Jerry on the February 11, 1955 *Colgate Comedy Hour*. Photo courtesy of Kayley Thompson.

them a party at their Las Vegas opening on January 12. "Where you fellahs are concerned, money is nothing. I know that, because I'm getting
nothing for what I'm doing here.") Finally, "Every Street's a Boulevard"
was the same arrangement as on last season's show, including the reprise
at the close.

When *Daily Variety's* 'Helm' thinks a Martin & Lewis show is lackluster, you can take it to the bank. "The Madmen of the Megacycles... were
not up to their usual antics, or perhaps not up to enough of them.... The
sketches and incidental dialogue fashioned for them by Artie Phillips and
Harry Crane lacked the snap and dash to bring out M&L's zaniest quali-
ties." Helm noted that the Ohio State University football team was in the
audience, "but not one football gag was used."

"The duo relied on material rather than themselves," wrote *Variety's*
'Jose,' "and the writing unfortunately was based on clichés.... The material seemed to have had some hard usage in many show biz fields. The café
sketch and the bit in which the Dean Martins select an orphan (Lewis)
for adoption had a familiar design. There's something basically unfunny
in an orphan submitting himself to a prospective parent that doesn't lend
itself completely to comedy treatment.... There were some moments
when individual efforts seemed to rise above the material, but these were
the exceptions."

"Dean and Jerry were very unhappy with their first show," wrote
Humphrey in his column a month later. "They blamed themselves, which
in itself is a refreshing comment. Most performers can cite a hundred
reasons why a show is a flop, none of which has anything to do with them.
'We were tired and trying to do too much. We hadn't finished our movie
at Paramount and you can't do two things at once. This has been a lesson to us,' said Jerry. Personally, I wasn't as disappointed in [the] show as
Dean and Jerry and many of the critics, but it's tough to argue with them
when they tell you the old spark just wasn't there."

The "old spark" between them had been in jeopardy for several
months, namely because they now had to work at it. As this show demonstrated, Lewis was still favoring the "sad stuff," and Martin, truly reduced
to singing straight-man, was visibly irritated; he gets off a few amusing
ad-libs, but they're nearly all when Lewis is off-screen or otherwise occupied. Arthur Penn, who'd moved from floor manager to assistant director, remembered that Dean kept himself in check when on camera. "The
only discomfort that was ever in evidence was when I would go into the
dressing room, and I would see him drinking." Penn also recalled that

Lewis' craziness had given Kingman Moore a bleeding ulcer in 1952, "to the point where he hemorrhaged in the control room." Now Bud Yorkin, whose final go-round with Martin & Lewis this was, had also reached the saturation point; he ended up reuniting with Simmons and Lear, who were writing *The George Gobel Show*. Within a few years, Yorkin and Lear would form the production company that would eventually fashion *All in the Family*, *Maude*, *Sanford and Son*, *The Jeffersons* and others, remaking the television sitcom into a vehicle for social justice.

Meanwhile, Dean and Jerry soldiered on: after wrapping up *You're Never Too Young*, they did their two week gig (at a record-setting $50,000 per week) at the Sands Hotel, and returned in time to rehearse their next Colgate show.

* * * * *

THE COLGATE COMEDY HOUR: Dean Martin & Jerry Lewis Show #24.

Airdate: February 13, 1955; NBC-TV.
With: Micki Marlo, The Four Step Brothers, Franklin Pangborn, Wyck, Bird and Kaylick
Cast: Robert S. Carson, Stanley Price
Announcer: Wendell Niles
Writers: Arthur Phillips, Harry Crane
Musical Direction: Dick Stabile
Choreography: Hal Belfer
Production Design: Furth Ullman
Television Director: Dick Weinberg
Producer & Director: Ernest D. Glucksman

OPENING / DEAN SOLO #1: The show opens in a facsimile of the Sands Hotel's Copa Room, where the boys had their Vegas engagement. A line of chorus girls introduce Dean, who sings "Belle From Barcelona." He starts "Melancholy Baby," when a parking attendant (*Lewis*) asks him to read an announcement that a car in the driveway needs to be moved. He reads the license number, hands it to Dean and departs. Dean resumes his song, and the attendant returns, miffed that the announcement hasn't been made: "There's a car parked in the driveway, cars aren't goin' in, they ain't comin' out, we ain't made a quarter all night!" He reads the license number again, and leaves. Dean resumes singing, and the attendant, now really angry, yells at him for not making the announcement. "I was co-min' to it," Dean says, but the attendant replies, "We ain't got time to wait for it; there's cars parked on top of one another out there!" He asks again and walks off, and Dean finishes the song. Dressed in a tuxedo, but still made up as the parking attendant, Jerry comes out and asks Dean, "Has my brother been out here? He asked you to make a little announcement, didn't he?" Dean replies he could tolerate his brother but not him, grabs Jerry and wrestles him upon a table.

SKETCH #1 / JERRY SOLO: Dean's in his dressing room and Sy Devore (*Franklin Pangborn*) is fitting him for a new tuxedo. Sy comments on the sumptuousness of the dressing room, but discovers that the jacket needs adjusting. He rips off the collar just as Jerry enters, and when he rips off a sleeve, Jerry rebels and tears Sy's coat to shreds, then peels off his moustache. Furious, Sy leaves the room; equally furious, Dean yells at Jerry, which he doesn't want to do because he has a sore throat and his voice is fading. Jerry tries to apologize, but Dean will have none of it. Explaining that the sponsor is coming up to discuss business, he urges Jerry not to do anything but mention how happy he is with Colgate's products. Mr. Larrabee (*Robert Carson*) and his wife arrive, and Jerry tries to be help-ful: he mentions all the products incessantly, tries to serve refreshments but distributes too many of them until they all spill. Jerry convinces the couple that he and Dean brush with Colgate every five minutes, but he gets toothpaste on Mr. Larrabee's tuxedo jacket, then tries to wash it in the sink with Fab, ruining the satin collar. After messing up her hair, Jerry forcibly shampoos Mrs. Larrabee with Halo. Finally they storm out and Dean loses his voice from yelling at his partner. He's called down to sing in the showroom, and Jerry has an idea. We cut to the stage, and Jerry appears, lip-synching to Dean's recording of "Sympatico."

GUEST ACT: As Dean gets some cough drops from the box office, he spies Micki Marlo in line and invites her to perform. She sings "St. Louis Blues."

SKETCH #2: Dean's asleep in his dressing room bed, and the doctor (*Stanley Price*) instructs Jerry that his partner needs to stay warm and rest. Jerry watches over him and tries to keep quiet, but the apple he eats is too crunchy and awakens Dean. He switches to a banana, but it's just as loud. Now Dean has a headache and asks for an aspirin. There's only one left and Jerry's dropped it. He thinks it's under the bed, so he lifts up the bed and sends Dean out the window. Jerry looks for Dean, who crawls back into bed just as Jerry decides to look under it, sending him out the window again. A call comes for Dean; the phone's across the room so Jerry carries him over and back again, twice. Now *Jerry's* exhausted, but there's a noisy fly in the room. He tries swatting it, but keeps missing (and hitting Dean). Dean tells him to open the door and shoo the fly out, which he does, successfully. But just as he's getting back into bed, the doorbell rings; when Jerry opens it, the fly returns. Inspired, Jerry gets a candy, sprays it with a poisonous disinfectant and drops it in a vase of water. The fly drinks it and tries to fly away, but conks out. In the interim, Dean has recovered his voice, and the two celebrate by singing "We Belong Together," with new lyrics by Sammy Cahn.

DEAN SOLO #2: A young couple arrives for the show, but there are no seats available. Dean overhears and he offers them his table. As they enter, he sings "Young and Foolish."

FINALE: Dick Stabile introduces the Four Step Brothers, who come on with a group tap. After this, Martin & Lewis join them with the routine they'd done twice before: each of the Steps takes a turn with some flashy dancing, followed by Dean and then Jerry.

ANALYSIS AND REVIEWS: Built entirely around Martin & Lewis, with both character sketches and elaborate production numbers jettisoned, the result was the funniest *Comedy Hour* for the team in a long time. Not that it surpassed or even equaled the best of their early TV shows, but still a breath of fresh air compared to more recent efforts. Even Dean, toward the end, says, "I never enjoyed a show as much as I did this one, believe me." Considering he was suffering a cold (he coughs at intervals throughout the program), it's a surprising statement; he must have been delighted to not have to play in another "sad stuff" sketch.

The show opens like the old ones used to close: Dean does a solo number and the team does a nightclub bit. This one in particular harkens back to their earliest years together, when Jerry would heckle a singing Dean while posing as a waiter, a cab driver or, as here, a parking lot attendant.

Both sketches take place in the dressing room between shows. The first is a reworking of the "Balaban Family" sketch from the previous season. In this case, it's not the head of the Paramount theater chain that's

"Ed Solomon" thinks Veto is a "rilly beeeg deodorant!" Scene from the opening of
the May 8, 1955 *Colgate Comedy Hour.*

paying a visit, it's the sponsor's representative. The end result is the same:
Jerry causes havoc. He plays it for sympathy, though; looking downcast
whenever Dean yells at him. Dean's lines are not as playful as in pri-
or years, which is always a minus. Still, the bit contains some genuine
laughs, especially when Jerry shampoos "Mrs. Larrabee's" hair. The ending gives Jerry the opportunity to mime to a record, but since it's one of
Dean's, it puts him in the position of having to burlesque and exaggerate
his own partner's style. Whether due to inhibition or a lack of preparation, he doesn't quite pull it off.

The second sketch is better, with Jerry playing nursemaid to the ailing
Dean. It's mostly visual, with reactions tied to sound effects such as the
overly-crunchy fruit and the pesky fly. Apart from twice getting dumped
out the window, Martin expends very little energy here, leaving Lewis
to carry the ball, which he does very well. However, the ending evolves
into yet another "we'll-always-be-a-team" lyric from Sammy Cahn, this
one a rewrite of last season's "We Belong Together." The new lyrics are in
the same vein as the originals ("Like welcome and mat / Hedda and hat /

Alley and Oop / Louella and scoop"), and the question is why Cahn even bothered writing them.

Although Micki Marlo lacked Kitty Kallen's staying power—her singing career lasted less than two decades to Kallen's five—she certainly brings more muscle to her rendition of "St. Louis Blues" than had Kallen three years before. And though his voice is a little ragged from the virus, Martin pulls off his two solos admirably, especially "Young and Foolish."

The finale with the Four Step Brothers is the same routine as seen in '52 and '53, adding to the old-time feeling that the show as a whole generates. Having been asked to stretch during the closing minutes, they proceed to thank everyone associated with the show, as was their custom when faced with extra time over the years. In the midst of this, Jerry tells the audience, "We do want to say, ladies and gentlemen, and to the viewers, and to the wonderful people who have been kind enough to have faith and to be nice enough to stick by Dean and I throughout the past year-and-a-half, we want to thank you for being so very kind to us." Apart from its long-windedness, the time frame specified in this discourse is notable. Their feud was reported only eleven months earlier. Possibly it refers to the brouhaha over the reviews of their London Palladium engagement of June 1953 and their subsequent ill-advised attacks on the British press. Or maybe the difficulties with each other actually began eighteen months ago; as previously noted, it was their 7th anniversary and their career ambitions were beginning to diverge. Whatever his intention, even if it was just something extemporaneous meant to fill time, Jerry's curious thanks to their various audiences raises more questions than it answers.

"Dean Martin and Jerry Lewis…showed tremendous improvement over their first [show this season]," wrote John Lester. "Apparently, the universal bad press reaction they received after that first outing, even allowing for the fact that Jerry had been ill, shocked them out of the complacency or whatever it was that made them think they could get by without trying. Dean and Jerry and their guests, singer Micki Marlow (sic) and the wonderful Step Brothers, worked hard right from the start last night and were rewarded with screams of delight from the studio audience." Associated Press critic Wayne Oliver agreed: "Sometimes Dean Martin and Jerry Lewis go through a television show with all the enthusiasm of small boys picking up their toys at bedtime. But once in a while they pull out the stops and give it everything they have. That's what happened in their 'Comedy Hour' appearance Sunday…. When he's trying, as he was in his latest appearance, Lewis is one of the best clowns of the era. He lacks the finesse of the accomplished comic who achieves laughs by well-timed quips and situations. It's pure buffoonery by a naturally funny guy. The skit...involving the fly in the room could have fallen flat if attempted by many comedians, but with Lewis it was hilarious.... Martin provides an excellent foil as straight man and his singing, while not great, provides pleasant interludes. It's too bad Dean and Jerry sometimes seem to give their TV shows the brushoff treatment, because they can be tops when they try."

'Helm' of *Daily Variety* said simply, "The laughs may not have been as sustained as on their previous melees, but when they popped, it was with explosive force. Most of the yocks stemmed from prop gags, the writers having been short on dialog magic. It was rough house most of the way [and] enough to keep the tempo bristling with hilarity." *Variety*'s 'Rose', never a fan of slapstick, didn't like the "long-accepted clichés" of roughousing during the first sketch but enjoyed the "real scripting cuties" of the second. "At least the two skits were a revelation in terms of a then-and-now transition of the comedy team into a more—let's hope—composed duo. The 'now' part seems to fit them better these days—at least on TV." Rose also thought the "teamup of the Step Bros. and Martin & Lewis made for a whammo closer with the two comics registering solidly on their hoofing assignments."

After this, the team went to work on their next picture for Wallis, *Artists and Models* (1955), interrupted only by a tribute dinner in their honor hosted by The Friars' Club in New York on March 11, and a brief appearance on the Academy Awards ceremony, which aired over NBC-TV and radio, on March 30. Lewis introduced his partner, who sang the nominated song "Three Coins in the Fountain," which would take the Oscar for its composers, Jules Styne and Sammy Cahn. The film wrapped at the beginning of May, so Martin & Lewis went straight from Paramount to the El Capitan for their next *Colgate Hour*.

* * * * *

THE COLGATE COMEDY HOUR: Dean Martin & Jerry Lewis Show #25.

Airdate: May 8, 1955; NBC-TV.
With: Ray Malone, Frances Weintraub
Announcer: Wendell Niles
Writers: Arthur Phillips, Harry Crane

Production Design: Furth Ullman
Television Director: Dick Weinberg
Producer & Director: Ernest D. Glucksman

OPENING/SKETCH #1: Announcer Art Hanazkrocksdorferplincka-dougal (*Martin*) welcomes us to the "Toast of the Colgate Town," hosted by "the famous columnist of the Hoboken News," Ed Solomon (*Lewis*). Art and Ed review the "rilly big" Colgate products that are sponsoring, then Ed introduces a celebrity in the audience: Cary Grant (*Martin*). Cary stands up and says hello to his wife, "Judy, Judy, Judy," and when he sits down, he notices that Jimmy Durante is next to him. Next, Ed introduces atomic bomb scientist Col. Arthur Wyatt, "who only last week ignited a rilly big bomb from Las Vegas." A heavily-bandaged man stands up, tries to wave, and collapses. Ed introduces another big star, "one of the great brothers," Groucho Marx (*Martin*), who says, "Welcome to the Adam and Eve Show: You Bet Your Leaf." After sitting down, he notices Janet Leigh is seated to his left. Ed introduces one of the stars of "20,000 Large Leagues Under the Big Sea," Kirk Douglas. A man in a diver's suit stands and waves. "Good to see you, Kirk," says Ed. "Happy seaweed!" Next, he introduces "Clark, stand up and take a bow, Gable." Clark (*Martin*) stands and says hi to Ed, adding, "Scarlett couldn't make it. She's home burning down the house." Gable sits and is surprised to see George Raft to his right. Ed introduces Martin & Lewis, who stand and wave, after which he observes, "That little one's a cutie, isn't he?" Ed talks briefly about next week's show, to feature "on this stage, 45,000 penguins smoking Kools." He introduces Ben Hogan (*Martin*), who happens to be seated next to Tony Curtis. Ed invites Ben to the stage, where he will hit a golf ball off the nose of a volunteer from the audience. No one steps up, so Ed does it. Ben places the ball on Ed's mouth, into which it keeps falling. Finally, Ben takes a swing…and knocks Ed out. "There you are and here's the show," says Dean, as the curtain opens for a production number.

GUEST ACT: The Martin & Lewis Show Tour train is standing by. Ray Malone and his dance troupe perform to "Take the A Train," augmented with a brief sax solo by Dick Stabile. At the conclusion, everyone boards the train and it leaves the station.

DEAN SOLO #1: The mothers of both Dean and Jerry are on board the train, and as the conductor (*Hal Smith*) chats with her, Mrs. Lewis

(*Frances Weintraub*) relates how Mrs. Martin used to take in laundry to make ends meet. We dissolve to a rooftop where Mrs. Martin is hanging clothes. Dean enters, chides her for working so hard, and takes over the laundry basket while singing. "For You."

SKETCH #2: The conductor brings Mrs. Martin to the compartment to join Mrs. Lewis. Together, the two mothers recall how Jerry was Dean's baby sitter. In a flashback, we see Dean and Lola Martin trying to care for their baby, when Mrs. Lewis arrives. Unfortunately, she can't watch the baby tonight, but her son, Jerome, can do it. However, Jerome is afraid of the strange apartment and of Mr. Martin. He cries when his mother leaves, but Dean encourages him to get comfortable, pointing out where everything is, with the sink last. Then he says, "Sit down," so Jerome sits in the sink. At first he mistakes a stuffed elephant for the baby, but Lola returns the infant to the crib. Jerome talks with the child and offers him some bubble gum. Dean argues that the baby can't chew without teeth, but suddenly a bubble starts growing in the crib. They remove the gum and as Dean goes to the window, the bubble carries him into the air. Jerome pops it with a pin, and Dean crashes to the fire escape. When the Martins get ready to leave, Jerome cries and grabs onto Dean's leg. Dean sends his wife to hail a cab while he convinces Jerome to play a game of hide-and-seek. As Jerome counts in the bedroom, Dean tries sneaking out the door, but suddenly Jerome is in the hallway. Dean tells him to order a quart of ice cream. As Jerome uses the bedroom phone, Dean tries sneaking out again, but the ice cream delivery man (*Lewis*) has arrived. Dean gives it to Jerome, telling him to eat it in the bedroom. As Dean sneaks out, the delivery man has returned, asking if he can have a tip. Jerome has finished the ice cream, but now he's sleepy, so Dean encourages him to lie down in the bedroom. He does and quickly passes out. Dean listens to him snore, as his wife returns telling him the cab driver is waiting. He starts to leave, but doesn't have the tickets, and looks around for them. After finding them, he double-checks the bedroom, then heads for the door, where the cab driver (also *Lewis*) asks him does he want the cab or not. In frustration, Dean tears up the tickets.

JERRY SOLO: With the help of some lovely showgirls, Jerry plugs each city and venue of the team's upcoming tour of eleven one-night stands, after which his disheveled wife pulls him offstage by his ear.

DEAN SOLO #2: After thanking Colgate for allowing them to satirize Ed Sullivan, Jerry introduces Dean, who sings "Is It True What They Say About Dixie?"

FINALE: Jerry wants to utilize the band for "something a wee bit classical" and "a little more highbrow." Dean picks up the trombone, as Jerry takes the podium to conduct. The band launches into a scorching rendition of "Fascinating Rhythm," during which Dean interjects a few less-than-spectacular solo passages. After this, they introduce Ray Malone who performs an energetic tap routine. He's joined by two other male dancers, and then by Dean and Jerry.

ANALYSIS AND REVIEWS: "It was Ed Sullivan night on both NBC and CBS for about 15 minutes after 8 p.m., one the real thing, the other a satirical takeoff by Jerry Lewis that was one long howl," wrote 'Helm' at the start of *Daily Variety's* review the next morning, without exaggeration. Thanks to the omnipresent Elvis and Beatles tributes that never fail to include scenes of their appearances with him, the passing of time has only slightly dimmed Ed Sullivan's unique reputation in television history. His self-conscious mannerisms and delivery have long been pop culture fodder, as witness his brief "cameo" (via Robin Williams) in Disney's *Aladdin* (1992). Lewis has a lot of fun exaggerating all of them: folding and unfolding his arms, leaning backward and cracking his knuckles (accompanied by an effect that sounds like bones being broken). The sketch sticks closely to the script, except when Martin, dressed as Groucho, apparently does something off camera to make Jerry break up. At one point, while rubbing his finger across fake teeth, Jerry says, "How does he talk with all of them?" Apart from that, he doesn't break character. The crux of the routine is "Solomon's" introductions of entertainment and sports stars that are in the audience, a Sullivan staple. It's always Dean unconvincingly made up as the celebrity (his fake "Clark Gable" ears are priceless), and each time there's a genuine star seated right next to him that is ignored. When Martin & Lewis themselves are announced, they appear together in a brief scene that was filmed ahead of time. The routine closes with an old gag: Dean attempts to hit a golf ball from Jerry's mouth, into which it keeps falling. The added challenge is that Lewis must also contend with the fake teeth and he manages it quite well. The payoff is less funny than it was in April 1951: here, Solomon is knocked out, and Martin introduces the rest of the show. Lewis crossing the Sullivan impersonation with his punch drunk might have made for a sharper finish.

Instead, we segue to a theme: the upcoming Martin & Lewis tour of one-nighters. A production number, Dean's first solo and the second sketch are linked together through the motif of a tour train, with Dean's and Jerry's (not real-life) mothers on board. The production number is the typical song-and-dance that has previously heralded the *Colgate Hour*; in this instance, it's appended to an opening sketch, and consequently makes less of an impression. For their remaining shows, Martin & Lewis would keep to opening with a lengthy sketch and mercifully drop the production number altogether.

In their pre-teaming days, Jerry actually did babysit for Dean and his first wife Elizabeth, which helped cement their friendship. Needless to say, those events looked nothing like what we see in the second sketch, where Jerry's a frightened child in a grown man's body, while Dean's wife Lola comes across as a one-dimensional shrew. Aside from these clichés, the sketch plays quite well, thanks to some better-than-average writing. When Jerry mistakes the stuffed elephant for the baby, Dean (in the next room) asks, "Hasn't he got my eyes?" Jerry agrees: "Yeah, and he's got your nose; your old one!" Bits such as the baby's bubble and Lola comforting the frightened babysitter are very funny, while Dean's responses garner a fair share of the laughs. Near the close, the sketch veers into some familiar territory, when Lewis appears as both the delivery boy and the cab driver, but while Martin's disbelieving reactions are good, the situation as a whole is nowhere near the psychological horror of the original "Everyone is Jerry Lewis" sketch.

One moment, though, really stands out: Jerry is clinging to Dean's leg as Lola leaves to hail a cab. As he's being helped to his feet, Lewis deliberately wipes the sole of his sneaker across the top of one of Martin's suede shoes, laughing even as he's still play-crying "Don't leave me." Martin looks down and laughs, but also responds with a loud, legitimate slap across his partner's face. As Martin dodges, Lewis continues trying to step on his shoes. Trying to stay in character, Dean cries, "Not the suedes! Jerome!" but Jerry's determined and this awkward "dance" between them continues. Finally, Martin pleads, "There's fifty million people watching!" to which Lewis says, "I'm not interested; if I want to dirty your suedes, I'll dirty 'em!" Unsurprisingly this gets an ovation, throughout which Jerry continues to attack Dean, who continues to dodge, finally saying, "Aw, c'mon, Jer!" They swing back into the sketch, but after a minute, Jerry's trying again. "Get off of the suedes!" Dean yells at him, seriously this time. The moment encapsulates how the dynamic between them has changed.

No longer the hero-worshipping little brother, Lewis now brashly asserts himself, as Martin slowly grows weary and less indulgent.

There's little the program can do to match the pair of above-average sketches, so it doesn't even try. The remainder of the show is, to put it nicely, perfunctory. With little originality, Lewis and the glamour girls detail all the cities on the team's upcoming tour. Martin sings his number pleasantly. The closing routine lacks the energy of their older nightclub bits (although, to be honest, throughout the *Colgate* shows, the least memorable Martin & Lewis routines are those in which either or both toot on brass instruments). And the dancing with Ray Malone and his troupe isn't a patch on the pants of their encounters with The Four Step Brothers.

As far as Helm was concerned, "Toast of the Colgate Town" was the show. "The maniacal member of the M&L team affected all the mannerisms of 'The Toaster' with a row of flashing white teeth and exaggerated diction in a gem of mimicry that must have caught and held a high percentage of the audience that switches back and forth…. Scripters Artie Phillips and Harry Crane gave them some whopping material and the comics waded into every line with gusto. It was the high spot of the M&L season and perhaps, at Sullivan's expense, gave Comedy Hour a long-awaited pull in the ratings." *Variety's* 'Trau' labeled the sketch "a howler," but also enjoyed the babysitting scene, "largely a Lewis credit on his bizarre antics." The critic also opined, "Producer Ernie Glucksman whipped up the neatest trick of the week midway by having Lewis unreel the pair's upcoming one-nighters (May 11-26) via enunciators held by oolala femmes. It was a terrific commercial for the junket."

For this show and the next one, Lewis handled all of the guest and interlude introductions, a task that previously had been divided between them. A reporter for *TV Guide* happened to sit in on at least one rehearsal for this show, and observed first-hand the growing ennui of Dean Martin and absolute control of Jerry Lewis:

"Martin arrived an hour-and-a-quarter late, while Lewis was auditioning for skits. Lewis put down his script and applauded. 'Here comes that famous actor,' he announced. 'Have you seen his latest record?' Martin, looking sleepy and cross, slumped into a chair. 'Ah, shut up,' he said. 'I hate television. *I hate television*,' he repeated, glaring at Dick Weinberg, the director. 'Well, don't look at me,' Weinberg said. 'I didn't invent it.'

"Jerry constantly expresses his affection for his partner by tapping cigaret (sic) ashes into Martin's hair, then smiling in cross-eyed innocence. Except for rehearsing his songs, when he comes to life with a snap, Martin is relaxed to the point of indifference—kidding the chorus girls, swapping jokes with engineers, phoning his tailor or simply napping. Lewis buzzes around like a souped-up bee, working out camera angles, orchestra introductions, sight gags, dance routines and script problems. He passes with dizzying rapidity from one personality to another.... Deadly serious, keenly analytical, Lewis becomes the final authority on what's funny. 'That's no good,' he says. 'We'll do it like this.' Martin listens patiently and obediently."

The anonymous author observed Lewis taking over from Ernie Glucksman the direction of "80 actors, dancers and technicians on their cues...leaving no doubt in anyone's mind that every detail of the program, from the opening fanfare to a minor bit in a sketch, was of great importance." It had been like that for several years... but unbeknownst to *TV Guide*—and even to Jerry Lewis—the days of a patient and obedient Dean Martin were drawing to a close.

* * * * *

SIDEBAR: *The Colgate Changeover*

As the current *Comedy Hour* season wound down, it was clear that Colgate-Palmolive was no happier than NBC with the producing acumen of the Bates agency, and in April they announced that responsibility for the show would be turned over to William Esty and Company. However, Colgate's other agency didn't actively produce shows; as Samuel H. Northcross, Esty's V.P. of Television, told *Sponsor* magazine, "When an agency gets into producing, it gets involved in too many extraneous things, like real estate, unions. It's all expensive and alien to the agency business.... No agency can make money producing shows." So, while Martin & Lewis cavorted across the country, behind-the-scenes negotiations were finalized to give their York Productions a piece of Colgate's action.

"The producing company is York Pictures, owned partly by Paramount and Martin and Lewis," said Northcross. "Next fall, the show will be entirely a variety show, with a continuous m.c., topical headline acts, to be directly competitive with Sullivan. We're fairly well decided on an actor, one who's sufficiently mature to carry authority with the people in his business. We're also planning to put more stress (and money) on names than on production values." To that end, $85,000 per week would be allocated toward production, which according to *Broadcasting-Telecasting* magazine was $20,000 higher than Sullivan's budget. Dean and Jerry each got to keep $4,000 of this as a perk for allowing their company to produce, over and above what NBC would be paying them for hosting.

Colgate again decided to keep sponsorship through the summer weeks, so the newly-christened *Colgate Variety Hour* would begin on June 12. Until the ambitious fall plans could be put into action, the show would focus on promoting new motion pictures. With Paramount naturally taking the lead, most other major studios were willing to participate. The audience would get a small preview of this approach when time was taken on Martin & Lewis' next hour to showcase their latest picture.

* * * * *

THE COLGATE COMEDY HOUR: Dean Martin & Jerry Lewis Show #26.

Airdate: June 5, 1955; NBC-TV.
Guest Star: Buddy Rich
With: The Ebonaires, Sonny King
Cast: Peggie Castle
Announcer: Wendell Niles
Writers: Arthur Phillips, Harry Crane
Television Director: Dick Weinberg
Producer & Director: Ernest D. Glucksman

OPENING/SKETCH #1: Tim Sellman (*Lewis*) introduces the program and the sponsoring products. After explaining how the Colgate company strives for dignity and good taste, we see that he isn't wearing any pants. Sellman introduces newsman Tedward R. Burrow. Emerging from a thick cloud of cigarette smoke, Burrow (*Martin*) welcomes viewers to "Person to People," where tonight he'll be interviewing the famous Hollywood luminary, Harlan Sando (*Lewis*). Sando greets the host while seated on his motorcycle, which he keeps inside the house (*Sando:* "It's my hobby." *Burrow:* "Oh, motorcycling?" *Sando:* "No, sitting!"). A set of bongo drums are mounted on the handlebars, and Burrow asks about them. Sando explains, "These drums come from an animal… You sneak up on this animal in the jungle, and when his back is turned, you steal his bongos." Burrow asks him about the items on his mantle, one of which we see is an Academy Award. Sando prefers talking about the "resister plug" and "carbonation vacillator" that rest on either side of the statuette. Finally Burrow asks, "Isn't that an Oscar?" Sando says it is: "They gave that to me for makin' a picture." When Burrow asks what picture, Sando says, "How do I know? I never go to the movies." Burrow wants to meet Harlan's family, so Sando introduces his "twin sisters," who are ages six and twenty-four. Burrow's confused: "If one is six and the other's twenty-four, how can they be twins?" Starting with the little girl, Sando says, "This one's my half-sister, and this one lies about her age!" Just before signing off, Sando asks Burrow, "How about getting a look at your family once?" Burrow agrees, and a curtain parts to show his family, a group of nine people of various ages all puffing away on cigarettes.

DEAN SOLO #1: Accompanied by The Ebonaires, Dean sings "Kentucky Babe."

SKETCH #2: Dean and his wife (*Peggie Castle*) are celebrating their anniversary as a second honeymoon: one week in their beachside house, all alone. Unfortunately, the bliss is short-lived: a publicist arrives with a brace of reporters and the winner of a contest for which the prize is a week with Dean Martin. Clad in a sweater and football helmet, the excitable young fan (*Lewis*) cries out "Dean Martin! My favorite movie star!" and faints. After the boy comes to, the newsmen gather around for photographs, which makes him even more excitable. Finally, Dean throws the reporters out and talks with the boy, whose name is Georgie. He asks for an autograph, and dictates a lengthy salutation. He also shows him his "What Dean Martin Doesn't Use" scrapbook that contains Dean's old mustache and a half-eaten candy bar, which has since melted. Georgie gathers new souvenirs: a button from Dean's suit (which ruins the jacket), the telephone (after Gary Cooper calls) and his butler's uniform. Dean draws the line when Georgie tries to put Mrs. Martin in his scrapbook. She wants to be alone with her husband, and Dean remembers the contest rules, one of which is Georgie has to pass a screen test, or else he must go home. Dean reads a lengthy monologue and tells Georgie he must get it right on the first try. Amazingly, Georgie does just that, and Mrs. Martin leaves to prep the guest room. Georgie confesses he'd like to be an actor but has neither talent nor good looks. Dean encourages him by singing "(You've Gotta Have) Heart" from *Damn Yankees*. As the curtain closes, they try it together, with special lyrics.

Newspaper advertisement for the June 5, 1955 *Colgate Comedy Hour*. The following week, the show would be renamed *The Colgate Variety Hour*, and Martin & Lewis' company would produce it.

INTERLUDE: Jerry introduces a clip from the team's latest picture *You're Never Too Young*; the "Relax-Ay-Voo" number from the barber scene is shown.

GUEST ACT / JERRY SOLO: Jerry introduces drummer Buddy Rich and asks if he can play alongside him. Jerry tries a few simple beats to warm up, but Buddy outclasses him every time and eventually takes over with a lengthy solo. Finally, he and Jerry play together along with the orchestra.

DEAN SOLO #2: "Carolina in the Morning"

FINALE: Jerry introduces Sonny King, who sings "If I Didn't Care" in the style of The Ink Spots. Dean tries to interject, but Sonny holds him off until the bridge. Throughout, Jerry stands still, moving only when Dean gives him a stick of gum to chew. At the show's conclusion they plug the *Colgate Variety Hour* and thank Sonny King and Buddy Rich. Jerry also thanks the firemen who would be heading up the MDA's fundraising campaign for the second year in a row.

ANALYSIS AND REVIEWS: The final *Colgate Comedy Hour* takes aim at another CBS stalwart, Edward R. Murrow and his *Person to Person* interview show, for the opening sketch. Unfortunately, the result lacks both the spark and satire of the previous show's Ed Sullivan takeoff. Dean makes no effort to mimic Murrow; instead he gets laughs by reclining in ridiculous positions in his easy chair while incessantly smoking. Cigarettes were as much Murrow's trademark as stiffness was Ed Sullivan's; a three-pack-a-day habit would ultimately claim Murrow's life when he succumbed to lung cancer at age 57. As for Jerry, he's costumed like Brando in *The Wild One* (1953), but uses his punch-drunk voice throughout, with no attempt to capture the actor's distinctive delivery.

Dean appears on a barren stage, and as he explains how they set the scene for television, the appropriate background scenery and props are moved into place, The Ebonaires get situated, the orchestra plays and he begins singing "Kentucky Babe." It's the exact same arrangement as in 1951, except Dean is a more confident performer. His performance is outstanding, making it doubly curious that he never recorded the song for Capitol. As it is, he'd recently released a Dixieland-themed album, from which were drawn his second solos from both the last show and this one.

The second sketch repeats, for the third time, the device of having everything just stop so the team can sing a special duet. This one, "Heart" from *Damn Yankees*, also has special lyrics, but only intended to replace the baseball-themed verses with lines about showbiz. Dean's suede shoes take another beating (you'd think he'd learn *not* to wear them) when a hyper Jerry pulls off a tablecloth, sending plates and food crashing to the floor and upon Dean's feet, after which he can't resist trying to step on them again. Lewis seems to be going for a combination of what he called "the monkey" and "the poor slob," but the material isn't especially memorable, except perhaps the moment when Georgie demonstrates how he won the contest: by singing "The Ballad of Davy Crockett" backwards and sideways.

For those who enjoy drum solos, the extraordinary Buddy Rich delivers a gem, and even though Lewis gets into the act, it's wisely set up so that Rich improves on Jerry's licks and eventually takes over. The minute or so that both play along with Stabile's orchestra makes for a fine finish. The routine with Sonny King dates back to Dean and Jerry's pre-team days; Jerry even explains that they used to do it informally at Leon & Eddie's Bar in New York ten years before. It's an interesting and funny change of pace, with Jerry practically comatose, just staring at the camera with a deer-in-the-headlights look. It's Dean who carries the comedy ball, caught between trying to get to the microphone while the overly-dramatic Sonny keeps pushing him away and reacting to the immobile Jerry. Even when Dean gets to do his part, Sonny insists on whispering the lyrics into his ear. Finally, during the second chorus, Dean snatches the mic from Sonny and points it at Jerry, who plaintively asks, "After this song, will we sing another one?"

"Last night's seasonal windup...to close out five years of Colgate sponsorship, rose rather than fell," wrote *Daily Variety's* 'Helm.' "The lunacies were not as extreme, but the volume of comedy was full measure with added factors to round out an evening of high carnival and a rich blend of melodies from the pipes of Dean Martin…. What they've done three times this season they should have repeated last night, that of topping 'Toast of the Town' in the overnight Trendex." The only thing Helm didn't like was the movie scene, calling it "devoid of laughs," which might be the reason it was cut from the film before release. 'Rose' of *Variety* was more generous, labeling the clip "a pleasant interlude," and calling "Person to People" "the best bit on the show…. With Martin as the interviewer and Lewis talking like a punchy pug, there were some genuinely funny episodes here. The bit in which Lewis emulated a contest winner who gets a chance to spend a week with a Hollywood star was basically funny, but this bit managed to recall so many similar things done by the combo." As for the show as a whole, Trau felt "the pair didn't have a brilliant setup, but hard work and application pushed some fairly mediocre situations into payoff territory."

John Lester's review consisted of a sentence: "While Dean Martin and Jerry Lewis were doing last Sunday's 'Colgate Comedy Hour' on NBC-TV, a little girl guest in our house suddenly asked: 'Don't those two men like each other?'" It was a fair question. After coming off a personal appearance tour, the two could've either been razor sharp or exhausted. Neither was the case. Each turned in an energetic, professional performance that pointedly lacked the intimacy and joy normally associated with Martin & Lewis. At times during the show, they laughed at each other; what they didn't do once was laugh *with* each other.

Good thing *TV Guide's* reporter wasn't covering the preparation for this show. "Martin complained that he was a fifth wheel," wrote columnist Aline Mosby less than a week later. "He didn't show up for many rehearsals, shrugging, 'Why should I? I got nothin' to do.'" Instead, "Dean practiced his golf swing on the NBC set and, observers report, 'needled Jerry about his trying to direct the show.'" Another anonymous eyewitness would tell columnist Dick Williams, "You never saw two colder guys than last Sunday night at their TV show. They just ignored each other off camera. You could feel the tension around them."

That coldness was in the interest of self-preservation. In less than 48 hours, all hell would break loose.

* * * * *

SIDEBAR: *Martin vs. Lewis, Round Two*

Monday, June 6: Jerry—literally seconds from boarding a train that would take the team to New York for a gala premiere of *You're Never Too Young*—was told by Mack Gray, Dean's personal assistant, "your partner isn't making the trip.... He said he's tired. He's going to take Jeanne on a trip to Hawaii."

The premiere was being held at Brown's Hotel in the Catskill Mountains of Sullivan County, New York, where Lewis had made his professional debut as a teen; the hotel picking up the tab. When owner Charles Brown made the offer at the start of the year, it was eagerly accepted by the two-thirds of York that weren't Dean Martin, who flatly rejected it but wasn't interested in proposing an alternate venue. Finally, while winding up their Vegas engagement in early February, he told his partner, "I don't give a f--- where we hold it," and Lewis took this as a default approval to open the film at Brown's.

That's the official story, which Lewis repeated in both *Jerry Lewis in Person* and *Dean and Me*. "I felt like somebody had kicked me in the stomach," he wrote in the latter volume. And yet, something doesn't quite ring true. There was a seventeen week stretch between closing at Las Vegas and arriving at Union Station depot, during which the team filmed *Artists and Models*, made a two-week personal appearance tour, and hosted three *Colgate* hours. Was *nothing* discussed about the premiere during that span? Train tickets and overnight reservations in New York City would've been required for Dean, who would have had to say whether or not he'd be bringing his wife. Discussions and possibly rehearsals of what they'd do or say upon arrival at Brown's would have at least been scheduled. Would the usually all-controlling Jerry have simply sidestepped all this, trusting he'd interpreted his partner correctly and expecting Dean would follow through on his own? Or did Dean simply nod his head in agreement when conferring with Jerry and/or Paramount, silently biding his time until the last possible moment before dropping a bombshell?

Make no mistake: it *was* a bombshell. After dispatching his "go-fer" to deal with Jerry, Dean met with his agent at MCA to discuss lining up a solo TV gig. While Lewis was brooding aboard the Super Chief, Martin was confiding to columnist Earl Wilson, "I want a little TV show of my own, where I can sing more than two songs in an hour, and I don't want to go out on the road anymore and travel around." Wilson, who like other journalists received an invitation—signed by both partners—for the premiere, asked Dean about it and got an earful:

"I think Jerry jumped on the train to New York, but my wife and I are taking off for Honolulu. Because, outside of back east, who knows about the Catskills? I'd go anywhere in the world, but it didn't seem right just to go to Brown's Hotel because it's not in everyone's reach. I told Paramount three months ago I wasn't going, but somebody down at Paramount didn't pay attention to me," said Martin, clearly willing to assign blame to York's third party.

"This is no big split-up," Martin assured Wilson. "I just love to sing. I'm about 10 years older than the boy. He wants to direct. He loves work. So maybe he can direct and I can sing." Wilson asked Dean how Jerry felt about these solo aspirations. "'Oh I don't even think anybody has mentioned it to him,' Jerry's elder partner replied airily."

Martin's assessment of the Catskills didn't win him any supporters "back east." Officers of the Sullivan County Hotel Association reminded the press of the many names that had started there: Ethel Merman, Danny Kaye, Moss Hart, Judy Holliday, Sid Caesar, Red Buttons and Eddie Fisher. "Martin was unkind and unfair," said the Association's vice-president Milton Kutsher. "We aren't known only in the east; we have a national reputation. We're on the map, no matter what Mr. Martin says. Maybe he should stop being Rip Van Winkle."

The wire services picked up on Wilson's column and proceeded to distribute a "Martin-Lewis Split Rumored" piece to the nation's dailies, which hit the front pages on Tuesday. This got Dean back on the telephone: to the Associated Press he denied there was any split-up, only "a misunderstanding." He reaffirmed that he'd rejected the press junket to Brown's months earlier, but this time it wasn't over who did or didn't know about the Catskills. "Martin felt that, because Lewis had once worked as a busboy and has a lot of friends there, so much of the limelight would be on Lewis that it would practically be a solo performance," read a follow-up dispatch on June 8. "Martin insisted he actually didn't know Lewis was going without him until after Lewis left for New York Monday night."

"I'm not mad at Jerry about this," Dean assured the press, "but naturally I'm upset about it. All this publicity makes me look like a heel." As for requesting a solo TV show, it had nothing to do with splitting up the team. "I just want to sing a little more, that's all." He and Jeanne left for Hawaii, assuming everything was smoothed over. Little did he know.

On Thursday, Lewis (accompanied by his wife) arrived at Penn Station and stepped onto a platform filled with reporters hoping to hear his side of the story. "I was completely unprepared for their questions," and so kept silent. The next morning he took a car to the Catskills, brooding and weeping as he passed billboard after billboard advertising the team's presence for the June 11 premiere. He managed to get through the weekend, surrounded by over 100 newspaper people, plus time on NBC radio's brand new *Monitor* series, with little more than a solemn "No comment..." concerning Martin's absence, until it was nearly over. He even narrated a Paramount newsreel of the event. Finally, on Sunday evening he broke down and, weeping, told reporters, "Maybe the lawyers wouldn't want me to say anything...but you've been wonderful. You know we have a cross to bear up here, and I want to thank you for saving me embarrassment by not asking questions I couldn't answer. Frankly, I don't have the answer."

At first, few believed the team was in any real danger of splitting. An unnamed Paramount executive told the *New York Post*, "There's no real panic about it. These are two smart boys, too smart to give up a $5,000,000 operation because of a spat." Their most perceptive critic, John Lester, also thought money would settle the matter: "The feeling in many quarters, this time, is that they're through as a team. I'm sure they are, too, in the sense that they'll never be the carefree, uninhibited performers of the past. But I'm just as sure they'll never break permanently. Too many people are associated with them business-wise who can and will prevail on them to continue. Also, there's too much money involved for either to be so foolish as to effect (*sic*) a complete break."

Yet hell hath no fury like Jerry Lewis scorned. By refusing to attend the premiere and sounding off to the press, Martin not only publicly defied Lewis' authority as their business manager, but also denigrated one of his sentimental partner's cherished memories. Wasn't a partnership supposed to involve give-and-take? When Steubenville arranged a celebratory "Dean Martin Day," Jerry was by his side throughout. More recently, when Jeanne Martin asked Dean to entertain at an event benefiting her pet children's charity, SHARE (Share Happily and Reap Endlessly), Jerry at first refused to join him because Abby Greshler was also involved, yet ultimately set his animosity aside and performed for his partner's sake. This cut deeper than a spat over a movie script.

Having spent a few days in Florida to recuperate, Lewis came home and went right to MCA chief Lew Wasserman, Paramount's Y. Frank Freeman and his attorney's office, and told them all he'd no longer work with Dean Martin. Lewis and his lawyers would spent the rest of June and all of July angling to get of every contract to which Martin & Lewis were committed… tersely repeating "No comment" to any reporter that asked what was going on.

Some of Jerry's friends were willing to plug the gap, albeit anonymously. Referring to "the inevitable bust up of Martin & Lewis," Earl Wilson reported, "Jerry, who's a sentimentalist, gets almost tearful now when he's asked by friends about lawyers trying to terminate their partnership as soon as possible. To one friend, Jerry said, 'Dean is a great talent and I know he will do well on his own. I hope I will too.'" Another unnamed Lewis associate was blunter: "Jerry thinks the team should do more… [to] keep active in clubs, theaters, benefits and public relations work, as well as pictures and TV. He thinks the other member of the team should participate to the fullest extent or else get out. For that reason, he has asked for release from their various contracts." Concurrently, MCA's bush beaters tried shopping a Martin solo show to various sponsors, until NBC reminded them they already had him under an exclusive TV contract that called for team appearances only. A similar stipulation was built into their contract with Hal Wallis.

In a front page story, *Variety* pragmatically looked at the brouhaha from the business side, pointing out the team's York Productions co-owned the newly christened *Colgate Variety Hour*, which had just started on June 12 with a show designed primarily to plug a new Paramount release, *Strategic Air Command*. "Paramount and other companies are in line for some hefty bally of their new pictures," read the piece in their June 15 issue. Moreover, "York…has the corporate commitment to provide Martin and Lewis for six of the shows beginning in the fall. [They] are York's key working assets, outside of equities in M&L pictures. If the combo dissolves, York, too, would cease to be a going concern. Meaning, no more *Colgate* show and the end of the opportunity for film companies to showcase their late product.

"This, of course, would be only one ripple in the wake of events that would follow an M&L rift. Their pictures… have been consistently strong, with domestic distribution grosses of about $4,000,000 each, and there's no sign of any box office slide. [Paramount] would have a tough time filling the void in its lineup that would be created with a M&L divorce."

News like that travels fast, even to a Hawaii that wasn't yet a state. When "the other member of the team" got wind of what his partner was doing, he cut short his vacation and returned home. Although a stop in Acapulco had also been on the Martins' summer agenda, he cancelled that, telling columnist Harrison Carroll he and Jeanne would "just stick around here for a while." *Now* he was angry, and despite all the uncertainty he refused to reach out directly to Lewis: "I wouldn't take a step to make up with that boy."

Faced with such childishness, *Daily Variety* editor Joe Schoenfeld saw fit to administer a spanking in the July 13 issue:

Hey, Kids! Meaning you, Dean and Jerry! Wake up! Grow up!

   Since it isn't so serious a matter as a split of the spoils, there can't possibly be any breach in your personal relationship that can't be repaired by the application of a lot of understanding and a little common sense. Friends once, surely you should be able to find the common ground of amicability if not outright devotion to one another. Obviously – to you as well as to outsiders – there's considerably more reason for you to remain as a team than there could possibly be in your separation.

Yes, you are fine individual talents! But until you blended those talents you were individual nonentities as entertainers. While you may believe that your earning powers will be as great in solo appearances, that's to be tested and cannot be guaranteed. The public made you a top boxoffice attraction because they loved you as a team; because together you have that indefinable chemistry that makes for top entertainment. Why break up a winning combination? Why commit the cardinal sin of disappointing your public?

There have been other show biz teams that, for one reason or another, didn't quite remain palsy walsy through their careers together. Yet, they saw the light of common sense and obvious economics and remained in tandem. The same should go for you, Dean and Jerry.

Grow up! Wise up! Make up!

Assuming he even read it, Dean saw no reason to comply. They were expected to start another York picture, a western comedy tentatively titled "Where Men Are Men" in August; surely Jerry would come to his senses before then. Yet after a couple of weeks' worth of golf rounds and no change in the status quo, Martin sensed damage control was in order. First, he instructed his attorneys to fire off a letter to MCA, Hal Wallis, Paramount and NBC that categorized his partner's stance—and his own desire for a solo show—as hearsay: "Gentlemen: Notwithstanding any statements or rumors which you may have heard to the contrary, please be advised that I recognize the existence of an employment contract with you dated September 1, 1954, and that I am and will continue to be and hold myself ready, willing and able to render and perform my services pursuant thereto." Journalist Herbert Kamm was at Lewis' home when a copy arrived. He recalled in 1957, "Written in the cold, formal phrasing one invariably finds in the language of lawyers… it closed with, 'Sincerely yours, Dean Martin.' Lewis held the letter in his hand, shook his head and said sadly, 'If he had only used the telephone.'"

Second, any reporter to which Jerry refused to comment found Dean more than willing to talk: To one: "I don't want to break up the team. It's a damn fine living and I want to hold on to it." To another: "What's the difference if we don't chum around? To me, this isn't a love affair; this is big business." And in every case, Martin referred to his partner as "the kid" or "the boy," never failing to point out that he was "ten years older" (actually nine). What was once a term of endearment from his "older brother" now sounded condescending… and Lewis fumed.

At the beginning of August, Lloyd Shearer of *Parade* magazine called on Jerry and caught him at the right—or wrong—psychological moment. After assuring Shearer that a split was "inevitable," the cork flew out of Lewis' bottle: "Dean was the guy who told the newspapers he was ready to do a single. Don't forget that. I didn't open my mouth. Now I will, and I want you should know the truth. This mess is my fault…. I made the mistake of worshipping this man. I thought more of Dean than my own wife, my own family. For years I thought I couldn't get along without him. I accepted everything we did on his terms, his standards, his values. Now I've grown up.

"A theatre-owner in Detroit, a guy who took care of us when we were struggling—he calls up. Business is lousy. He's going broke. For old time's sake, won't we play his house? I'm ready to fly to Detroit in the morning. But I gotta turn the guy down. Why? Can I tell him my partner wants to play golf? It's the same way with benefits. Hospitals, orphanages, worthwhile charities. They phone; will we give them a few minutes, a few hours? I'm dying to say 'Yes'—but I can't unless I show up without my partner." He was also dying to emulate Bob Hope: "I feel that when Dean and I get a few weeks off, we should be entertaining the troops in Korea, or Japan, or Greenland."

By now, Lewis was thoroughly worked up: "A guy in show business has obligations. God gave me a little comic ability… I must use what he gave me to make people laugh. Not only the fellas that can afford $6.60 for the first row, but also for the sick and the shut-ins…. I don't wanna preach, but I can't tell you how deeply I feel about these things. Twenty-nine years old, and I've got ulcers and I spit blood and I can't sleep and I lose weight. Who needs this? I don't care if Patti and me *(sic)* gotta go back to a one-room apartment in Newark. I gotta live with my conscience. You can't run a partnership, you can't run your life without principles. And if the only principle in this setup is to make money and to hell with everything else, I'm not buying it."

Needless to say, Shearer found Martin just as eager to talk. "I think the kid's bein' silly. We gotta (*sic*) company together, the York Corporation. We got one of the greatest deals of all time. Both of us gets $4,000 a week from TV. Then, after five years or six pictures, Paramount gives us five or six million dollars to split." Then Dino let his own cork fly: "Jer is willin' to throw this out the window because I don't love him. Who says I gotta love him? Business is business. Does Abbott love Costello? Why can't we have a business-like partnership?"

With that question, Dean had effectively thrown down a gauntlet toward his sentimental partner, but there was more to come: "To hear some of the gossip you'd think I was a criminal 'cause I don't wanna work 365 days a year. I can't help it if I'm not built like the kid. Jer'll work 24 hours a day if you let him. He'll put on a benefit for the kid who sells papers on the corner. I admire, respect him for it. But Jeez! He's ten years younger'n me. I can't take that routine. End of the day this guy jumpin' up and down my back, I'm tired. I'm beat. I like to go home. I gotta wife, six kids. They're entitled to my time, my companionship. I didn't get married so that I could spend my life on the stage doin' benefits for the campfire boys." Pointing out the telethons and Muscular Dystrophy events under their belts, Martin added, "We done (*sic*) as many benefits as anyone in the business. There's been no shirkin' on that score.

"I can't change the way I'm built to suit Jerry. They talk about my golf and all that. I never missed a show or rehearsal yet. Work is work an' play is play, an' a man's gotta have time for both… for his family, his kids. A guy should be allowed to step into a church for a few minutes without playin' a benefit."

Parade was one of countless mainstream magazines, newspapers and movie fan publications that served up takes on the feud; Maurice Zolotow even dusted off his 15-month-old *American Weekly* piece, brought it up to date and sold it to *Cosmopolitan*. But before any of them reached print the situation had changed. On August 8, Martin and Lewis walked into a Paramount conference room and sat down with Lew Wasserman, Y. Frank Freeman, Hal Wallis and their lawyer, Joe Ross—all of whom proceeded to explain the facts of their professional lives. Freeman had asked Paramount's board of directors if they'd approve a split. The answer was no. Wallis, whose contract with them—like NBC's—specified they could only work as a team, was adamant about enforcing it. Wasserman assured them NBC was of the same mind, and their lawyer affirmed these contracts were ironclad.

Moreover, the team had an outstanding tax debt of $650,000 that had come due. Lewis had borrowed the full sum from Y. Frank Freeman in July with a promise to pay it all back in two months. Although there was percentage money coming in from their pictures that would cover the debt, it would empty the till and Lewis now realized he'd have to continue working with Martin in order to refill it.

Despite promising he "wouldn't take a step to make up" with Jerry, Dean made the first move that morning; entering his partner's dressing room, extending his hand and asking, "Shake, Jer?" Martin and Lewis shook—and that was the summit of their interaction that day. There would be no hijinks at *this* meeting, no snipped ties, no water poured anywhere except into a glass and down a dry throat. As their agent and employers spoke, Lewis would later write, "their voices turned into a hum in my head that repeated the same message over and over: *You're stuck boy—stuck good and proper. For now, anyway.*" Once they'd all had their say, Lewis quickly and quietly agreed to everything, then dashed over to the set of George Gobel's first film, *The Birds and the Bees*, which had been written by Sidney Sheldon, author of the screenplays for *You're Never Too Young* and "Where Men Are Men" (soon to be retitled, with all due irony, *Pardners*), and directed by Martin & Lewis' favorite old pro, Norman Taurog. He spent the next hour or so working off his frustration. Earl Wilson was there, and noted "Jerry was his old self—clowning, pulling people's hats down over their eyes, chasing stagehands. 'Quiet on the set!' he shouted, clumping heavy-footed on the floor, making a great racket." In the midst of this madness, Wilson, who'd heard about the meeting, asked him if he and Dean would be working together again. He got a quiet, impassive response; a one-word scoop.

"Yeah."

The official announcement came from Paramount that afternoon: Martin and Lewis would continue as a team and *Pardners* would commence production in the fall. Unlike their first reconciliation, there would be no joint press release—they would make their own separate statements later in the day—and questions about the personal relationship between the two principals were answered, once again, with journalism's equivalent of the Fifth Amendment: "No comment."

The love affair had ended, but they were staying together for the kids: Wallis, Paramount, NBC and all that money. On August 8, 1955, Martin and Lewis embarked on "a business-like partnership," until neither man could bear it any longer.

8

1955–56:
THE COLGATE VARIETY HOUR AND A PARTNERSHIP END

DEAN: "Not too much was said. We both agreed to fulfill the contracts, go back to work, and try and make the best of everything."

JERRY: "We are attempting to get this thing started again. And the best way to do that is to keep my mouth shut."

DICK STABILE: "Thank God! Now I don't have to sell my drums!"

– Separate statements to the press, August 9, 1955

IN THE WEEKS AFTER PARAMOUNT'S press statement, a joke made the rounds in Hollywood: "Martin and Lewis have finally made up. Now if they'd only start speaking to each other." Except it wasn't a joke. The two continued to keep their distance until the beginning of September, when it was time to rehearse their first appearance of the TV season.

At that point, columnists were fed blurbs that the two were "back in business again" and "getting along nicely." NBC even issued a press release that claimed "Dean and Jerry, having rested all summer, are readying a typical wild Martin and Lewis show," completely ignoring the trauma that overshadowed this so-called "rest."

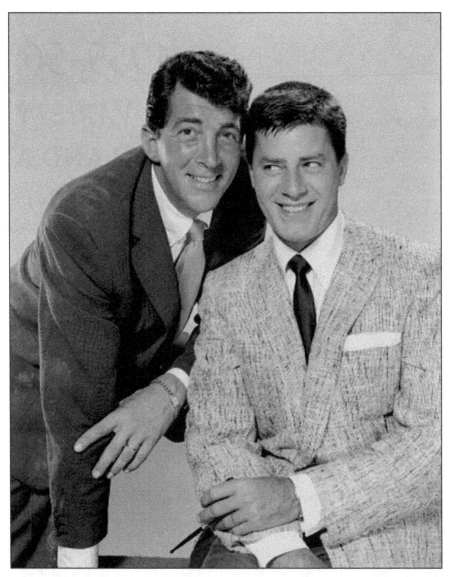

Forced togetherness and fake smiles characterize this 1955 publicity photo.

"They met at NBC's Hollywood studios the other day," wrote John Lester for his September 7 "Radio and Television" column, "greeted each other cordially, expressed their desire to 'get on with the show,' after which began the roughhouse, madcap antics." In light of this information, Lester concluded, "I now feel they'll stay together indefinitely. By the time current contracts run out in about three years, they will have realized how childishly they acted and have become good friends again, valuing each other more than ever."

Two days before their *Colgate* program was to air, Earl Wilson printed an even more optimistic tidbit. Dean and Jerry "were at a party at songwriter Sammy Cahn's when Jerry got into a friendly argument with another famous comedian. Dean busted over to Jerry and said, 'Hey, you're not supposed to be fighting with anybody but ME!'—and they've been back in love since."

Sadly, whatever intimacy remained between Dean and Jerry existed on paper: in contracts that could not be broken, in Jack Keller's rose-colored press releases, and in yet another piece of special material written by Cahn for their opening *Colgate* show.

* * * * *

THE COLGATE VARIETY HOUR: Dean Martin & Jerry Lewis Show #27.

Airdate: September 18, 1955; NBC-TV.
With Freddie Bell & The Bell Boys, Frank Sinatra (voice only)
Cast: Bob Carson
Announcer: Wendell Niles
Writers: Arthur Phillips, Harry Crane.
Staged and Directed by: Robert S. Finkel
Produced by: Ernest D. Glucksman
A York Pictures Production

OPENING/SKETCH #1: The Colgate-Palmolive company presents "The $64 Million Dollar Question," hosted by Hal April (*Martin*). After reviewing the Colgate products that are sponsoring the program (with extra emphasis on Veto deodorant), April introduces the returning contestant who has won $16 million: a Western Union messenger boy named Morty M.M. Morton (*Lewis*). Morton explains that his initials also stand for Morty, because his mother "used to get very exasperated with me, and say 'Morty, Morty, Morty....'" He's opted to keep the $16 million and go home, but April ignores this and places him in the isolation booth for a six-part $32 million question. Morton correctly guesses the answer, and decides to try for the whole jackpot. For this, he's told the isolation booth is insufficient protection against cheating, and is submerged in a tank of water with a headset. April begins reading the question, but time runs out and two guards enter the tank to ensure Morton stays put until the following week.

DEAN SOLO #1: "Nevertheless"

SKETCH #2: At a poolroom just off Broadway, "the aspiring stars of tomorrow while away the hours dreaming of the big chance." Dean is nearing the end of a game and trying to win a $5 bet, when a poor soul (*Lewis*) comes in from the rain. He watches Dean play, but gets too close and water spills from his hat onto the table. Dean directs him to take a seat, but the guy doesn't sit still for very long. As Dean tries to make a shot, the fellow, whose name is Harold, buys a Coke from a very noisy machine and loudly sips. Dean ties his straw in a knot and orders him to sit. The Coke has made the cue sticky, so Harold gets him some powder, which he liberally sprinkles over Dean's hands (and under his armpit). He offers to clean off the powder with a fan, but it doesn't work, so he uses a broom to dust off the table and gets more powder on Dean. After more mishaps with the powder and pool cues, Dean tells him to get out, but Harold refuses, saying he's also an actor, specifically a joke teller. Dean invites the other patrons to gather around for "free entertainment." Harold attempts to tell jokes, but as each one falls flat, he gets more distraught, and the others walk away. Dean goes back to his game, and tells Harold he's a singer. Harold replies that he also writes songs; his newest is called "Yetta, I Can't Forget 'er." He sings it, and Dean thinks it's terrible: "You can't write songs! Who would sing that?" As Dean goes back to his game, Harold looks at his watch and turns on the radio in time to hear Frank Sinatra sing "Yetta." As Sinatra croons, Dean finds himself alternating between singing along and banging his head in disbelief. When it's over, Harold explains that he made $200 from his first song and shows him the money. Dean immediately invites him to play poker, but after watching Harold unsuccessfully shuffling cards, he decides not to take advantage of him. At that point, a song plugger enters and Harold pays him the $200 for placing "Yetta" with Sinatra. The plugger tells him to tune in Perry Como at 7 to hear him sing Harold's new number, "Shirley, Her Teeth are Pearly." Given all this, Dean decides he's wrong about the kid's songwriting and wants to team with him. When Harold says they have no money to get started, Dean assures him "The only thing you need to build a team is us." They sing "Side By Side," followed by a special-lyric version.

JERRY SOLO: After naming some of the former prizefighters who have entered show business, Bob Carson introduces the newest of this circle: former welterweight contender Rocky Lachmann (*Lewis*), who, in punch drunk fashion and with a nose literally out of joint, sings "Learnin' the Blues."

DEAN SOLO #2: "I Like Them All"

GUEST ACT & FINALE: Jerry plugs *You're Never Too Young*, then introduces Freddie Bell and the Bell Boys, who sing "Rock-A-Beatin' Boogie." Dean and Jerry join them in an up-tempo rendition of "Shake a Hand." At the conclusion, they thank Frank Sinatra for recording "Yetta" and plug his appearance on NBC Tuesday in *Our Town*, wish Rocky Marciano luck on his upcoming championship bout with Archie Moore, say hello to two children who are suffering with muscular dystrophy, and plug next week's *Variety Hour*. They close with a reprise of their "Side By Side."

ANALYSIS AND REVIEWS: CBS-TV's *The $64,000 Question* (hosted by Hal March and sponsored by Revlon cosmetics) was a surprise smash and would even surpass *I Love Lucy* as the highest-rated show of 1955-56. Contestants that claimed expert knowledge of a certain subject would answer questions of escalating difficulty in that category, the value of a correct answer doubling each time, until the titular jackpot was reached. Featuring outlandish gimmicks such as a soundproof isolation booth and a bank guard that secures the most valuable questions, it was inevitable that parodies would appear—and they did. (Milton Berle would do his own take-off a couple of weeks later, in which Martin & Lewis made a cameo appearance.) The show, which actually began life as radio's *Take It or Leave It* (with a jackpot $64 question), would also lead to a plethora of "big money" quiz programs on television during the next two years, which in turn led to the quiz show rigging scandal and a subsequent congressional investigation during 1958-59.

The sketch all but accuses the original of "fixing" contestants ahead of time. Hal April convinces the reluctant Morty, whose area of knowledge is tobacco, to try for the $32 million. As April blows the smoke from six cigarettes into the soundproof isolation booth, Morty must name: 1) which cigarette has the cork tip, 2) the location of the plantation where the tobacco was grown, 3) the name of the plantation's foreman, 4) the store where the first pack was sold, 5) the name of the man who bought it, 6) the size of the bill he paid with, and 7) the serial number of that bill. He has 30 seconds to come up with the answer.

A brilliant parody of the contestant's tension within the isolation booth follows, intercut with the equally tense reactions of Hal April, the bank guard, and Morty's father and mother (photos of Jerry in makeup and drag, of course). When Morty admits he doesn't know the answer, April encourages him to guess. Of course, all six guesses are right on the nose, with Lewis's emotional reactions building with each correct answer. Topping it all, an incredulous Martin looks right into the camera: "What guessing!" It's impossible to escape the feeling that everyone knew *exactly* what was happening on these programs and decided to spill the beans. Revlon certainly took offence at the inference; they and CBS threatened a lawsuit against the team and NBC. (Ironically, the first quiz show for which contestant-fixing was proved, instigating the scandal, was *Dotto*, sponsored by Colgate-Palmolive.)

The sketch was well-written enough for Martin & Lewis to follow it to the letter… until Jerry got into a 10-foot tank of water, and Dean proceeded to push him under while reading the $64 million dollar question. After the third dunking, Martin immediately attempts to force his partner down again, but Lewis grasps the side of the tank. "Let me catch a breath here," he calls out. Pushed under again, Lewis returns with the old code phrase, "You're overacting!" Down he goes again, and re-emerges with, "A joke's a joke… but I'm drowning!" Now laughing along with the audience, Dean sends him under again. Jerry immediately pops up: "READ FASTER, WILL YA?" After one more submerging, a gasping Lewis grabs the tank and eyes Martin with suspicion: "Haven't you heard? The feud is over!" The line stopped the show.

Lewis's ad-lib, of course, wasn't the only comment on the team's well-publicized outburst. Sammy Cahn's lyrics for the special rendition of "Side By Side" performed after the second sketch, while not as good-naturedly satiric as the version they'd sung on their radio program back in 1953, still made light of the cause and scope of the event:

DEAN: *Oh, the road gets a little bit bumpy.*
JERRY: *And our nerves get a little bit jumpy.*
DEAN: *We beef and complain!*
JERRY: *But we remain…*
BOTH: *SIDE BY SIDE!*

JERRY: There are times when his smile ain't so sunny.
DEAN: Times when his fun isn't funny.
JERRY: So we fuss and we pout,
DEAN: But still we come out...
BOTH: SIDE BY SIDE!

DEAN: Life can be demandin'.
JERRY: Life isn't always play.
DEAN: We reached an understandin':
JERRY: It's gotta be HIS way!

DEAN: There are some who had parted us neatly.
JERRY: But we have fooled them completely.
DEAN: Had us both on the shelf!
JERRY: Look for yourself...
BOTH: SIDE BY SIDE!

DEAN: Like Topsy and like Eva, we'll always roll along!
JERRY: We had our own Geneva: He admitted that I was wrong!

DEAN: So, please allow us to sum up:
JERRY: If ever a problem should come up...
DEAN: We'll fight like before,
JERRY: But after the war...
BOTH: SIDE BY SIDE!

As for the sketch itself, it was another example of Jerry the put-upon innocent, inadvertently ruining Dean's game, not to mention the pool table. Dean gets a few moments to shine when he directs Harvey to take a seat, guiding the poor schnook into position with his hands, as if by magic. Harvey tries doing the same to himself shortly thereafter and winds up missing the chair. Later, when Dean continues playing pool as Sinatra is crooning Harvey's ridiculous "Yetta," his reactions are very good. But, as in prior shows, the sketch doesn't conclude so much as it is suspended for the special-lyric duet.

Dean's two songs and Jerry's solo spot are fine interludes, although the latter is not as funny as some of his other stunts. Here he just sings a song in his "punch drunk" voice and with his nose visibly taped so that it's pointed to the right. When Freddie Bell and the Bell Boys (whom Jerry erroneously introduces as "the Bellhops") start rocking, it's a little surprising. By now, of course, white rhythm and blues was on the ascent; Bill Haley and the Comets had already reached number one (with "Rock Around the Clock") on *Billboard's* music charts, and Elvis Presley was beginning to draw attention. Each would record one of the songs performed here: Haley would cut "Rock-A-Beatin' Boogie" and Presley would do "Shake a Hand." Even though popular music was changing, it's still a shock seeing a balladeer like Dean and a big band enthusiast like his partner freely indulging in rock and roll, even if Dean's vocalizing has a touch of satire to it.

Reviewers were ecstatic: "Easily one of their funniest shows of any season," raved *Daily Variety's* 'Helm,' who added, "Setsiders haven't seen the last of caricaturing '$64,000 Question' but they'll never see it done with more sock boffs than generated by the M&L version... Their other sketches also had high laugh contents." *TV-Radio Life's* critic agreed: "One of their best shows to date. Bob Finkel can take a deep bow for his initial chore of directing and staging an M&L epic." *Motion Picture Daily* proclaimed, "The pair, in their expected and welcome brand of comedy—largely slapstick—were aces high, [sending] the series off to a rollicking start."

"Except for the numerous commercials and one rock-n-roll number," wrote *Variety's* 'Herm,' "Martin & Lewis were on camera for the full hour and were socko all the way." All the critics made mention of the feud references and the special "Side by Side," with *Motion Picture Daily* terming it "an inspirational reply to a loud, if unspoken, question in the minds of all viewers.... It was real showmanship." *TV Radio-Life* noted, "As a matter of fact, the boys made it clear to viewers that their feud was a thing of the past." 'Herm,' on the other hand, hedged his bets: "Whatever the realities in the case, the boys worked together with as much rapport as ever."

The rapport was strictly that of two professionals determined to subsume any unpleasantness for the sake of the audience. Privately, observers recognized that nothing much had been resolved between them. When rehearsing earlier in the week, Jerry continued to involve himself in every aspect of production, spending as little time beside Dean as he could get away with. At one point, Lewis ducked into the soundproof booth used in the "$64 Million Dollar Question" sketch to check the wiring on the floor. Martin was overheard muttering, "Maybe we'll get a break; he'll electrocute himself down there." Whether because of this or (more likely) to simply assert himself, Lewis got his revenge on the air: during a quick reprise of the "Side By Side" rewrite at the close of the show, he pointedly changed his punchline to "I admitted that *he* was wrong."

Singing "Side By Side" and not meaning it on the September 18, 1955 *Colgate Variety Hour*.

Almost from the start of the team's career, Lewis had touted the strength of his and Dean's relationship as the basis of their mass adulation. The undercurrent of mutual affection that drove their antics was such a keystone of the act, the public had no trouble carrying it over to their private lives. Seeing them on television making light of their "misunderstanding" with a special song convinced the audience and most critics that all was well again. To be sure, the two *wanted* to enjoy themselves when working together. Whatever degree of animosity he was harboring, Martin still found Lewis funny; whatever professional frustration he was feeling, Lewis still loved his partner. Yet the stumbling blocks remained: Martin hated the "sad stuff" that Lewis kept encouraging the writers to produce, and Lewis hated that Martin was unwilling to give one performance more than was specified in their contracts.

A performance that was contracted was their guest appearance on the *Variety Hour* of October 16, a special tribute to Rodgers and Hammerstein, tied in with the release of the motion picture version of their classic show, *Oklahoma* (1955). The telecast originated from the Hollywood Bowl. Gordon MacRae and Shirley Jones were on hand to re-create numbers from the film, while other guests (Yul Brynner, Jan Clayton, Will Rogers, Jr., Bambi Lynn and Rod Alexander) paid tribute in their own specialties. According to *Daily Variety's* review, Jerry "conducted the orch of 52 in an R&H overture, but couldn't suppress the urge to take a pratfall after Martin gave a soothing version of 'Some Enchanted Evening.'"

A kinescope for the show hasn't surfaced as of this writing, but Lewis shot some 16mm footage of the dress rehearsal earlier in the day, in color and sound. It's a marvelous piece of history that deserves inclusion in *Oklahoma's* next home video upgrade, assuming there is one. Both MacRae and Jones perform their numbers and Rogers' monologue is also included. Everyone hits their marks and follows the script, even Lewis before he takes the podium to conduct. When he's through, he introduces Dean who treats it as he would any other rehearsal: not seriously. "Jerry, you did a hell of a good job there," he says, and of course his partner has to respond in kind: "Christ, Dean, thanks a lot!"

An *uncontracted* performance request came from their boss at Paramount, Y. Frank Freeman; the man who'd rescued the pair from the ire of the IRS just a few months before. Freeman was chairing a benefit for underprivileged children to be held at the Shrine Auditorium, and requested that Martin & Lewis make an appearance. The story is told in both of Lewis' books and other biographies as well: Jerry goes to great lengths to obtain Dean's verbal assurance that he'd be there and insists on sealing the deal with a handshake, as they had done long ago to inaugurate their partnership. The afternoon of the benefit, Thursday, November 10, Dean is nowhere to be found, so his nervous partner goes to even greater lengths, writing a note of reminder and having three copies made. One is left in Dean's dressing room at Paramount, and a messenger delivers the copies to his wife, his assistant Mack Gray, and the Lakeside Country Club. Ultimately, Dean fails to show up and Jerry does twenty minutes solo. The next morning, he confronts Dean in his dressing room and the latter asserts, "Nobody told me there was going to be a benefit." Adding insult to injury, Dean grabs a piece of paper, and scribbles a request for "two prints of *Living It Up*" on it before leaving the room. Jerry flips the paper over and sees his reminder.

The problem with this story is that, on November 10, the two of them would have been rehearsing their next starring *Colgate Variety Hour*, which was to air in three days. Possibly Lewis simply misremembered the El Capitan dressing room as Paramount, but the fact is they both should have been working together all week. If Martin blew off Thursday's rehearsal—and he would claim more than once that he "never missed" one in all the years they worked together—then Lewis' angst and notes are wholly justified.

Certainly they were rehearsing together on Friday, because that evening they appeared via remote on NBC's *Tonight*, hosted by Steve Allen from New York City. *Tonight* was then much more loosely constructed than the slick talk show it became under the Paar and Carson regimes; conversation was low-key, and Allen's announcer, Gene Rayburn, would even provide weather updates. On this segment, Allen made a game of turning his sponsors' advertising slogans into tongue-twisters, and he'd close out the program with an audience sing-along.

When the cutover was made to the El Capitan, Hy Averback introduces Dean and Jerry, who are seated within the set for the show's second sketch. Jerry was trying to flip a spoon into a coffee cup, while Dean was watching… and scowling, until he knew the camera was on him too, at which point he asked, "Steve, what's on the agenda there?" The first order of business was a song: with Skitch Henderson and the band playing in New York, via split-screen Dean took a flyer at "Almost Like Being in Love" and the results were very impressive. There's no discernable delay between West Coast voice and East Coast music, although Martin at one point says he can't hear the band. If true, he carried on admirably, always in pitch and with a steady rhythm that Henderson matched.

After that, Allen challenges them to the tongue-twisters; each is given a slogan to say five times fast. Averback gets the first: "Stretch mesh." Lewis is next with Armour's "Specially bred for a broad breast." When he succeeds, Jerry almost—but not quite—licks the side of Dean's face. Martin's is "we re-weave," and this being Dean he doesn't even try, saying "we-we-weave" each time and concluding with, "I sound like a baby!" Jerry agrees: "I think it's time for me to burp him!" Finally Lewis challenges Allen, asking him to say "I sat and tried my best" five times fast, which Allen does. "It's not much of a tongue-twister," Allen tells him, and Lewis agrees: "Oh, I know. I just like hearing people say 'I sat and tried my best!'"

Lewis plugged the upcoming *Variety Hour*, and Allen surprisingly asked Martin about this being muscular dystrophy month. Unsurprisingly, Lewis does the talking on this subject; the nation's firefighters were again collecting contributions as they had the previous year. And that was it; Allen said goodnight, and since it was almost 10:00 pm in Hollywood, presumably everybody went home. Two days later, although n one yet knew it as such, the *Variety Hour's* final "Dean Martin & Jerry Lewis Show" would air.

* * * * *

THE COLGATE VARIETY HOUR: Dean Martin & Jerry Lewis Show #28.

Airdate: November 13, 1955; NBC-TV.
With: The Norman Luboff Choir
Cast: Evelyn Lovequist, Isobel Elsom, Pat Sheehan, Frances Weintraub, Ave Lax, Milton Frome.
Writers: Arthur Phillips, Harry Crane.
Producer: Ernest D. Glucksman
Director: Robert Finkel

OPENING / SKETCH #1: Dean welcomes us to "Martin's Mighty Midnight Matinee Movie," sponsored by Colgate-Palmolive, their products displayed by his lovely assistant, Mildred (*Pat Sheehan*). Martin tells us the show will be premiering "a genuine talkie." The movie is actually a Japanese import: "Egg Roll is a Many Splendored Dish," starring Tab Yataguchi (*Lewis*). The opening titles have barely faded away when Martin is back with a commercial for Kralik Coffee, the coffee "with the flavor removed...so you can't form a habit," and which pours like maple syrup. "Ask for it by name. And if you can't think of the name, ask for tea." The picture resumes, and Tab enters the home of his geisha sweetheart, but the subtitles tell us he can't stay very long. His girl asks "Why not?" Just as he's answering, we return to Martin for another commercial; this one demonstrates a "dandy handy gadget" for housewives. His assistant Mildred places some raw whole vegetables into the drum, a button is pushed, and Martin opens a drawer to reveal the contents: "Instant garbage!" We return to the film: Tab says he can't say why he must leave, so his girl asks in to sing a love song before he goes. Picking up a shamisen, he does so, 's girl coyly fans herself. However, his plucking becomes so passion- instrument is quickly smashed into kindling. The film gives way 'in, who is nuzzling Mildred when he realizes he's on the air. He es a surprise guest: the star of the film. Tab enters; he and Dean few seconds until he becomes nauseous. Dean asks him what 'American women. Yataguchi gives a lengthy answer in Japanese, miming the hourglass figure, dancing and embracing. Dean asks, "What does that mean?" and Tab says, "Ecchhh!"

Martin says they will recreate a scene from Yataguchi's new picture, "Rice Cake Jungle." As the theme for *Dragnet* plays, we are shown scenes of Tokyo, and Martin's narration tells us the plans for a top secret aircraft have been stolen. He's brought into the interrogation room by two uniformed guards. Yataguchi enters and interrogates Martin, who mocks the way he talks (*Yataguchi*: "What about *pwans*?" *Martin*: "I don't got no *pwans!*"). During the interrogation, Martin keeps pulling a gun on Yataguchi, who gets angry with his guards for not stopping him ("He's gonna *bwow* my *bwains* out!"). Yataguchi and a guard resort to a torture that Martin selects from "Column B": they each grab one of his legs, pull them apart and advise him to "Make a wish." Martin hands over the "pwans," and Yataguchi is so pleased he sings his love song again, once more smashing his instrument while Martin coyly fans himself.

DEAN SOLO #1: "Beside a Shady Nook"

SKETCH #2: The wealthy Mrs. Cartwright (*Isobel Elsom*) is throwing an engagement party for her daughter Lorraine (*Evelyn Lovequist*) and Dean, who is uncomfortable because he doesn't know anyone. His fiancée asks him why he didn't invite his friend. "Sidney? He hasn't got a tuxedo; he couldn't come to these places." Mrs. Cartwright has engaged a renowned violin virtuoso to entertain; just as he begins playing, Sidney (*Lewis*) rides by on his bicycle. He stops to listen, notices the formal appearance of the guests, takes off his beanie and straightens his hair, using a nearby fountain to wet his comb. Looking around, he spots his friend, waves and yells, "HEY, DEAN!" Dean and Lorraine are mortified. Sidney carries his bike through the seated guests, bumping into them. Martin tells him to take a chair, so he snatches one from under one of the guests. Dean points to an empty chair, which makes a lot of noise when Sidney unfolds it. "I came over to congratulate you for marrying a rich girl!" says Sidney, who explains to Miss Cartwright how he and Dean were childhood buddies: "We used to steal fruit from pushcarts together!" Embarrassed, Dean explains, "Ah, that was a long time ago, wasn't it?" to which Sidney replies, "Yesterday!" They listen to the virtuoso, but Sidney's hungry, and this creates several disturbances. He eats peanuts but begins choking. He tries to reach a bowl of fruit, but passes his hand through a harp, making discordant sounds. He spots a low-hanging fruit on a tree, but when he grabs

Rehearsing their guest appearance on *The Colgate Variety Hour* of October 16, 1955, performed at the Hollywood Bowl. The show is lost, but this rehearsal exists in a 16mm Lewis home movie. Photo courtesy of Kayley Thompson.

the branch, the fruit won't dislodge. Dean takes the branch away from him, causing fruit to liberally fall upon the guests, who depart in anger. Dean tells Sidney he just doesn't belong in these high class surroundings and that Lorraine is important to him. He shows Sidney the engagement ring he bought; Sidney accidently drops it in the punch bowl. The butler pours out some drinks, one of which contains the ring. Dean and Sidney surreptitiously check each of the guests' drinks; the ring is in Mrs. Cartwright's glass. She catches Dean fishing it out, but Sidney explains that it was his fault: he told Dean to take her drink because "I don't think he wants you to be a boozer." Mrs. Cartwright announces the engagement, and as the guests offer congratulations, Sidney enthusiastically kisses all the women, ending up with Lorraine in a lengthy clinch. "Hey," Dean tells him, "that happens to be the girl I'm gonna marry." "I'd like to wish you the best of luck," says Sidney, who resumes kissing her. Dinner is served; Sidney sits beside Dean and starts eating, but Dean wants Lorraine in Sidney's chair. Sidney offers to switch with her, and asks another guest if he can sit across from Dean, eventually he stands upon the table (with one foot on Dean's hand) and directs a mass seating change. Dean pulls him off and again says he doesn't belong here. A furious Lorraine tells Dean that his "common" friend Sidney has ruined the party and storms off. As Dean chases after her, Sidney looks around sadly. Dean returns, though, and tells Sidney he forgot something: "I don't belong here myself." Together they sing "Two Lost Souls."

JERRY SOLO: Jerry explains that there are three extra minutes he needs to fill, which he'd like to use to sing his Kangaroo Patrol song, "Pouches Forever." Before he can start, director Bob Finkel, over the loudspeaker, asks Jerry to hit his mark. Jerry can't seem to get where Finkel wants him, so a technician (*Milton Frome*) places him in the correct spot. Jerry attempts to start again, but another technician places him somewhere else. Angry now, Jerry yells at Finkel and the others, but as he calms down he realizes this will get him in trouble with the union. Sure enough, as Jerry introduces the song, the spotlight lowers to the floor. He drops to the floor, but the first technician tells him the time is up. Angry again, Jerry tells him he's going to sing anyway, but someone grabs him by the legs and he's swiftly yanked from the stage.

DEAN SOLO #2: Accompanied by the Easy Riders, Dean sings his newest release, "Memories Are Made of This."

FINALE/GUEST ACT: Jerry argues that Dean should have asked him for a group to sing with, as he has one. When Dean asks to see the group, the Norman Luboff Choir surrounds him. Under Jerry's direction, they accompany Dean's rendition of "Sometimes I'm Happy."

ANALYSIS AND REVIEWS: A few days after this broadcast, Eve Starr reported in her "Inside TV" column, "Dean Martin and Jerry Lewis, fed up with the almost bored reaction of the "regulars" who predominate (*sic*) Hollywood's studio audiences, turned all the tickets for Sunday's show over to the student body of Woodbury College. The reaction was close to atomic." "They were the hottest audience in the last seven years," Lewis told *Newsweek*. "They applauded louder and they laughed harder...like a servicemen's audience. We're going to invite U.C.L.A. students for our next show." It was a worthwhile idea, but unfortunately they'd not get to utilize it.

Topical references were few and far between on Martin & Lewis' shows, which is one reason why they've held up despite the technological disadvantage of existing on kinescope. Even if the originals are obscure to modern viewers, the television programs spoofed by the team utilized formats that have endured; nearly everyone has seen at least one variety, celebrity interview and game show. The satire of this opening sketch, however, requires some background for context. While practically every TV station had at least one movie program at the time, major Hollywood studio films weren't available. The features that TV distribution and syndication companies offered were haphazardly-assembled packages culled from independent producers, defunct B-movie factories and European studios. Few such packages contained anything produced later than 1942, unless it was a foreign film like Italy's *The Bicycle Thief* (1948). It was big news in 1954 when the Bank of America sold 30 independent productions it had obtained via foreclosure to syndicator General Teleradio, a package that included *Body and Soul* (1947), *One Touch of Venus* (1948), *Magic Town* (1947) and *The Miracle of the Bells* (1948); prior to this sale, most features on TV starred Saturday afternoon cowboys, barely-remembered names from the 1920s and '30s, and Laurel & Hardy. A month after this sketch aired, it was out of date: R.K.O. Radio Pictures sold its pre-1948 library to television in December, followed shortly thereafter by Warner Bros; within two years, all the major studios had capitulated, consigning ancient ad-hoc film packages to oblivion.

"Martin's Mighty Midnight Matinee Movie" was specifically based on *The Late, Late Show*, which aired at midnight on New York's WCBS-TV, channel 2, even using the same theme song (Leroy Anderson's "The Syncopated Clock"). The sketch came under fire even before it aired. "The skit burlesques various long-winded commercials on such items as garbage disposals, vacuum cleaners and coffee," reported columnist James Bacon the day before the broadcast. "Without exception, groups representing various segments of those industries have asked, in legal queries, the comics' intent with regard to these products." Since there is no vacuum cleaner commercial in the finished sketch, their letter must have been particularly intimidating. Additionally, the "Matinee Movie" was originally titled "Egg

Roll is a Many Splendored Thing," but according to Lewis, "Twentieth Century-Fox got wind of this so now the movie title has been changed to 'Egg Roll is a Many Splendored Dish.'" Added Martin, "It's getting so you can't say 'Hello' on television anymore without the telephone company claiming 'That's our line.'"

Needless to say, the bits with "Tab Yataguchi" are extremely politically incorrect, but those who aren't sensitive to such matters will find much to laugh at, as Dean clearly does throughout his "Rice Cake Jungle" scene. The buck-toothed Asian was a staple of Lewis' night club shtick, and he'd briefly essayed a similar type in *Living it Up*.

The Engagement Party sketch is another Lewis venture into pathos. Twice during the bit, Martin calls him "Jerry" instead of "Sidney," which at least implies he was as disinterested during rehearsals as he appeared in the *Tonight* segment. The gags are all good and Lewis puts them over with panache, but once again, the sketch just stops so a Sammy Cahn-penned lyric meant to reassure viewers can be trotted out, this one based on "Two Lost Souls" from *Damn Yankees*:

DEAN: *We're two lost souls, that's all that we are,*
JERRY: *One of us sings,*
DEAN: *The other is jerky.*
JERRY: *But to us, we'll stick*
DEAN: *Through thin or through thick,*
BOTH: *Like 'Alba' and 'querque'*

DEAN: *It's Jerry and Dean, and no one in between,*
JERRY: *Like let's say Gallagher and let's say Shean.*
DEAN: *Of course we complain; we fuss and strain,*
JERRY: *But after the fussin' there's always us'n.*

DEAN: *Ah, we're two lost souls, each wedded to each,*
JERRY: *We go hand in hand, in all kinds of weather.*
DEAN: *On the bottom or top,*
JERRY: *A hit or a flop,*
BOTH: *It's both together. We got each other.*

This time, the performance feels sterile, plus the two barely look at each other. In fact, they hardly look at each other throughout the show. Asked to be harsh or angry with Lewis, Martin is all-in, with no implication that he's kidding around as in prior years. Asked to be sweet, Martin mostly looks away when speaking his lines, and persistently turns away when Lewis is speaking to him. For his part, Lewis plays directly to the audience, never to his partner.

Martin even looks a little disinterested during the acoustic guitar-driven "Memories Are Made of This." It's been reported that he didn't think much of the song or the arrangement, but went along with it at Capitol's insistence. His earlier rendition of the fully orchestrated "Beside a Shady Nook" was more to his liking and it shows in his performance.

The finale with Jerry's "group" takes the old "choir-ee" arrangements like "Once in a While" to a new extreme. The bizarre arrangement is very funny, and of course Jerry's (mis)direction and Dean's reactions are spot on. The vocal gymnastics required of the Luboff choir must have been a challenge, but when they suddenly produce water pistols and fire into the air while continuing to sing, it stops the show.

Daily Variety's 'Helm' admitted, "Martin & Lewis have had funnier shows.... Last night's...didn't abound in the continual uproar that generally explodes from M&L antics." Helm enjoyed the closing most, calling it "a howling burlesque worthy of Spike Jones." Conversely, *Variety's* 'Chan' opined, "Martin & Lewis turned in their best show by far of the past couple of seasons.... It was a crowded hour of M&L only and virtually all of it off the top shelf in the laugh department, all solid material with no stretching or stalling." Both *Varietys* singled out "Memories are Made of This" for praise; Chan calling it "a potential hit."

The usually perceptive John Lester was evidently too busy laughing to notice any lack of rapport between the two stars: "The boys were up to some of their old time laugh antics and threw in a few new ones for good measure. Their opener was one of the latter, a take-off on CBS-TV's late movie series.... [They'll] probably have a lawsuit on their hands some time today. The number was also pretty rough on the Japanese, and the boys can expect criticism from this angle, too.... Controversial or not, I have to admit I laughed all the way through the number and continued to the excellent finale with the Norman Luboff choir—and beyond. I thought it was a very funny show.... Dean and Jerry weren't brilliant or sensational, they were just 'crazy' and they were a delight."

One critic at least suspected something was amiss: "Maybe I'm imagining things, but if Dean Martin and Jerry Lewis have really made up, I'll eat this column," wrote Walter Hawver of the *Albany Knickerbocker*. "The tension between the two was evident at all times last night, and it affects their comedy. Not that the takeoff on late, late television shows or the garden-party fiasco script were as good as TV fans have come to expect of the combo, but with the same material several years ago the pair would have scored more laughs than they did.

"'It's Jerry and Dean, and no one in between,' the boys sang...but don't you believe it. Jerry was at his best when he was on stage alone. His 'time filler' jousting with the director and cameramen was a gem."

* * * * *

Variety was correct: "Memories are Made of This" became a huge hit and would sit comfortably at number one on the Hit Parade at the start of 1956. More importantly, Martin was being openly courted by two studios for solo roles: Warner Brothers offered him *The Pajama Game* opposite Doris Day, while MGM sought him for an original story, *Ten Thousand Bedrooms*. With all this temptation, the thought of playing a one-dimensional heavy alongside the sympathetic schnook was becoming unbear-

It's their final starring *Variety Hour* and Dean can barely look at his partner playing "the poor schnook."

able. Yet a $2 million individual gross income the previous year, with many more millions on the horizon, kept him rooted to the status quo.

Pardners had finally started shooting on November 21. Four days later, NBC announced that Colgate's request to be relieved of sponsoring the *Variety Hour*, despite a contract that ran through May, had been granted. The series that began with such promise five years and three months earlier had its final broadcast—a simple hour of holiday music by Fred Waring's Pennsylvanians—on Christmas Day. The week before, Martin & Lewis made their final appearance, via a clip from *Artists and Models*.

The *Colgate Variety Hour* had been a flop; only the two Martin & Lewis starring hours outdrew *The Ed Sullivan Show*. The actor that Esty and Company had selected as host was Charlton Heston, who didn't make it beyond the summer run. Then they tried comedian Jack Carson, and finally settled on another actor, Robert Paige. All of them bombed. Now the network had its own ideas for the timeslot, as reported by the *New York Times'* Val Adams: "A new comedy series will replace the 'Variety Hour' on January 8. Having decided that an all-comedy show might be the best in combating 'The Ed Sullivan Show' on [CBS], NBC now has embraced the assumption that television desperately needs new comedians. As a result, relatively unknown comedy performers will have prominent roles on the new series." Despite the former *Colgate Hour* tandem of production supervisor Sam Fuller and producer-director Ernie Glucksman, plus a writing staff of ten, the outcome was even more disastrous than its predecessor. *Film Bulletin's* Dick Bretstein, having watched the first two weeks, rightly concluded *The NBC Comedy Hour* "will in no way suffer from the effects of longevity. The combined efforts of such acknowledged talents as Ernie Novacks (*sic*), Jonathan Winters, Bob and Ray, Dick Shawn, Paul Gilbert, and others, succeeded in producing no more than two hours of weak, tasteless, and almost consistently unfunny 'entertainment.' Improbable as it seems, the new show makes the recently departed 'Colgate Variety Hour' appear far better than it really was."

Losing the big-budgeted *Colgate* show also spelled the end of the network's deal with York Pictures, and thus with Martin & Lewis. Negotiations were reopened, and on December 19, NBC announced the signing of a "new agreement, giving NBC exclusive rights to Martin's and Lewis' services on both radio and television. [It] was negotiated by NBC and York Pictures, Inc., corporation to which the comics are under contract for all show business activities." The terms were five years; four hour-long shows per season; $7.5 million per year. For a team whose very existence had become tenuous, locking into a five year deal would seem an unwise move, but the contract had been written in a way that would, in just a few months, take NBC by surprise. York Pictures guaranteed to deliver Martin and Lewis for five years. Nowhere did it guarantee they'd deliver a team.

It was as a team, though, that they kicked off the deal with a guest shot on *The Milton Berle Show* on December 20. Times had changed for "Uncle Miltie" since the days of *Texaco Star Theater*: no longer TV's top banana, he was now appearing once per month, alternating with *The Martha Raye Show* (which was written by Simmons and Lear) and the occasional color spectacular. Berle's show was also "in tint," as *Variety* might say, enabling Hal Sawyer to introduce him as "Mr. Color Television."

After a monologue and a parade of bathing beauties that sashay across the stage with placards for his sponsors, Berle introduces Lewis, who takes on the persona of an awestruck fan. "You're the same, like on television," he tells the host. "You're funny and make out yourself like a nut." He asks for Milton's autograph for his "Aunt Sylvia Hillmannnnnn," and proceeds to dictate a lengthy salutation. Disgusted, Berle leaves the stage and Lewis gets around to introducing Martin with a rather harsh conclusion: "Let's give him a big hand right across his mouth."

"I thought for a minute you had another partner," says Martin. "You were out here a long time, buddy." The two go into a routine: Dean wonders what he should sing, and suggests perhaps "a jump number." Jerry enthusiastically agrees, but then Dean has second thoughts, and Jerry agrees with those as well. Dean suggests a ballad, and Jerry likes the idea; Dean reconsiders, thinking it could get "too draggy," and Jerry agrees again. And so it goes, with Dean suggesting, then reconsidering, a rhythm and blues number, an "old American folk song" and a tune for dancing. With each suggestion, Jerry's enthusiasm for the idea gets more pronounced; with each second thought, he switches to serious, concerned concurrence. It's an amusing routine, but oddly rigid, with no spontaneity to either man's performance. Moreover, there's nothing inherently "Dean-and-Jerry" about it. It's simply a well-rehearsed routine that any two people could have performed to the same reaction.

Finally, Jerry suggests "Memories are Made of This." Martin pointedly waits until his partner has left the stage before starting the song. It's basically the same performance as delivered on the team's last starring *Variety Hour*, although Dean's backing group, The Easy Riders, are too far from the microphone and barely audible, at least on the surviving kin-escope. When the song is over, Jerry comes out with a gold record of the song and presents it to Dean. Unlike the presentation for "That's Amore," Dean doesn't even pretend surprise, nor does he smile at his partner. Then, a proud moment was shared between friends; now, Martin's award for a solo accomplishment is delivered not by the record company, but by his controlling partner.

With that out of the way, the two go into an up-tempo tap routine lifted directly from their appearances with The Four Step Brothers, except it's just the two of them. Jerry even uses the same lines when Dean begins dancing: "There goes Speedy! Notice that at no time do his feet leave his legs." After this, they go back even further in time to the "Swanee River" vaudeville dance performed on the February 4, 1951 *Comedy Hour*. It's expanded here, since it was originally performed in haste when the team had five minutes left over. Added are some tricks with their batons, at which Jerry fails, of course. The difference between this and the earlier performance is a noticeable lack of intimacy. There are no spontaneous

The closing scene from *Hollywood or Bust* (1956), the final Martin & Lewis movie. The two barely spoke to each other off-camera throughout its production.

smiles at one another; they simply perform the routine, which had been in the act for years, take their bows and curtain call with Berle, and that's all.

Unlike any other variety show, where the special guest star would have come on toward the end, Martin & Lewis' appearance was scheduled for Berle's first half, and for good reason: it put them opposite CBS's sitcom *You'll Never Get Rich*, which had been winning the time slot every week. In the next morning's review, 'Daku' of *Daily Variety* noted the team's "wildly funny antics must have clobbered the ratings out of Phil Silvers on the other network.

"[Martin & Lewis] made it more than a guest shot. Anyone tuning in a few minutes late would have guessed they were watching the Martin & Lewis show…. The team was in top form."

After this, they went back to work on *Pardners*, the shooting of which continued into January 1956 and, according to Lewis, was a period of "silence" and "coldness" between them. "Both Dean and I had become cynical and tough," he'd write in *Dean and Me*. "When I'd catch my partner's eye— or try to—he would be staring over my shoulder." Singing the title song, which concluded with "You and me will be the greatest pardners, buddies and pals," was "the hardest thing about the picture." The lyrics, unsurprisingly, came from the pen of Sammy Cahn, who was making a second career out of writing "we really still like each other" songs for Martin & Lewis.

If Jerry was through pretending to himself that all was well between him and Dean, he was still reassuring the press that their feuding days were over. "The team is better off now than it ever was," he told Bob Thomas during the waning days of *Pardners'* production. "We know exactly where we stand with each other. There are no misunderstanding, no jealousies. We couldn't be happier." He affirmed that their dispute over working apart was resolved: "Now we agree that I can do anything I want as long as it isn't a coast-to-coast TV show or something like that. I've played about 20 benefits in the past month—things nobody ever hears about. I go out and have a ball." Lewis also told Thomas he was "really peeved" at reports that "I was jealous of Dean because of his hit records. Dean's success in records is the greatest thing that could happen to us. That's his own form of expression—something that can give him satisfaction because he does it all by himself. I get mine out of playing before live audiences at benefits. It's a perfect arrangement."

Columnists Tom O'Malley and Bob Cuniff, while noting that Lewis "was hotly denying gossip reports that he was 'jealous' of Dino's gold record achievements," also cited an anonymous source who claimed that difficulties between the two roared to life whenever Martin's record sales climbed higher than usual. "When Dean comes up with a record smash," said the nameless informant, "he thinks wistfully of doing a single—on his own terms and without the helter-skelter schedule he must meet as Jerry's partner. A big seller fires up his confidence that he wouldn't starve without Jerry. So he gets a little independent, rhubarbs start springing up between him and Jer and pretty soon they're fighting like a couple of alley cats.

"As for Jerry—well, let me say this, I don't know whether he's jealous, like the columnists say, but there's a good and sound reason that he isn't turning cartwheels when Dean cuts a big song hit. A financial reason. Jerry thinks be should be cut in on the record profits—fifty-fifty! You see, when a songwriter is hired to do a score for a Martin and Lewis movie, the songwriter is technically hired by both Dean and Jerry. So Jerry gets the comedy songs, which never sell and Dean gets the ballads, which do. So when 'That's Amore' was written for one of their films and turned out a smash, Jerry argued he should be cut in on the loot. He thinks it's a team proposition."

Whatever the truth about Martin's record sales—despite Lewis' denials, the "informant" probably had a point about "That's Amore," a song commissioned by the team for a York picture—Lewis kept himself busy, both with and without his partner. In addition to the nameless "benefits," he was called upon by his peers: on January 29, he served as toastmaster for the Screen Producers' Guild "Milestone Awards" banquet at the Beverly Hilton Hotel. One week later, he hosted the Humanitarian Awards Dinner honoring Tony Martin for "humanitarian and patriotic contributions to nation, philanthropic groups and individuals." Held at the Beverly Hills Hotel, event proceeds went to the American Medical Center in Denver, Colorado. And during his and Dean's engagement at the Sands Hotel, he was tapped to emcee the Academy Awards Ceremony, held March 21 at Hollywood's Pantages Theater. In his monologue, Lewis thanked Jack Entratter for allowing him and Martin to appear, adding, "And I must publicly thank my good partner, Dean Martin, because last night in Las Vegas, at the roulette wheel, he arranged it so that we would be in Las Vegas for five more years." Martin later came on to sing "(Love is) The Tender Trap," one of the Best Song nominees with another Sammy Cahn lyric. Alas, Cahn and composer Jimmy Van Heusen couldn't overtake the powerhouse hit "Love is a Many Splendored Thing," which copped the prize. Martin also engaged in a little byplay with his partner, but the crux of the evening was Lewis alone, and his performance won several plaudits from critics and industry members.

It was during the Vegas engagement that Lewis, still inwardly hoping that his relationship with Martin could be restored, conceived the idea of doing a contemporary take on the Damon and Pythias story: two men whose friendship is tested when one lays his life on the line for the other. To drive the point home, Dean would play Mike Damon, sympathetic policeman and Jerry would be Sidney Pythias, juvenile delinquent. This would be their next York picture, after finishing their upcoming assignment for Wallis, *Hollywood or Bust* (1956).

Unfortunately, Lewis assigned the writing of "Damon and Pythias" to his pal Don McGuire, the man who wrote *3 Ring Circus*. McGuire's opinion of Martin didn't bode well for the project: "Dean was a terrible actor. He could barely talk. Jerry was the guy who made him a hit, made him funny." Still, he strove to create a story that gave both men "a close relationship" and Lewis campaigned with Freeman for the opportunity to direct the film.

While that was going on, the restriction on separate appearances over "coast-to-coast TV" was evidently lifted, provided both partners got the same perk. On April 10, Martin and Lewis made individual guest shots on NBC: Jerry on Tennessee Ernie Ford's morning program and Dean on Dinah Shore's prime time variety hour. Neither man was at his best, but of the two, Lewis comes off better. Ford's show was broadcast from the Coast at 9:00 am, so Jerry pretends to be somnambulant throughout, even to falling asleep on Ford's shoulder while the latter is delivering a commercial. While singing the Blue Bonnet margarine jingle, Ford notices that Lewis is mouthing along, so he moves his head behind Jerry's so it becomes a lip synch performance. Martin is mentioned twice and only in passing; first in a reference to their recent Vegas appearance that he and Ford turn into a comic exchange, Ford telling him the team's act "comes on like a truckload of turkeys. That means it's good," and Lewis responding, "In New York, when you have a turkey *one*, you're in trouble!" Later, Lewis plugs Dean's appearance on the evening's Dinah Shore program. Like most morning shows, it's a low-key affair but the studio audience audibly enjoys Jerry's antics, no matter how subdued.

Martin doesn't fare quite as well. At the start, it's implied that he's sold the network to two gullible laborers (*Stubby Kaye* and *Johnny Silver*) for $500. His solo is "Inamorata" from *Artists and Models*, and during his conversation with Dinah, he admits to having fleeced the two rubes, while surreptitiously changing a sign that reads "Dinah and Dino" so that the billing is reversed. Dinah switches it back, but Dino is persistent: "I get top billing on the Martin and Lewis Show!" "But it's *my* show," she rejoins. Eventually they sing a special lyric duet of "Let's Call the Whole Thing Off" in which they argue about their respective merits and eventually rethink their argument:

> *DINAH: If that's your decision, I'll have to call Perry,*
> *DEAN: I just had a vision: you know I'm with Jerry,*
> *DINAH: But Jerry is crazy,*
> *DEAN: And Perry's so lazy,*
> *DINAH: Let's call the whole thing off!*

Eventually Dinah acquiesces billing priority to Dean, and they duet on "You Made Me Love You."

The problem with the routine is that Dean comes off looking as slimy as he does in the Martin & Lewis films: he cheats a pair of simpletons and cares more about his billing position than he does his hostess. A similar mock battle, on radio opposite Tony Martin, was woefully unfunny; on television opposite Dinah Shore, it's that *and* distasteful; no romantic crooner should be so ungallant. Later on, Martin engages in some amusing repartee with Kaye and Silver, and performs a closing dance with Dinah and her other guests, Marge and Gower Champion. Yet the billing issue continues right to the end of the show; as Dinah sings "Dean and Dinah," he loudly chimes in, "That's right, Dean and Dinah!" About the most that can be said is he looks perfectly at home without Jerry, but except for his one solo, he's never on stage alone.

The following month, the script for "Damon and Pythias" was finished. If Lewis harbored any hope that his and McGuire's opus would touch Martin's heart and possibly rekindle their friendship, it was dashed almost as soon as Martin got hold of his copy. The next day, he let his partner know that he would in no way play a uniformed cop, claiming it was "low class." Assuming that Martin didn't read the script beyond his costume requirement, Lewis blew his stack: "Then we'll have to get somebody else." "Start looking, boy," Martin retorted and stormed off.

Almost simultaneously, the pair reported to work on *Hollywood or Bust*, only speaking to each other when cameras rolled. For the first few weeks, Lewis sabotaged the production, intentionally blowing lines and breaking character; partly to retaliate against Martin, but mostly with the intent to force Hal Wallis to renegotiate—or release them from—his restrictive contract. The gambit failed; director Frank Tashlin, no doubt with Wallis' blessing, simply threw Lewis off the set, forcing the comic's hand. With nowhere else to vent, he returned to work, performed perfunctorily and kept his anger in check until the inevitable happened. On May 18, he emceed yet another industry event, a testimonial dinner for Jean Hersholt held by the Screen Actors Guild. Lewis "covered himself with glory," according to Louella Parsons. "He was never funnier or better." Then he went home and was overcome with nausea and chest pains. Patti drove him to the doctor's and he wound up in the hospital for three days, diagnosed with a heart flutter brought on by stress. Martin never paid a visit.

Once more, Lewis returned to *Hollywood or Bust* and, in his words, "tried for the miracle." "You know, it's a hell of a thing," he suddenly said to Martin during a break. "All I can think of is that what we do is not very important. Any two guys could have done it. But even the best of them wouldn't have had what made us as big as we are."

"Yeah? What's that?"

"Well, I think it's the love that we still have for each other."

Martin thought long and hard about what to say, and then said it. "You can talk about love all you want. To me, you're nothin' but a (bleep) in' dollar sign."

"He may have wanted to say more," Lewis wrote for *Jerry Lewis In Person*. "God knows he probably could've gone on for hours about all the real and imagined injustices I had heaped upon him during the past couple of years. Maybe he would have, if I had stayed to listen." The distance between them remained carefully concealed until the evening of June 18, when a press preview of *Pardners* was held at Newhall Ranch. Martin failed to show up; two hours later, Jack Keller phoned his home and was told he had "an upset stomach." To Lewis, knowing his partner had blown off the previous day's press meet-and-greet to play golf, this was one York Pictures snub too many. There wouldn't be any vague talk about "a cross to bear" and what "the lawyers" would or wouldn't want him to say. Lewis was blunt: "No more. It's over."

Back at Paramount the next morning, he went straight to Y. Frank Freeman for permission to make "Damon and Pythias" (which would eventually be titled *The Delicate Delinquent*) with another costar. The now-sympathetic Freeman got Barney Balaban's okay and forcibly persuaded Wallis to agree; the producer reluctantly waived his "team-only clause" for one solo picture apiece. Not long after, York arranged to loan Martin to MGM for *Ten Thousand Bedrooms*.

Years later, Lewis would credit his father with advice that helped sway his decision. "You and Dean have been the greatest shooting star in the history of show business. Recognize that it tails off," Danny reportedly told him. "But don't wait until it's gone before deciding [to] do something. You gotta do it while the star is still cresting." Asked about the split by Bob Thomas, however, Danny Lewis professed, "At first, I was shocked. The boys were like Sears, Roebuck, or Montgomery Ward, or Marshall Field. Not just an act, but an institution. But Jerry explained to me that he wanted to keep working and Dean would rather play golf. He said he wasn't happy not working. I told him in that case maybe it was better to split."

Now that it was out in the open, Martin insisted to the press that his primary gripe was Lewis in the director's chair, although the costume rankled: "Jerry wrote this story, and he plans to co-produce and co-direct it. If he wants to be a director, okay, but I think he ought to start on something simpler than a million dollar film, especially one with my money in it. Besides, I didn't like the role. I didn't want to go through the movie wearing a policeman's suit. I [also] didn't think the story was too good." Lewis simply responded, "Dean had approved the [story] idea. Mr. Freeman was to be our partner in this picture. I'm going to do what I am told." One thing Mr. Freeman agreed with Dean about was the budget: Lewis' first film without Martin would not be a million dollar, color-and-stereo spectacular but monochrome and monophonic, with a negative cost of $485,000.

For his part, Lewis insisted the issue was Dean's work ethic. To Joe Hyams he griped, "I'm tired of being restricted. I don't want to work 12 weeks and sit around for 40. He wants to work 12 weeks and play golf for 40 weeks. In those 40 weeks I can do a lot of good. I'm not a happy man unless I can perform and entertain and make people happy. I feel like a completely frustrated cripple when I'm not allowed to do it. I want to do everything I can, to use myself to the fullest."

"I want to keep working," he told Louella Parsons, "fifty-two weeks out of the year. I want to learn every branch of this business. I want to direct, to produce and I want to continue to be as successful as we are now. I am grateful to Dean for getting me where I am today, but my gratitude does not permit him the right to tear me down.... I cannot let anybody restrict me in my comedy scenes. I have to do comedy as I see it."

Before that could happen, however, Dean and Jerry faced a month of confirmed personal appearances, which they had to meet through sheer force of will. There was a muscular dystrophy telethon scheduled to begin Friday, June 29, airing locally in New York City. They were set for ten

Dinah Shore looks at him adoringly, but Dean still comes off like a heel in his solo
appearance on her April 10, 1956 TV show.

days at The 500 Club beginning July 1, immediately followed by separate
two-week engagements at the Copacabana and the Chez Paree. Sifting
through these obligations, Lewis noted that, serendipitously, their final
show at the Copa would conclude in the early hours of July 25—ten years
to the day since their official teaming. He decided to cancel the Chicago
gig; Martin, undoubtedly eager to wrap things up quickly, voiced no ob-
jection, assuming he was even consulted.

Columnist Dorothy Kilgallen heard through her grapevine that Martin was actually responsible for the Chez Paree cancellation: "[A] bizarre rumor... has it that Dean scuttled the Windy City engagement because he 'was afraid of some mobsters there.' According to the story circulating among his pals, Dean received a telephone threat, which he chose to take seriously, and he promptly sent along word that as far as he was concerned the Chicago date was off." Asked about this while at the Copa, Martin replied, "Ridiculous," adding that his first nightclub appearance as a solo would be in Chicago.

There were some rough patches during this final month together, one of them being an appearance on NBC's news show for dawn-risers, *Today*, on June 26, which was arranged to be broadcast from The 500 Club. Earmarked as a celebration of Dean & Jerry's 10th Anniversary, the network touted it as an "early morning spectacular," which it assuredly wasn't. For one thing, The 500 Club, in size and décor, was every bit the 2nd-tier venue it had been in 1946. For another, "Dean and I [could] hardly bear to look at each other," as Lewis put it fifty years later. A surviving kinescope, which is actually from a 10:00 am performance for the West Coast airing, bears him out.

The show opens with the leggy Boots McKenna Girls and a modest orchestra helping to introduce the hosts: Jack Lescoulie, Faye Emerson (substituting for vacationing Dave Garroway), newsman Frank Blair, 1955's Miss America winner, Lee Meriwether, and the ever-popular chimpanzee, J. Fred Muggs. Concurrently, a governor's conference was taking place in the city, so the tables are occupied by the governors and their families; Miss Emerson interviews two during the course of the surviving hour. This being a "spectacular," there is other entertainment: Joan Kayne, a former Miss New York and one of the original June Taylor Dancers from *The Jackie Gleason Show*; Joe Maize and His Chordsmen, a novelty music act; Pip Walters, a 19-year-old juggler; singer Joey Stevens, the club's crooner-emcee. None of them escaped the supper club circuit, although Maize also recorded three albums for Decca. Stevens, whose real name is Dave Boyer, conquered alcohol and pill addiction through the intercession of his minister brother; he's still active as an inspirational speaker/singer.

Martin & Lewis come on during the final quarter-hour, and it's depressing; there's no spark between them at all. Muggs, resting his head on the table, appears to be dozing, so Dean sends Jerry over to "wake your brother up" and laughs when the monkey takes a swing at him. While his partner picks up a microphone, Dean, in a Chaplinesque move, kicks his cigarette with his heel and catches it again. When the audience cheers this, Jerry, who wasn't watching, assumes the applause was for him. "I just picked up the microphone! Why are they applauding? I don't understand what was so terrific about that!" They sit down on the stage and Jerry starts interviewing Dean, peppering him with questions about why he's in town and what he plans to do, never giving him a chance to answer. The camera cuts away to Muggs, looking bored; when it returns, Dean's got his eyes closed and his fingers in both ears. The monkey actually upstages them both when he appears to be passionately embracing a woman guest and has to be pulled off her. But Jerry gets a bigger laugh with a topical gag: "Thank you, Arthur and Marilyn," a reference to the red hot romance between a certain playwright and movie actress.

"Dean is gonna sing one of the songs that kept him from getting into the big time for about ten years," Jerry tells us. The band kicks off "Embraceable You," and Jerry gets on a camera, which is out of focus and pointed at Dean's knees. As Dean sings, Jerry points the camera at Muggs: "Hey Dean, you're not even moving your lips!" Jerry plays around with the lenses, zooming in and out and messing with the focus. Between verses, Dean says, "I could've phoned this in!" Throughout the song, Jerry keeps talking and nothing he says is particularly funny. The biggest reaction he gets is on an old gag; he looks into the viewfinder, laughs and says, "Dirty pictures!"

Once the song has mercifully ended, Jerry requests applause for Faye Emerson's work as Garroway's sub, and for the cameramen and director Jack Hines. "And I think I did great by showin' up," says Dean, not untruthfully. With a minute and a half to go, he simply leaves the stage, as Jerry dances with Faye during the closing theme. Before the fade, he dances with Frank Blair and provokes Muggs some more.

The Philadelphia Inquirer's Harry Harris watched and decided, "If the boys hate each other's guts, it didn't show. The official reason for their being on tap at what, for them, was the middle of the night was to celebrate their 10th anniversary as a team at the night club where they first became partners.... The only cognizance they took of that fact was at 8:43 A.M., when this dialogue took place:

JERRY: We're at the 500 Club here.

DEAN: It's miserable.

JERRY: It's very early. We started here.

'Nearly Killed Each Other'

Martin, Lewis Come to Blows, Lester Reveals

DEAN MARTIN and JERRY LEWIS
Before the Team Split Up

A front page story from the July 6, 1956 *Long Island Star-Journal*.

"End of sentimental reminiscences.... Lewis was his usual dynamic self, chattering and clowning all over the place. Martin seemed rather subdued, but maybe the time of day was to blame. 'Even the air,' he observed mournfully, 'isn't up this early.'"

Variety's 'Jose' saw the same show as Harris and was disgusted: "Instead of providing the basis of a morning spectacular, Dean Martin & Jerry Lewis made a spectacle of themselves on NBC-TV's 'Today.' It was evident that the team isn't talking to one another. Whatever communication there was between them gave further proof of what is being headlined—the split is permanent and from their work, which was strictly lower case, it seems irrevocable."

Jose contrasted Martin & Lewis with other teams that "harbored personal animus—yet they could all work together," and fully recognized the difference. "[These] combos were formed primarily on the basis of respect for each other's talent. Starting from that basis, they can survive personal splits. In the case of Martin & Lewis it seems to have been born on the basis of personal regard. In their early years, they laughed at and with each other; each gave the other a lift that communicated itself with the audience. Now that the personal warmth is gone, the base of the team is gone, as reflected in their 'Today' contribs. They are now two talented performers and nothing else." *Motion Picture Daily* was a tad more charitable: "The boys were noticeably cool toward one another, but provided some wonderfully relaxed nonsense when dealing with J. Fred Muggs and Dave Garroway's cool summer replacement, Faye Emerson."

Another difficult task was the telethon, which was broadcast locally on New York City's WABD-5, the flagship station of the soon-to-be-defunct Du Mont network. Its goal was to collect one million dollars toward the construction of an MDA research center. As noted previously, there's no surviving kinescope for this 21-hour program that originated from Carnegie Hall; all that remains are the reviews. 'Jose' was again watching and was guardedly impressed: "The talents of Dean Martin & Jerry Lewis appeared to have become fused again as a team. The feuding duo was seemingly united under the common bond of charity.... The [box office] of Martin & Lewis is still tremendous, and their prestige is also big enough to bring out some of the top names in show biz for a cuffo contribution. Unfortunately, the bond that makes them a great team is uncertain and tenuous. There were moments of fusion and there were times when they spoke around and over each other. During these moments, they're just two guys, but as this show proved—with a heart."

The *New York Post's* Barry Gray reported, "At a time when telethons are generally worn thin, the almost-divorced comedy team managed to rack up collections, mostly checked for authenticity, in excess of $500,000." Gray was especially impressed with Ernie Glucksman's producing skill: "Glucksman, a marvel on spectaculars and hour-long fiestas, like a chef arranging a banquet for 1,000 had to multiply every normal recipe by 20: Acts, comedy, dance and talk, interspersed in entertainment order, remote pickups from mountain resorts [there were occasional cutaways to the Catskills, specifically Grossinger's and Brown's Hotel], watching WABD monitors and enabling mountain viewing with hometown collections.... It was the type of job generally reckoned to contain a thousand mishaps— amazingly enough, tribute to genius, it went on and off the air without a boo-boo. Except one little one perhaps: The appearance of comic after comic, Milton Berle, Jan Murray, all making quips about the upcoming separation of the Martin-Lewis goldmine. Jerry roared and took them in humor. Dean merely stood, unsmiling. Phil Silvers...picked up the theme, then noting the Martin frown, quickly apologized for being in 'poor taste' and noted, for all of us, 'I love you both.' It is to Silvers' credit that he showed this sensitivity to the Martin mood." In an article published after the split, *Coronet's* Morton Cooper noted one aspect of "the Martin mood" while on the air: "Martin made constant references to the quarts of liquor he had allegedly consumed in the dressing room between appearances on camera. At one point, when Lewis announced that either would do anything in order to receive a big contribution for MD research, Martin upstaged him, smiled at the millions of viewers looking in, and asked, 'How much will you give to see me get drunk?'"

Upstaging between the two during the show led to an argument that led to punches thrown...or so John Lester reported in a front page *Star Journal* story. "Word is Dean Martin and Jerry Lewis got into 'a terrific argument' after arriving in Atlantic City to play The 500 Club there, 'and nearly killed each other.' The incident was hushed for several days but sources close to the boys—none of whom will allow identification—confirmed it last night and said a fight grew out of a screaming session in which Dean claimed he was 'upstaged' throughout the team's recent highly successful 21-hour muscular dystrophy telethon on WABD.... The situation is so serious that out-of-town friends of the team are being urged to stay away from Atlantic City 'until things quiet down—if they ever will!'"

Evidently things quieted down, as the two made it through the engagement without incident, and then moved on to the Copa. On their second night there, things heated up again: *New York Herald-Tribune* columnist Marie Torre reported, "During a rough-house clown routine... Martin's heel came down hard on Lewis' left foot, and the comedian shrieked out in pain. He later dismissed the accident, but early [the following] morning continued pain necessitated an examination by an orthopedist." The diagnosis was two fractured toes. "Lewis will be forced to limp through his act for the next few days, and to ease the strain, he will wear soft velvet slippers." He also canceled a booking to co-host *Today*, scheduled for an unspecified morning during the week of July 23.

He did, however, show up as the mystery guest on *What's My Line?* the evening of July 22. Unlike his 1954 appearance with Dean, he played along and disguised his voice to the blindfolded panel. Coincidentally, Vivian Blaine was a panelist and when she asked, "Do you work alone?" the studio audience laughed at Jerry's facial expressions until he finally answered "No." But the laugh was enough to cue Bennett Cerf, who asked, "Are you *about* to work alone?" and the audience reaction to *that* narrowed the identity to two possibles. "Now we have to know which one," observed Arlene Francis. Even though it wasn't her turn, Vivian blurted out "Are you Jerry Lewis?" and that ended the game. Arlene, clearly hoping the split was either a rumor or publicity stunt, asked, "Mr. Lewis? You are going to have a new movie coming out pretty soon called *Pardners*, aren't you?" That led to a Lewis plug for the picture, which would open mere hours after the team closed at the Copa. He tried to keep it light, but then host John Daly turned serious: "I think what Arlene was getting to, Jerry; I think I speak for the panel as well as a lot of people—you know the reception you got here tonight. As I say, it's none of our business, but we kind of hope that *Pardners* as a picture title means that you and Dean really aren't gonna break up; that you'll stay together." Visibly uncomfortable from both Daly's oration and the applause that followed, Jerry tiptoed around the topic: "I just hope people go to see this picture, because it's a fun picture, actually, and we had a great deal of fun making it." Gently prodded by Cerf, Jerry added, "Let me just say this: I think that the entertainment medium, whether its television, night clubs or motion pictures, I think that once we're in front of this particular entertainment medium, we should make it strictly entertainment and not anything other than that."

Their final show, which ended in the early hours of July 25, has been written up as the stuff of legend. The celebrity-studded audience; the typical clowning tinged with added significance; the final duet ("Pardners," of course); the deafening ovation; a more-than-tipsy Jackie Gleason grabbing the mic and pleading for a reconciliation; the final bow-off, with Martin and Lewis exiting, for the first time, to opposite sides of the stage. "Those used to being on the other side of the laughs," wrote INS reporter Ralph Villers, "laughed it up but loud—Phil Silvers, Nanette Fabray, Jack E. Leonard, Jerry Colonna. Together and singly, Dean and Jerry just about popped to give a great last show. They breezed from the stage once and returned to dish out more in the wake of continuous applause." Morton Cooper's perspective was different; he saw a show that was "subdued, occasionally dragging, sometimes downright dull. All the proven ingredients were there: the Crosby-out-of-Jolson voice of Martin, the seal with a strained larynx voice of Lewis, the dirty words in Italian and Yiddish, the almost unceasing impersonations of homosexuals, the kibitzing with the customers, the friendship songs. It was all pretty good, rowdy night club, but it wasn't good, rowdy Martin and Lewis. They obviously had had it. Their lack of *sympatico* glared....

"It was more than apparent that the whole bit was an act, that they were not planning to miss one another too soon."

Later that day, moviegoers would behold two shadows in Technicolor and VistaVision promising each other in song, "You and me will be the greatest pardners, buddies and pals," while two flesh and blood men quietly and separately made their way to California to begin individual careers and lives.

9 THE AFTERMATH: "WHY WE BROKE UP"

JERRY: Why we broke up, I'll never know.

DEAN: Me either!

JERRY: I have no idea what happened.

DEAN: It was because I was a Jew and you were a dago.

JERRY: No, no, *you're* the dago, *I'm* the Jew!

DEAN: Oh. I knew it was something like that.

JERRY: That's what we could never get straightened out.

– On stage at Bally's Grand Hotel,
Las Vegas, June 7, 1989

MARTIN & LEWIS have two legacies: they were the most financially successful comedy team in show business history, and they are the pop culture template for two people who were once close and can no longer tolerate each other.

To cite one example of the latter: in the Disney film *The Princess Diaries 2: Royal Engagement* (2004) —a movie targeted toward adolescent girls—we learn that Lord Crawley (*Paul Vogt*) has a twin brother (*Peter*

The MDA Telethon Reunion, September 6, 1976. Photo courtesy of ABCDVDVIDEO.

Vogt) with whom he's not on speaking terms. Forced into contact by the plot, they limit their interaction to curtly greeting each other by their first names: "Jerry" and "Dean."

"I keep reading about our 'tumultuous' relationship. That annoys me," said Lewis to *TV Guide's* Hal Hinson in 2002. "It appears to me that people want to know there was angst between us. Look at my house. Look at all the memories I have all around me." By that point, though, Martin had been dead nearly seven years and Lewis was in the throes of writing an intimate memoir of their partnership; one that, while not wholly dishonest, tended to gloss over their conflicts (the Brown's Hotel fiasco being a notable exception), not to mention the many times one would snipe at the other in the press after the final separation; something of which, surprisingly, Dean was more guilty than Jerry.

"Why did Martin & Lewis split up?" It was a question they'd spend the rest of their careers answering, or sometimes *not* answering because they were bored with it. It was a question put to mutual friends, former associates and ex-wives. Even their children, who were so young at the time (or not yet born), were and still are asked why their fathers parted ways. Amazingly, the question of how two such opposite personalities could have teamed so successfully to begin with falls distantly behind the one asking how it all ended. Along with ancient film footage depicting screaming hordes of young fans blocking city streets in order to catch a glimpse of their heroes, the persistence of this one question puts Martin & Lewis in the same legendary class as The Beatles.

And the answer is the same in both cases, and it's a simple one: they didn't want to work together anymore. The unit had become too confining.

There's another question concealed within the first, however: "Why couldn't they remain friends?" *That* answer is much more complicated.

"The animosity was that of two people that loved one another very much, that split up, that did what they had to do," Lewis recalled in 1990; in other words, like a married couple going through divorce. The evidence doesn't contradict him. Throughout the nine months of "business-like partnership," each still nursed feelings of betrayal, and the contractually-forced togetherness only frayed them further, which is why a blow-up over costuming for a film—the least impressive item on anyone's grievance list—could end it all.

In a later interview, Lewis likened his feelings to that of a husband whose wife had been unfaithful, adding, "We're talking about the same thing. This relationship was very strong. When you scar a relationship, you're never gonna have it right again. Let's assume you forgive your wife. Whatta you think you've got? You've got staying up at night waiting for the other shoe to fall…. Once a relationship is scarred, everything you do is a façade. All the cheer and the happiness and the giggling is bullshit. You can only do that without scars. Then it's real. So I knew in my heart this could not be retrieved."

There's a legend that goes hand-in-hand with the legacy: from the day they split up, Martin and Lewis neither saw nor spoke to each other for twenty years, until Frank Sinatra brought Dean onto Jerry's 1976 Muscular Dystrophy telethon. Both persistently endorsed this myth. The reality is there were several encounters prior to that celebrated reunion, two in front of audiences. Sadly, there were also several more scars to come.

As with many a failed marriage, they tried to separate amicably. "Jerry's a great partner; the greatest," Dean assured Broadway columnist Hy Gardner the day of the team's final Copa performance, "but we'd both like to seek new worlds. We'll still be together at least once a year living up to our movie commitments to Hal Wallis." Almost simultaneously, Jerry was pledging to TV columnist Marie Torre "if there's a good property – a movie or spectacular – with meaty roles in it for both of us, we'll do it. A great part of Dean's unhappiness had to do with the fact that he was limited in his movie roles on account of us being a team."

At least in print, Dean sounded especially reluctant to pull the plug for good. "It doesn't seem like we've split," he'd say a month after the final Copa show. "We still get along with each other. By separating we're just trying to prove a point to ourselves. What we can do on our own. How the public will react to seeing one of us without the other." The public was, of course, the main reason why, at first, they were tiptoeing around the subject.

Ever fearful that his celebrity would wane, Lewis also wanted to keep his options open...until the evening of August 6, 1956. He'd been vacationing in Las Vegas with Patti for a few days when Sid Luft – Judy Garland's then-husband – asked him to sub for his wife, who'd contracted laryngitis, at the Frontier Hotel that evening. Tux-less as well as Dino-less, Jerry, wearing an ordinary suit and tie, tentatively walked on stage that evening, with the ailing Miss Garland seated nearby for moral support. Fifty-eight minutes of mostly ad-lib later, nobody doubted Jerry Lewis would thrive on stage alone. He did two shows, each time closing with Judy's finale, singing "Rock-A-Bye Your Baby (With a Dixie Melody)" straight; each time it earned him a standing ovation. One month later, he told columnist Aline Mosby, "That was the greatest night in my show business career."

Emboldened by the reaction to his singing, Lewis returned to Hollywood and recorded a handful of demos, which he then shopped around to various labels. Decca offered to release "Rock-A-Bye Your Baby" as a single, along with a 12-track album. Both disks came out in November and became huge sellers; within five months of its release, "Rock-A-Bye" would earn a gold record.

Behind the scenes, NBC canceled their 5-year, $7.5 million contract, citing the team's split-up, via telegram; whereupon York Productions immediately filed a $5 million lawsuit against the network, charging breach of contract. NBC took a closer look at the agreement and saw that it was between them and a company owned by two comedians and a movie studio, not specifically with a comedy team, "a loophole 18 of [York's] attorneys rushed through," wrote one TV journalist, who labeled it "the legal blunder of the year." NBC quickly settled with the two: figuring they'd already done three of the original twenty shows (*Milton Berle, Today* and the two solo appearances), the revised deal called for seventeen shows apiece over five years, for a total of $5 million.

As his lawyers conferred with NBC, Lewis set to work on "Damon and Pythias," now titled *The Delicate Delinquent*. Darren McGavin, who'd recently played a dope pusher in *The Man with the Golden Arm* (1956), was cast as the patrolman, Mike Damon. "I didn't read for the part or anything," he told Bob Thomas. "I just came to Jerry's office and we talked for a long time – how we felt about delinquency, our own boyhood experiences and so forth. At the end, Jerry said he'd like to have me do the part, and I said I'd like to do it."

Since everyone knew the role had been written for Martin, McGavin spoke to a UPI reporter about the inordinate amount of attention he'd been getting: "Song pluggers have chased me like bill collectors. They all think I'm a singer.... People are working overtime comparing me to Dean. I'm not a comic. I'm not a singer. I'm a legitimate actor. I've done my best to keep Jerry from breaking me up while I work. It's a game with us. He's a very funny, brilliant young man. Jerry doesn't talk much about Dean, and Martin hasn't visited the set since we started shooting," to no one's surprise. The picture, directed by its scenarist Don McGuire (and co-directed, without credit, by Lewis), would gross over six times its cost domestically, as much as any recent Martin & Lewis picture.

All of these accomplishments jump-started Lewis' ego. "I've never been happier in my life," he'd tell the New York press in November, "because, for the first time in ten years, I am rid of a cancer." Of course, everyone interpreted *that* as him labeling Martin a malignant tumor that needed to be removed, but the real malignancy had been his fear of going it alone. Now that he knew for certain he could thrive without Dean, Jerry was eager to embark on what he would later term a "furious tear, a single-minded quest to become the King of Show Business."

Only one obstacle remained.

DEAN: I don't want to work with Jerry Lewis again, but if Hal Wallis insists, I'll do it.

JERRY: If Wallis expects us to work together, he'll have to be prepared to do the scenes at the Menninger Clinic.

– Separate comments to the press, November 1956

Back in September, Jerry told Louella Parsons, "I have no plans to work again with Dean Martin." She promptly asked him about the contract with Wallis. "Oh, I think Hal will take care of that if our solo pictures are good," he replied. Wallis, however, already had a script prepared for the two of them: another service comedy, *The Sad Sack*. In October, he sent start-up notices to both Martin and Lewis that said, in effect, solo pictures and hit records be damned, they were expected to fulfill their obligation. "We really hoped Wallis would let us do our jobs separately," Dean told columnist Harold Heffernan, "but it looks like it's not going to be that way, and around January 1, Jerry and I will be at it again."

"They've shaken hands and agreed to get together professionally," wrote Heffernan, but that was either a misunderstanding or outright fabrication. Terming Wallis's edict a rumor, Lewis told Hedda Hopper that a reteaming wouldn't happen. After Jerry's "Menninger's" comment appeared in her column, Wallis gleefully gave Hopper a tongue-in-cheek exclusive: "I've changed the title of their film. It's now 'Martin and Lewis in Menninger's.' I'll do it on a split-screen with Jerry's scenes at the clinic."

Perhaps he wasn't as eager as he was telling the press to resume an expensive battle of wills against Martin and Lewis; perhaps he wanted to see how *Hollywood or Bust*, a Christmas release, would fare at the box office in the face of all the headlines. Whichever it was, Wallis pushed the official start date of *The Sad Sack* to March 1. In the interim, Jerry played the Sands Hotel in Las Vegas, the Chez Paree in Chicago and New York's famed showcase, RKO's Palace Theater, where he shattered box office records with a $90,000 pre-sale gross.

He also authored a piece for *LOOK* magazine that tore asunder any chance that Dean and he would work together anytime soon.

* * * * *

Martin's first year apart from Lewis was shaping up to be a disaster.

He went straight to work on *Ten Thousand Bedrooms* and enjoyed the time spent on location in Rome and Paris, but as filming progressed, he suspected the finished product would be nothing special. It turned out to be less than that. The picture, which beat *The Delicate Delinquent* to theaters by three months, had a whopping negative cost of $1,800,000; after both domestic and foreign box offices were tallied, it wound up losing $1.1 million.

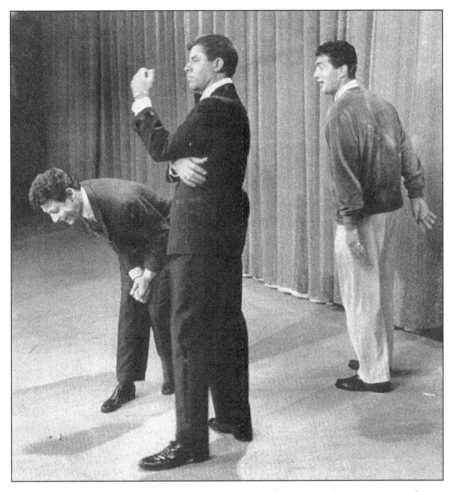

"Just don't sing!" Dean bursts in on *The Eddie Fisher Show*, September 30, 1958, much to Jerry's feigned annoyance and Fisher's uncontrollable glee.

During production, reporters and columnists showed little interest in the picture, choosing instead to ask Dean about the split. His answers were always the same: he and Jerry, "as close friends as we ever were," only parted "to prove to ourselves we could go it separately." He'd tired of "the pat formula" of their pictures, where he "was a heel for 60 minutes, then during the last 20 minutes proved I was a good guy by coming to Jerry's rescue." Nevertheless, they'd not only honor their contract with Wallis, but would "probably do one together for our own company," which they had no intention of dissolving. "After four or five years, we'll have some real dough to divide…in the neighborhood of $5 million."

To that last point, columnist Armand Archerd noted in late November that York received $150,000 as a loan-out fee for Martin's services, of which his ex-partner was entitled to a third. Meanwhile, even before its release, *The Delicate Delinquent* was expected to realize at least $2 million in profit for York, also due for a three-way split between Lewis, Paramount and Martin. Concluded Archerd wryly, "You can bet this remaining paper partnership will not last much longer."

Once *Ten Thousand Bedrooms* wrapped, Dean had little to keep himself occupied except to record an album and renegotiate with NBC over how many appearances he'd make per season (they eventually settled for four: two starring specials and two guest shots). Independent producer Robert Aldrich sought him for the lead in *A Machine for Chuparosa*, a tale of a small Mexican farming village that gets its first tractor. Aldrich hoped to start shooting in January 1957, but had difficulty in casting the remaining parts before his rights to the property expired. The film was never made; it would have been Martin's first dramatic role.

He even made it known he'd consider a sitcom. "That's what's here to stay, I'm convinced of it," he told Heffernan. "Situation comedy – something the folks at home can identify themselves with. If I could get such a series, I'd sure like to do it." Although he, like Jerry, was under contract for NBC's spectaculars, he had little faith in them: "As far as I can see, those specs add up to nothing but a big bore. I don't think this is what the public actually wants. Variety, as in *The Ed Sullivan Show*, yes… but specs, no." He'd been booked at the Sands for March (at $25,000 per week, which was $10,000 less than Jerry); his first solo TV show was set for April. Until then, all he could do was sing and play golf.

Like Lewis, he preferred to work alone; unlike Lewis, he was willing to swallow his pride and make an occasional team picture for the sake of his bank balance. Then, on January 22, Lewis' *LOOK* article came out… and the easy-going, unsentimental, 'who-the-hell-cares-anyway' Italian hit the proverbial ceiling.

The pertinent quotes have appeared in each man's biographies over the years. Dean, asserted his partner, "only likes to work a few weeks a year and play golf the rest of the time." Jerry "would put in a couple of months preparing for our shows" and Dean "would show up the day before the actual performance and say 'What do I do?'" Dean only "wanted wild, crazy noise without rhyme or reason," while Jerry "tried to work bits into the act in which the comedy developed out of pathos." Most damaging of all, Dean "divorced Betty and married his second wife, Jeanne, and suddenly our families weren't friendly anymore."

That last made Martin feel like he'd been hit "below the belt," which is what he told columnist Sidney Skolsky, who'd brought him an advance copy of the magazine. "I thought we broke up an act, a partnership, not a friendship…[but] Jerry talks about Jeanne and that's going too far. I respect other wives. I could talk about Patti, and Jerry knows it, but I wouldn't." When Aline Mosby asked him about the piece, he said, "It should have been called 'I've Never Been Scared.' He's never been frightened, and I really know this kid. Nothing that Jerry wrote is true. It's maudlin and ridiculous," and confessed he was "especially hurt because we parted friends."

Mosby's column was printed on January 28. That evening, NBC introduced its newly-formatted *Tonight!* program. Titled *Tonight! America After Dark*, it became something of a nocturnal *Today*, with news breaks and remote interviews across the country; an intimate look, so the network intended, at America's night life. Pick-ups on premiere night were split between New York, Chicago, Kansas City and Los Angeles. Hollywood columnists Paul Coates and Vernon Scott made their way around town, and the latter happened upon Dean and Jeanne dining at the Beverly Hilton. Martin had been drinking…and evidently stewing. When Scott asked the inevitable questions about "I've Always Been Scared," the quotes appearing in the next morning's reviews show Martin didn't stem his fury:

What did he think of the article? "Everything in it was full of lies but one thing: he wrote it." What Lewis said about his work ethic? "He doesn't know what he's talking about." Did he really object to Lewis' desire for pathos? "I wouldn't have objected if he knew how to do it – or felt it." Would he and Lewis ever team up again? "Get back together? Hah! Not even in the same country." Is he considering authoring a response? "What I'd say about him, *Confidential* wouldn't even print."

Years later, Lewis would admit the inflammatory parts about Dean were "definitely the hurt talking," but at the time, he asserted he was just being honest. "I'm sorry my article was misinterpreted, but it was all the truth," he told Earl Wilson. "How do you break up a partnership and not a friendship? The partnership must have been based on friendship." Meanwhile the critics, none of whom were particularly impressed with *America After Dark*, were positively aghast at the Scott-Martin segment. Jack Gould: "Martin spoke of Jerry Lewis in terms so utterly nauseating

TV GUIDE

15¢

A strange, sad story:
JERRY LEWIS'S FLOP
By Richard Gehman   see page 18
LOCAL PROGRAMS • DECEMBER 14-20

Rosemary Clooney,
Frank Sinatra,
Dean Martin,
Kathryn Crosby,
Bing Crosby
prepare for a special

The press liked to keep the feud going, as in this 1963 *TV Guide* cover where the head of a laughing Dean appears to be pointing to the story about his ex-partner's failed variety show.

as only to invoke sympathy for his erstwhile partner." John Lester: "Dean Martin's personal and professional blasts at his ex-partner… were in the worst possible taste." Harry Harris: "Martin lashed out with snarling comments…. It was a shocking exhibition of no fun after dark, but [also] had the harsh sound of truth, and exposed most of the program's conversation for the contrived oohing and ahing it was."

Leo Guild of *The Hollywood Reporter* noted Jeanne Martin literally gave Dean a surreptitious kick beneath their table "because she felt he was being too frank in his criticism" of Jerry. Later, Martin would call NBC and tell officials he was trying "to gag it around as much as he could and was just sort of kidding." But it was too little, too late. The next day, he alerted his lawyers that he wanted out of York; they were to sell his stock back to Lewis and/or Paramount as quickly as possible. Nothing, not even the promise of "real dough to divide," was worth his remaining tied to Jerry Lewis in any fashion. He was clearly desperate: when the deal was done, Martin still owed York over a half-million for advances taken over the years.

With that, Hal Wallis was finally convinced. Even though *Hollywood or Bust* was cleaning up—it would out-gross *Pardners* by a million—he officially threw in the towel and renegotiated his three remaining Martin & Lewis pictures into six: three with Martin, three with Lewis. David Wayne would take Martin's role in *The Sad Sack*—it was the last time a Jerry Lewis picture required a faux Dean—and Wallis would chortle gleefully after a gross of $3.2 million (which was $100,000 more than *Hollywood or Bust* took in) ensured a tidy return. With or without Martin, Lewis was profitable.

Wallis wasn't much interested in Martin anyway, not after *Ten Thousand Bedrooms* stiffed. By April 1957, Dean's career consisted of recording sessions, infrequent appearances on NBC, six weeks per year at the Sands, and small, second-rate clubs in places like Pittsburgh; the kind of joints from which he and Jerry had graduated back in 1948. It got so bad that when *TV Guide's* Dan Jenkins came calling to talk about his first solo special, he assumed they'd want to hear about the split. Jenkins subsequently wrote that Martin "spoke like a man who was getting a load off his mind. He never stopped long enough for anyone to get a question in."

And what a load it was: "You know, I'm getting a little tired of being the heavy in this thing. Every time Jerry opens his mouth, it comes out that Dean Martin is lazy or something and doesn't like to work. People have been hearing that for a long time now and they believe it…."

"I always liked to work. Jerry liked to play. I'd walk into rehearsal on a Monday and Jerry and all his flunkies would be sitting there… Jerry would say, 'We're thinking.' And I'd say, 'So think. When you're ready to go to work, call me.'" The next day, "they'd be tossing a football around the stage. And I'd say, 'So O.K., if you fellas want to play football, I'll go out and play a little golf. Call me when you're ready to go to work.'" Then, "when we'd finally get down to work…there'd be some flunky standing in for him. And I'd say, 'Hey, where's Jerry?' And some voice out of a speaker somewhere would say, 'He's up here in the control booth lining up the shots.' So I'm supposed to stand there are rehearse with some stooge who can't even ad lib? So I'd call some guy and say, 'You stand here and be me until Jerry is ready to do the work he's supposed to be doing, like rehearsing, maybe.' And that's the way it would go…."

There was more; about Lewis' comedy ("Jerry is a very funny man, but he's a visual slapstick comic… But somewhere along the line he read a book about Chaplin and all of a sudden goes with this pathos stuff. It's not his bit"), about his *LOOK* article ("It's not so bad, maybe, that he has to take off on me, but why does he have to take off on my wife?"), about his career aspirations ("He's spending too much time being everything but a comic. He's got to be a director and a writer and a producer."), about his singing ("If Norman Brooks couldn't make it imitating Jolson, what makes Jerry think he can make it? It's ridiculous.")

He summed up with, "Look, I'm not sore. I've just severed all connections… Far as I'm concerned, Jerry Lewis doesn't exist any more in my life. I like it just fine that way. But I'm tired of being the heavy, that's all." To that end, *TV Guide* did him no favors, putting "Dean Martin Blasts Jerry Lewis" on the front cover of the April 13 issue. Shortly thereafter, the magazine printed a letter from one Calvin T. Beck of North Bergen, NJ, who spoke for many fed-up fans: "Martin and Lewis' feud is neither interesting, inspiring or wholesome. It's no credit to the entertainment field to hear such moronic outbursts repeated over and over. While those who follow show business are, unfortunately, aware of the fact that many of the personalities are emotionally unstable or immature, why destroy the illusions of us all by dragging their ugly private affairs into print? About the only thing that the Martin and Lewis flare-up seems to remind us is that these boys lack something badly: a good, old-fashioned paddling with the hairbrush."

Martin's reps at MCA were beating the bushes for a prestige picture with a decent co-starring role alongside a strong lead. They found one:

The Young Lions. Even better, there were *two* strong leads: Montgomery Clift and Marlon Brando. Convinced the part of Michael Whiteacre could do for Martin what *From Here to Eternity's* Angelo Maggio did for Frank Sinatra, MCA let the producers know they could have the crooner-actor for a $20,000 song. The ploy worked. Finally required to really *act*, Dean positively dazzled in the role.

In February 1958, just ahead of the picture's release, Dean appeared on *Person to Person* with Ed Murrow, this time with his wife by his side. He talked about his performance in the film and the hopes for his career. He and Jeanne introduced their children, he dealt a hand of Showdown (the stakes were $10 toward either man's favorite charity; Dean won), did a few card tricks and spoke of his early days as a croupier. Toward the end, Murrow asked him what he considered "the biggest break" of his life. As Jeanne stared right at him, Dean looked directly into the camera, mustered every ounce of sincerity he could, and replied, "Outside of meeting my wife Jeanne, I think the biggest and most wonderful break of my life was meeting Jerry...Jerry Lewis. We had ten wonderful, great years, and I enjoyed every minute of it. And I think that was a real lucky, lucky break for me." It was the high moment of the interview; an astonishing atoning for the previous year's headlines before a coast-to-coast audience that, Martin knew, needed to like him if they were to give his new picture a chance.

Among the most astonished was Lewis, who reportedly gave Martin a call after the broadcast. "Did you mean those things you said about me?" he asked. "Of course," Dean replied, adding, "I always mean everything I say about you." Left unspoken was the obvious caveat: "both good and bad." Not that it mattered; once *The Young Lions* came out, and won him both popular and critical acclaim, Dean would never again need to say a kind word about his former partner.

Not long after, he convinced Sinatra, who was then only a casual buddy, to cast him as the southern gambler in *Some Came Running* (1958). It proved a landmark in more ways than one: again, Dean's natural ability enhanced an important picture, and Frank—much as Jerry had years before—fell in love with him. From that time on, Dino would consider Frank his best friend; keenly aware, though, of Sinatra's ambition and intensity, he deliberately kept that friendship at arm's length. They'd record together, appear on stage, screen and TV together, even hang out together... but of genuine warmth such as Dean had openly bestowed upon Jerry during their glory years, there would be not a trace. Once-burned, twice-shy.

A third successful picture, *Rio Bravo* (1959) opposite John Wayne, proved Dean Martin had become a bankable star, and that was good enough for Wallis. The producer would call in Martin's debt to him just as he was wrapping his second Jerry Lewis solo vehicle, yet another service farce called *Don't Give Up the Ship* (1959).

* * * * *

So it was that by the autumn of 1958, both Martin and Lewis were bona-fide successes apart. They rarely appeared in newspaper columns during the year, except separately when promoting their individual work. As for the gossip mongers, they were too busy covering a juicy new Hollywood scandal: Eddie Fisher had left his wife, Debbie Reynolds, and their two young children, ending what had been described in fan magazines as a storybook marriage to take up with the recently widowed Elizabeth Taylor.

Lewis had known Fisher for years; like him, Fisher had logged time in the Borscht Belt, and they'd become close friends. He eagerly accepted a guest spot on the singer's first TV show of the season, set to air on September 30. A bit was written where Fisher would introduce his special guest, building him up as one of the greatest of comedians. Jerry would then come out and sing straight, much to Eddie's annoyance, and the two would get into a mock argument. During rehearsals the afternoon before, Bing Crosby stopped by to chat with Fisher and wish him well; he was headed to an adjoining studio to rehearse his own show, scheduled for October 1. What Bing didn't mention was that *his* special guest was Dean.

On the air, the interplay between Lewis and Fisher was nicely handled. "If I wanted to have a singing guest," says Eddie, "I could get, uh, Mary Martin. Or, uh, Dude Martin. Or, uh, Tony Martin. Or..." Jerry's heard enough: "YOU'RE GETTING VERY CLOSE, BIG MOUTH!" This being Lewis, there's some ad-libbing; at one point, Fisher turns away to laugh, and Lewis pulls him back, smacking him on the arm: "You face me! I haven't worked with a singer in years!" This sends Fisher over the brink and he collapses from laughter into Lewis' arms.

After a few more ad-libs, Lewis gets back on script: "Will you do me a plain personal? Leave the stage and let me do what I have to do." Just as Fisher is delivering his line, the curtain parts, and out steps a casually dressed Dean Martin: "Just don't sing! Do whatever you want to, but don't sing! That's all!" The studio audience lets out a shriek (which drowns out the second half of this outburst, but Dean's lips are easily read); Jerry turns away from Dean and faces the audience, scowling—but has to cover his mouth to hide a smile. Meanwhile, Dean heads toward the curtain, but turns again toward Jerry, making a clapping gesture with his hands and saying something that cannot be deciphered thanks to the still-screaming audience. At that moment, Crosby emerges from behind the curtain and forcibly pulls Martin away. Throughout, Fisher is doubled over in hysterics.

Jerry grabs the laughing host once again and steadies him while laughing himself. He releases Fisher and runs over to peek behind the curtain, but Martin and Crosby have vanished. He returns downstage, holds up his hand to silence the audience and, turning presumably toward the adjacent studio, loudly sings "Returrrrrn to Meeeeee" —Dean's hit from earlier that year. Lewis and Fisher swing back into their routine,

The Journal-News

A MEMBER OF THE GANNETT GROUP   ROCKLAND COUNTY, N.Y., TUESDAY, SEPTEMBER 7, 1976

Carter rips Ford as drive begins

Frank Sinatra, center, brings Dean Martin and Jerry Lewis together

Surprise reunion

Frank Sinatra, appearing as a performer on the annual Muscular Dystrophy Telethon in Las Vegas hosted by Jerry Lewis, brought on Dean Martin to the surprise of Lewis Sunday night. It was the first time Martin and Lewis had appeared together since their comedy team broke up more than 20 years ago. A spokesman said the surprised Lewis was genuinely touched. The telethon raised more than $21 million.

Dean Martin, left, and Jerry Lewis reunited

Probation chief backed in plea for larger staff

As big as the upcoming Presidential election: Martin and Lewis' 1976 Labor Day reunion hits the front page.

but Dean's surprise appearance has inspired Jerry to kick it up a notch. As in the early *Colgate* shows, he runs offstage and between cameras to harass a crew member, takes even more liberties with the material, and treats Fisher as he once did his partner: "I ad-libbed! You don't know where we are, do you?" The audience howls while Fisher, laughing again, can only shake his head.

Newspaper critics jumped on the "reunion" as the only noteworthy part of the show, especially since Fisher—under strict orders from NBC—made no mention of his personal situation. "A routine variety show with a routine theme…Eddie's 'very special guest' Jerry Lewis converted it into a wacky—and hilarious—shambles," wrote Harry Harris. After describing Martin's surprise appearance, Harris added, "The show never again came anywhere near that pixilated peak."

The rumor mill immediately began churning. "Apparently, that was a good deal more than a routine gag the other night when Dean Martin did his surprise walk-on," wrote Sturgis Hedrick. "A tip from the West Coast tells us that the feuding Martin & Lewis will reunite for an NBC-TV spectacular this season. The walk-on was the opening gun in the publicity barrage." Conversely, Bob Williams asserted, "There was nothing pre-arranged about the surprise party Bing Crosby and Dean Martin sprang on the *Eddie Fisher Show*. It was Crosby's own puckish little plot…. Martin's willingness to join in Crosby's gag gave rise to immediate but unfounded rumors of a possible Martin-Lewis reconciliation. Jerry's shouted remark to Dean, 'Return to me,' was most generous. It was a healthy plug for Martin's record of the same title…no more."

Martin confirmed the spontaneity of the moment: "It was a gag. Bing and I were rehearsing for his show and decided to have a little fun." Asked why he didn't linger awhile, he replied, "If I'd stayed longer, they'd think we're together again," which some of "them" apparently did anyway. Meanwhile, now that he knew it wasn't Dean's idea, Lewis—still angry with Crosby over the snub during the 1952 Olympic Telethon—told Williams he thought the stunt was unprofessional and "dangerous with a kid like that on his first show of the season."

Not long after, an article appeared in which the Muscular Dystrophy Association thanked Lewis for his support of their cause, and let the world know the research center they were building in New York—the funding of which had been the focus of the team's 1956 telethon—would be known as "the House That Jerry Built." Maybe Martin wouldn't have cared had it not been publicized—the organization's dealings had always been with Lewis alone—but since it was, he took exception. "Those millions Lewis raised were raised by both of us over a 10 year (*sic*) period, if anyone's interested. We did it, not he. I just don't want him taking credit for something he didn't do alone."

That outburst coincided with Lewis going to the hospital with a perforated ulcer on October 31, forcing him to cancel a muscular dystrophy telethon set for Thanksgiving weekend. Although the official diagnosis was "overwork," Dick Stabile informed columnist Mike Connolly that Lewis had told him, "I'm sick. I can't work. This time, if Dean wants a feud, he'll go it alone. I pray to God I'll never say a word against him, even in my defense." Stabile added his own thoughts: "Comedians are the most sensitive, worrisome, easily upset people in show business. Dean must realize this. He's worked with Jerry long enough to know it. There's no other man alive who can hurt Jerry as Dean can, and of this I believe Dean is well aware."

Lewis wanted to make his feelings known about the matter once and for all, so columnist Sheilah Graham handed her December 3 space over to him. He framed it as a slam on "the less imaginative members of the press," specifically ones who harp on two irksome issues. The first: "Periodically some scribe, seeking a provocative subject, chooses to interpret some of my wild gestures and grimaces as mercilessly burlesquing the pathetic, the mentally retarded and the handicapped. This is a lie!

"Practically every move I make on stage, I have learned from my four sons who, thank goodness, are normal healthy boys, but it destroys me to think that some people would believe that, as a father, I could be so unfeeling and callous as to ape those who are less fortunate. As national chairman for the Muscular Dystrophy Association and dedicated to help wipe out one of the most crippling killers known to medicine, how could I face these stricken children if they thought for a moment I was ridiculing them?"

The second "pet peeve is the reporters who, at this late date, still print that my ex-partner, Dean Martin, and myself are either feuding or on the verge of getting together again. Every time we run into one another publicly, they interpret every word we say as having some deep inner meaning. It just isn't true. The same differences exist today as did at the time of our split. We both have very definite ideas as to the conduct of our professional careers and it just so happens they take different directions."

Sadly, three weeks after the column saw print, he and Martin *were* feuding again, with poor Eddie Fisher caught in the middle.

The all-but-unknown August 23, 1977 reunion. Photo courtesy of Kayley Thompson.

It started when Martin, who'd been booked for Fisher's December 23 show, "walked out in a salary hassle, leaving Eddie in the lurch," UPI reported the previous afternoon. Upon learning Fisher had lost his guest star—he'd later claim he had no idea it was Dean until after the fact—Lewis offered to fill in; moreover, he'd do it for free, "because it's Christmas."

That set Dean off like a July Fourth fireworks display: "It's a grandstand martyr play. Jerry's full of baloney, always has been. It's not good for show business when performers work for nothing. But then, Jerry never did anything good for the business anyhow. He never has. He just wanted to make me look bad. I wouldn't do that to anybody."

Meanwhile, Fisher—who'd been told by NBC at the start of the season not to invite Elizabeth Taylor to the studio "because her appearance would seem to be flaunting things that are not too wholesome" —was stunned. Worse, and to the network's chagrin, Taylor ignored the edict and slipped in a side door, kept her boyfriend company for a half-hour prior to air, watched the program from the director's booth, then sat in Fisher's dressing room, holding his hand as he detailed his dispute with Martin to Vernon Scott after the broadcast:

"It all started with a kitchen…complete with stove, sinks and all the rest of it. [Dean and I] had a reciprocal agreement. I appeared on his show with the understanding that he would appear on my show. I had a $7,500 kitchen installed at my home after the show and Dean liked it. He was a good friend of mine, and said he would appear on my program if he could have a kitchen installed at his home like the one I had.

"But when it came time to install his kitchen, he said it would cost $11,400. I couldn't understand why his should cost more, so I balked. Then his representatives said if I didn't come through he would appear on the *Dinah Shore Show* for $20,000. I had no choice. I agreed to have the $11,400 kitchen installed.

"Then, all of a sudden, I was notified that he wanted $25,000 for the show or he wouldn't appear. That did it. I couldn't go that high, and that was the end of the deal. Even if he wasn't a friend of mine, I still couldn't understand why I should be treated like that. Maybe he just got too big, too fast.

"And then he had to go and blast Jerry Lewis. It wasn't fair. Jerry appeared on my show with very little notice. He didn't want to be a hero or show anybody up. He knows how hard it is to find guest stars of the Dean Martin, Jerry Lewis caliber. He offered to help me out—and brother, he did."

Asked to comment, and aware that NBC was considering cancelling the show over "the moral aspects" of the Fisher-Taylor relationship, Lewis went on record that the issue was Fisher, not his ex-partner: "Eddie was my friend before he got himself in trouble and he's my friend now. Dean's not the only one to turn his back on Eddie. It's about time people let up on [him]. The point is, if a man makes a decision that's his business, and his friends should be able to draw the lines. I'm not condoning what Eddie did, but it has nothing to do with his entertainment value or his talent. I figure when a guy does a stretch for a year, he's paid his debt. And believe me, Eddie's been through the mill.

"I'm not mad at Dean or anyone else. Remember, it takes two to make a feud. I'm not a party to any disagreements. I just went on to help Eddie. I hope everyone has a Merry Christmas."

As 1959 began, Martin was preparing for *Career*, his first obligatory assignment for Hal Wallis, when *Newsweek* caught up with him. The first thing he told them was what he'd told Ed Murrow nearly a year earlier… with an addendum: "The best thing that ever happened to me was when I met Jerry Lewis. The best thing that's happened to me since then was when we split up." He spoke of the split; his film roles; his NBC contract (now two shows a year at $200,000 each); his partnership in the Sunset Strip restaurant Dino's Lodge and in the Sands Hotel (the latter was "like an oil well—it pays every month"). He'd earned close to a million in 1958 and no longer had to endure the night club circuit, just "two weeks a year at the Sands." Asked if he'd ever consider reuniting with Lewis, he replied, "Sure…when we get to the moon."

Six months later, Lewis was in a position to *purchase* the moon. On June 7 (ironically, Martin's 42nd birthday), Paramount signed him to a seven-year, 14-picture contract worth "in excess of $10 million," according to *Motion Picture Daily*. It was, Paramount's Barney Balaban said, "the biggest price ever paid for acting talent in movie history." Anyone who questioned Balaban on the wisdom of such a deal in the modern age, was informed of the $400 million Lewis' pictures (with and without Martin) had grossed to date. "Look at the money he's made the studio," said Balaban, "If he wants to burn it down, I've got a match."

* * * * *

JERRY: "I can't forget that Dean's the fellow that helped build my house."

DEAN: "I am 100% better off since Jerry and I broke up."

– *Separate statements to interviewers, 1960*

On March 12, 1960, we didn't get to the moon…but Martin and Lewis reunited anyway, for 15 minutes, on stage at the Sands.

This reunion, for which neither film nor audio apparently exists, began with a phone call placed weeks earlier. Martin, making *Ocean's 11*, complained of head pain and dizzy spells, and a rumor broke that he'd developed a brain tumor. Lewis, in Miami making *The Bellboy*, heard the rumor and telephoned his ex-colleague. "The call was formal, like Truman calling Eisenhower," said one of Jerry's associates, "but Dean knew that Jerry was sincerely worried." Martin told him it was just overwork; after a few days' rest, he was fine.

Jerry was due to open at the Sands beginning Wednesday, March 9, but needed a few more days to finish *The Bellboy* ahead of an actor's strike. He asked Jack Entratter if someone could cover for him until Sunday. Someone could: Dean.

Lewis arrived on Saturday evening in time for Martin's closing show and took a seat. "It was the first time I had seen him work alone since we split, and I was surprised and delighted," he told Alfred G. Aronowitz of the *New York Post* the next day. "I shouldn't say 'surprised' because I know Dean is great. But it was a beautiful show."

"Now, folks," announced Dean, "I want you to meet that brilliant young comic, Jerry Lewis, my partner." Jerry came up on stage, and then walked to the wings. When he came back, he was wearing a giant pair of boxing gloves. "The audience," he recalled, "reacted like Castro and Eisenhower got married.... We strained trying to remember what we used to do, and for 15 minutes there wasn't a dry eye in the house, including ours." The pair finished up with a comic rendition of "My Heart Cries For You," presumably near to their performance on the May 20, 1951 *Colgate Comedy Hour*. They reportedly chatted for 10 minutes in Dean's dressing room before Martin had to catch a train back to Los Angeles. "Lewis went with him to the front of the hotel," UPI reported. "They shook hands and embraced."

By his own admission, Lewis was "walking on a cloud all day" Sunday. "I was never happier in my life to see my ex-partner and he felt, or at least he showed, the same feeling. We're going to go on as we are, except that we're not going to have any more childish, unnecessary battling.... It was a beautifully emotional thing with two people who cared for each other for very many years, and then, because of their own insecurities, led the world to believe that they didn't care anymore. You just don't turn off caring. Your subconscious lets you think you do.

"Of course, this doesn't mean we're going to team up again, but that [decision] isn't based on something distasteful, just something logical. Dean is doing just great; he doesn't need anybody to help him in what he's doing, and I'm doing fairly well, too."

It was clearly a joyous milestone in Jerry's life, but after speaking with Aronowitz, he never again mentioned or even acknowledged this event, as the Martin-Lewis relationship once more turned to ice. Director and unabashed Lewis fan Peter Bogdanovich was told about the reunion by publicist Jack Keller, who added a postscript: "Now get this: Not long afterward, in [an] interview, Dean slams into Jerry like crazy. So go figure."

The interview, which appeared in *Pageant* magazine's August issue, took place shortly after "The Summit" in Las Vegas, where Martin, along with his *Ocean's 11* cohorts Frank Sinatra, Sammy Davis, Jr., Peter Lawford and Joey Bishop, were tearing up the stage at the Sands. The piece briefly references the "so-called reconciliation in Las Vegas," adding, "Martin delivered himself of a most blunt outburst on the current status of his former partner...scornful of Lewis' present efforts."

Some of the ground had been covered in Dean's "blast" to Dan Jenkins three years earlier, but was now directed not at Jerry but toward his advisors. It also de-personalized their recent reunion: "Even though I'll fill in for Jerry—or anybody, for that matter—I still think he's on the wrong track. God gave him a gift to be the funniest comic the world ever saw, but whoever it is that advised him to direct, sing, dance, write and produce—what he's doing now—is just plain stupid... He's let his hair grow too long, he's speaking beautifully, he's trying to be an intellect. He's not an intellect; he's a comic...."

"Jerry'd better come to his senses and get rid of the idiots around him, the yes-men. Yes-men kill you. The men around Jerry are complete idiots. Underline that. Complete idiots.... You can say that for me." Small wonder that, as Dorothy Kilgallen reported, "Jerry Lewis' chums consider Dean Martin's quotes in the current issue of *Pageant* magazine as 'below the belt.'" It was *their* belts receiving the blows.

There's no question Lewis surrounded himself with loyalists; he was too insecure *not* to indulge that luxury. The question is how much influence they had on his career decisions, and the answer is not much. Martin had missed the point: Lewis was a producer and director because he'd been aiming to be one since that very first scripted home movie in 1951. He sang because audiences and record buyers, enchanted by his sincerity, told him he could. In fairness, if Dean saw his ex-partner solely as a "brilliant young comic," it was because he valued making an audience laugh even more than winning them over with a song. In his opinion, comedy was Jerry's greatest gift; when you're that good at it, why be anything else? But, however well-intentioned Martin's outburst, it came over as an attack that Lewis was bound to take personally.

A few months later, *Pageant* sought Lewis out and got his response: "It hurts me when Dean belts me in print. But it doesn't give me the right to belt him back. There is back-biting in every business, but I don't have to indulge. Dean has a 'Jerry Lewis' routine in his night club act in which he belts me. I have no anti-Dean Martin material. I put out an album a few years back: 'Jerry Lewis Just Sings.' Some people nicknamed it: 'Music to Get Even with Dean Martin By.' But it wasn't my name, [or] my idea."

To be fair, there wasn't a "Jerry Lewis" routine per se; Dean would just make an occasional crack. On stage alone, he'd remove the microphone from the stand, then say "Excuse me, Jerry" as he moved it out of the way. Or he'd say something like, "See these muscles? I got them carrying Jerry all those years." Or he'd warn his pianist Ken Lane to quit "adding to your part. That's what happened to Jerry!" With the Rat Pack, Sammy, during a celebrity imitations routine, would advise Dean to be nice to him "or I'll do Jerry." Dean would respond, "Jerry who?"

And so "Jerry who?" decided he'd simply avoid any contact with Dean, which wasn't easy since they both worked at Paramount. "I'd see him tooling around the lot in his little golf cart with his name on it in lights. When he saw me, he'd duck around a corner," Dean told the *Saturday Evening Post's* Pete Martin (no relation). After the third or fourth time, Martin barged into Lewis' office, saying, "You little so-and-so... why do you keep ducking me?" Dean took Jerry to his own office, told him to sit and have a drink, and tried to reassure him that there was no reason to be so childish. "I said, 'Now, isn't this better than ducking me?' He said, 'Yep,' and I felt pretty good about it. Then he left. And the next time he saw me, he ducked me again." Lewis unsurprisingly never mentioned this incident either.

Interviewers and columnists couldn't get enough of this stuff, and when nothing new was forthcoming they'd occasionally stir the pot by revisiting the partnership. When Lewis opened a tony restaurant on the Sunset Strip just three blocks west of the less formal Dino's Lodge, Erskine Johnson built a February 1962 column around a mythical "food feud," likening it to the Berlin Wall: "There is no Iron Curtain wall separating Dino's and Jerry's but the emotionalism is high and thick. Rioting and head clobbering with breadsticks could happen.... There are underground rumbles about non-aligned friends and how the stars will line up in this now-divided Sunset Strip world. There is talk that passports and loyalty oaths may be demanded.... There could be a showdown between the rival chefs—supreme of young capon vs Long Island ducking hurled from 50 paces apart at high noon." A lengthy and more serious James Bacon article, "The Great Martin and Lewis Feud," appeared in March 1963. In what could only have been an attempt to elicit more juicy outbursts from Martin, the piece begins, "Dean Martin, who wants to live like Bing Crosby, and Jerry Lewis, who can afford to but doesn't, have been solo almost seven years now. But the feud that broke them up still lingers on. What has happened...could be summed up this way: Dino would be richer if he had stuck with Jerry—but more miserable. One of Martin's business partners reports that he might become a rich man soon. Lewis is a millionaire already...."

"Moviewise, Lewis is the winner going away. In their heyday as a team, Martin and Lewis were among the top 10 box office attractions. Since they split, Lewis is still there. Martin never made it..,. [His] solo career almost floundered at the start. After the split with Lewis, Martin was cast in a movie called '10,000 (*sic*) Bedrooms.' He was the star with the only marquee name. The picture died a horrible death although it was an entertaining movie and Martin was good in it. His agents called an emergency meeting. 'It was decided that Martin henceforth should be cast only in movies where other stars would carry the box office lure,' one recalled."

Bacon also theorized, "The main cause of the split is basic. As one who practically grew up in the business with Martin and Lewis, I can say flatly that Martin hates Lewis'—er, well...vice versa." On the latter point, Lewis begged to differ... somewhat. "I love Dean," he told *TV Guide's* Richard Gehman a couple of months later, "but I don't like him much anymore."

* * * * *

For Lewis, the year 1963 began with the release of *The Nutty Professor*, the most critically and financially successful of his self-directed films. It ended with ABC-TV's *The Jerry Lewis Show*, a live two-hour variety series that remains one of the most expensive and infamous disasters in the history of television. Lewis convinced the network to give him two hours of prime time live—nothing taped in advance—for five years and $35,000,000. His vision for the show was grandiose, if unspecific: "The live communication on this show is going to stimulate the audience and the performers," he told Gehman. "We're going to have people who know how to perform and how to talk.... I'm going to have the wildest combination of things you ever heard of."

He had ABC purchase the El Capitan—where so many *Comedy Hours* had originated—renamed it the Jerry Lewis Theater and oversaw its complete refurbishment. In explaining the show's failure a couple of years later, he said, "I was busily building that theater... for camerawork and everything else. I was so busy at getting the proper facilities...and making it the kind of perfection I think our business warrants, I forgot the show. I forgot a minor thing called, 'Get Funny.'"

His ex-partner could have said, "I told you so," but didn't. Instead, he said it with wisecracks. After the requisite 13 weeks, with its host growing more disenchanted with each broadcast, ABC canceled *The Jerry Lewis*

Show and re-renamed the theater. Now it was called the Hollywood Palace, and the network turned over what had been Lewis' first hour to a Sullivanesque variety series of the same name. Each show had a different celebrity host; when Martin took a week, he told the viewing audience, "I want to thank Jerry for building this wonderful theater for me." And now, when calling his microphone stand "Jerry" on stage, he couldn't resist adding, "They took your show away, huh?"

They did, and although the financial pain was minimized—contractually, ABC had to buy him out—the public embarrassment lingered. Lewis took it out on the network, on the writers and producer, and even on Ernie Glucksman, who was fired after fourteen years' loyal catering to his star's every whim. But he knew who was to blame for the debacle, which marked the beginning of a decline in popularity. From here on in, each subsequent Jerry Lewis movie would gross less than the one before, until finally Paramount dropped him as well.

As for Martin, his *Hollywood Palace* stint led to yet another "lucky break" for his career. He told producer Nick Vanoff he'd host if he could rehearse for only one day. Vanoff agreed to this, as well as to have cue

The fourth, and final, reunion in Las Vegas: June 6, 1989.

cards at the ready, and Dean called it his happiest experience with television yet, informing his agent that "if they could all be that easy," he wouldn't be averse to doing his own variety show.

With that, NBC came calling. Even then, it took time to convince Martin they were serious. "First, I asked [for] a ridiculous sum," he told Melvin Durslag. "Then I said I wanted to own the package 100% after the first showing of the series. I also said I wanted to work Sunday only, and I reserved the right not to sing on the show if I didn't want to. What I asked should have been thrown back into my face, but the network accepted it." *The Dean Martin Show* debuted in September 1965 and it wasn't long before Martin realized it was doing "wonderful things for my records and has given me a recognition that one doesn't get from movies."

That same month, David Susskind—the former MCA agent who hired Simmons and Lear for *Colgate* and had become a producer/host himself—presented Lewis over a two-part interview session for his *Open End* series. Susskind's subject, who brought his own tape recorder to the interview, dwelled on his successes and failures, focusing mainly on the former. When, however, the host brought up the subject of Martin & Lewis and asked how such an "incredible, successful marriage" ended, Lewis became visibly uncomfortable, yet markedly candid in an answer worth printing in full:

"Well... *(pause)* I think it has to start with *(pause)* me. I think I was one of the very, very strong forces in the destruction of the relationship, in that... psychologically, I guess, or sub-consciously, both Dean and I were aware that the life of a team such as this had so many years in it.

"We had put in ten years; ten very successful years and we built the kind of a theatrical empire the likes of which no one had ever seen. It was motivated by a tremendous love one man had for another. Dean was my father, my brother, my friend. He was the big strong guy that I could lean on and depend on. And I was a kid brother to Dean, and someone who knew the theatrical aspect of things, and... and understood Dean so well. And there was a very, very strong relationship there.

"But egos get pulled into this kind of a thing. I began to want to do more things. I was hoping that Dean would live by the standards that I set for myself. I had no right to expect him to do that. At that time, I really was terribly hurt because I said we should now go and do *this* for our career, and he didn't concur. I took offense at his not being able to live by a standard or a pinnacle that I had set as a... as a goal. Well, that was wrong. I had no right to expect it. Dean is a very easy going, marvelous man who likes to do what he does as he does it, and as you can't expect me to change what I believe, I couldn't expect him to change, but I didn't know it then.

"Moreover, I wanted to do so many other creative things, and he wanted more *time*. He wanted to play more golf and be with his family; I wanted to be with my family, but *work* when I wasn't. And it was just a matter of two men wanting different things.

"There were terrible rumors that really were terribly unfair. Nobody would ever print the real truth because it didn't read well. It wasn't something that would sell papers. And the truth (*pause*) is simply that, uhh (*pause*) we loved one another, and... if... if... Dean feels this day as I feel about him, I can say we still love one another. We just didn't like working together anymore."

There it was: egos, ambition, "artistic differences," as Lewis' official biography press release would put it, "destroyed" their relationship. There's no mention of "outside forces" or "shit-stirrers" (as he'd later claim in *Dean and Me*) pulling them apart; just "me." It was remarkably and brutally honest. And the pauses are nearly as revealing as the words as he says, "…if Dean feels this day as I feel about him." That he didn't really *know* how Dean felt was the biggest hole in his heart; one for which all the honors and successes and braggadocio in the world couldn't compensate.

As for Dean, he was still brooding over that eight-year-old *LOOK* article. In August he'd told an Associated Press interviewer, "I like Jerry. I even kiss him when we run into each other, but I don't like the things he said about me." That same week, he told Bob Thomas, "You know, when Jerry Lewis and I broke up, he said I wouldn't last two years in show business. So now what happens? He gets dropped by Paramount." For all Jerry's reputation as the overly sentimental, easily hurt partner, it sometimes seemed to be Dean who couldn't let go of the past.

By 1967, Martin's earnings were approaching $5 million per year, and with *The Dean Martin Show*, which was then sponsored by Colgate, nestled among the top 15 in ratings, NBC effectively tripled that number by signing him to another three years at $35 million. No one was more surprised than Dino: "God! I am not worth it. What do I do? I do an hour: I sing maybe ten songs [and] talk. I make fun of my wife, of my children, of my mother-in-law, of myself, of my drinkin'."

Ten years earlier, Martin griped about Jerry being so preoccupied doing other things that he was expected to rehearse with "some flunky." Now guest stars on Dean's show were expected to do the same during the week, although in this instance the "flunky" was producer Greg Garrison.

Dean would come in on Sunday (having run through his lines on the golf course during the week), watch a run-through, then tape the show, relying on cue cards whenever his memory failed him. This method occasionally rattled his guests, but also made for the kind of spontaneous fun that always tickled audiences, as Dean well knew. In a sketch that aired early in the series, Bob Newhart played a customer attempting to return a defective toupee to Martin, portraying the sales clerk. Dean, an admitted fan of the comedian, kept breaking up at both the material and Newhart's delivery. At one point, Newhart's character requests "a straight man who didn't laugh," but this just cracks up Martin even more. Finally, Newhart eyes him with suspicion: "You're sure you worked with Jerry?" "Yeah," laughs Martin, "but our stuff wasn't this funny."

Curiously, in May, Colgate decided to revive their *Comedy Hour* as a one-shot special and pre-empted Dean's show to air it. The result more closely resembled the 100th episode than any other vintage *Comedy Hours*: jam-packed with comedians (Bob Newhart, Phyllis Diller, Nipsey Russell, Allan Sherman, Nanette Fabray and two teams: Mel Brooks & Carl Reiner, and Dan Rowan & Dick Martin), each had a specific amount of time in which to perform one of their classic routines. "It was an all-star game filled with bits and pieces of good moments," wrote *Newsday's* Murry Frymer. "The comedians barely had a chance to warm up when, in a jiff, the next one came on.... It was most upsetting to meet them and then not get to know them." Publicity about the revival didn't fail to mention Martin & Lewis' appearances on the original, and it evidently got NBC thinking that if Dean could thrive with a variety show, so might his ex-partner, who was offered, and accepted, an hour of his own.

That news, naturally, got the columnists going, with speculation about trading guest spots and what might take place should the two encounter each other during rehearsals. Of the former, Martin had already made clear that he'd never have Jerry on ("Not for a million dollars"); of the latter, there was no logistical chance: Jerry rehearsed on weekdays and taped on Friday, while Dean's only day at NBC was Sunday. Other faces from the past were involved: the executive producer was Bob Finkel, who'd directed Dean and Jerry's final *Colgate* programs, and the head writer was Ed Simmons.

There was, however, a day when Lewis did make the trip to NBC on a Sunday. Martin's father had died on August 29. "Jerry came to Dean's dressing room and offered Dean his condolences," wrote a columnist. "They embraced and it looked like old times again. Then Dean, without prompting from anyone, gave a plug to Jerry's opening show on his own. But that's as far as it has ever gone."

Then, just like old times, another Martin blast appeared in print, this one in *LOOK* of all places. Italian journalist Oriana Fallaci, who would become better known for interviewing such political figures as Golda Meir and Yasser Arafat, queried Martin for the magazine's holiday issue. Fallaci didn't even ask about his days with Lewis; a simple question about work in general brought it out: "I enjoy it so much because it's all so easy for me...bein' an actor. Why do you think I split with Jerry? 'Cause I was doin' nothin' and I was eatin' my heart out.... Everything was Jerry Lewis, Jerry Lewis, and I was a straight man. I was an idiot in every picture.... I knew I could do so much better. And I proved it. Not to the public, not the country or the world. To myself, to my wife.

"When I said to Jeanne I quit with Jerry, she said, "Wow." And she gave me the biggest kiss I ever had. And the lawyers said, 'You can't break this team up.' And I said, 'Oh, yes, I can. Watch me.' And my own lawyer said, 'You're crazy.' And I said, 'Yeah, but I'm walkin' out. I'm through.' And Jerry calls me, and says, 'Let's go on.' And I say, 'You go to . . . you . . .' And I hang up.... Two of the greatest turnin' points in my career were: First, meetin' Jerry Lewis; second, leavin' Jerry Lewis. I became a real actor because of those two things."

Both men had come full circle. Lewis, older and on a downward slope, could express regret at how utterly his relationship with Martin had dissolved. Meanwhile, having achieved success beyond anyone's wildest imaginings, including his own, Martin was happy to take full responsibility for ending their partnership, whether deserved or not. It was a reversal from the press of 1956, where Jerry, charged with confidence, was bent on working exclusively alone, while an uncertain Dean hedged. And although Martin's pride in becoming "a real actor" was justified, it had been a few years since he'd done any real acting. He was then immersed in the self-parody of the Matt Helm pictures and inane comedies such as *How to Save a Marriage and Ruin Your Life* (1968); all made at Columbia, which is where Lewis went after Paramount dismissed him. From Paramount, to Columbia, to NBC: they seemingly couldn't escape proximity to one other.

Ed Simmons gave *The Jerry Lewis Show* his best shot, even to dusting off the ventriloquist sketch from the November 3, 1951 *Comedy Hour*, and giving Dean's role to guest star Ben Gazzara. It's painful to watch: Gazzara has none of Martin's charm, while the middle-aged Lewis has com-

Jerry Lewis hits Broadway in *Damn Yankees*, 1995. Dean, who would pass away that Christmas, sent his partner a congratulatory telegram on opening night.

pletely lost his youthful zest and physical limberness. Some of this was unavoidable and some chemical: Lewis had injured his spine two years prior and was taking Percodan for the pain, which would over time cause him serious problems. The sketch, however, plays to raucous laughter and applause: all of it canned because the show wasn't taped in front of an audience; everything was carefully edited and pieced together. Although not a smash success like Dean, Jerry did well enough to be renewed for a second year.

With the start of a new season, speculation rose anew whether Dean would ever guest on Jerry's show, or vice versa. When asked point blank by columnist Kay Gardella, Lewis "played it straight from the shoulder – and heart. 'Dean was 12 years ago. I don't see any reason for appearing together.' He fell silent; after a moment he added softly, with a catch in his throat:

"'Dean can kid about me the same as he does about his wife and booze—because he's doing it in character, not as the real Dean Martin. If I kidded about our old partnership, the hurt and pain would show. You don't live and work with a guy as long as I did without the split-up being painful. How do you tell your audience you loved the guy? To kid about what was, and is, painful would be beneath my dignity. Dean can do it because the CHARACTER he plays on his show lets him do it. I can't. I'm still too sensitive about it.'"

Given a new timeslot, *The Jerry Lewis Show's* ratings dropped precipitously. Halfway through the new season, Lewis insisted on taping in front of a live audience, performing from start to finish as much as possible. When NBC acquiesced, Simmons sensed that Lewis would once again be meddling in everything but performing, and resigned. It didn't matter: no amount of tampering could save the show, which was canceled.

Which actually suited Lewis just fine, for by then he'd found an outlet on television in which he was not only welcomed, but rewarded and honored.

* * * * *

In 1966, Jerry Lewis did something he'd not done since November 1959: hosted a telethon on behalf of the Muscular Dystrophy Association. During the years in between, he'd remained involved with the organization but, according to MDA's then-Executive Director Bob Ross, "management at the time thought telethons no longer interested audiences and they decided to drop it as a fund-raising device." Management still had little faith in the idea when Ross suggested it seven years later but authorized it anyway, telling him, "Have your failure." The 21-hour program aired on New York City's Metromedia station, WNEW-5 over the Sunday and Monday of Labor Day weekend. Subsequently, wrote journalist Joyce

Gabriel of the Newspaper Enterprise Association, MDA "discovered, to its delight, that a whole new generation, which had never seen a telethon before, was enthusiastic about it."

The broadcast ultimately raised, verifiably, over $1 million. It was a record for any telethon and MDA was convinced. Ross made the show an annual event. The following year, over $1.1 million was donated. In 1968, four additional stations were added; in 1969, there were 20; and in 1970, the telethon went coast-to-coast with 65 stations, which Lewis labeled "the Love Network." Donations that year exceeded $5 million. The "Love Network" kept growing. Longtime MDA supporters such as the letter carriers' and firefighters' unions were joined by corporate sponsors like the nation's 7-11 stores. The telethon moved from New York City to Las Vegas, the better to attract A-list celebrities who wanted to participate.

The Jerry Lewis Telethon for Muscular Dystrophy became not just a tradition, but a pop-culture institution, as did various elements: the phrase "Jerry's Kids" to describe dystrophy sufferers; Lewis interacting with MDA's annual "poster child;" co-host Ed McMahon predicting the final tote board amount; Lewis' plea for "just a dollar more" than the prior year's total; his closing, a usually-tearful rendition of "You'll Never Walk Alone."

"It's Jerry who makes a national show possible," Ross told Gabriel. "People are attracted to the telethon because of him. There's not another performer who could do the show Jerry does. He has the dynamism, the desire and the dedication to see it through." Lewis was, indeed, the main attraction; his identity became indivisible from the cause, and together they'd so entranced the nation that he could even get away with saying, as he did in 1973, "God goofed, and it's up to us to correct it." The total that year exceeded $10 million for the first time.

With film obligations having ended and no new ones lined up, Lewis' career by then was all but subsumed by his charity work. Most weeks he flew back and forth between MDA research facilities (for progress updates), local television stations (to add to the network), and corporate boardrooms (to line up additional sponsors), and he did it while abusing his mind and body with no fewer than 10 Percodan per day, all of which he obtained illegally.

Where Martin was concerned, Lewis evidently decided that maybe he *could* give as good as he got. In October 1972, Hy Gardner quoted him: "I decided to end the partnership when I found I could look him in the eye on the stage and didn't like him. I still don't like him. I haven't seen him in years. Ours was a love relationship and the relationship ended. I still love him as a performer. If anyone criticized him in my presence, I'd kill them. But see him? No." During personal appearances, Lewis would have a Q&A session; inevitably someone would ask if he'd ever appear on *The Dean Martin Celebrity Roast*. He had a ready answer: "I was roasted by him years ago."

With the 1976 telethon, there were 216 stations carrying the broadcast, a new peak. Frank Sinatra, who hadn't appeared live on a telethon alongside Jerry since Martin & Lewis' very first in 1952, came on…but he didn't come alone. After singing, he handed Lewis a couple of checks from local businesses, pledged his own $5,000 donation, then said, "I have a friend who loves what you do every year, and who just wanted to come out and… would you send my friend out, please?" A curtain parted and a tuxedo-clad Dean Martin, cigarette in hand, casually strolled from the wings.

One of Martin's children, daughter Deana, was watching at home and let out a scream. "I got chills," she told *Vanity Fair* in 2016. "My jaw dropped. I called my sister. She said, 'I can't believe this.'" Presumably the rest of the telethon's 84 million viewers had similar reactions.

One of Lewis' children, son Gary, was part of the staff, serving as his dad's "go-fer." Martin, disguised as a waiter, had been smuggled backstage and secreted into McMahon's dressing room. While running an errand, Gary spotted him, telling *Vanity Fair*, "I thought, 'What the heck is going on?'… but I didn't say anything to my dad just to be safe. He always told me he hates surprises, so I wasn't going to give him this one." Still, Gary, who hadn't seen "Uncle Dean" since he was 10 years old, couldn't resist saying hello. "It was the '70s and I had real long hair and was wearing weird clothes. I said, 'I'm Gary.' He said, 'I know.' And he called me 'Pally.'"

The orchestra and several staffers had been tipped off, but the host was caught completely unawares. As Martin approached center stage, Lewis froze and gave Sinatra a look that said, "How could you?" A grinning Sinatra snatched Lewis' microphone; the conductor took the papers he was holding. Martin, beaming, walked past Sinatra to Lewis, who'd already opened his arms, and while the two embraced, Martin closed his eyes and kissed his ex-partner on the cheek. The audience had already risen for a standing ovation that would last more than a minute, still cheering as Frank asked Dean, "I think it's about time, don't you?" "And thank *you*," replied Martin, kissing Sinatra. Lewis wiped his eyes; Martin brushed a single tear away.

"There they are, folks," says Frank, handing Dean his microphone.

JERRY: So, how've you been?

DEAN: You know, it seems like we haven't seen each other for 20 years!

JERRY: Well you know, there was all those rumors about our breaking up, and then when I started the show and you weren't here, I believed it.

Sinatra walks over with a candle and offers to "show you guys to your room... the lights are out upstairs," which prompts Martin to comment, "Oh, he drinks a lot, this kid." He turns back to Lewis.

JERRY: So, you workin'?

DEAN: I work... six weeks a year at the 'Megum' [the MGM Grand Hotel]. And in six days, I do a roast....

Sinatra wanders over again, and Lewis turns to him: "Would you excuse us a minute?" "I just wanna see if the wires are alright," says Frank, walking away again. Jerry turns back to Dean, saying, "Gee, it's nice to see ya," but Dean is looking away, determined to continue playing the drunk. "I'm over here!" says Jerry.

DEAN: I had to... I had to come in here because I had to... you know... I had to 'go' and this was the closest place.

JERRY: You always have to 'go!'

DEAN: I always drink!

Finally, Martin and Sinatra tell Lewis that they're got a "meldey" – Dean's word for "medley" – to do. "A 'meldey?'" asks Jerry. "Okay." Sinatra says, "Goodbye, Jerry," and Jerry, looking at Dean, says, "Well, there we go again!" Looking back at Jerry, Dean throws a kiss and says, "Thanks for comin' over!"

Sinatra and Martin sang; the former, straight; the latter, cutting up, while Lewis watched from his podium, biting a fingernail, in awe. Occasionally during the "meldey," Martin shot a few glances at his ex-partner. Lou Brown was playing piano, just like old times; Dean even asked him, "Are you playin' in the cracks?" Tiring of the difficulty he had reading lyrics off the cue cards, Dean put his glasses on… whereupon Jerry did the same.

When their performance ended, Dean started to walk toward Jerry but Frank pulled him back by the microphone cord. Martin attempted a joke about the meager amount pledged so far, citing what was actually the phone number, but Sinatra didn't catch on so Martin delivered the punch line himself. "So long, Jer!" he said, blowing a kiss, and the two conspirators left, as Jerry called out, "Thank you, Dino."

Several hours later, while the show was still in progress, Lewis "had to run a videotape to see what happened because I was told that Dean and I were on television." Such were the perils of mixing Percodan with a stimulant like Dexedrine, which Lewis needed to stay awake for the 48-hour ordeal (preparation and performance) that was the *Jerry Lewis Telethon*. And his instinct then was still to keep his distance. "I love him now," he'd tell the press shortly after the show, "But I still wouldn't work with that old drunk, I guarantee you."

It didn't matter, though: the reunion hit all the papers, made the news broadcasts, sent columnists scurrying to their papers' morgues for past articles about the team. As always, it went hand-in-hand with speculation about a reteaming. Alvin Cooper, the production coordinator for NBC's *The Big Event*—a 90 minute Sunday night showcase —received what he termed "a soft 'no'" from both men to reunite on his show, which he found more encouraging than the "hard 'no'" he got when he asked the same of The Beatles. Regardless, it didn't happen, although both appeared— separately—on NBC's four hour 50th Anniversary special in November. Martin even introduced a segment on comedy teams: "I work alone these days, but as most of you know I started out with a partner…and a great one." In December, Lewis made clear his feelings about reteaming: "It's like asking a man who got rid of his wife if he'll remarry her."

Dean added a lengthy monologue to his stage show about how Frank summoned him to Vegas without telling him why, which scared him ("Hot damn, I'm wonderin' what I done now?"). Getting in Frank's car, Dean fretted over where he was being driven, but "luckily, Jilly [Rizzo, Sinatra's right-hand man] made a left and we ended up at the back of the Sahara, and the rest y'all know." More seriously, he'd conclude, "I want to thank Frank for doin' that, and I especially want to thank Jerry Lewis for doin' that telethon every year for those beautiful little children…. He's a good guy."

Lewis might not have desired a remarriage, but he wasn't averse to the pledges another Dean Martin appearance could bring to the *Jerry Lewis Telethon*. The '76 show had ended with over $20 million on the tote board. In his autobiography *Jerry Lewis: In Person*, he wrote that the following August he tried to invite Dean, then working in Vegas, onto the '77 program. He called the hotel, left messages, wasn't called back. He sent his assistant Joey Stabile to deliver the invite personally, adding, "Whatever he decides, make sure he knows I want a meeting." Dean, "as charming as ever," told Stabile he'd meet with Jerry at the Sahara, and then never showed up. "I'm still waiting," concluded Jerry.

Martin was then appearing with Sinatra at Caesar's Palace where the latter was under contract. What Lewis *didn't* write was that, on the 23rd – less than two weeks from the telethon date – he dashed over there after his own first show. Dean and Frank were at the point where a portable bar had been wheeled on stage and the two would kibitz; Sinatra mainly playing it straight. Martin was about a minute into a long-winded story of how Benjamin Franklin didn't actually discover electricity ("It was his wife, Aretha!"), when the crowd suddenly began cheering. Dean turned, saw that Jerry had emerged from the wings, and laughed nervously, "Oh-h-h-h boy!"

Audio and photos exist of the event. After nearly a minute of cheers and laughs, Jerry takes a microphone and acts indignant:

> JERRY: I just want to say one thing. They told me that you two guys were gonna be on at a certain time. Look at me! I just came off the stage; I almost busted my ass to get over here! I get here and you two guys are doing a goddamned career!

> FRANK: Your ass is whole, it's all right. You didn't bust it.

In a mincing voice, Frank asks, "Are you in town long?" Jerry turns to Dean and, sounding equally campy, says, "Hi, big guy!" The audience cheers after this, signaling that they'd embraced at this point. When the applause dies down, Frank says, "How are ya, Jerry? Say something here."

Jerry responds, "It's such a lovely thing, I really don't want to disturb you, the beauty of this marquee that says, 'Sinatra and Martin.'" Followed by a loud, mocking laugh directed at his ex-partner. The audience, immediately getting that it's a rib at Dean's billing position, explodes with laughter.

DEAN: Did you say "mahkee?"

JERRY: No, no, "Martin." "Martin."

DEAN: But you said "the mahkee."

JERRY: No, "the mar*quee!*"

DEAN: Oh, I thought you said "mahkee."

JERRY (to Frank): Is he drinking again?

As a way of answering the question himself, Dean bumps into the microphone, then apologizes: "Sorry, Mike!" Jerry continues: "And I just wanted to come and say hello to these two lovely, wonderful persons, who I have known over the years personally. And that the beauty of Dean working with this band singer is such a joy." When the laugh dies down, he concludes, "And I just wanted to come here and see that, and to tell all of you that are here present tonight that I am going to be working with George Burns."

DEAN: "Burns and Lewis?"

JERRY: Well, it ain't gonna be "Lewis and Burns"—you fixed that!

With that, Lewis leaves the stage. "Jerry Lewis, ladies and gentlemen," says Frank as Dean also says, "Jerry Lewis!" As the applause dies down, Dean comments, "That was a beautiful surprise." He might have said more, but Frank immediately pulled him back into his Ben Franklin story, and that was that. As for Jerry, he would never mention this spontaneous appearance. Perhaps by the next morning, thanks to the Percodan and with no videotape to review, he'd forgotten it ever happened.

* * * * *

The two former partners soldiered on as the '70s gave way to the '80s. *The Dean Martin Celebrity Roast* specials ended in early 1979, when the producers "ran out of major stars," according to Vernon Scott. For a while, Martin restricted himself to Vegas, Atlantic City (usually with Sinatra) and an occasional TV guest appearance. That same year, Lewis produced, directed and starred in his first movie in nearly 10 years, *Hardly Working*. Thanks to the Jerry Lewis fans in Europe, the film turned a profit even before it got its US release, which happened in 1981, where it also performed surprisingly well.

By then, Martin had mellowed and could reminisce with a degree of nostalgic warmth, even if his chronology wasn't very accurate. Sitting with the 500 Club's Paul "Skinny" D'Amato at the Resorts International Casino after a 1980 performance, the two recalled that night in July 1946, and writer David J. Spatz was present:

"'Jerry opened the show, then Dean would come on and sing,' the club owner recalled. 'Then one night, Jerry decided to have some fun and break in on (Martin's) act. He ran across the stage like some sort of crazy waiter, breaking dishes and clowning around while Dean tried to sing.' 'It really broke me up,' Martin interjected. 'It was funny stuff, and the audience started to go crazy. Then one night I dumped a pitcher of water on his head and Jerry went into this monkey bit.' 'By the end of the summer, nobody wanted them to leave,' D'Amato said. Martin admitted the act was about as bizarre and off-the-wall as anything going. 'It was a whole different time, and we were getting away with murder,' he said. One night between shows at the 500 Club, he recalled, he and Lewis stripped down to their shorts and chased each other through the club. 'Yeah, you almost got me closed down,' D'Amato said with a laugh. 'Nah, pal, we were just breaking it in there,' Martin shot back. 'A few weeks (*sic*) later we did it on the dance floor at the Copacabana.'"

Still, the ex-partners remained out of touch, even after Lewis suffered a heart attack and underwent double bypass surgery in December 1982. "I don't think it's in the cards," he told *People* the following February. "Our lifestyles and careers are separate and apart. But if you told me he was outside right now, it'd be a joy to jump on his neck." Only a month before the attack, he spoke about Dean at length with Ed Bark, a reporter from Gannett News Service, while in Dallas for a public appearance. "I love him. I never have stopped. I'm not ashamed of that. How do I not love him? He took me out of a toilet and put me in a castle. What would I have, no gratitude? That'd be stupid."

As he had in his interview with Susskind, Lewis described the main conflict between them: "He never had the same energy to perform as I did. That was one of the things that I really had to wrestle with—how to get him to come up to my energy level. That was wrong. You can't do that. It would have changed his own persona, and he's never had the need that I have. The need I have is to move and be active. He does what's comfortable for him, and that's as it should be."

When Bark asked him if he ever wanted to see his ex-partner, Lewis replied, "My only interest is on a totally social, friendship level. Nothing professional whatsoever. That would be totally out of the question. We might just sit down and have a beer and just reminisce. That would be nice." But he also knew that Dean was "a loner. He's always been such a loner. But how can you argue with that, if that's his lifestyle?" Consequently, he concluded, if a chance to sit and talk old times "doesn't happen, I respect the why of it. It's okay."

Sadly, the next time Dean and Jerry talked it wasn't for old times' sake, but due to a death in the family. On March 21, 1987, Dean Paul Martin, Jr. —Dean's first born child with wife Jeanne and a member of the California National Guard—took off from March Air Force Base in an F-4C Phantom jet to perform a practice low-level bombing run. The day was overcast; there was snow in the high altitudes. Dean Paul's was one of four jets participating in the maneuver. Only three returned. It took four days before searchers found the wreckage in the foothills of the Little San Gorgonio Mountains.

Although the two had divorced in 1972, in recent years Dean and Jeanne had reconciled, dating now and again. About the only comfort each had in the face of this tragedy was that they could endure the loss together, although Jeanne would later say they never spoke of it. When the Air National Guard performed its "Missing Man" maneuver at the close of the funeral service, Dean lost it. "That was the only time I ever saw my father cry," his daughter Deana would later write. "His shoulders shook violently as he collapsed into himself, unable to take anymore."

Back at Martin's home, friends and family hugged him and those who were capable tried to offer words of sympathy. Finally, Dean's agent Mort Viner told him, "You know, Jerry was there today." Dean looked at him, "his eyes not his own," according to Deana.

"Jerry?"

"Jerry Lewis," said Viner. "He slipped in the back and didn't let anyone know he was coming." Martin's producer, Greg Garrison, who'd also spotted Lewis, confirmed it.

"Well, why didn't he say hello?" asked Martin.

"I guess he didn't want to bother you," said Viner. Garrison would later say that Lewis "didn't want any cameramen from a hundred feet away taking pictures of the two of them together."

Martin mulled this over and asked Viner, "Can you get him on the phone?"

"Sure." Mort put in the call to Jerry, and Dean went to the privacy of his den and picked up the extension. Accounts vary as to how long they spoke, from twenty minutes to two hours, but it was long enough. Lewis would later write that he tried to offer words of consolation and encouragement, but all his partner could say was, "Jer, I just can't tell you." However, Deana and Dean Paul's younger brother Ricci would write in their memoirs that the partners had expressed their love for each other at the close of the call. And from that point on, if there wasn't exactly a resumed friendship, at least there was peace.

In November of that year, Frank Sinatra conceived the "Together Again Tour," in which the three senior Rat Packers—he, Dino and Sammy—would travel to 29 cities across the country, playing the kinds of venues that usually hosted the biggest selling rock and country artists. Dean was dubious, but acquiesced to his friend's wishes.

The tour opened on March 13, 1988 at Oakland Coliseum, to a sellout crowd. Martin went on first, and from the start he was uncomfortable. Used to the intimacy of a Vegas showroom, he sang too softly and the sound system couldn't always compensate. When the three of them were on together, Frank asked Dean if he wanted to do something. "I want to go home," he cried, not necessarily joking.

Six days later, in Chicago, Sinatra griped that they hadn't been given suites on the same floor of the hotel. When it turned out management couldn't accommodate the request, a furious Sinatra wanted to change hotels, but Martin had already settled in and refused to leave. After the next evening's performance, Sinatra bluntly told Viner that Dean wasn't singing well enough and needed to do better. Mort informed Dean.

And that did it. Dean's greatest fear was happening: Frank was turning into Jerry. If they continued together, there was only one possible outcome and he was in no shape physically or emotionally to deal with it. He told Mort to charter a plane; they were leaving. For the sake of appearances, after returning to Los Angeles, he checked into a hospital for a day, claiming a kidney problem had flared up. Within six weeks he was back in Vegas on familiar turf: the old MGM, now named the Bally Grand Hotel. Although Lewis had offered to sub for his ex-partner, Sinatra eventually replaced Martin with Liza Minelli, and the tour was renamed "The Ultimate Event."

From the stage at one of his first shows at the Bally that April, Dean "praised Lewis' work with the Muscular Dystrophy Association," according to the AP. Somehow this news led to another rumored professional reunion. In early May, the *New York Daily News* reported, "Dean Martin and Jerry Lewis will appear on the same stage later this month for a benefit performance. [They] will perform at the sold out May 14 Friars Club event for Barbara Sinatra's charities." Frank and Sammy were also scheduled, as were several other celebrities. Lewis was invited and made the trip, but even if he hadn't walked out on Sinatra and Davis only weeks before, Martin had no desire to travel to New York. There hadn't been a planned Martin & Lewis performance since July of 1956, and there would never be another.

There was, however, one more surprise to come.

* * * * *

On June 7, 1989, Dean Martin turned 72. He celebrated by doing his usual show at the Bally; pretty much the same show he'd been doing since 1957. A few songs, some with all the original words, but most with at least one joke lyric, or some visual shtick, slipped in. Some patter with his longtime pianist Ken Lane. A lot of jokes about drinking. Even a little ad-lib, if something struck him as funny. It was as comfortable as a worn-in pair of shoes.

Every show included a moment when Dean would bow off and exit, only to return moments later for an encore. This night, however, as Martin strode back to the stage, Lane and the band stopped playing and a voice came from the wings: "How the hell long are you gonna stay on?" As Dean turned toward the voice, Jerry emerged, asking "Do you know how long I've been waiting in this goddamned wing here?" The two embraced and Jerry brought out a birthday cake "on behalf of Bally's…for 72 years of joy that you've given to the world."

In the midst of the presentation, Dean turned to his former partner, nudging him on the arm. "I've gotta kiss you on the lips," he said and did just that, adding "mwah" for emphasis. As Lewis assumed a stunned expression (and the audience applauded), Martin turned his attention to the cake. A remarkable moment followed: Jerry tapped Dean on the arm and in an effeminate voice asked, "Are you busy later?" Before the words were out of Jerry's mouth, Dean had turned and placed a hand on his hip, and his lisping reply to the question was instantaneous: "Yes, I am." Unlike the 1976 reunion, Martin didn't cling to his "drunk" persona. Despite 33 years having passed since their professional parting, for a few seconds the "telepathy that could put Western Union out of business" was again in evidence between them.

Newspapers reported on the surprise, of course, and at least one Los Angeles columnist added that various talk shows were sending out feelers about whether Martin and Lewis could be booked together. As always, it was not to be. His health now visibly deteriorating, Martin would restrict his appearances to Bally's until retiring in 1991. Lewis continued acting in films, guesting on television, playing Las Vegas and hosting MDA telethons. In February 1995, he made his Broadway debut as Mr. Applegate, the devil, in a revival of the musical *Damn Yankees*. It was another first in a long list: when the contract was signed, Lewis became the highest-paid actor in Broadway history. The show would be a success both critically and popularly, and for a few months, thanks to a Major League work stoppage that had cancelled the prior year's World Series, it was the only baseball in town.

On opening night, Lewis received scores of congratulatory telegrams from well-wishers. Only one has ever been quoted: DEAR JERRY, LEAVE IT TO YOU TO PLAY BASEBALL DURING A STRIKE. HIT A HOME RUN. LOVE, DEAN.

* * * * *

Dean Martin passed away on Christmas Day, 1995, of respiratory failure at age 78. Although he'd finally stopped smoking the year before ("I woke up one day and didn't smoke anymore," he told Deana), six decades of Lucky Strikes and Kents had already taken their toll. At the funeral, Jerry spoke movingly of his partner, and closed with, "Rest well Dino—and don't forget to short-sheet my bed when I get there."

Jerry Lewis "got there" on August 20, 2017, dying of end-stage heart failure at age 91. Amazingly, after all the stress, ulcers and heart problems; decades of smoking; drug addiction; a lengthy bout with pulmonary fibrosis, he still managed to live as long as any and longer than most of his generation. As he'd often predicted, bouquets were tossed his way by obituary writers; he was now "an undeniable comedic genius," to cite the notice in *Variety*.

Both men's obits, naturally, mentioned their partnership, focusing less on the decade of work and success than on the quarter-century plus of acrimony. No one mentioned the final televised exchange between them, which had come on *Entertainment Tonight's* segment about their last stage appearance:

DEAN: Aww, you surprised me. I mean it: I love you.

JERRY: I love you, Dino.

It's a cinch Jerry meant it; he'd spent most of their years apart admitting it. But did Dean *really* mean it? Were these the words of a showman kowtowing to a paying audience, or did a lifetime of tides high and low finally wash away any lingering bitterness and hurt from the heart of the man? Those who knew Dean Martin, and those who think they knew him, will argue for one side or the other. But whatever may have been his deepest, most heartfelt sentiments, one thing is certain: Dean *knew* Jerry would love to hear him say it.

And he loved his partner at least that much.

Epilogue
Martin and Lewis Sum Up Martin & Lewis

DEAN: With Jerry and me, it was mostly just doin' what we felt. Those were great times.[1]

JERRY: Two guys who had more fun than the audience: that's the legacy.[2]

Endnotes

1. "NBC: The First 50 Years" (NBC-TV, 1976)
2. "Martin & Lewis: Their Golden Age of Comedy," Part 3 (The Disney Channel, 1994)

Vera Vague (Barbara Jo Allen) is flanked by Dean, Jerry and Red Skelton in this backstage photo from the November 25, 1948 *Elgin Thanksgiving Day Greeting to America* broadcast. Photo courtesy of Kayley Thompson.

APPENDIX I
MARTIN & LEWIS RADIO GUEST APPEARANCES

MERRY-GO-ROUND
AIRDATE: *November 1946 (exact date unknown); WDAS-AM, Philadelphia*

UNKNOWN PROGRAM
HOST: *Arnold Fine*
AIRDATE: *December 1946 (exact date unknown, but day/time was Saturday, 5:15pm); WWDC-AM, Washington DC*

SCOUT ABOUT TOWN
AIRDATE: *August 5, 1947;Mutual Broadcasting System (MBS).*
    Dean and Jerry, along with Dorothy Sarnoff, pay a visit to Barry Gray's show, which spotlighted acts that were in New York. Dean sings "Peg O' My Heart." The team was appearing at Loew's State Theater at the time. See Chapter Two for additional details. 15 minutes.

THE BOB HOPE SWAN SOAP PROGRAM
AIRDATE: *October 26, 1948; NBC.*
    Bob Hope visits Martin & Lewis in their dressing room at Slapsie Maxie's nightclub, and invites them to guest on his show. Dean sings "Everybody Loves Somebody (Sometime)." See Chapter Two for additional details. 30 minutes.

THE BOB HOPE SWAN SOAP PROGRAM
AIRDATE: *November 23, 1948; NBC.*
   30 minutes.

ELGIN THANKSGIVING DAY GREETING TO AMERICA
AIRDATE: *November 25, 1948; NBC.*
HOST: *Don Ameche*
   Also known as "Two Hours of Stars," this was a Thanksgiving special sponsored by Elgin Watches. Martin & Lewis appear near the end of the show for about 13 minutes. Dean sings "Rambling Rose" and the two interact with Vera Vague. They close with "That Certain Party." 2 hours.

MARCH OF DIMES
AIRDATE: *January 31, 1949; NBC.*
   A benefit program for the National Foundation for Infantile Paralysis. The team did a guest spot from Hollywood.

CHESTERFIELD SUPPER CLUB
AIRDATE: *February 10, 1949; NBC.*
   A daily program with different vocalists rotating as its host. This edition stars Peggy Lee. Dean and Jerry sing "The Money Song" and Dean duets with Miss Lee on "You Was" (which they'd recorded for Capitol Records on December 14, 1948). 15 minutes.

SEALTEST VARIETY THEATER
AIRDATE: *February 17, 1949; NBC.*
HOSTESS: *Dorothy Lamour*
   30 minutes.

THE BOB HOPE SWAN SOAP PROGRAM
AIRDATE: *March 29, 1949; NBC.*
   30 minutes.

THE BOB HOPE SWAN SOAP PROGRAM
AIRDATE: *April 12, 1949; NBC.*
   30 minutes

Photo courtesy of Kayley Thompson.

HI! JINX
AIRDATE: *May 9, 1949; WNBC-AM, New York City.*
HOSTESS: *Jinx McCrary*

COMMAND PERFORMANCE, **Program #397**
RELEASE DATE: *October 18, 1949; Armed Forces Radio Service.*
   Martin & Lewis perform a skit with hostess Alexis Smith that repeats material from their own show of May 1, 1949. 30 minutes

NEXT, DAVE GARROWAY
AIRDATE: *April 11, 1950; NBC from Chicago.*

THE WAYNE HOWELL SHOW
AIRDATE: *November 11,1950; NBC.*

THE SIXTH ANNUAL HARVEST MOON BALL
AIRDATE: *November 18,1950; WMAQ-AM, Chicago.*
   A benefit performance hosted by the *Chicago Sun-Times.* 30 minutes.

GUEST STAR, Program #194
RELEASE DATE: *December 3, 1950; syndicated by the Treasury Department.*
15 minutes.

THE BIG SHOW
AIRDATE: *December 17, 1950; NBC.*
The boys come on during the second half-hour, interact with hostess Tallulah Bankhead, and perform in a sketch with Bob Hope. See Chapter Three for additional details. 90 minutes.

THE BIG SHOW
AIRDATE: *February 11, 1951; NBC.*
The boys come on during the second half-hour, interact with hostess Tallulah Bankhead, and perform in a sketch with Groucho Marx. Jerry,

At the microphone for *Premiere*, December 29, 1952.
Photo courtesy of Kayley Thompson.

without Dean, does a sketch with Groucho, Tallulah and Joan Davis. See Chapter Three for additional details. 90 minutes.

THE BING CROSBY SHOW
AIRDATE: *November 7, 1951; CBS.*
   30 minutes.

THE BOB HOPE SHOW
AIRDATE: *November 10, 1952; NBC.*
   15 minutes.

THE MARTIN & LEWIS CHRISTMAS SEALS SHOW
RELEASE DATE: *Syndicated during December 1952.*
   Helen O'Connell helps the team promote the Christmas Seals charity fund. 15 minutes.

PREMIERE
AIRDATE: *December 29, 1952; NBC.*
   Broadcast from the Academy Theater in Hollywood, during the opening of the Martin & Lewis picture, *The Stooge*.

THE PHIL HARRIS - ALICE FAYE PROGRAM
AIRDATE: *March 29, 1953; NBC.*
   Phil is worried that Martin & Lewis will be funnier than him. 30 minutes.

GUEST STAR, **Program #315**
RELEASE DATE: *April 2, 1953; syndicated by the Treasury Department.*
   15 minutes.

MARTIN & LEWIS RADIO & TELEVISION PARTY FOR MUSCULAR DYSTROPHY
AIRDATE: *November 25, 1953; ABC* (Eastern US only. West Coast transcription aired December 1, 1953.)
   See Chapter Six for details of this broadcast. 2 hours.

ACADEMY AWARDS PRESENTATION
AIRDATE: *March 30, 1955; NBC.*

Jerry introduces Dean, who sings the Oscar-nominated song "Three Coins in the Fountain."

ACADEMY AWARDS PRESENTATION
AIRDATE: *March 21, 1956; NBC.*

Jerry is the emcee; Dean sings the Oscar-nominated song "(Love is) The Tender Trap."

MONITOR
AIRDATE: *June 24, 1956; NBC.*

Separate taped interviews with Dean and Jerry aired during the course of this program.

APPENDIX II
MARTIN & LEWIS TELEVISION GUEST APPEARANCES

TOAST OF THE TOWN
AIRDATE: *June 20, 1948; CBS-TV*
HOST: *Ed Sullivan*
   See Chapter Two for more details.

TEXACO STAR THEATER
AIRDATE: *August 3, 1948; NBC-TV*
HOST: *Morey Amsterdam*

WELCOME ABOARD
AIRDATE: *October 3, 1948; NBC-TV*
HOST: *Russ Morgan and His Orchestra*

WELCOME ABOARD
AIRDATE: *October 10, 1948; NBC-TV*
HOST: *Russ Morgan and His Orchestra*

WELCOME ABOARD
AIRDATE: *October 17, 1948; NBC-TV*
HOST: *Russ Morgan and His Orchestra*
NOTE: A kinescope of this show exists in the Jerry Lewis Collection, which is housed at the Library of Congress' Motion Picture Division.

Dean and Jerry flank Milton Berle at the Friar's Club.

THE DAMON RUNYON MEMORIAL FUND TELETHON
AIRDATE: *April 9, 1949; NBC-TV*
HOST: *Milton Berle*

TEXACO STAR THEATER
AIRDATE: *October 18, 1949; NBC-TV*
HOST: *Milton Berle*
NOTE: A kinescope of this show exists in the Jerry Lewis Collection.

SATURDAY NIGHT REVUE
AIRDATE: *April 15, 1950; NBC-TV from Chicago*
HOST: *Jack Carter*
NOTE: A kinescope of this show exists in the Jerry Lewis Collection.

BROADWAY OPEN HOUSE
AIRDATE: *May 30, 1950; NBC-TV*
GUEST HOSTS: *Dean Martin & Jerry Lewis*

SHOW OF THE YEAR (Cerebral Palsy Telethon)
AIRDATE: *June 10, 1950; NBC-TV*
HOST: *Milton Berle*

TEXACO STAR THEATER
AIRDATE: *June 13, 1950; NBC-TV*
HOST: *Milton Berle*
NOTE: A kinescope of this show exists in the Jerry Lewis Collection. See Chapter Three for more details.

THE COLGATE COMEDY HOUR
AIRDATE: *May 6, 1951; NBC-TV*
HOST: *Phil Silvers*
NOTE: A kinescope of this show exists in the Jerry Lewis Collection. See Chapter Three for more details.

MARTIN & LEWIS TELETHON FOR THE NEW YORK CARDIAC HOSPITAL
AIRDATE: *March 14-15 1952; WNBT-TV, New York, NY*
NOTE: A kinescope of the first hour of this show exists in the Jerry Lewis Collection. See Chapter Four for more details.

BING CROSBY & BOB HOPE TELETHON FOR THE US OLYMPIC TEAM
AIRDATE: *June 21-22, 1952; NBC-TV*
NOTE: A kinescope of the Martin & Lewis appearance exists in the Jerry Lewis Collection. See Chapter Four for more details.

THE COLGATE COMEDY HOUR
AIRDATE: *November 2, 1953; NBC-TV*
HOST: *Bud Abbott*
Dean and Jerry assist host Bud Abbott, whose ailing partner Lou Costello was not present. They basically take over the final quarter-hour of the program. Dean sings "I Love Paris," after which he and Jerry reprise the "You're Just in Love"/"My Heart Cries For You" routine from the May 20, 1951 broadcast, augmented with exchanges used in *Sailor Beware* (1952). This is followed with an "old-time vaudeville" dance-off to "Tony's Bop."
NOTE: A kinescope of this show exists in the Jerry Lewis Collection and has been released on DVD and Blu-ray by Thunderbean.

WHAT'S MY LINE?
AIRDATE: *January 24, 1954; CBS-TV*
HOST: *John Daly*

Dean and Jerry are the "mystery guests" in this segment that took place between the team's shows at the Copacabana. See Chapter Six for more details.

NOTE: A kinescope of the Martin & Lewis appearance is in the Jerry Lewis Collection. As of this writing, the complete show is not known to exist in any archive.

THE JACK BENNY PROGRAM
AIRDATE: *May 23, 1954; CBS-TV*
GUEST STAR: *Bob Hope*

Martin & Lewis make a surprise cameo appearance at the conclusion of "The Road to Nairobi," a comedy sketch starring Benny and Hope. The latter have been captured by cannibals and are in a giant soup pot, but the natives can't get the fire going. "They have no matches!" yells Hope. Suddenly Jerry's voice is heard: "I've got a match!" He and Dean come running from the back of the theater, light the pot and begin sampling the soup. Near the end, Benny invites them out for a bow, but when Jerry starts talking, Dean has to pull him offstage.

PERSON TO PERSON
AIRDATE: *July 2, 1954; CBS-TV*
HOST: *Edward R. Murrow*

In one of the two segments of this 30-minute show, Martin & Lewis are interviewed at Jerry's home. They talk briefly about their recent feud, and show Murrow the "Gar-Ron Playhouse" where they rehearse. They play a tape of one of their "rehearsals," and it's mostly Jerry griping about having to appear on Murrow's show. See Chapter Six for more details.

NOTE: A kinescope of the Martin & Lewis appearance is in the Jerry Lewis Collection.

TODAY
AIRDATE: *July 16, 1954; NBC-TV*
HOST: *Will Rogers, Jr.*

It's "Martin & Lewis Day" in Atlantic City. The team is there to celebrate their 8th Anniversary and for the opening of *Living It Up* (1954).

Martin & Lewis make a cameo appearance on *The Jack Benny Program*, May 23, 1954.

THE RED SKELTON SHOW
AIRDATE: *November 23, 1954; CBS-TV (8:00 p.m.)*

Martin & Lewis make a surprise appearance to plug the Muscular Dystrophy Association's Thanksgiving campaign.

TRUTH OR CONSEQUENCES
AIRDATE: *November 23, 1954; NBC-TV (10:00 p.m.)*
HOST: *Jack Bailey*

Martin & Lewis make an appearance to plug the Muscular Dystrophy Association's Thanksgiving campaign.

TEXACO STAR THEATER
AIRDATE: *November 27, 1954; NBC-TV*
HOST: *Jimmy Durante*

Martin & Lewis make an appearance to plug the Muscular Dystrophy Association's Thanksgiving campaign.

ACADEMY AWARDS PRESENTATION
AIRDATE: *March 30, 1955; NBC-TV*

Jerry introduces Dean, who sings the Oscar-nominated song "Three Coins in the Fountain."

THE MILTON BERLE SHOW
AIRDATE: *September 27, 1955; NBC-TV.*

Martin & Lewis make a brief cameo appearance at the conclusion of a sketch that parodies (what else?) *The $64,000 Question.* The show bankrupts the network and they have to offer Berle as a prize. Martin & Lewis win him, and he carries them piggyback off the stage.

Martin & Lewis help Ralph Edwards surprise Milton Berle for *This Is Your Life*, June 6, 1956.

THE COLGATE VARIETY HOUR: A Tribute to OKLAHOMA and Rodgers & Hammerstein.
AIRDATE: *October 16, 1955; NBC-TV.*
HOST: *Gordon MacRae*
 Martin & Lewis make a mostly non-humorous guest appearance in this program, which was broadcast live from the Hollywood Bowl. Jerry conducts the orchestra on a Rodgers & Hammerstein medley, and also while Dean sings "Some Enchanted Evening" from *South Pacific.*

TONIGHT
AIRDATE: November 11, 1955; NBC-TV
HOST: Steve Allen
 Martin & Lewis appear live from the El Capitan where they are rehearsing the *Variety Hour* for November 13. They converse via split-screen. See Chapter Eight for details.
NOTE: A kinescope of the Martin & Lewis appearance is in the Jerry Lewis Collection.

THE MILTON BERLE SHOW
AIRDATE: *December 20, 1955; NBC-TV.*
Martin & Lewis "took over the first half of the Berle program" (*Daily Variety*). See Chapter Eight for details.
NOTE: A kinescope of the Martin & Lewis appearance is in the Jerry Lewis Collection.

ACADEMY AWARDS PRESENTATION
AIRDATE: *March 21, 1956; NBC-TV*
 Master of Ceremonies Jerry Lewis introduces Dean, who sings the Oscar-nominated song "The Tender Trap." They do a brief routine together.

THIS IS YOUR LIFE
AIRDATE: *June 6, 1956; NBC-TV*
HOST: *Ralph Edwards*
 Martin & Lewis help Edwards surprise the "principal subject," Milton Berle.

TODAY
AIRDATE: *June 26, 1956; NBC-TV*
HOSTS: *Jack Lescoulie, Faye Emerson (subbing for Dave Garroway),*

Frank Blair, Lee Meriwether

For "TV's first early-morning spectacular," Martin & Lewis appear live from the 500 Club, where they'd be opening for 10 days on July 1. See Chapter Eight for more details.

APPENDIX III
THE COMPLETE COMEDY/ VARIETY HOUR BROADCAST LOG

FOLLOWING IS A BASIC LIST of all the *Comedy/Variety Hours* sponsored by the Colgate-Palmolive-Peet Company (renamed Colgate-Palmolive Company as of November 1953) from September 10, 1950 – December 25, 1955. It includes the ten *Comedy Hours* sponsored by Frigidaire during season one; these are noted and separately numbered. It includes the *Colgate Summer Comedy Hour* from 1954. It does not list the 90-minute Max Liebman-produced spectaculars that aired every fourth week during the 1954-55 and 1955-56 seasons, nor does it include the *NBC Comedy Hour*, which replaced the *Colgate Variety Hour* in January 1956.

THE *COLGATE COMEDY HOUR* THEME SONG LYRICS:

At last it's show time; you know there's no time left to worry 'bout old man blues,
Forget your cares and join the fun,
We'll put your troubles right on the run.

Remember, this is play time; you'll have a gay time 'til we're taking our final bow,
Your cares will disappear while we are here,
If you'll join our show right now!

A publicity photo for a teaming that never happened. Harpo Marx made several guest appearances on *The Colgate Comedy Hour*, but never when Martin & Lewis were hosting.

SEASON ONE:

SEPTEMBER 10, 1950
Broadcast 1-01
HOST: Eddie Cantor
WITH: Tommy Wonder; Yma Sumac; Danny Daniels; Helen Wood; Janet Gaylord; Charlotte Fayne; Lou Wills, Jr; Rudy Tone; Joseph Buloff; Lew Hearn; Robert Gari; Jack Albertson; Val Buttingnol & Joy Williams. Music by Al Goodman and His Orchestra.

SEPTEMBER 17, 1950
Broadcast 1-02
HOST: Dean Martin & Jerry Lewis
  See Chapter Three.

SEPTEMBER 24, 1950
Broadcast 1-03
HOST: Fred Allen
WITH: Monte Woolley; Peter Donald; Risë Stevens; Sono Osato; Hugh Laing; Zachary Solov; David Burns. The voices of Kenny Delmar, Minerva Pious and Parker Fennelly are heard in a puppet show version of "Allen's Alley." Music by Al Goodman and His Orchestra.

OCTOBER 1, 1950
Broadcast F-01, Sponsored by Frigidaire
HOST: Bobby Clark
WITH: Joan Blondell; Sigmund Romberg.

OCTOBER 8, 1950
Broadcast 1-04
HOST: Eddie Cantor
WITH: Al Goodman and His Orchestra.

OCTOBER 15, 1950
Broadcast 1-05
HOST: Dean Martin & Jerry Lewis
See Chapter Three.

OCTOBER 22, 1950
Broadcast 1-06
HOST: Fred Allen
WITH: Ella Logan; Anthony, Allyn & Hodges; Mort & Art Havel; Portland Hoffa; Parker Fennelly; Peter Donald; Al Goodman and His Orchestra.

OCTOBER 29, 1950
Broadcast F-02, Sponsored by Frigidaire
Michael Todd's Revue
HOST: Bobby Clark
WITH: Mel Allen; Frances Langford; Gussie Moran; Atilio & Hector Peiro; The Albins.

NOVEMBER 5, 1950
Broadcast 1-07
HOST: Eddie Cantor

WITH: Ida Cantor; Robert Gari; Charlie Cantor (no relation); Fred & Sledge; Leslie Scott; Bil and Cora Baird's Marionettes; Dick Barstow; Al Goodman and His Orchestra.

NOVEMBER 12, 1950
Broadcast 1-08
HOST: Dean Martin & Jerry Lewis
See Chapter Three.

NOVEMBER 19, 1950
Broadcast 1-09
HOST: Fred Allen
WITH: H. Allen Smith; Sheila Bond; Billy Tabbert; Al Goodman and His Orchestra.

NOVEMBER 26, 1950
Broadcast F-03, Sponsored by Frigidaire
HOST: Bob Hope
WITH: Marilyn Maxwell; Jimmy Wakely; The Taylor Maids; The High Hatters; Judy Kelly; Nelson Case; Les Brown and His Band of Renown.
NOTE: This show was performed before a military audience.

DECEMBER 3, 1950
Broadcast 1-10
HOST: Eddie Cantor
WITH: Joe Bushkin; Jack Albertson; Dick Van Patten; Connie Sawyer; The Armandis; Junie Keegan; Les Zoris (Robert Gross & Claudine Baudin); Al Goodman and His Orchestra.

DECEMBER 10, 1950
Broadcast 1-11
Tickets, Please! A Broadway revue starring The Hartmans (Paul & Grace).
WITH: Jack Albertson; Tommy Wonder; Dorothy Jarnac; Patricia Bright; Bill Norvas; Mildred Hughes; Warde Donovan; The Upstarts.

DECEMBER 17, 1950
Broadcast 1-12
HOST: Fred Allen

WITH: Doc Rockwell; Eileen Farrell; The Christianis; Kenny Delmar; Minerva Pious; Peter Donald; Parker Fennelly; Al Goodman and His Orchestra.

DECEMBER 24, 1950
Broadcast F-04, Sponsored by Frigidaire
HOST: Bob Hope
WITH: Lily Pons; Eleanor Roosevelt; Bob Cummings; Robert Maxwell; Betty Bruce; New York Mayor Vincent Impellitteri; the Choir of the Cathedral Church of St. John the Divine.

DECEMBER 31, 1950
Broadcast 1-13
HOST: Eddie Cantor
WITH: Danny Thomas; Ed Wynn; Sigmund Romberg; Al Goodman and His Orchestra.

JANUARY 7, 1951
Broadcast 1-14
HOST: Bud Abbott & Lou Costello
WITH: Evelyn Knight; Hal Le Roy; Paul Remos and His Toy Boys; The Jimmy Ford Four; Art and Mort Havel; Patricia Shea; Valerie de Cadenet; Al Goodman and His Orchestra.

JANUARY 14, 1951
Broadcast 1-15
HOST: Jerry Lester
CAST: Dagmar, David Street, The Mello-Larks, Milton DeLugg, Wayne Howell, Jack Adrian.
WITH: Fred Allen; Joan Bennett; Kukla, Fran & Ollie; Pat O'Brien.

JANUARY 21, 1951
Broadcast F-05, Sponsored by Frigidaire
HOST: Bobby Clark
WITH: Julie Wilson; Willie, West and McGinty; Bobby Lane and Claire; The Maxwells; Jack Mann; Dick Dana; Miriam Wakefield; Tom Jones and His Orchestra.

JANUARY 28, 1951
Broadcast 1-16
HOST: Eddie Cantor
WITH: Estelle Sloan; Dave Powell; Lee Fairfax; Joe Marks; Basil O'Connor (of the March of Dimes); Al Goodman and His Orchestra.

FEBRUARY 4, 1951
Broadcast 1-17
HOST: Dean Martin & Jerry Lewis
See Chapter Three.

FEBRUARY 11, 1951
Broadcast 1-18
HOST: Spike Jones and The City Slickers (Laverne Pearson, Doodles Weaver, George Rock, Sir Fredrick Gas, Freddy Morgan, Dick Morgan, Bill King, Lois Ray, Joe Siracusa, Dick Gardner).
WITH: Gale Robbins; The Wayne Marlin Trio
NOTE: The telecast originated from Chicago. Dave Garroway makes a cameo appearance.

FEBRUARY 18, 1951
Broadcast F-06, Sponsored by Frigidaire
Would-Be Gentleman starring Bobby Clark
WITH: Basil Rathbone; Sarah Churchill; Fran Warren; Walter Abel; Mary Boland; Danny Scholl; Nelson Case.

FEBRUARY 25, 1951
Broadcast 1-19
HOST: Eddie Cantor
WITH: Lena Horne; Jack Albertson; Charlie Cantor; the Bil and Cora Baird Marionettes; Landre & Verna; Phil Kramer; Marcia Walter; Al Goodman and His Orchestra.

MARCH 4, 1951
Broadcast 1-20
HOST: Tony Martin
WITH: Milton Berle; The Andrews Sisters; Leonard Sues.

MARCH 11, 1951
Broadcast 1-21
HOST: Bud Abbott & Lou Costello
WITH: Lon Chaney, Jr.; Jarmilla Novotna; Sid Fields; Milton Frome; Gregg Sherwood; Jesse, James and Carnell; Al Goodman and His Orchestra.

MARCH 18, 1951
Broadcast F-07, Sponsored by Frigidaire
HOST: Beatrice Lillie
WITH: Rex Harrison; Jean Sablon; Valerie Bettis; Wally Cox; Nelson Case.

MARCH 25, 1951
Broadcast 1-22
HOST: Eddie Cantor
WITH: Jimmy Durante; Eddie Jackson; Al Goodman and His Orchestra.

APRIL 1, 1951
Broadcast 1-23
HOST: Eddie Cantor
WITH: Eddie Fisher; Marion Colby; Evelyn Gould; Joel Grey; William Warfield; Tony & Eddie; Miche'le Auclair; Phyllis Gehrig & Don Weismuller; Al Goodman and His Orchestra.

APRIL 8, 1951
Broadcast F-08, Sponsored by Frigidaire
HOST: Bob Hope
WITH: Rex Harrison; Lilli Palmer; Arthur Treacher; Janis Paige; Frank Robinson. Cameo appearances by Frank Sinatra, Eddie Cantor, Ed Wynn, Sid Caesar, Imogene Coca, Tex and Jinx McCrary, Ken Murray, Jimmy Durante, Faye Emerson, Toots Shor.

APRIL 15, 1951
Broadcast 1-24
HOST: Tony Martin
WITH: Fred Allen; Celeste Holm; Kathryn Lee; Peanuts Hucko; Joe Silver; Richard Loo; Lynn Loring; Art & Mort Havel; Al Goodman and His Orchestra.

APRIL 22, 1951
Broadcast 1-25
HOST: Eddie Cantor
WITH: Anne Jeffreys; Robert Gari; Charlie Cantor; Gehrig & Weismuller; Hal Loman; Joan Fields; Al Goodman and His Orchestra.

APRIL 29, 1951
Broadcast 1-26
HOST: Dean Martin & Jerry Lewis
See Chapter Three.

MAY 6, 1951
Broadcast 1-27
HOST: Phil Silvers
WITH: Dean Martin & Jerry Lewis; Vivian Blaine; Joey Faye; Al Goodman and His Orchestra.

MAY 13, 1951
Broadcast F-09, Sponsored by Frigidaire
HOST: Beatrice Lillie
WITH: Dick Haymes; Wally Cox; Victor Moore; Harold Lang; Helen Gallagher.

MAY 20, 1951
Broadcast 1-28
HOST: Dean Martin & Jerry Lewis
See Chapter Three.

MAY 27, 1951
Broadcast 1-29
HOST: Eddie Cantor
WITH: Joel Grey; Connie Haines; Charlie Cantor; Herbert Coleman; Monsieur Crayone; Joe Silver; Lou Wills Jr; Al Goodman and His Orchestra. Eddie Fisher makes a cameo appearance.

JUNE 3, 1951
Broadcast 1-30
HOST: Dean Martin & Jerry Lewis
See Chapter Three.

JUNE 10, 1951
Broadcast F-10, Sponsored by Frigidaire
HOST: Jackie Gleason, sponsored by Frigidaire.
WITH: Fred Allen; Harold Lang and Helen Gallagher; John Carroll; Vivian Blaine.

JUNE 17, 1951
Broadcast 1-31
HOST: Eddie Cantor
WITH: Milton Berle; Jack E. Leonard; Phil Foster; Dagmar; Junie Keegan; Ida Cantor. Cantor's daughter Marilyn and Berle's daughter Vicki also appear. Al Goodman and His Orchestra.

JUNE 24, 1951
Broadcast 1-32
HOST: Dean Martin & Jerry Lewis
See Chapter Three.

SEASON TWO:

SEPTEMBER 2, 1951
Broadcast 2-01
HOST: Jackie Gleason,
WITH: Rose Marie; Johnny Johnston; The Esther Junger Dancers; Al Goodman and His Orchestra. Eddie Cantor makes a cameo appearance at the end.

SEPTEMBER 9, 1951
Broadcast 2-02
HOST: Eddie Cantor
WITH: Cesar Romero; Barbara Ashley; Stanley Prager; Bill Gray; Jimmy Russell & Aura Vainio; Siri; Robert Gari; Al Goodman and His Orchestra.

SEPTEMBER 16, 1951
Broadcast 2-03
HOST: Spike Jones and The City Slickers.
WITH: Helen Grayco; Jan Peerce; The Wayne Marlin Trio.

SEPTEMBER 23, 1951
Broadcast 2-04
HOST: Ezio Pinza
WITH: Milton Berle; Paul Winchell & Jerry Mahoney; Colette Marchand; Martha Wright.

SEPTEMBER 30, 1951
Broadcast 2-05
HOST: Eddie Cantor
WITH: Judy Kelly; Martin Freed & Ernie Stewart; Sid Fields; Ida Cantor; Jack Slattery; Al Goodman and His Orchestra.
NOTE: This was the first *Comedy Hour* to originate from Hollywood.

OCTOBER 7, 1951
Broadcast 2-06
HOST: Donald O'Connor
WITH: Ed Wynn; Arlene Dahl; Mary Hatcher; Walter Catlett; Douglas Fowley; The Ungar Twins; Sidney Miller; Al Goodman and His Orchestra.

OCTOBER 14, 1951
Broadcast 2-07
HOST: Bud Abbott & Lou Costello
WITH: Phil Regan; Gale Storm.

OCTOBER 21, 1951
Broadcast 2-08
HOST: Jack Carson
WITH: Robert Alda; Betty Garrett; The Honey Brothers; Hal March; Jack Norton; Peter Leeds; Tommy Wells; Bud & C.C. Robbins; Dean Elliott and His Orchestra.

OCTOBER 28, 1951
Broadcast 2-09
HOST: Eddie Cantor
WITH: Cesar Romero; Verna Felton; Sheilah Graham; The Caprino Sisters; Al Goodman and His Orchestra.

NOVEMBER 4, 1951
Broadcast 2-10
HOST: Dean Martin & Jerry Lewis
See Chapter Four.

NOVEMBER 11, 1951
Broadcast 2-11
HOST: Donald O'Connor
WITH: Harpo Marx; Yvonne De Carlo; Sidney Miller; Roger Price; Pat Patrick; Gale Robbins.

NOVEMBER 18, 1951
Broadcast 2-12
HOST: Bud Abbott & Lou Costello
WITH: George Raft; Louis Armstrong; Rosette Shaw; The Pied Pipers; Sid Fields; Joe Kirk; Al Goodman and His Orchestra.

NOVEMBER 25, 1951
Broadcast 2-13
HOST: Eddie Cantor
WITH: Cesar Romero; Betty Graham; Eddie Fisher; Al Goodman and His Orchestra.

DECEMBER 2, 1951
Broadcast 2-14
The American Guild of Variety Arists (AGVA) Show
HOST: Bob Hope
WITH: Bob Crosby; Toni Arden; Eddie Bracken; Frank Faylen; Marilyn Maxwell; Georgie Price; Billy Daniel; Lita Baron; The Skylarks; Wally Blair; Joe Mole; Sid Marion; Pat C. Flick; The Rio Brothers; Al Goodman and His Orchestra.
NOTE: A benefit for AGVA. All performance fees were donated to the union's welfare fund.

DECEMBER 9, 1951
Broadcast 2-15
HOST: Eddie Cantor
WITH: The Nilsson Twins; Norman Brown; Tom D'Andrea; Larry Blake.

DECEMBER 16, 1951
Broadcast 2-16
HOST: Jack Paar,
WITH: Carmen Miranda; The Three Stooges; Alan Young; Roy Rogers, Dale Evans & Trigger; The Whippoorwills.

DECEMBER 23, 1951
Broadcast 2-17
HOST: Eddie Cantor
WITH: Farley Granger; Bobby Breen; Sharon Baird; Stuffy Singer.

DECEMBER 30, 1951
Broadcast 2-18
HOST: Dean Martin & Jerry Lewis
See Chapter Four.

JANUARY 6, 1952
Broadcast 2-19
HOST: Donald O'Connor
WITH: Harpo Marx; Gale Robbins; Pat Patrick; Sidney Miller.

JANUARY 13, 1952
Broadcast 2-20
HOST: Bud Abbott & Lou Costello
WITH: Errol Flynn; Rhonda Fleming; Bruce Cabot; Sid Fields; Joe Kirk; The Pied Pipers; Al Goodman and His Orchestra. George Raft makes a cameo appearance.

JANUARY 20, 1952
Broadcast 2-21
HOST: Eddie Cantor
WITH: Adele Jergens; Robert Clary; Jimmy Dobson; Shirley Mitchell; Doris Singleton; Sharon Baird; Herman McCoy's UCLA Swing Choir; Al Goodman and His Orchestra. Kirk Douglas makes a cameo appearance.

JANUARY 27, 1952
Broadcast 2-22
HOST: Danny Thomas
WITH: Dorothy Lamour.

FEBRUARY 3, 1952
Broadcast 2-23
HOST: Donald O'Connor
WITH: Kay Starr; Ben Blue; Sidney Miller; Frank Nelson; Scatman Crothers; Corinne Calvet; Gwen Carter O'Connor; Al Goodman and His Orchestra.

FEBRUARY 10, 1952
Broadcast 2-24
HOST: Dean Martin & Jerry Lewis
See Chapter Four.

FEBRUARY 17, 1952
Broadcast 2-25
HOST: Eddie Cantor
WITH: The Will Mastin Trio featuring Sammy Davis Jr.; Reggie Rymal.

FEBRUARY 24, 1952
Broadcast 2-26
HOST: Danny Thomas
WITH: Carmen Miranda; Grace Hartman; Bunny Lewbel; The Beatrice Kraft Dancers.

MARCH 2, 1952
Broadcast 2-27
HOST: Donald O'Connor
WITH: Buster Keaton; Broderick Crawford; Patricia Morison; Cecil Kellaway; Eddie Gribbon; Sidney Miller.

MARCH 9, 1952
Broadcast 2-28
HOST: Bob Hope
WITH: Anna Maria Alberghetti; Georgie Tapps; Martha Stewart; Les Brown and His Band of Renown.
NOTE: Broadcast from Camp Elliott, San Diego County, California.

MARCH 16, 1952
Broadcast 2-29
HOST: Eddie Cantor

WITH: The Will Mastin Trio featuring Sammy Davis Jr.; Dorothy Kirsten; Sharon Baird; Betsy Mills; Mabel Butterworth; Harry Von Zell.
NOTE: Broadcast from March Air Force Base, Riverside, California.

MARCH 23, 1952
Broadcast 2-30
HOST: Dean Martin & Jerry Lewis
See Chapter Four.

MARCH 30, 1952
Broadcast 2-31
HOST: Tony Martin
WITH: Chico & Harpo Marx; Kay Starr; St. Paul Choir; Al Goodman and His Orchestra.

APRIL 6, 1952
Broadcast 2-32
HOST: Bud Abbott & Lou Costello
WITH: Charles Laughton; Three Beaus and a Peep; Isabel Bigley; Johnny Conrad and His Dancers; Sid Fields; Joe Kirk; Milton Frome; Bobby Barber; Jill Kraft; Helen Donaldson; Anita Anton; Alex Fossell; Al Goodman and His Orchestra.

APRIL 13, 1952
Broadcast 2-33
HOST: Eddie Cantor
WITH: Joe E. Brown; Constance Moore; Dave Barry; Sharon Baird; The Los Gatos Trio.

APRIL 20, 1952
Broadcast 2-34
HOST: Donald O'Connor
WITH: Andy Devine; Mindy Carson; Ben Blue; Sidney Miller.

APRIL 27, 1952
Broadcast 2-35
HOST: Dean Martin & Jerry Lewis
See Chapter Four.

MAY 4, 1952
Broadcast 2-36
HOST: Bud Abbott & Lou Costello
WITH: Vera Zorina; Tony Bavaar; The Ashtons; Monique Van Vooren; "Sport" Morgan; Three Beaus and a Peep; Gemze de Lappe; Sid Fields; Joe Kirk; Bobby Barber; Jean Cleveland; Charlie Bollinder; Al Goodman and His Orchestra.
NOTE: This broadcast originated from New York City.

MAY 11, 1952
Broadcast 2-37
HOST: Donald O'Connor
WITH: Hedy Lamarr; Tony Dexter; Martha Tilton; Sidney Miller; Scatman Crothers; Tom D'Andrea & Hal March; Al Goodman and His Orchestra.

MAY 18, 1952
Broadcast 2-38
HOST: Eddie Cantor
WITH: Cesar Romero, The Szonys; Rusty Draper.
NOTE: This show was performed before a military audience.

MAY 25, 1952
Broadcast 2-39
HOST: Ben Blue
WITH: Ann Sheridan; Peggy Lee; The Four Step Brothers; The Whippoorwills; Al Goodman and His Orchestra.

JUNE 1, 1952
Broadcast 2-40
HOST: Herb Shriner
WITH: Lily Pons; The Borrah Minevitch Harmonica Rascals.

JUNE 8, 1952
Broadcast 2-41
HOST: Eddie Cantor
WITH: Danny Thomas; Kay Starr; Harry Von Zell; Tom D'Andrea & Hal March; Pat O'Brien; Ida Cantor; Johnny Dugan; Sharon Baird; songwriters Jay Livingston, Nacio Herb Brown, Harry Akst, Harry Ruby, and Jimmy McHugh.

JUNE 15, 1952
Broadcast 2-42
HOST: Bob Hope
WITH: June Hutton; Paul Douglas; Johnny Mack; Bess Myerson & Randy Merriman; Les Brown and His Band of Renown.
NOTE: Broadcast from the Douglas Aircraft plant, Santa Monica, California. Myerson & Merriman would cohost the show's summer replacement, the quiz series *The Big Payoff*.

SEASON THREE:

SEPTEMBER 21, 1952
Broadcast 3-01
HOST: Dean Martin & Jerry Lewis
See Chapter Five.

SEPTEMBER 28, 1952
Broadcast 3-02
HOST: Eddie Cantor
WITH: Dorothy Lamour; Eddie Fisher; The Will Mastin Trio featuring Sammy Davis Jr.; Sharon Baird; Tom D'Andrea; Henry Slate; Sid Fields; Al Goodman and His Orchestra.
NOTE: Cantor suffered a mild heart attack shortly after arriving home from performing this show; contrary to legend, the attack did not come while he was on the air.

OCTOBER 5, 1952
Broadcast 3-03
HOST: Donald O'Connor
WITH: Broderick Crawford; Ben Blue; Lisa Kirk; Sidney Miller; Andy Clyde; Chester Conklin; Eddie Gribbon; Scatman Crothers; Al Goodman and His Orchestra.
NOTE: This show was performed live at 8:00 pm Pacific Time, and aired in Los Angeles.

OCTOBER 12, 1952
Broadcast 3-04
HOST: Bob Hope

WITH: Fred MacMurray; The Clark Brothers; Connie Haines; Les Brown and His Band of Renown.

OCTOBER 19, 1952
Broadcast 3-05
HOST: Bud Abbott & Lou Costello
WITH: Gisele MacKenzie; Lizabeth Scott; The Four Pipers; Les Dassie; Sid Fields; Dudley Dickerson; Bobby Barber; Milt Bronson; Al Goodman and His Orchestra.

OCTOBER 26, 1952
Kinescope of Broadcast 3-03
HOST: Donald O'Connor
WITH: Broderick Crawford; Ben Blue; Lisa Kirk; Sidney Miller; Andy Clyde; Chester Conklin; Eddie Gribbon; Scatman Crothers; Al Goodman and His Orchestra.
NOTE: This was a network rebroadcast of the October 5 show, which had only been seen live in Los Angeles due to a three-hour labor strike by NBC's Hollywood engineers.

NOVEMBER 2, 1952
Broadcast 3-06
HOST: Judy Canova
WITH: Cesar Romero; Liberace; Zsa Zsa Gabor; Hans Conried; Carl Ravazza; The Lancers; Charles Dent and His Orchestra.

NOVEMBER 9, 1952
Broadcast 3-07
HOST: Bob Hope
WITH: Rosemary Clooney; The Four Step Brothers; Bill Goodwin; Les Brown and His Band of Renown.

NOVEMBER 16, 1952
Broadcast 3-08
HOST: Donald O'Connor
WITH: Ann Sheridan; The Bell Sisters; Patti Moore; Ben Lessey; Tom D'Andrea & Hal March; Sidney Miller.

NOVEMBER 23, 1952
Broadcast 3-09
HOST: Bud Abbott & Lou Costello
WITH: Peggy Lee; The Shaller Brothers; Fisher and Ross.

NOVEMBER 30, 1952
Broadcast 3-10
HOST: Dean Martin & Jerry Lewis
See Chapter Five.

DECEMBER 7, 1952
Broadcast 3-11
HOST: Bob Hope
WITH: Frances Langford; Tony Martin.

DECEMBER 14, 1952
Broadcast 3-12
HOST: Bud Abbott & Lou Costello
WITH: Margaret Whiting; The Nicholas Brothers; Buster Shaver & Olive; Sid Fields; Bobby Barber; Tom and Jerry; The Hollywood Stunt Group; The Four Pipers; Jack Lomas; Dorothy Granger; Gordon Jones; Al Goodman and His Orchestra.

DECEMBER 21, 1952
Broadcast 3-13
HOST: Ray Bolger
WITH: Rise Stevens; Betty Kean; Bill Sands; Roger DeKoven.

DECEMBER 28, 1952
Broadcast 3-14
HOST: Ben Blue
WITH: Hedy Lamarr; Peggy Lee; Phil Harris; Al Goodman and His Orchestra. Donald O'Connor introduces Blue at the show's start.

JANUARY 4, 1953
Broadcast 3-15
HOST: Bob Hope
WITH: Marilyn Maxwell; Don Cherry.

JANUARY 11, 1953
Broadcast 3-16
HOST: Bud Abbott & Lou Costello
WITH: Victor Borge; Gisele MacKenzie; Allan Jones; Grace Hartman; Sid Fields; Bobby Barber; Harry Lang; The Four Pipers; R. J. Otis & Abner; The Hollywood Stunt Group.
NOTE: Broadcast from Washington, D.C. for President Eisenhower's inauguration.

JANUARY 18, 1953
Broadcast 3-17
HOST: Eddie Cantor
WITH: Dinah Shore; Arnold Stang; Joel Grey; The Tokayers; Al Goodman and His Orchestra.

JANUARY 25, 1953
Broadcast 3-18
HOST: Dean Martin & Jerry Lewis
See Chapter Five.

FEBRUARY 1, 1953
Broadcast 3-19
HOST: Bob Hope
WITH: Margaret Whiting; Marion Colby; Nelson Eddy; Monte Montano; The Blackburn Twins; Bob Sweeney.

FEBRUARY 8, 1953
Broadcast 3-20
HOST: Ben Blue
WITH: June Havoc; Bob Crosby, Mimi Benzell; Sid Fields; Snag Werris; The Sportsmen.

FEBRUARY 15, 1953
Broadcast 3-21
HOST: Eddie Cantor
WITH: Frank Loesser; Connie Russell; Billy Daniel; Tom D'Andrea & Hal March; Sharon Baird; Sara Berner; Danny Richards; Frank Jenks; Ben Wrigley; Ray Kellogg; Sid Fields; Al Goodman and His Orchestra. A scene from *Hans Christian Andersen* (1952) with Danny Kaye is shown.

FEBRUARY 22, 1953
Broadcast 3-22
HOST: The Ritz Brothers
WITH: Kay Starr; Corinne Calvet; Colleen Gray; Jack Webb; Al Goodman and His Orchestra.

MARCH 1, 1953
Broadcast 3-23
HOST: Bob Hope
WITH: George Jessel; Robert Alda; Contance Moore.
NOTE: The show celebrates Hope's 15th Anniversary with NBC, and includes a clip from a Friar's Club banquet held in his honor.

MARCH 8, 1953
Broadcast 3-24
HOST: Donald O'Connor
WITH: Hedy Lamarr; Marilyn Maxwell; Cecil Kellaway; Sidney Miller; Tom D'Andrea & Hal March.

MARCH 15, 1953
Broadcast 3-25
HOST: Eddie Cantor
WITH: George Jessel; Connie Russell; Sharon Baird; Billy Daniel; Danny Richards Jr.; Harry Ruby; Bob Sweeney; Al Goodman and His Orchestra.

MARCH 22, 1953
Broadcast 3-26
HOSTS: Bob Hope; Eddie Cantor; Abbott & Costello; Donald O'Connor; Martin & Lewis
WITH: Sid Fields, Bobby Barber, Sidney Miller.
Colgate's 100th *Comedy Hour*. See Chapter Five.

MARCH 29, 1953
Broadcast 3-27
HOST: Bob Hope
WITH: Rosemary Clooney; The Bell Sisters. Mickey Rooney makes a cameo appearance.

APRIL 5, 1953
Broadcast 3-28
HOST: Donald O'Connor
WITH: Brian Aherne; Vivian Blaine; Tom D'Andrea & Hal March; Scatman Crothers; Tony Dexter; Sidney Miller; the winners of the "Most Handsome" and "Most Beautiful" Centenarians contest; Al Goodman and His Orchestra.

APRIL 12, 1953
Broadcast 3-29
HOST: Eddie Cantor
WITH: Connie Russell; Gloria Grahame; The Will Mastin Trio featuring Sammy Davis Jr.; The Billy Daniel Dancers; Al Goodman and His Orchestra.

APRIL 19, 1953
Broadcast 3-30
HOST: Bob Hope
WITH: Phil Harris; Marilyn Maxwell; Les Brown and His Band of Renown.

APRIL 26, 1953
Broadcast 3-31
HOST: Bud Abbott & Lou Costello
WITH: Teresa Brewer; Hoagy Carmichael; The Four Pipers; The Amin Brothers; Jack Lomas; Sid Marion; Sherry Morland; Evelynne D'Smith; Sid Fields; Michael Ross; Bobby Barber; Al Goodman and His Orchestra.

MAY 3, 1953
Broadcast 3-32
HOST: Dean Martin & Jerry Lewis
See Chapter Five.

MAY 10, 1953
Broadcast 3-33
HOST: Eddie Cantor
WITH: Billy Daniel; Connie Russell; Si Milano; Jan Peerce; Nanci Crompton; John Robertson; Mel Blanc (voice only); Bonzo the chimpanzee; Al Goodman and His Orchestra.

MAY 17, 1953
Broadcast 3-34
HOST: Donald O'Connor
WITH: Nelson Eddy; Thomas L. Thomas; Beatrice Kay; Sidney Miller; Tom D'Andrea & Hal March; Al Goodman and His Orchestra.

MAY 24, 1953
Broadcast 3-35
HOST: Bob Hope
WITH: Don McNeill; Gloria De Haven; The De Castro Sisters; Rocky Marciano.
NOTE: Broadcast from the Blackstone Theater, Chicago.

MAY 31, 1953
Broadcast 3-36
HOST: Dean Martin & Jerry Lewis
See Chapter Five.

JUNE 7, 1953
Broadcast 3-37
HOST: Eddie Cantor
WITH: George Jessel; Dinah Shore; Ralph Edwards; Billy Daniel; David Rubinoff; Herman Hover; Ticker Freeman; The Notables; Ida Cantor; Lita Baron; Al Goodman and His Orchestra. **NOTE:** Eddie & Ida Cantor celebrate their 39th wedding anniversary.

JUNE 14, 1953
Broadcast 3-38
HOST: Bob Hope
WITH: Rosemary Clooney; Frankie Lane; Randy Merriman; Bess Myerson.
NOTE: The telecast originates from the S.S. Los Angeles, to an audience of sailors.

SEASON FOUR:

OCTOBER 4, 1953
Broadcast 4-01
HOST: Dean Martin & Jerry Lewis
See Chapter Six.

OCTOBER 11, 1953
Broadcast 4-02
HOST: Jimmy Durante
WITH: John Wayne; Jack Roth; Eddie Jackson; Candy Candido; Jules Buffano; Roy Bargy and His Orchestra.

OCTOBER 18, 1953
Broadcast 4-03
HOST: Eddie Cantor
WITH: Jack Benny; Connie Russell; Billy Daniel; Sheldon Leonard; Peter Leeds; Sandra Gould; Rex Ramer; Jack Boyle; Michael Ross; Al Goodman and His Orchestra.
NOTE: The show celebrates the forthcoming biopic *The Eddie Cantor Story* (1953).

OCTOBER 25, 1953
Broadcast 4-04
HOST: Donald O'Connor
WITH: Lauren Bacall; Joanne Gilbert; Elaine Stewart; Tom D'Andrea & Hal March; Sidney Miller; Al Goodman and His Orchestra.

NOVEMBER 1, 1953
Broadcast 4-05
HOST: Bud Abbott
WITH: Peggy Lee; Dean Martin & Jerry Lewis; Jimmy Thompson; Pat Horn & Gene Nelson; The Pied Pipers; Al Goodman and His Orchestra.

NOVEMBER 8, 1953
Broadcast 4-06
HOST: Jimmy Durante
WITH: Frank Sinatra; Danny Thomas; The Gay Tyroliers; Jackie Barnett; Jan Arvan; Hy Averback; Wanda Smith's Cover Girls; Charles Smith; Allen Henderson; The Mad Hatters; Jack Roth; Eddie Jackson; Jules Buffano; Roy Bargy and His Orchestra.

NOVEMBER 15, 1953
Broadcast 4-07
HOSTESS: Martha Raye
WITH: Irene Dunne; Cesar Romero; Rocky Graziano.

NOVEMBER 22, 1953
Broadcast 4-08
HOST: Donald O'Connor
WITH: Ralph Bellamy; Dorothy Dandridge; Sidney Miller; Corinne Calvet; Jack Albertson; Snag Werris; Al Goodman and His Orchestra.
NOTE: This was the first commercial network telecast using RCA's all-electronic color system. *Variety:* "...a 60-minute visual treat including a single tinted Colgate commercial on behalf of Halo that demonstrated beyond doubt the qualitative aspects of 'rainbow video.'" For their impersonations routine, O'Connor and Miller presented "The Colgate Dramedy Hour," which interpreted *Death of a Salesman* as performed by Martin & Lewis.

NOVEMBER 29, 1953
Broadcast 4-09
HOST: Eddie Cantor
WITH: Frank Sinatra; Brian Donlevy; Eddie Fisher; Harold Arlen; Connie Russell and The Debonairs; Joan Shawlee; Al Goodman and His Orchestra.

DECEMBER 6, 1953
Broadcast 4-10
HOST: Jimmy Durante
WITH: Ethel Merman; Keye Luke; Eddie Jackson.

DECEMBER 13, 1953
Broadcast 4-11
HOST: Perry Como
WITH: Martha Raye; Ben Blue; Mike Mazurki; The Fontaine Sisters.

DECEMBER 20, 1953
Broadcast 4-12
HOST: Donald O'Connor
WITH: Charles Coburn; Scatman Crothers; Sidney Miller; Jana Mason; daughter Donna O'Connor; the Rose Bowl Queen and Court; Al Goodman and His Orchestra.

DECEMBER 27, 1953
Broadcast 4-13
HOST: Eddie Cantor

WITH: Donald O'Connor; Jimmy Durante; Connie Russell; George Gobel; Dennis Day; Al Goodman and His Orchestra.

JANUARY 3, 1954
Broadcast 4-14
HOST: Jimmy Durante
WITH: Eartha Kitt and Paul Douglas.

JANUARY 10, 1954
Broadcast 4-15
HOST: Dean Martin & Jerry Lewis
　　See Chapter Six.

JANUARY 17, 1954
Broadcast 4-16
　　Two distinct parts make up this show. The first half is variety featuring Frank Sinatra, Alan Young, Stan Freberg and acrobats Chiquita & Johnson. The second half originates from Bing Crosby's Pro-Amateur Golf Tournament at Pebble Beach, California. Players include Dean Martin, Phil Harris, Don Sherry, Lloyd Mangrum, baseball players Lefty O'Doul, Ralph Kiner and Jerry Pretty; and professional golfers Doug Ford, Bud Ward, Peter Haig, Jimmy Demaret and Dutch Harrison.

JANUARY 24, 1954
Broadcast 4-17
HOST: Ethel Merman
WITH: Jimmy Durante; Gene Nelson, Decola & Rubini, Sid Marion; Al Goodman and His Orchestra.
NOTE: The Hollywood Foreign Press Association presents Merman with a Golden Globe award for Actress in a Leading Role: Musical or Comedy, for her performance in Call Me Madam (1953).

JANUARY 31, 1954
Broadcast 4-18
HOST: Eddie Cantor
WITH: Groucho Marx; Connie Russell; Wally Cox; Billy Daniel; Ricky Vera; Ida Cantor; Marilyn Cantor; Jesse, James and Cornell.
NOTE: The program is a celebration of Cantor's 62nd birthday.

FEBRUARY 7, 1954
Broadcast 4-19
HOST: Jimmy Durante
WITH: Carol Channing; Tallulah Bankhead; Eddie Jackson.

FEBRUARY 14, 1954
Broadcast 4-20
HOST: Donald O'Connor
WITH: George Prentice; Beatrice Kay; Scatman Crothers; Sidney Miller.

FEBRUARY 21, 1954
Broadcast 4-21
HOST: Gene Wesson
WITH: Bud Abbott and Lou Costello; Keefe Brasselle; Sonja Henie; Carolyn Jones; Will J. White; Joyce Jameson; Norman Abbott; Michael Ross; Glen Stangle; The Jud Conlon Singers.

FEBRUARY 28, 1954
Broadcast 4-22
Anything Goes by Howard Lindsey and Russell Crouse. Music by Cole Porter
WITH: Ethel Merman, Frank Sinatra; Bert Lahr; Sheree North; Arthur Gould-Porter; Al Goodman and His Orchestra.

MARCH 7, 1954
Broadcast 4-23
HOST: Eddie Cantor
WITH: Eddie Fisher; Jack Palance; William Holden; Audrey Hepburn; Brandon de Wilde; Billy Daniel; Al Goodman and His Orchestra
NOTE: Holden, Palance, Hepburn and de Wilde are named the winners of *LOOK* magazine›s annual movie awards.

MARCH 14, 1954
Broadcast 4-24
HOST: Jimmy Durante
WITH: Eddie Cantor; Robert Montgomery; Patrice Munsel; Marion Colby; Eddie Jackson; Jack Roth; Jules Buffano; Roy Bargy and His Orchestra.

MARCH 21, 1954
Broadcast 4-25
HOST: Bud Abbott & Lou Costello
WITH: Les Paul and Mary Ford; Veola Vonn; Janik & Arnaut; Fred Darian; Harry Mendoza; Danny Richards, Jr.; Norman Abbott; Al Goodman and His Orchestra.

APRIL 4, 1954
Broadcast 4-26
HOST: Eddie Cantor
WITH: Connie Russell; Billy Daniel; Chiquita & Johnson; Manolo Mera; Ricky Vera.

APRIL 11, 1954
Broadcast 4-27
HOST: Jimmy Durante
WITH: Marilyn Maxwell; Liberace and brother George Liberace; Eddie Jackson; Ben Wrigley.

APRIL 18, 1954
Broadcast 4-28
HOST: Bud Abbott & Lou Costello
WITH: Jane Russell; Rhonda Fleming; Connie Haines; Beryl Davis; Tony Martinez; Nestor Paiva; Benny Rubin; Jim Hayward; Baby Mistin; Al Goodman and His Orchestra.

APRIL 25, 1954
Broadcast 4-29
The Ice Capades of 1954
WITH: Donna Atwood & Bobby Specht; Herb Shriner; The Old Smoothies (Orrin Markus & Irma Thomas); Paul Castle; Larry Jackson & Bernie Lynam; Rosemary & Bobby Maxson; Sonya Kaye; Hugh Forgie & Stig Larson; Helen Davidson.
NOTE: The telecast originates from Will Rogers Memorial Coliseum in Ft. Worth, Texas

MAY 2, 1954
Broadcast 4-30
HOST: Dean Martin & Jerry Lewis
See Chapter Six.

MAY 9, 1954
Broadcast 4-31
HOST: Jimmy Durante
WITH: Shelley Winters; Eddie Jackson; circus performers George Perkins and his crazy car, Linda the trapeze artist, Kirkman the magician, Harold De Garro (stilt walker), Pansy the Horse; Wally Blair (juggler) and Art Larue and His Dogs.

MAY 16, 1954
Broadcast 4-32
HOST: Eddie Cantor
WITH: Milton Berle; Connie Russell; Eddie Fisher; Andre, Andree & Bonnie.

MAY 23, 1954
Broadcast 4-33
HOST: Bud Abbott & Lou Costello
WITH: Peggy Lee; Hoagy Carmichael; Ricky Vera; Eddie Sauter & Bill Finegan

MAY 30, 1954
Broadcast 4-34
HOST: Dean Martin & Jerry Lewis
See Chapter Six.

THE COLGATE SUMMER COMEDY HOUR:

JUNE 6, 1954
Broadcast S-01
Holiday in New York
WITH: Jackie Cooper; Kaye Ballard; Jules Munshin; David Daniels; Elise Rhodes; Bart Mayo; Al Goodman and His Orchestra.

JUNE 13, 1954
Broadcast S-02
Let's Go Places
WITH:: Bobby Van; Paul Lynde; Mary McCarty; Paul Gilbert; Barbara Ruick; Vic Schoen and His Orchestra.

JUNE 20, 1954
Broadcast S-03
Continental Holiday
WITH: Kaye Ballard; Jules Munshin; Andy Griffith.

JUNE 27, 1954
Broadcast S-04
Away From It All
WITH: Bobby Van; Paul Lynde; Nat 'King' Cole; Mary McCarty; Gene Sheldon.

JULY 4, 1954
Broadcast S-05
Holiday, U.S.A.
WITH: Charlotte Rae; Jules Munshin; Johnny Bachemin; Dino Dante; Al Goodman and His Orchestra.

JULY 11, 1954
Broadcast S-06
WITH: Bobby Van; Paul Lynde; Mary McCarty; Martha Stewart.

JULY 18, 1954
Broadcast S-07
Free and Easy
WITH: Jules Munshin; Kaye Ballard; Betty Madigan; Jonathan Lucas.

JULY 25, 1954
Broadcast S-08
WITH: Bobby Van; Pearl Bailey; Jeff Chandler; Jack Prince; Jay Lawrence.

AUGUST 1, 1954
Broadcast S-09
WITH: Kaye Ballard; Jules Munshin; Jeff Chandler; Mindy Carson; Buddy Lester; Jonathan Lucas; Marshall & Farrell.

AUGUST 8, 1954
Broadcast S-10
WITH: The Will Mastin Trio featuring Sammy Davis Jr.; Connie Russell; Gene Sheldon; Jay Lawrence; The Gaylords; The Nita Bieber Dancers; Don Wilson; Vic Schoen and His Orchestra.

AUGUST 15, 1954
Broadcast S-11
WITH: Kaye Ballard; Ronny Graham; Willie Mays; Miss Universe Miriam Stevenson; The Chords.

AUGUST 22, 1954
Broadcast S-12
WITH: Margaret Whiting; The Hamilton Trio; Dick Contino; Gene Sheldon; Alan King.

AUGUST 29, 1954
Broadcast S-13
WITH: Kaye Ballard; Ronny Graham; Mimi Benzell; Louis Prima; Dania Kropska; Peter Gennaro.

SEPTEMBER 5, 1954
Broadcast S-14
WITH: Nat "King" Cole; Larry Storch; Dorothy Lamour.

SEASON FIVE:

SEPTEMBER 19, 1954
Broadcast 5-01
HOST: Eddie Fisher
WITH: Louis Armstrong; Peggy Lee; Mischa Elman; The Vagabonds, Maria Tallchief & Frederic Franklin; Rocky Marciano and his manager Al Weill; Gordon Jenkins and His Orchestra.
NOTE: The broadcast originates from the Hollywood Bowl.

SEPTEMBER 26, 1954
Broadcast 5-02
Lou Walters' Latin Quarter Revue: Made in France
WITH: Johnnie Ray; Jane Morgan; Joe E. Lewis; The Seven Ashtons; The Debonairs; Art Maner; Leo Durocher and the New York Giants (who would win the 1954 World Series later that week); Al Goodman and His Orchestra.

OCTOBER 3, 1954
Broadcast 5-03
WITH: Dinah Shore; Phil Harris;William Bendix; Tom D'Andrea & Hal March; and The Charlivel Trio.

OCTOBER 17, 1954
Broadcast 5-04
Friar's Frolics (a celebration of the Friar's Club's 50th Anniversary)
HOST: Milton Berle
WITH: Janis Paige; Mitzi Green; Smith & Dale; Georgie Price; Joel Grey; Beau Jenkins; Marilyn Ross; Al Goodman and His Orchestra.

OCTOBER 24, 1954
Broadcast 5-05
Revenge with Music by Howard Dietz & Arthur Schwartz
WITH: Anna Maria Alberghetti; Harpo Marx; Ray Middleton; Ilona Massey; Jerry Colonna; Edward Everett Horton.

OCTOBER 31, 1954
Broadcast 5-06
HOSTESS: Terry Moore
WITH: Paul Winchell; Don Cornell; Connee Boswell; The Minevitch Harmonia Rascals; Giselle & Francois Szony; Al Goodman and His Orchestra.

NOVEMBER 14, 1954
Broadcast 5-07
HOST: Gordon MacRae
WITH: Dorothy Kirsten; The Will Mastin Trio featuring Sammy Davis Jr.; Larry Storch; Gene Sheldon; Josanne Mariani; Carmen Dragon and His Orchestra.

NOVEMBER 21, 1954
Broadcast 5-08
Let's Face It by Cole Porter
WITH: Vivian Blaine; Gene Nelson.

NOVEMBER 28, 1954
Broadcast 5-09
HOST: Gordon MacRae

WITH: Gale Storm; Jack Carter; Meredith MacRae; Debra Paget; Gene Sheldon.

DECEMBER 12, 1954
Broadcast 5-10
HOST: Gordon MacRae returns as host.
WITH: Tony Curtis, Gloria De Haven, Gene Nelson, Paul Gilbert and Mara Corday from *So This is Paris* (1954); Terry Brennan, coach of Notre Dame; the 1955 Rose Bowl Queen; Gene Sheldon; Carmen Dragon and His Orchestra. Cameo appearances by Rock Hudson and Jeff Chandler. Scenes from *So This Is Paris* are shown.

DECEMBER 19, 1954
Broadcast 5-11
HOST: Dean Martin & Jerry Lewis
See Chapter Seven.

DECEMBER 26, 1954
Broadcast 5-12
Hollywood Ice Revue
HOST: Gordon MacRae
WITH: Gundi Busch, Skippy Baxter, Andra McLaughlin, Freddie Trenkler, The Bruises, Jimmy Grogan, Bobby Blake.
NOTE: The show originates from Chicago Stadium.

JANUARY 9, 1955
Broadcast 5-13
HOST: Bob Hope
WITH: William Holden & Brenda Marshall; Hedda Hopper; Margaret Whiting; Anita Ekberg; Robert Strauss; Jerry Colonna; The Nick Castle Dancers.
NOTE: The program was filmed at Goose Air Base in Labrador and Thule Air Base in Greenland.

JANUARY 16, 1955
Broadcast 5-14
HOST: Gordon MacRae
WITH: Jack Carter; Patti Page; The Vagabonds; The Lecuona Cuban Boys with Neil Castell; Gene Sheldon; The Aquaclowns; The 1955 Orange Bowl Queen; Cypress Gardens Aqua-Maids; Carmen Dragon and His Orchestra.

NOTE: The program originates from the Fontainebleau Hotel, Miami Beach, Florida.

JANUARY 23, 1955
Broadcast 5-15
HOST: Gordon MacRae
WITH: Paul Winchell; Ronny Graham; Joyce Bryant; The DeMarco Sisters; The Mayo Brothers; 1955 Maid of Cotton De Lois Faulkner; Franchot Tone & Gloria Vanderbilt.

FEBRUARY 6, 1955
Broadcast 5-16
WITH: Bobby Van; Spike Jones and the City Slickers; Paul Gilbert, Nat 'King' Cole; Billy Barty; Senor Wences; Helen Grayco. Gil Lee and John Halvorson cover the Jai Alai game live from Tijuana, Mexico.
NOTE: The telecast alternates from San Diego, Hollywood and Tijuana.

FEBRUARY 13, 1955
Broadcast 5-17
HOST: Dean Martin & Jerry Lewis
See Chapter Seven.

FEBRUARY 20, 1955
Broadcast 5-18
HOST: Gordon MacRae
WITH: Peggy Lee; Louis Armstrong; Gene Sheldon; The New Orleans Jazz Saints; Skeets & Pete; and Carmen Dragon and His Orchestra.
NOTE: Broadcast is live from Mardi Gras in New Orleans' French Quarter.

MARCH 6, 1955
Broadcast 5-19
HOST: Gordon MacRae
WITH: Ronny Graham; Jaye P. Morgan; The Gabor sisters (Eva, Zsa Zsa, Magda and Jolie); The Wiere Brothers; Carmen Dragon and His Orchestra.
NOTE: Broadcast from the ocean liner S.S. United States while docked on the Hudson River.

MARCH 13, 1955
Broadcast 5-20
HOST: Gordon MacRae
WITH: Bud Abbott & Lou Costello; Debra Paget; The Dassies; Middleweight champion Carl 'Bobo' Olson.

MARCH 20, 1955
Broadcast 5-21
HOST: Gordon MacRae
WITH: Kaye Ballard; Cornel Wilde; Jean Wallace; Bert Lahr; Caterina Valente; The Marquis Chimps.

APRIL 3, 1955
Broadcast 5-22
WITH: Tennessee Ernie Ford; Kitty Kallen; Phil Harris; Dave Brubeck; Harry Mimmo; The Mazone-Abbott Dancers.

APRIL 10, 1955
Broadcast 5-23
Roberta by Jerome Kern and Otto Harbach
WITH: Gordon MacRae; Reginald Denny; Nina Foch; Jack Carter; Lucille Norman; Agnes Moorehead; Luba Malina, Fritz Feld.

APRIL 17, 1955
Broadcast 5-24
HOST: Gordon MacRae
WITH: Edgar Bergen & Charlie McCarthy; Leigh Snowden; Ronny Graham; Sue Carson; The Treniers.

MAY 1, 1955
Broadcast 5-25
HOST: Liberace
WITH: George Liberace and His Orchestra.
NOTE: Broadcast live from the Riviera Hotel in Las Vegas, Nevada.

MAY 8, 1955
Broadcast 5-26
HOST: Dean Martin & Jerry Lewis
   See Chapter Seven.

MAY 15, 1955
Broadcast 5-27
HOSTS: Rhonda Fleming and Gordon MacRae
WITH: Bud Abbott & Lou Costello; The Clark Brothers; Jana Mason; The Singing Sergeants of the Air Force; Carmen Dragon and His Orchestra. A filmed appearance by President Eisenhower is shown.
NOTE: Broadcast from March Air Force Base, Riverside, California. During the program, the Thunderbirds are shown flying, and an F-100 jet travels to the base from Tuscon, Arizona.

MAY 29, 1955
Broadcast 5-28
Highlights of Broadway 1955
HOST: Eddie Fisher hosts this revue, which includes scenes from the shows *Palace*, *Damn Yankees*, *Fanny*, *La Vie* and *House of Flowers*.

JUNE 5, 1955
Broadcast 5-29
HOST: Dean Martin & Jerry Lewis
    See Chapter Seven.

THE COLGATE VARIETY HOUR: Summer Edition

JUNE 12, 1955
Broadcast SV-01
HOST: Charlton Heston
WITH: Vera-Ellen; Sarah Vaughan; Johnny O'Brien; Billy Ward and His Dominoes; The Dagenham Pipers; The Chadulis; Paul Mantz; Frank DeVol and His Orchestra. A cameo appearance by Richard Arlen, star of *Wings* (1927)
NOTE: Clips from Paramount's *Wings* and *Strategic Air Command* (1955) are shown.

JUNE 26, 1955
Broadcast SV-02
HOST: Charlton Heston
WITH: Fred MacMurray; Chiquita & Johnson; Louis Prima; Dick Kerr.
NOTE: A scene is shown from Paramount's *The Far Horizons* (1955), which stars Heston and MacMurray.

JULY 3, 1955
Broadcast SV-03
HOST: Guy Lombardo
WITH: Sheree North; The Fontaine Sisters; Morey Amsterdam.
NOTE: Telecast from Lombardo's restaurant Eastpoint House in Freeport, Long Island. The program showcases the water show "Arabian Nights in Jones Beach."

JULY 10, 1955
Broadcast SV-04
Tribute to Composers Richard Adler & Jerry Ross
HOST: George Abbott
WITH: Stars of Broadway's *The Pajama Game* and *Damn Yankees*, including Gwen Verdon; John Raitt; Helen Gallagher; Eddie Foy, Jr.; Ray Walston; Jimmie Komack, The Four Aces; Fran Warren; Mary Stanton; The DeMarco Sisters; Abbe Lane; Hal Hastings and the orchestra from *Damn Yankees*.

JULY 24, 1955
Broadcast SV-05
HOST: Jack Webb
WITH: Ella Fitzgerald; Peggy Lee; Ray Anthony; Pete Kelly's Big Eight; Miriam Nelson & Jack Regis; Ray Heindorf and Orchestra.
NOTE: A promotion for the release of Warner Brothers' *Pete Kelly's Blues* (1955); produced and directed by Webb, who also portrays Kelly.

JULY 31, 1955
Broadcast SV-06
HOST: Edgar Bergen & Charlie McCarthy
WITH: Anna Maria Alberghetti and The Alberghetti Family; Mitzi McCall.
NOTE: A scene from the Martin & Lewis movie *You're Never Too Young* (1955) is shown.

AUGUST 7, 1955
Broadcast SV-07
HOST: Edgar Bergen, with Charlie McCarthy, Effie Klinker and Mortimer Snerd
WITH: Hedda Hopper; Bob Cummings; The Vagabonds; The Dorman Brothers; The Merriel Abbott Dancers; Paule Desjardims; Conrad Hil-

ton. Celebrities interviewed by Miss Hopper include Celeste Holm; Art Linkletter; Irene Dunne; Thomas Mitchell; Charlotte Greenwood; Audie Murphy; Shelley Winters; Mr. & Mrs. Walt Disney; Dan Dailey; Merle Oberon; Charlton Heston; Mamie Van Doren; Richard Boone; Ann Miller and Jim Backus.

NOTE: Telecast from the grand opening of the Beverly Hilton Hotel, Beverly Hills, California. A clip is shown from Paramount's *To Catch a Thief* (1955) starring Cary Grant and Grace Kelly.

AUGUST 21, 1955
Broadcast SV-08
HOST: Edgar Bergen & Charlie McCarthy
WITH: Harry Belafonte; Carol Ohmart; Millard Thomas; Augie & Margo.
NOTE: A scene from the Paramount release *Ulysses* (1955), starring Kirk Douglas, is featured.

AUGUST 28, 1955
Broadcast SV-09
HOST: Charlton Heston
WITH: Edgar Bergen & Charlie McCarthy; The Marjorie Fields Moppets; Bob Williams & Red Dust; Tim Hovey and Julia Adams.
NOTE: Clips from Heston's *The Private War of Major Benson* (1955), a Universal-International release, are shown, plus scenes are performed live by Heston and co-stars Adams and Hovey.

SEPTEMBER 4, 1955
Broadcast SV-10
HOST: Charlton Heston
WITH: The Bob Hamilton Trio; The King Sisters; Frank DeVol and His Orchestra.

THE COLGATE VARIETY HOUR:

SEPTEMBER 18, 1955
Broadcast 6-01
HOST: Dean Martin & Jerry Lewis
  See Chapter Eight.

SEPTEMBER 25, 1955
Broadcast 6-02
HOST: Jack Carson
WITH: Anna Maria Alberghetti and The Alberghetti Family; Thelma Ritter; Frank Cady; The Cabots; Byron Foulger; Emory Parnell.
NOTE: Scenes are shown from Paramount's *Lucy Gallant* (1955), starring Charlton Heston and Jane Wyman.

OCTOBER 2, 1955
Broadcast 6-03
HOST: Jack Carson
WITH: Harry Belafonte; Martha Scott; Mel Allen; New York Yankees Yogi Berra, Whitey Ford and Hank Bauer; Brooklyn Dodgers Duke Snider, Carl Erskine and Pee Wee Reese. (The Yanks would lose the World Series to the Dodgers two days later.)
NOTE: Miss Scott introduces scenes from Paramount's *The Desperate Hours* (1955), in which she co-starred with Humphrey Bogart and Fredric March.

OCTOBER 16, 1955
Broadcast 6-04
Salute to OKLAHOMA (1955) and Rodgers & Hammerstein
HOST: Robert Paige
WITH: Gordon MacRae; Shirley Jones; Gene Nelson; Dean Martin & Jerry Lewis; Bambi Lynn & Rod Alexander; Yul Brynner; Will Rogers Jr.; Jan Clayton.
NOTE: Broadcast live from the Hollywood Bowl. See Chapter Eight for more details.

OCTOBER 23, 1955
Broadcast 6-05
Salute to College Football
HOST: Jack Carson
WITH: Jack Haley; Mickey Rooney; Rudy Vallee; Ray Milland; Stan Freberg; Helen Grayco; The Compton College Comets cheerleaders; Roger Williams; The Bob Hamilton Trio; UCLA's Ronnie Knox and coach Henry "Red" Sanders.
NOTE: Mel Allen appears on film interviewing members of the Los Angeles Rams. Milland shows a scene from his new film, *A Man Alone* (1955), which he also directed.

OCTOBER 30, 1955
Broadcast 6-06
WITH: Anna Maria Alberghetti; The Bob Hamilton Trio; Jack Webb; Spike Jones; Robert Cummings.

NOVEMBER 13, 1955
Broadcast 6-07
HOST: Dean Martin & Jerry Lewis
See Chapter Eight.

NOVEMBER 20, 1955
Broadcast 6-08
HOST: Robert Paige
WITH: Gordon MacRae; Harry Belafonte; Jonathan Winters; Ray Anthony; Fran Warren; The Bob Hamilton Trio; The Norman Luboff Choir; The Merriel Abbott Dancers; Frank DeVol and His Orchestra
NOTE: Broadcast from Palmer House in Chicago. During the show, the finalists for the Harvest Moon Talent Contest are announced by *Chicago Sun-Times* columnist Irv Kupcinet.

NOVEMBER 27, 1955
Broadcast 6-09
Modern Screen Magazine 25th Anniversary
WITH: Claudette Colbert; Joan Collins; Kirk Douglas; Bob Hope; Rock Hudson; Jimmy McHugh; Debbie Reynolds; Leigh Snowden; Russ Tamblyn; Lana Turner; John Wayne; Anna Maria Alberghetti; Eddie Fisher; Gordon MacRae; Louella Parsons.
NOTE: Telecast from the Cocoanut Grove nightclub in Los Angeles, the magazine celebrated its milestone by handing out awards to various stars.

DECEMBER 11, 1955
Broadcast 6-10
Salute to George Abbott
WITH: Gwen Verdon; Pat Stanley; Helen Hayes; Eddie Albert; Elaine Stritch; Bob Fosse; Edie Adams; Nancy Walker; Jack Straw; John Raitt; Russell Nype; Sam Levene; Peter Gennaro.

DECEMBER 18, 1955
Broadcast 6-11
HOST: Robert Paige
WITH: George Raft; Mickey Rooney; Ben Alexander; Richard Carlson; Broderick Crawford; Eddie Mayehoff; Anna Maria Alberghetti and The Alberghetti Family.
NOTE: A clip is shown from the Hal Wallis-produced Dean Martin & Jerry Lewis film *Artists and Models* (1955), released by Paramount.

DECEMBER 25, 1955
Broadcast 6-12
HOST: Robert Paige
WITH: Fred Waring and his Pennsylvanians.
NOTE: A program of Holiday music, which includes a scene from Paramount's *White Christmas* (1954).

Acknolwedgements

I WOULD LIKE TO ACKNOWLEDGE the existence of two previous books about Martin & Lewis. The first is *Everybody Loves Somebody Sometime (Especially Himself)* by Arthur Marx (Hawthorne Books, Inc., 1974), which was a good source of quotes from intimates who are no longer with us, but otherwise is hopelessly marred by the author's palpable anti-Lewis bias and tendency to favor his own sarcastic quips while ignoring or misrepresenting pertinent facts. The second is Lewis's own (in collaboration with James Kaplan) *Dean and Me (A Love Story)* (Doubleday, 2005), also a source for quotes included herein. Like Marx's book, *Dean and Me* struggles with facts (such as the year he and Martin met), and a few private conversations between the two read more like something an older, wiser Lewis imagined having, rather than the likely reality. Yet the book is a heartfelt tribute to the dispassionate, reticent partner from the sentimental, gregarious one, and for that reason alone is immensely valuable.

The following biographies of the two principals contained valuable information: *Jerry Lewis In Person* by Jerry Lewis with Herb Gluck (Athenium, 1982); *Dino: Living High in the Dirty Business of Dreams* by Nick Tosches (Doubleday, 1992); *King of Comedy: The Life and Art of Jerry Lewis* by Shawn Levy (St. Martin's Press, 1996); *Inventing Jerry Lewis* by Frank Krutnik (Smithsonian Institution Press, 2000); *That's Amore: A Son Remembers Dean Martin* by Ricci Martin with Christopher Smith (Taylor Trade Publishing, 2001); *Memories Are Made of This: Dean Martin Through His Daughter's Eyes* by Deana Martin with Wendy Holman (Three Rivers Press, 2004). Other books that were important: *How Sweet It Was* by Arthur Shulman and Roger Youman (Bonanza Books, 1966); *The Golden Age of Television* by Max Wilk (Delacorte Press, 1976); *Prime Time* by Marlo Lewis & Mina Bess Lewis (J.P. Tarcher, Inc., 1979); *The Tonight Show* by Robert Metz (Playboy Press, 1980); *The Box: An Oral History of Television, 1920-61* by Jeff Kisseloff (The Penguin Group, 1995); *As Long As They're Laughing* by Robert Dwan (Midnight Marquee Press, 2000).

As for the book in your hands, I must begin by thanking my own ex-collaborator, Chuck Harter, for unearthing copies of at least 60% of the newspaper and magazine articles referenced within this book, which in turn gave me guidance to seek out additional material from two key websites: *Lantern* (http://lantern.mediahist.org) and *Old Fulton New York Post Cards* (http://fultonhistory.com/Fulton.html). Harter's primary archive was that of the Motion Picture Academy Library; to them for maintaining copious files of articles, vignettes and blurbs, and to Chuck, a fine author in his own right, for combing through and copying this material, I'm forever grateful.

The list of shows in Appendix I were mostly discovered at the Library of Congress, either in Patti Lewis' clipping scrapbooks or in the micro-filmed NBC card files; the remainder came from J. David Goldin's *RadioGOLDINdex* website (http://www.radiogoldindex.com/). The *Colgate Hour* entry at Jim Davidson's *Classic TV Info* website (http://www.classictvinfo.com/ColgateComedyHour/index.htm) is the source for much of the information found in Appendix III.

Most of the Martin & Lewis *Colgate Hours* have made their way to home video and YouTube, while Chuck Harter provided complete copies of those that were not otherwise available as such, for which I owe him another debt of thanks. Rob Stone and Rachel Del Gaudio of the Library of Congress each gave me an opportunity to view rare Martin & Lewis TV appearances and home movies that were included in the Jerry Lewis Collection. I'm proud and honored to count both as friends, as well as collaborators during the Library's annual film identification workshop, Mostly Lost, about which you can learn more by searching "Mostly Lost" here: https://www.loc.gov/. The Library is also home to many uncirculating M&L radio shows, a handful of scrapbooks originally compiled by Patti Lewis, and a script from the team's first radio series, all of which proved extremely useful.

To John McElwee, author and acknowledged expert on classic movie exploitation, my sincere thanks for providing the box office performance figures that were cited in the forgoing.

Kayley Thompson is the source for many of the photographs contained herein, as well as for the audio and photo from the August 1977 Las Vegas reunion, plus many rare videos and radio show outtakes at her

YouTube account. She also provided many press clippings surrounding the ex-partners' other reunions during 1957-76. Thank you, Kayley for your dedication and willingness to help me.

Other friends and colleagues who provided rare clippings, radio show recordings, background information and lots of encouragement include Martin Grams, Jr., Derek Tague, Richard Rieve, Mike Henry, Steve Massa, Ben Model, Robert Farr, James L. Neibaur and my fellow members of the Metropolitan Washington Old-Time Radio Club. Thank you all.

Work on this project began in the late 1990s; it was actually the first book I ever discussed with my publisher, Ben Ohmart. It was put on hold when *Dean and Me* was announced, after which other projects took center stage. To Ben for his patience and continued willingness to publish this book nearly twenty years after receiving the first proposal, my deepest appreciation. Many thanks to John Teehan for the splendid design of these pages.

To my wife Myra and our four children: thank you for your patience and understanding, and for loving me.

As always, praise and humble prayers of thanks to the Father, Son and Holy Spirit for Their guidance and love.

Referenced Magazine
and Newspaper Articles

In **ADDITION TO** the books and websites cited in the Acknowledgements, along with radio and television reviews quoted within the text, the following magazine and newspaper articles provided much information and several quotes:

Adams, Val; "NBC Will Drop Colgate TV Show"; *New York Times*; November 21, 1955

Anderson, Nancy; "Big Ones Make 'The Big Event'"; *Greenfield Recorder*; October 21, 1976

Anonymous; "Nothing Like Praising Your Competitor, CBS Learns From Godfrey"; *Variety*; January 12, 1949

Anonymous; "Lewis-Martin Show to Slug it Out with O&H"; *Variety*; February 23, 1949

Anonymous; "Sealtest May Back Martin-Lewis Show"; *Variety*; March 9, 1949

Anonymous; "The Talk of Show Business"; *Time*; May 23. 1949

Anonymous; "Martin & Lewis TV Bow Pushed Up"; *Variety*; October 26, 1949

Anonymous; "NBC Star-Rotating Show Set for Sun; Colgate Sponsors"; *Variety*; June 28, 1950

Anonymous; "C-P-P Sign With NBC-TV"; *Broadcasting-Telecasting*; July 3, 1950

Anonymous; "NBC Signs Wynn To Long-Term Radio-TV Pact"; *Broadcasting-Telecasting*; July 17, 1950

Anonymous; "Colgate's 3-Out-of-4 Series to Run 60G Weekly; Max Liebman Alternate"; *Variety*; August 9, 1950

Anonymous; "Bulletins"; *Broadcasting-Telecasting*; September 18, 1950

Anonymous; "'Colgate Comedy Hour' Rated by Hooper"; *Broadcasting-Telecasting*; September 18, 1950

Anonymous; "Colgate Comics to Get Schwerin Test"; *Variety*; September 20, 1950

Anonymous; "Martin-Lewis Rib of Pic Indy On TV Brings COMPO Into Action"; *Variety*; September 20, 1950

Anonymous; "Industry Up in Arms Against Martin-Lewis Television Slur"; *Harrison Reports*; September 23, 1950

Anonymous; "Looks Like Film Biz Can't Block Kine on Martin-Lewis; COMPO Threats"; *Variety*; September 27, 1950

Anonymous; "Martin and Lewis Recant"; *Harrison Reports*; September 30, 1950

Anonymous; "NBC Ignores COMPO Protest on M&L's Pix Lampoon; Kine Sent Out"; *Variety*; October 4, 1950

Anonymous; "Martin & Lewis Talent Quest Gets A Sophie Tucker (At $7,500) Rebuff"; *Variety*; October 11, 1950

Anonymous; "Was It All in Fun?"; *Broadcasting-Telecasting*; November 6, 1950

Anonymous; "Second Glances: We Point With Pride"; *TV-Radio Life*; January 12, 1951

Anonymous; "Crackpots Hit Jackpot"; *Life*; August 13, 1951

Anonymous; "3-Way Rhubarb on 'Tandem' Setup; NBC, Sponsors Differ on Programs"; *Variety*; September 5, 1951

Anonymous; "Martin and Lewis In New Crack at AM"; *Variety*; September 5, 1951

Anonymous; "Million Dollar Madmen"; *Quick*; October 8, 1951

Anonymous; "Martin and Lewis Raise $1,148,419"; *Philadelphia Inquirer*; March 16, 1952

Anonymous; "His Story About Like Cinderella's"; *Binghamton Press*; April 29, 1952

Anonymous; "How Fab Caught Up"; *Sponsor*; September 22, 1952

Anonymous; "Martin-Lewis Map Pick-Up"; *The Billboard*; October 18, 1952

Anonymous; "Jerry Lewis in Hospital"; *Rochester Democrat-Chronicle*; January 14, 1953

Anonymous; "Jerry Lewis Records Show in Wheelchair"; *Albany Times-Union*; January 18, 1953

Anonymous; "NBC-TV 'All Star Revue' Fades in April: Talent Contracts a Poser"; *Variety*; January 21, 1953

Anonymous; Untitled Column; *Syracuse Post-Standard*; January 25, 1953

Anonymous; "Martin-Lewis Comedy Will Roll on Feb 12"; *Brooklyn Eagle*; February 1, 1953

Anonymous; "Screen Secrets: Those Glorious Goons"; *Screen Magazine*; May 1953

Anonymous; "Martin, Lewis Fail to Wow British Critics"; *Los Angeles Examiner*; July 23, 1953

Anonymous; "Those Feudin' Comics"; *TV Guide*; October 16, 1953

Anonymous; "Simmons, Lear's 52G As M&L's Scripters"; *Variety*; October 28, 1953

Anonymous; "Unions Studying Telethon Demands"; *Broadcasting-Telecasting*; November 9, 1953

Anonymous; "As We See It"; *TV Guide*; November 27, 1953

Anonymous; "Writers Confused on M&L Status"; *Variety*; December 9, 1953

Anonymous; "Dean Martin Scouts Talk of a Feud"; *Spokesman-Review, The*; December 27, 1953

Anonymous; "Zany Comedians Frighten Blonde"; *Rochester Democrat-Chronicle*; January 10, 1954

Anonymous; "Martin & Lewis Bypass Scripters In Expensive Feud"; *Variety*; January 13, 1954

Anonymous; "$3,342,000 is Raised in Nation Drive by Mailmen for Muscular Dystrophy"; *Fredonia Censor*; January 14, 1954

Anonymous; "M&L Back to AC 500 Club To Fete 8th Anni as Team"; *Variety*; February 23, 1954

Anonymous; "Report Martin, Lewis To Continue as Team; *Buffalo Evening News*; March 17, 1954

Anonymous; "'Citizen of Year' Award Bestowed on Martin, Lewis"; *Hollywood Citizen News*; August 28, 1954

Anonymous; "NBC's 'Hey, There' On Bates Contrib; 20 for MacRae"; *Variety*; September 1, 1954

Anonymous; "'Comedy Hour' Just One Frantic Ad Lib Booking"; *Variety*; September 29, 1954

Anonymous; "M&L Vs. 'Toast' Bally; *Variety*; December 22, 1954

Anonymous; "NBC's 'If M&L Fail to Deliver, That's All, Boys'"; *Variety*; December 29, 1954

Anonymous; "Esty to Produce 'Comedy Hour'"; *Broadcasting-Telecasting*; April 4, 1955

Anonymous; "How Do They Ever Get on the Air? A Glimpse of a Martin and Lewis Rehearsal"; *TV Guide*; May 14, 1955

Anonymous; "Agency Profile: Samuel H. Northcross"; *Sponsor*; May 30, 1955

Anonymous; "'Unknown' Catskills Tell Off Dean Martin"; *New York Post*; June 8, 1955

Anonymous; "That Spat Makes Jerry Cry"; *New York Post*; June 13, 1955

Anonymous; "Cut Dean-Jerry Umbilical Cord; Biz Falls Off"; *Variety*; June 15, 1955

Anonymous; "Martin-Lewis Near Complete Split-Up; *Daily Variety*; July 13, 1955

Anonymous; "Hollywood: Films - TV - Radio"; *Gloversville Leader-Herald*; July 28, 1955

Anonymous; "Martin-Lewis Feud is $20 Million One"; *Los Angeles Mirror-News*; August 2, 1955

Anonymous; "Martin and Lewis Continue as Team"; *Motion Picture Daily*; August 9, 1955

Anonymous; "The Pay's the Thing: Dean, Jerry Sign Truce"; *New York Post*; August 9, 1955

Anonymous; "Jerry Lewis, Martin to Continue"; *Rochester Democrat-Chronicle*; August 9, 1955

Anonymous; "$5 Million A Week: That's The 1955 Production Bill for Nighttime Network TV"; *Broadcasting-Telecasting*; October 10, 1955

Anonymous; "Anything For Laughs"; *Newsweek*; December 5, 1955

Anonymous; "Martin, Lewis Score in New Comedy Show"; Unsourced Clipping; March 20, 1956

Anonymous; "Jerry Lewis Warming Up for Telethon"; *New York Post*; May 22, 1956

Anonymous; "Dystrophy Telethon Slates Live Pickups in Yonkers"; *Yonkers Herald-Statesman*; June 16, 1956

Anonymous; "Martin, Lewis Agree To Go Separate Ways; Team Breakup 'Final'"; *Gloversville Leader-Herald*; June 19, 1956

Anonymous; "Martin, Lewis May Stay Team"; *Albuquerque Journal*; June 19, 1956

Anonymous; "Final Barrier Removed: Dean Martin, Jerry Lewis to End Profitable Partnership in July"; *Jefferson City Post-Tribune*; June 19, 1956

Anonymous; "Martin and Lewis Will Break Up Team"; *Aiken Standard and Review*; June 19, 1956

Anonymous; "Still Martin & Lewis For Film Plug in A.C."; *Variety*; June 27, 1956

Anonymous; "Martin and Lewis Chirp: 'Mostly We're Divorced'"; *Variety*; July 25, 1956

Anonymous; "Comedians File $3-Million Suit Against NBC"; *Albuquerque Journal*; August 15, 1956

Anonymous; "TV Coast-to-Coast"; *Council Bluffs Non Pareil*; September 23, 1956

Anonymous; "Lewis Partnership Won't Last"; *Galveston Daily News*; October 14, 1956

Anonymous; "Martin Happy Without Lewis"; *Dallas Morning News*; November 11, 1956

Anonymous; "Dean Martin Blasts Lewis"; *San Mateo Times*; January 29, 1957

Anonymous; "What Martin & Lewis Can't Forgive"; *TV Star Parade*; May 1957

Anonymous; "Re-union With Martin Is Surprise to Lewis"; *Buffalo Evening News*; October 1, 1958

Anonymous; "Dean Martin Quits; Lewis Takes Over"; *Schenectady Gazette*; December 23, 1958

Anonymous; "Martin, Lewis Feud About Fisher"; *Long Beach Independent*; December 24, 1958

Anonymous; "People: $1 Million a Year"; *Newsweek*; February 9, 1959

Anonymous; "Martin and Lewis Back Again - Briefly"; *Albany Times-Union*; March 14, 1960

Anonymous; "Dean, Jerry Kiss, Make Up At the Sands"; *Dallas Morning News*; March 14, 1960

Anonymous; "Jerry Lewis $140 Mil Grosser"; *The Hollywood Reporter*; November 23, 1962

Anonymous; "142 Guests Will Visit Dean Martin's TV Show"; *Watertown Daily Times*; August 6, 1965

Anonymous; "Dino On Downward Slope"; *Journal-News*; June 8, 1973

Anonymous; Newsmakers; *Newsweek*; September 20, 1976

Anonymous; "Martin, Lewis Reunion Set"; *Auburn Citizen*; May 2, 1988

Anonymous; "Martin, Lewis to Share Stage Again"; *The Recorder*; May 2, 1988

Archerd, Armand; "Martin & Lewis Split Official"; *Evening Independent*; November 28, 1956

Arnold, Maxine; "Dean Martin - Vagabond Singer; Jerry Lewis - Sentimental Clown"; *Radio-TV Mirror*; June 1952

Aronowitz, Alfred G.; "Martin & Lewis: The Hearts Cried"; *New York Post*; March 14, 1960

Bacon, James; "Martin, Lewis Score Unhappy First"; *Los Angeles Mirror-News*; November 12, 1955

Bacon, James; "Dean 'n' Jerry Inc. Okay"; *Washington Post and Times-Herald*; June 17, 1956

Bacon, James; "Eddie Fisher Show Fireworks Backstage"; *Idaho Falls Port Register*; December 26, 1958

Bacon, James; "The Great Martin and Lewis Feud: It's Still Going Strong"; *Milwaukee Journal*; March 3, 1963

Bark, Ed; "New Images Emerge From a Day With Jerry Lewis"; *Gannett Westchester Newspapers*; November 5, 1982

Baskette, Kirtley; "Two Wives - Two Lives"; *Modern Screen*; October 1952

Bissell, Elaine; "Jerry Operates on Doctors"; *Yonkers Herald-Statesman*; December 5, 1974

Bretstein, Dick; "TeleViews: New 'Comedy' Hour"; *Film Bulletin*; January 23, 1956

Brookhouser, Peter; "A Dressing Room Named Bedlam"; *Philadelphia Inquirer*; October 30, 1949

Buchwald, Art; "Martin, Lewis, Takes and Fabrications"; *Los Angeles Times*; June 19, 1956

Burr, Ty; "The Song of the Soused"; *Entertainment Weekly*; January 12, 1996

Busch, Niven; "The Multi-Million Dollar Dilemma of Martin & Lewis"; *Redbook*; December 1955

Bushman, Leonore; "Cross Town"; *Philadelphia Daily News*; September 1946

Carew, Peter; "An Open Letter to the Trade on 'Multi-Vision'"; *Variety*; December 10, 1952

Carroll, Harrison; "Behind the Scenes in Hollywood"; *Union-Sun & Journal*; June 28, 1955

Carroll, Harrison; "Behind the Scenes in Hollywood"; *Vidette-Messenger*; June 22, 1956

Clark, Mike; "The Looney and the Tune"; *Memories*; Aug/Sept 1989

Clarke, George W.; "Man About Boston"; Unsourced Clipping; January 1947

Coates, Paul V.; "Confidential File"; *Los Angeles Mirror-News*; July 20, 1955

Coe, Richard L.; "One on the Aisle"; *Washington Post*; October 23, 1952

Cohen, Harold V.; "Martin & Lewis Make Lunacy Pay Off"; *TV Digest*; September 20, 1952

Cohn, Al; "Martin Plays It Straight When Lewis Drops In"; *Long Island Newsday*; June 11, 1989

Connelly, Lyn; "A Peek at the Stars"; *Virden Recorder*; September 1, 1956

Connolly, Mike; "Rambling Reporter"; *The Hollywood Reporter*; January 31, 1957

Connolly, Mike; Untitled Column; *Desert Sun*; November 15, 1958

Cooper, Morton; "The Rise and Fall of the Martin and Lewis Empire"; *Coronet*; January 1957

Corliss, Richard; "Crooning Toward Oblivion"; *Time*; January 8, 1996

Crosby, John; "Madcaps With Charm"; *Greenfield Recorder-Gazette*; February 16, 1952

Crosby, John; "Mr. Crosby Makes His Bow"; *Greenfield Recorder-Gazette*; June 27, 1952

Crosby, John; "Jerry Lewis Sat Down to Make TV History"; *Los Angeles Daily News*; February 5, 1953

Crosby, John; "Newspaper Columnists Flop On New 'Tonight'"; *Greenfield Recorder-Gazette*; February 5, 1957

Cunniff, Bob; O'Malley, Tom; "Facts Behind Feuds"; *Waterloo Daily Courier*; February 13, 1956

Davidson, Bill; "Anything For a Laugh"; *Collier's*; February 10, 1951

Eyman, Scott; "Ring-a-Ding-DINO!"; *Palm Beach Post*; December 2, 2001

Fallaci, Oriana; "Dean Martin"; *Look*; December 26, 1967

Fine, Arnold; "Tips on Tables: Here's a Yellow Cab Driver Who Admits It"; *Washington Daily News*; November 1946

Flaherty, Vincent X.; "Hope-Crosby Telethon to Bolster Olympic Funds"; *Albany Times-Union*; June 12, 1952

Foster, Bob; Untitled Column; *San Mateo Times*; January 30, 1957

Frymer, Murry; "Colgate Squeezes Tube, Squirting Out Too Much"; *Newsday*; May 12, 1967

Gabriel, Joyce; "Jerry Stars for Muscular Dystrophy"; *Gloversville Leader-Herald*; September 2, 1971

Gardner, Hy; "Coast-to-Coast"; *New York Herald-Tribune*; July 17, 1956

Gardner, Hy; "Coast-to-Coast"; *New York Herald-Tribune*; July 24, 1956

Gardner, Hy; "Jerry Lewis Thrives After His Split with Dean Martin"; *Oakland Tribune*; November 19, 1956

Gardner, Hy; "Dean and Jerry Still a World Apart"; *Albuquerque Tribune*; October 27, 1972

Gehman, Richard; "Dean Martin: Crown Prince of the Clan"; *Albany Times-Union*; August 30, 1959

Gehman, Richard; "The Zany Thinker"; *American Weekly*; May 20, 1962

Gehman, Richard; "That Kid, Jerry Lewis"; *TV Guide*; June 15, 1963

Gehman, Richard; "What Happened To Jerry Lewis"; *TV Guide*; December 14, 1963

Gerhard, Inez; Untitled Column; Unsourced Clipping; March 6, 1952

Glover, William; "Jerry Lewis Reflects On Life"; *TV Observer*; December 12, 1976

Glucksman, Ernie; "They Really Are For Real"; *TV Screen*; June 1951

Gould, Jack; "Martin And Lewis Score On TV Show"; *New York Times*; September 18, 1950

Gould, Jack; "Martin-Lewis Team Reveals Patience, Dignity and Understanding on Benefit TV Marathon"; *New York Times*; March 17, 1952

Gould, Jack; "Television: Peep Show"; *New York Times*; January 30, 1957

Gould, Jack; "Tawdry Television"; *New York Times*; February 3, 1957

Graham, Sheilah; "Dean, Jerry Split Enters Money Phase"; *Hollywood Citizen News*; January 9, 1957

Gray, Barry; Untitled Column; *New York Post*; November 17, 1953

Gray, Barry; Untitled Column; *New York Post*; December 24, 1953

Gray, Barry; "Barry Gray Speaks Out"; *New York Post*; May 31, 1956

Guild, Leo; "On The Air"; *The Hollywood Reporter*; January 30, 1957

Hanauer, Joan; "Martin Has No Regrets On Split With Lewis"; *Lima News*; November 2, 1956

Handsaker, Gene; "It's Crazy But Fun on Martin-Lewis Set"; *Evening Leader*; August 5, 1950

Handsaker, Gene; "Lear and Simmons In Hectic Living"; *Corning Leader*; June 27, 1952

Handsaker, Gene; "Split Not Sudden, Says Dean"; *Los Angeles Mirror-News*; August 27, 1956

Harris, Harry; "'Conflict' Keynote of Week's Listings"; *Philadelphia Inquirer*; June 24, 1956

Harris, Harry; "New 'Tonight!' No Fun After Dark"; *Philadelphia Inquirer*; January 30, 1957

Harris, Harry; "Screening TV"; *Philadelphia Inquirer*; October 1, 1958

Harrison, Bernie; "A Frantic Time Was Had by All"; *Washington Star*; January 30, 1957

Hedrick, Sturgis; "Martin, Lewis Feud Fanned By 'Friends'"; *Buffalo Evening News*; September 16, 1955

Hedrick, Sturgis; "Martin-Lewis Reunion Hinted At By Walk-On"; *Buffalo Evening News*; October 2, 1958

Heffernan, Harold; "Contract Puts Dean, Jerry Together Again"; *Yonkers Herald-Statesman*; October 1956

Hill, Gladwin; "The Borscht Belt's Latest Gift to the Movies"; *New York Times*; September 18, 1949

Hinson, Hal; "The Kings of Comedy"; *TV Guide*; November 23, 2002

Hollinger, Hy; "Jerry Lewis: Clown With A 'Problem'"; *Variety*; June 15, 1955

Hopper, Hedda; "It's Not Safe When Zany Martin, Lewis Cut Loose"; *Los Angeles Times*; June 24, 1951

Hopper, Hedda; "Wacky Duo - You Know Who - Serious About Comedy Quality"; *Los Angeles Times*; August 2, 1952

Hopper, Hedda; "Martin and Lewis Rift; Their Act Breaking Up"; *Los Angeles Times*; June 19, 1956

Hopper, Hedda; "Lewis Says 'No' Again To Make Film With Dean Martin"; *Newark Advocate*; December 6, 1956

Hughes, Alice; "Comics' Tiff Welded By Zany Show"; *Buffalo Courier-Express*; September 30, 1955

Humphrey, Hal; "Rehearsal With Martin & Lewis is Twin Bedlam for Director"; *Buffalo Evening News*; February 15, 1952

Humphrey, Hal; "Former Partners, Foes Now Studio Neighbors"; *Troy Record*; September 2, 1967

Jenkins, Dan; "'I'm Tired of Being the Heavy': Dean Martin Blasts Away at Jerry Lewis"; *TV Guide*; April 13, 1957

Johnson, Erskine; "Hollywood Today"; *Olean Times-Herald*; April 19, 1954

Johnson, Erskine; "In Hollywood"; *Portsmouth Herald*; July 5, 1956

Johnson, Erskine; "Split Costly, M&L Learn"; *Utica Observer-Dispatch*; July 13, 1956

Johnson, Erskine; "Jerry's Quotes About Dean's Wife Fire Up Feud Anew"; *Los Angeles Mirror-News*; January 31, 1957

Johnson, Erskine; "Jerry Lewis O.K. by Self"; *Walla-Walla Union-Bulletin*; December 16, 1956

Johnson, Erskine; "It's a Food Feud With Dean, Jerry"; *Jamestown Post-Journal*; February 22, 1962

'Jose'; "M&L: Miffed & Lousy"; *Variety*; June 27, 1956

Kaliff, Joe; "Magic Carpet over Broadway"; *Brooklyn Eagle*; April 13, 1961

Kamm, Herbert; "It's Quits for Martin and Lewis" (6-part series); *Schenectady Gazette*; January 7-12, 1957

Kamm, Robert; "Aftermath of a Friendship: Is the Martin-Lewis Feud Still On?"; *World-Telegram Magazine*; June 27, 1959

Kaufman, Dave; "On All Channels"; *Daily Variety*; January 29, 1957

Kilgallen, Dorothy; Untitled Column; *Gloversville Leader-Herald*; June 22, 1955

Kilgallen, Dorothy; "Did Threat Scuttle His Date?"; *Washington Times*; June 30, 1956

Lader, Lawrence; "The Slapsy Twins"; *Pageant*; April 1951

Lanigan, Bob; "Martin and Lewis Zaniest Pair Around"; *Brooklyn Eagle*; May 23, 1951

Lanigan, Bob; "Writer Urges TV Comics: Stick to Your Radio Scripts"; *Brooklyn Eagle*; April 26, 1953

Lardner, Rex; "Round and Round, Up and Down"; *New York Post*; March 18, 1951

Larkin, Lou; "Laughing on the Outside (Still Pouting on the Inside)"; <u>Modern Screen</u>; November 1955

Lester, John; "Radio and Television"; *Long Island Star-Journal*; September 21, 1950

Lester, John; "Talent Unions to Ban Telethon Appearances"; *Long Island Star-Journal*; November 6, 1953

Lester, John; "Ailing Jerry Lewis Off 'Comedy Hour'"; *Long Island Star-Journal*; September 16, 1954

Lester, John; "Dean, Jerry Won't Break"; *Long Island Star-Journal*; June 8, 1955

Lester, John; "Martin, Lewis 'Getting Along Nicely'"; *Long Island Star-Journal*; September 7, 1955

Lester, John; "Dean, Jerry to Honor Contracts"; *Long Island Star-Journal*; June 28, 1956

Lester,John; "Martin, Lewis Come to Blows, Lester Reveals"; *Long Island Star-Journal*; July 6, 1956

Lester, John; Untitled Column; *Long Island Star-Journal*; January 30, 1957

Lester, John; Untitled Column; *Long Island Star-Journal*; April 23, 1957

Lewis, Jerry; "I've Always Been Scared"; *Look*; February 5, 1957

Lewis, Jerry; "Lewis Tees Off Against Critics"; *Dallas Morning News*; December 3, 1958

Lewis, Patti; "My 13 Years With Jerry Lewis"; *TV-Radio Mirror*; July 1957

Liebenson, Donald; "When Jerry Met Dean - Again, on Live Television"; *Vanity Fair*; September 5, 2016

Lyons, Leonard; "The Lyons Den"; *New York Post*; February 1, 1952

MacArthur, Harry; "After Dark: Jerry Lewis and Dean Martin Find a Sure Way to Win Audiences"; *Washington Evening Star*; December 1946

Martin, Jeanne; "This is My Dino"; *Family Weekly*; September 27, 1959

Martin, Dean, Lewis, Jerry; "This Time We're Not Joking"; *Parade*; February 21, 1954

McNellis, Maggi; "Maggi's Private Wire"; *Screenland-TV Land*; July 1953

Mishkin, Leo; "Martin, Lewis Run Riot on Colgate Video Show"; *New York Morning Telegraph*; September 19, 1950

Mosby, Aline; "2 Comedians Offer Advice to Youngsters"; *Tonawandas News*; April 20, 1954

Mosby, Aline; "Second Fiddle-itis Blamed for Martin's Break With Lewis"; *Tonawandas News*; June 11, 1955

Mosby, Aline; "Martin and Lewis Negotiating Split On TV, Film Work"; *Tonawandas News*; August 2, 1955

Mosby, Aline; "Dean Martin, Jerry Lewis Breaking Up"; *Oxnard Press-Courier*; June 18, 1956

Mosby, Aline; "Think Split Martin and Lewis Will Team Up Again"; *Hammond Times*; June 21, 1956

Mosby, Aline; "Jerry Lewis Completes 25 Years in Show Business; He's a 'Single' Now"; *Coshocton County Democrat*; September 9, 1956

Mosby, Aline; "They All Laughed, But Now Jerry's Making Lots of Loot"; *Fairbanks News-Mirror*; December 31, 1956

Mosby, Aline; Untitled Column; *Beverly Hills Citizen*; January 28, 1957

Mosby, Aline; "Light Touch"; *Odessa American*; March 4, 1957

Newton, Mark; "Why Martin and Lewis Are Rifting"; *Screenland-TV Land*; November 1955

O'Neill, Lou; "Sports"; *Long Island Star-Journal*; July 9, 1952

Panitt, Merrill; "Martin and Lewis Wow Late Viewers on Telethon"; *Philadelphia Inquirer*; June 24, 1952

Parsons, Louella O.; "Dean Martin & Jerry Lewis"; *Los Angeles Examiner*; August 3, 1952

Parsons, Louella O.; "Martin, Lewis Really Part"; *Los Angeles Examiner*; June 19, 1956

Parsons, Louella O.; "In Hollywood"; *Anderson Daily Bulletin*; September 27, 1956

Parsons, Louella O.; "Dean Martin (Minus Jerry) Still a Great Star"; *Albany Times-Union*; September 7, 1958

Pelgram, Jane; "Two Serious Comedians"; *Radio & TV Life*; March 6, 1949

Quincy, Awfrey; "Static and Snow"; *Broadcasting-Telecasting*; October 2, 1950

Ross, Mildred; "TV in His Stride"; *TV-Radio Life*; January 1953

Rosten, Leo; "Slapstick With Sex Appeal: The Martin and Lewis Bonanza"; *Look*; April 22, 1952

Scheuer, Philip K.; "New Duo's Clowning Has Studio Howling"; *Los Angeles Times*; April 10, 1949

Scheuer, Steven; "Video Keynotes"; *Long Island Star-Journal*; April 21, 1955

Schoenfeld, Joe; "Time and Place"; *Daily Variety*; July 13, 1955

Scott, Vernon; "Liz Taylor Adds Fuel to Flareup Over Friend Eddie Fisher's Show"; *Tucson Daily Citizen*; December 24, 1958

Shales, Tom; "A Comedy Duo Joined at the Quip"; *Washington Post*; November 24, 2002

Sharbutt, Jay; "TV Can't Mold Jerry"; *Journal-News*; June 8, 1973

Shearer, Lloyd; "Why Martin and Lewis Fight"; *Parade*; August 28, 1955

Skolsky, Sidney; "Martin Hits Lewis: 'Jealous of Wife'"; *New York Post*; January 22, 1957

Smith, Bill; "Vaudeville: Loew's State, New York"; *The Billboard*; January 25, 1947

Smith, Bill; "Too Many Cooks Didn't Kill Martin and Lewis"; *The Billboard*; March 10, 1951

Smith, Bill; "Big Dough, Big Aches Wind Up M&L Story"; *The Billboard*; March 17, 1951

Smith, Bill; "Martin-Lewis Preview Riot For Atl'tic City"; *The Billboard*; July 24, 1954

Smith, Cecil; "Jerry Lewis: Man in Motion - He's Making It Alone, Bigger and Better Than Ever Before"; *Los Angeles Times*; February 18, 1958

Spatz, David J.; "How Jerry Lewis' Legendary Partnership was born in Atlantic City"; *The Press of Atlantic City*; August 20, 2017

Starr, Eve; "Martin and Lewis Agree to Agree"; *Rochester Democrat-Chronicle*; December 24, 1955

Sullivan, Ed; "FCC Survey Suggested for 'Telethons'"; *Philadelphia Inquirer*; July 13, 1952

Thomas, Bob; "Martin, Lewis Hot Names in Hollywood"; *Binghamton Press*; February 20, 1951

Thomas, Bob; "Dean, Jerry Must Decide"; *Hollywood Citizen News*; August 2, 1955

Thomas, Bob; "Location of Film Premiere Causes Martin, Lewis Bust"; *Niagara Falls Gazette*; August 3, 1955

Thomas, Bob; "Martin, Lewis in Perfect Harmony After Feud"; *Niagara Falls Gazette*; January 27, 1956

Thomas, Bob; "Will Martin, Lewis Team Again on TV?"; *Corpus Christy Times*; June 23, 1956

Thomas, Bob; "Irishman Jerry's Partner"; *Long Beach Press-Telegram*; August 31, 1956

Thomas, Bob; "Martin and Lewis Feud May Still Not Be Over"; *Niagara Falls Gazette*; April 24, 1957

Thomas, Bob; "'Lazy' Dean Martin?"; *Salmanca Republican-Press*; August 11, 1965

Thomas, Bob; "Dean Martin Gets $34 Million Birthday Gift"; *Niagara Falls Gazette*; June 28, 1967

Torre, Marie; "Martin Fractures Lewis; 2 Toes, That Is, in Copa Act"; *New York Herald-Tribune*; July 18, 1956

Torre, Marie; "To Jerry Lewis, It's Only the Beginning"; *New York Herald-Tribune*; July 25, 1956

Torre, Marie; "Dean and Jerry Get NBC Solo Roles"; *Philadelphia Inquirer*; November 20, 1956

Torre, Marie; "The New 'Tonight' Bows"; *New York Herald-Tribune*; January 30, 1957

Tusher, Bill; "Backstage Bedlam"; *TV Topics*; December 1951

Villers, Ralph; "Dean, Jerry Clown It Up--Then Leave Stage 'Singles'"; *Albany Times-Union*; July 26, 1956

Williams, Bob; "On The Air"; *New York Post*; October 1, 1958

Williams, Bob; "On The Air"; *New York Post*; October 15, 1958

Williams, Bob; "On The Air"; *New York Post*; October 21, 1958

Williams, Dick; "Martin & Lewis Feud Not Likely Split-Up"; *Los Angeles Mirror-News*; June 8, 1955

Wilson, Earl; "Jerry Knows What He's Doing (Making a Fortune)"; *New York Post*; July 9, 1951

Wilson, Earl; "Martin & Lewis 1/2-Split, Dean Wants to Solo"; *New York Post*; June 7, 1955

Wilson, Earl; "It Happened Last Night"; *New York Post*; June 28, 1955

Wilson, Earl; "Jerry Must Swallow $5,000,000 Bitter Pill, Dean Says"; *New York Post*; August 2, 1955

Wilson, Earl; "It Happened Last Night: Here a Hilton Opening And Ran Into Jerry Lewis"; *New York Post*; August 9, 1955

Wilson, Earl; "Honest Man"; *New York Post*; March 7, 1958

Wilson, Kay; Untitled Column; *Bluefield Daily Telegraph*; September 7, 1968

Zolotow, Maurice; "The Great Martin-Lewis Feud"; *American Weekly*; June 20, 1954

Zolotow, Maurice; "The Martin and Lewis Feud"; *Cosmopolitan*; October 1955

INDEX

CPSIA information can be obtained
at www.ICGtesting.com
Printed in the USA
FSHW011025280620
71378FS

9 781629 333526